D1267435

EDWARD HYAMS

A Dictionary of Modern Revolution

Allen Lane

Allen Lane
A Division of Penguin Books Ltd
21 John Street, London WC1

ISBN 0 7139 0476 3

Printed by Cox & Wyman Ltd,
London, Fakenham and Reading

Set in Monotype Plantin

INTRODUCTION

In the course of the last century the economic, political and social systems of a large part of the world have been transformed by more or less violent revolution. The absolutist Russian, Austrian, German, French, Ottoman and Chinese empires have vanished; but so has satisfaction with the potential for liberty and social justice once thought to be inherent in the parliamentary monarchies and republics. What were the motives and what the purpose of the revolutionaries whose energy wrought these changes?

'Life being what it is,' said Baudelaire, 'one dreams of revenge.' Feeling, thinking, reading men, facing the spectacle of life being what it was for the majority of their fellows in the nineteenth century, for the agricultural and industrial workers who produced the world's wealth, dreamed of revenge on the minority classes which imposed the injustice of a lifetime of suffering on that majority. Modern revolution was a violent repudiation of man's estate under capitalism.

But that repudiation would have been sterile indeed had it been no more than a furious tantrum provoked by the spectacle of injustice institutionalized in the political-economic system. The revolutions of the seventeenth and eighteenth centuries had transferred political power, and, in the case of agrarian reform, a certain amount of property, from the hands of the aristocracy into those of the burgesses and farmers. They had not called in question the basic institution of property. By the mid-nineteenth century it was vividly clear that revolution of that kind had failed to usher in the reign of social justice: about 1870 American factory-workers were, for example, little better off than factory workers in Tsarist Russia. But also by that time the theoretical foundations for a new kind of society, perhaps a just society, had been laid. These foundations were the works of a number of economists who had demonstrated that social justice was incompatible with the

5

Introduction

established system of property rights, a proposition which, indeed, had been put forward by some extremists, like the Levellers, in the English revolution, and by Gracchus Babeuf in the French revolution, but which was a serious issue in neither of those upheavals.

Thomas More had reached that conclusion as early as 1516: his *Utopia* is a communist state. But there was no science behind his communism; it was the product of Christian belief in an imaginary condition, immanent justice, of an imaginary divine code, natural law, an illusion which was not given up by intelligent people until the publication of Darwin's *The Origin of Species*, and which has never been quite abandoned by the less intelligent. Scientific criticism of property as the source of social injustice began with such eighteenth-century pioneers of socialism as Mably, Morelly in *Code de la nature* (1755), and such Englishmen as Spence, Ogilvie, Hall and, above all, William Godwin in his *Enquiry concerning political justice* (1793). What these men did was to rationalize the emotions which had given rise to *jacqueries* for many centuries and which were given popular expression in such ancient riddles as 'When Adam delved and Eve span, Who was then the gentleman?' Finally, there was the Frenchman Proudhon, who answered his own question 'What is Property?' with 'Property is Theft' and then proceeded to demonstrate it irrefutably.

For there can, of course, be no title to property in land or natural resources other than force, if you go back far enough. What all the pioneer political economists discovered, or believed that they had discovered, was the manifest but long masked truth that all early human societies were communist; and they believed that this was according to natural law – as I have said, it was Darwin who discovered the justification for capitalism when he demonstrated that if there was, indeed, a natural law, it had nothing to do with 'law' and knew not justice, a concept which man, finding his condition intolerable, had foisted on God.

Since there was, in nature, no title to property in land and natural resources, any revolution designed to establish a just society must begin by getting land and natural resources out of private hands so that it might be held in common as it had been in the Golden Age supposed to have existed in the remote past, and so as to bring about a new Golden Age, the Millennium. But it was clear that mankind's common estate must still be administered by someone. What part of mankind could, then, be shown to have a just title to economic and political power? To this the anarchist

socialists, originally from Godwin but effectively from Proudhon, answered, categorically, *nobody*. For political power, in any hands whatever, could not but entail social injustice and was, therefore, intolerable. So the anarchist solution was to do without politics, to rid mankind of the burden of the state. The basis of any kind of human society was, obviously, economic activity, that is, production: and therefore the absolute minimum, and at the same time utmost tolerable degree, of social organization must be cooperation in economic activity. So the aim of the anarchist revolutionary became the total destruction of those major evils, the existing political, economic and social institutions. They would then be replaced by communes of cooperating workers, linked in a nationwide, and ultimately worldwide, federation.

That was the anarchist solution: the numerically more important branch of socialism had a very different one.

Although it had been settled that nobody had title to property in land or natural resources, the question of who had just title to property in the means of production and their product was answered by an Englishman, David Ricardo, and a Swiss, Sismondi. Any manufactured article contains two kinds of component elements: raw materials and labour. Since it was agreed that the raw material belonged to nobody, that is equally to all mankind, the only valid way to value anything grown or manufactured by men was in terms of the labour which had gone to the growing or making of it. This argument produced one awkward anomaly: the value of socially useless articles the making of which required much skilled labour often worked out higher than the value of many socially useful articles whose making consumed less labour. This anomaly was later corrected by Karl Marx in his own refinement of the labour theory of value. The theory led also to the conclusion that the only just title to the product of labour was the labour which had produced it: in other words, labour was the rightful owner of what labour produced and it followed that economic power should be in the hands of the workers.

◊ Marx and ◊ Engels were foremost in drawing this revolutionary conclusion from the labour theory of value. Furthermore they reached the conclusion that political power should be in the hands of the working class, by an entirely different route. Their master in philosophy, ◊ Hegel, had explained the evolution of the universe, including human societies, in terms of the eternally repeated reconciliation by synthesis, of thesis and

7

Introduction

the antithesis it provoked, a process which he called the dialectic (the word was borrowed from Plato but its meaning altered). But for Hegel this process occurred on the plane of the ideal: thesis was idea, antithesis anti-idea and events followed their reconciliation by synthesis. Hegel's critic Feuerbach, perceiving that, historically, need and practice generate idea, retained the dialectic but got rid of the idealism. Marx seized on this to invent, or discover, an historical dialectic (dialectical materialism), one of whose manifestations was class war. The social class in power generates from its own needs a lower class which is forced as it grows to seek to oust the ruling class and seize power for itself: thus, in the revolutions in western Europe in the seventeenth and eighteenth centuries, the bourgeoisie won power from the feudal aristocracy in class wars. Being then established in power itself, the bourgeoisie generated the proletariat to serve its economic purpose; and the proletariat must now rise to take power from the bour-geoisie into its own hands. Marx saw this as inevitable because dictated by an ineluctable law of history. Would the proletariat, then, ultimately be ousted in its turn by some social class generated by its success? No; the process was not endless, and for the following reasons.

Ricardo, Sismondi, other economists and Marx himself had seen it as axiomatic, and in any case self-evident, that the absolute basis of human society is economic production (without it man is not man but a foraging animal). There can, therefore, be no social class more fundamental to society than the producing workers, so that once power was in their hands, it could go no further. Therefore the dictatorship of the proletariat must be the ultimate and permanent political and economic regime.

But the dialectic was not all that Marx got from Hegel. A true Prussian, Hegel revered the State, but even had his temperament not led him to do so, his own dialectic would have compelled him to glorify it. It was, of course, fundamental to his system that the synthesis is a higher manifesta-tion of being than its component thesis and antithesis. When his dialectic was applied to history, then the individual man was seen as thesis, and man at large, society, the collective, as antithesis: they were reconciled in synthesis – the State. It follows that the State is a higher order of being than the individual man. Marx, seeking an institution in which the dictatorship of the proletariat would be made manifest in action, that is to say at once an embodiment of its spirit and an instrument of administration of man's common estate, found it in the Hegelian State.

8

The socialist revolutionaries, other than the anarchists, therefore set out to overthrow the old orders – both absolutist and bourgeois parliamentarian – and to establish dictatorship of the proletariat made manifest in the power held and wielded for the proletariat by the State. That, at all events, was their immediate and socialist purpose: they also had, in theory, an ultimate and communist purpose, an 'ideology' generated by their actions. Marx, since he had rejected Hegel's idealism, did not have to regard the State as a transcendental being. The arguments and demonstrations of the anarchists to the effect that the State was and must by its nature be oppressive, and was therefore an evil to be rid of, could not be totally ignored. It was therefore laid down that whereas during the socialist phase of the post-revolutionary epoch (the phase of 'from each according to his capacities, to each according to his work), the State must be retained as a necessary evil, as the communist phase ('From each according to his capacities, to each according to his needs') was attained, by means of the perfection of economic cooperation, increased production, and political and social education, the State would become progressively less necessary and could be allowed to 'wither away'.

A number of socialist revolutions having been accomplished, directly affecting the lives of about half the human race, and indirectly those of all mankind, at great cost in suffering, blood and treasure, the just society failed to appear. A new generation of revolutionaries has arisen to seek the causes of failure and try again. On the whole socialist theory, beginning with people like Mably, Thomas Hall and Godwin, and completed by Lenin, has stood up very well to re-examination by the New Left, whose thinkers therefore conclude that it was practice which was at fault. And this was manifestly true: the State, instead of becoming at once the embodiment and instrument of the workers, became the instrument of oppression, as the anarchists had foreseen that it would, in the hands of the Communist Party bureaucrats; in the extreme case, of the archbureaucrat Joseph ◊ Stalin, whose rule turned out to be more tyrannous than that of Ivan the Terrible. But there was no need to do any inventing of new theories in order to correct this state of affairs. For, as well as the anarchists, the two greatest socialist revolutionaries of the century had foreseen the danger of this happening and shown ways to avoid it.

◊ Lenin in his later writings under the head of cultural revolution

9

had foreseen and warned against the rise of a tyrannous and inflexible communist bureaucracy: there was only one way to avoid it – direct democracy. The workers must not delegate their power to officials, they must all take part in wielding it, all be active politicians managing the common estate and the common labour of the proletariat; officials were necessary, but they must be kept under constant and vigilant pressure by the people.

Trotsky, too, foreseeing that the moment the revolution was regarded as complete and accomplished the new State would crystallize, and fossilize into a tyranny (albeit more or less benevolent) which could not but deny liberty to the people, preached a 'revolution in permanence'. This comes to much the same thing as Lenin's Cultural Revolution (fermented in China by Mao Tse-tung to get power out of the hands of party bureaucrats hostile to himself) although it envisages the nee for repeated recourse to violence against the State's tendency to become oppressive.

There is, then, a new wave of revolution which is still fundamentally Marxist-Leninist but which is bent on the overthrow not only of capitalism but also of the 'State capitalism' into which, it is held, Soviet socialism has degenerated.

For some years, during the past two decades, the revolutionary socialist movement known as Castroism, after Fidel ▷ Castro or Guevarism, after Che ▷ Guevara, was the most fashionably radical of the ▷ New Left movements. Its philosophy was drawn from the experience of the Cuban revolution (*q.v.*) in which the fighting was done not by a militant proletariat but by armed and politically conscious peasants. Resembling, therefore, the ▷ Chinese Communist revolution, it also had affinities, for example, with the Algerian nationalist-socialist revolution. It was, therefore, a model for other nations where social and economic conditions were such that the country was better able to bring the liberating revolution to the cities, than the cities to the country. That fact, and the Cuban revolution's success, stimulated similar movements in which rural guerrilla bands tried, by violent action against government forces and their 'imperialist' (i.e. foreign capitalist) allies, to 'create a revolutionary situation', in Latin America, and parts of Africa and Asia. In certain countries imitation of these methods by townsmen led to the emergence of 'urban ▷ guerrilla' bands, e.g. the ▷ Tupamaros.

But the Cuban revolutionary purity has been tarnished in the eyes of the real *gaucheiste* by the revolution's expedient reliance on Soviet aid.

The purest of the pure New Leftists are to be found among the Maoists. Although an entry under that head appears in the *Dictionary*, something must be said here about this present revolutionary advance guard. First, as to its name, Maoism is not simply an imitation of the communism of the People's Republic of China: inspired by certain of the *Thoughts* of ⟡ Mao Tse-tung, European Maoism is, in its purest manifestation, very much more radical, more *gaucheiste*, than Chinese communism, despite the fact that Chinese communist practice since the Cultural Revolution is apparently less bureaucratic than Russian communism. The Maoists are Marxist-Leninist, and claim that there is continuity from Marx and Lenin to Mao; but they utterly repudiate the Communist Party practices of going to the people with a readymade programme, arrogating to the Party militant leadership of the proletariat. The dictatorship of the proletariat must really come from the proletarians themselves. The Maoist intellectual becomes one of the people – here there are echoes of the Populist movement in late nineteenth-century Russia; and of the intellectual communism of Britain in the 1930s. The Maoist does not lead and teach the people, he is taught and led by them, though he should act as a spark to fire the mass. He should give his weight to pushing the spontaneous revolutionary movements in his factory or office or university towards the Left, away from moderation and negotiation, towards revolutionary action.

Reproached by the institutionalized Old Left with having no clear political line, no programme based on theory, the Maoist does not deny it: he answers that the masses, the people, are constantly pushing in a direction and sense favourable to their class; that the fundamental immorality from which stems all social evil is the exploitation of man by man and of this basic sin the masses alone are not guilty; and that it follows that the revolutionary movement of the people themselves cannot but be moral. Out of it will emerge, helped to birth by the Maoists, a revolutionary socialist and wholly democratic programme of the people, not of a small élitist and avant-gardist group such as those formed by the Trotskyists, or of a bureaucracy such as that of the Communist Party or the trade unions.

This *Dictionary* attempts to put at the student's disposal an easily accessible source of information about the men, events and institutions which have transformed the economic, political and social structures of a

Introduction

great part of mankind during the past century; and those which are continuing the work of transformation by creating, wherever it seems possible, a revolutionary situation.

E.H.

Note

◊ indicates cross reference to another entry. The following subjects, so frequently recurrent, are not thus marked: anarchism, capitalism, communism, democracy, socialism.

A

Action Française. A flamboyant, romantic and extreme rightwing political movement founded in France (1899) by Charles Maurras to overthrow democratic institutions beginning with the Third Republic and substitute an absolute monarchy. As an instrument of the ultra-Catholic, chauvinistic, anti-Republican Right which believed that Dreyfus, being a Jew, must be guilty, that the Army was sacred, and the Republic and all ◊ *Choseards* corrupt, the movement might have had more credibility if it had not hampered itself with anachronistic Royalism. Léon Daudet, son of the popular writer Alphonse Daudet, editor of its newspaper *Action Française* (suppressed in 1945), won the movement many adherents by his brilliant antidemocratic, antisemitic polemics; but, *c.* 1933, it became tarred with the by then rather dirty brush of ◊ Fascism and even ◊ Nazism and was soon being suspected of fifth column pro-German leanings, and (following the outbreak of World War War II) activities. Action Française adherents collaborated with the German Army of Occupation of France, and in the Vichy Government. As a result the movement was destroyed by the liberation of France in 1944. Maurras died in prison while serving a sentence for treason.

African National Congress (ANC): See South Africa and Rhodesia, Revolution in.

African Power Transfers. The meaning of the word *Revolution* in the title of this work is implied in the Introduction. That definition excludes many of the transfers of political power from white, formerly colonial governments to black African governments which have taken place since the end of World War II; it also excludes a number of well-known African political leaders who, however, as the first native African rulers of their countries often led nationalist movements and suffered persecution and imprisonment for their causes, and are thought of as revolutionaries. The names from which the reader has been referred to this explanation are those

13

of such militant nationalist but, in our sense, non-revolutionary leaders. For a transfer of political power from one bourgeois capitalist government albeit colonialist and white, to another, albeit African and black, is not a revolution, although this truth may be masked by the fact that new black African governments have received aid from communist powers, such aid being given as a move in the global struggle between the communist and capitalist blocs. Nor are the struggles of African nationalist militants to replace such white colonialist governments as the Rhodesian, or the Portuguese, but with the intention of retaining the political and economic structure and systems unchanged, directly 'revolutionary'. African revolutions and revolutionaries, that is people bent on replacing a bourgeois capitalist by a socialist or communist system are, of course, included under the appropriate headings.

All this being so, it is nonetheless true that a black ⟡ bourgeois takeover from a white imperial power has a revolutionary tendency. A Hastings Banda or a Jomo Kenyatta or a Julius Nyerere may be no Marxist ⟡ Leninist revolutionary, may even, like Banda, be a social reactionary, yet since he has had to fight against ⟡ imperialism, in the broad and general sense, he is necessarily, albeit stigmatized by the men on his left as a 'neo-colonialist', forced some way into the anti-imperialist camp, here using 'imperialism' in the specifically Leninist sense: thus, for example, even so rightist a leader as the Shah of Iran has been only a little less firm than, e.g. the revolutionary Ghadafieh of Libya, in appropriating more and more of his country's oil revenues, that is in fighting the 'imperialism' of the great concessionary oil companies; and has, in that context, declared a policy of total appropriation which even a communist leader could not better.

The 'Third World' state of mind is, in fact, of itself revolutionary in tendency. Kwame Nkrumah was overthrown by a *coup d'état* from the right, grounded in the complaint that he was guilty of malversation of public funds and of cultivating a personality cult; but his successors are unable to reverse his more or less socialist policy without creating a dangerously revolutionary situation. Furthermore, there is also the suspicion that his overthrow had a good deal to do with the fact that he was making life difficult for the bourgeois cocoa-farmers and the European and American gamblers in cocoa prices.

Black African and brown Asian power takeovers from former imperial powers may, indeed, be seen as manifestations of the bourgeois revolution which, in Marxist theory, must precede the socialist revolution, with the old imperial power playing, in each case, the role of 'Tsarism'. The black bourgeois leaders had to have mass support in their struggle to win nationalist independence; in other words they were forced, willy-nilly, to rouse the sleeping proletarian dog, and to give the people at large lessons in revolution which that people will, in due course, remember when it comes to the next stage of the struggle, be that struggle violent or otherwise.

A factor which has tended to make easier the task of some Arab and, in general, Muslim, leaders with socialist inclinations – the late Gamal Abdul Nasser is a case in point – has been Islamic religious hostility to capitalism. Although the difficulties in the way of the growth of capitalism entailed by religious hostility based on disapproval of the use of interest and the even stronger disapproval of speculative undertakings for contingent profit, have no doubt been much exaggerated, those difficulties did and to some extent still do exist. A number of leading Muslim propagandists and publicists of socialist leanings have argued that socialism, with its emphasis on public service as a motive, instead of private profit, and on welfare instead of *laissez-faire*, is actually implicit in Koranic and later Islamic teaching; and they have invented a rather ill-defined and idealist 'Islamic Socialism'.

Although, therefore, the black and brown leaders who have taken over political power from former white imperial governments without making a social revolution, have not, for the reasons given above, been treated in this dictionary as revolutionaries, their acts and movements have contributed very considerably to the general Third World revolutionary movement. The resistance of the native of colonial territories to the dominion of the 'mother' country – Portuguese Africa is a case in point – has even, to some extent, spread into the mother country, just as there was some identity of purpose between the various North African nationalist rebellions and the left-wing revolutionaries in metropolitan France. Thus, also, there is some identity of purpose between so conservative a ruler as Haile Selassie of Ethiopia, and his socialist and communist associates in the Pan-African movement which is a part of the larger Third World revolt against imperialism.

Al-Fatah. Palestine Revolutionary Liberation Movement: *See* Palestine, Revolution in.

Alternative Society is the society composed by those people, for the most part young, who reject the industrial-managerial consumer society, whether capitalist or Moscow communist, *in toto*. Neither an alternative nor a society its members are Hippies, Flower Children, the followers of such sects as Hare Krishna, and plain dropouts. They give expression to their rejection of existing society and to their apartness by the wearing of often peculiar secondhand clothes, the wearing of long hair and full beards by the males and the rejection of cosmetic make-up by the females, a more or less nomadic way of life, a cult of pop music listened to in communion, and the harmless but illegal practice of smoking *Cannabis sativa* instead of tobacco, in various forms and under various names, a practice which has been glamorized by police persecution. In so far as they can be called revolutionaries at all, the alternative society people seek not to overthrow established society by violence, which they repudiate, or political action, which they deprecate, but by withdrawal which, if practised by a sufficient number of people, would cause it to wither away. A similar method of destroying capitaliam was advocated by some of the anarchist philosophers. As, however, those of the alternative society's members who are not gathered together in communes which try to be self-supporting, live by some form of begging, they are, in practice, dependants of or parasites on the society they condemn, as indeed are the communes in the measure that they make use of manufactured goods and are indebted to that society for, e.g. the maintenance of public order and services. While it is difficult not to sympathize with the dropout's criticism of the consumer society, it is impossible not to be impatient with the alternative society's ineffectiveness in both the merely negative attack on established institutions and in the business of staying alive.

The phenomenon of the 'dropout' is not, of course, new in history. The early Christian eremitical movement in North Africa and the Middle East during the decline of the Roman Empire had many of the attributes of the alternative society movement – a woolly-minded mysticism without the discipline of the great mystics, condemnation of worldliness and material-ism, pacifism, rejection of rationalism and positivism, and heavy emphasis on love although in the case of the hermits they confined themselves to *agape* whereas the modern dropouts are much addicted to eroticism. As for the alternative society's communes, they may be seen as feeble reproduc-tions of the monastic establishments which came into being during the great *volkerwanderung* of the so-called Dark Ages with, once again, the difference that to the moderns love means both *eros* and *agape*.

Perhaps the most curious and significant phenomenon to be observed in connection with the alternative society is the ferocity of the hostility with which a majority of the members of established societies react to it. Such strong reaction implies a measure of self-doubt and uneasiness of alarming magnitude and tends to vindicate the criticism implicit in the attitudes of the alternative society's votaries.

Anarchism, from the Greek *anarkhia*, non-rule, is a political doctrine dedicated to the abolition of formal government. Its earliest literary exponent was William Godwin whose *Political Justice* (1793) had much influence on his son-in-law, Shelley. Anarchism first became an organized movement in Russia late in the nineteenth century, and from the beginning it had two wings: its left, led by ◊ Bakunin, preached the destruction by violence of capitalism, all state authority and formal political organization; and the assassination of kings and tyrants: its right, led by ◊ Kropotkin, rejecting the use of violence, contrived to believe that man's fundamental goodness could establish public order by voluntary cooperation. Both wings believed that the formal state and all forms of government are evil, and the fount of evil in individuals; and that a society of freely associating individuals without written law, police, courts or armed forces, should replace them. About 1880 a form of anarcho-communism emerged led by Bakunin and advocating the use of ◊ assassination: its adherents in various countries assassinated Alexander II of Russia (but see ◊ nihilism), King Humbert of Italy, President Carnot of France, the Empress Elizabeth of Austria, and President McKinley of the USA. ◊ Lenin was influenced by anarchist teaching when he argued, in his interpretation of Marxism, that the state must ultimately 'wither away', leaving a voluntary regime without class, force, formal organization or government. Tolstoy became a non-violent anarchist, holding any kind of state to be inconsistent with Christianity and advocating destruction of the state by refusal of military service, non-payment of taxes and refusal to recognize the law courts. International anarchist conventions were held in 1877 and 1907, but the rise of the social democractic movement and of communism aborted it as an international revolutionary movement except in Spain where it remained an important force until destroyed by the ◊ Stalinist Communists during the Civil War (1936–39). In France, Italy and Spain it became associated with syndicalism as anarcho-syndicalism, in the USA it had great influence on the syndicalism of the ⟡ Industrial Workers of the world; in Britain, the land of its origin, it made no impression on political life although professed, as it still is, by some intellectuals; in Russia it took the form of nihilism; its non-violent forms of resistance to established authority advocated by Kropotkin and Tolstoy were adopted in India by ⟡ Gandhi ⟡ and used with success against the British Raj.

Anarchism is still very much alive, although it now has no mass support. The anarchist parties, groups or associations in several European countries including Britain, and in the United States, are 'intellectual' bodies which are numerically unimportant; but anarchism survives in the spirit of the ⟡ New Left at large, for the defeat of libertarian socialism by the bureaucracies of the 'communist' countries has taught the younger revolutionaries a distrust of the state which has driven them to look again at the theories of such philosophers as ⟡ Proudhon, ⟡ Kropotkin and even Godwin; and while the New Left does not utterly reject the state, its internationalism and its insistence on direct democracy as opposed to representative democracy is tantamount to such a rejection.

Angola, Popular Movement for the Liberation of (MPLA): *see* Portuguese Africa, Revolution in.

APRA (American Popular Revolutionary Alliance): *see* Unceda (Luis de la Puente).

Arab Workers' Socialist Party: *see* PFLP.

Assassination as an instrument of revolution can be defined as murder for a political end by the disinterested agent of a revolutionary cause. The word is derived from *Hashishi*, a name given by Crusader Europeans to the trained political murderers employed by the Old Men of the Mountains, successive rulers of a sect of Fatimid Shias founded by Hasan Ibn al-Sabbah (1092). These agents were supposed to be doped into total obedience by being given a foretaste of paradise while under the influence of hashish, though Marco Polo says it was, in fact, opium.

Assassination has been justified or even urged, as a revolutionary means, by a number of respectable, and very considerable authorities. Predictably, the Nechaev-Bakunin ◊ *Revolutionary Catechism* contains the following: 'Between the revolutionary and society there is war to the death . . . he must make a list of those who are condemned to death and expedite their sentence according to the order of their relative iniquities.' But Alfieri also, the respectable prophet of Italian freedom and unity, propounded a 'theory of the dagger' as a political method; St Thomas Aquinas grants a right, based on 'natural law', to assassinate a tyrant for the common good; and ◊ Mazzini wrote, 'holy is the dagger which Harmodius crowned with flowers; holy the dagger of Brutus'. John Locke was of opinion that 'Whoever uses force without right . . . puts himself into a state of war with those against whom he uses it, and in that case all former ties are cancelled, all other Rights cease, and everyone has a right to . . . defend himself and resist the aggressor'. The subtitle of Milton's *The Tenure of Kings and Magistrates* is 'Proving that it is lawful and hath been held so through all ages to call to account any tyrant or wicked king and after due conviction . . . to put him to death if the ordinary Magistrates have neglected or denied to do it . . .'

During the century before 1870 there were more than a score of revolutionary assassinations in Europe, including those of King Gustavus III of Sweden, Tsar Paul I of Russia, Kotzebue the German dramatist who was an agent of the Russian government, and the Turkish Sultan, Selim III. But the 'golden age' of political, usually revolutionary, assassination began *c*. 1865: the list of important victims is as follows:

Abraham Lincoln, President of USA	1865
Mihailo Obrenović, Prince of Serbia	1868
Juan Prin, Prime Minister of Spain	1870
Earl of Mayo, Viceroy of India	1872
Gabriel Garcia Moreno, President of Ecuador	1875
Abdul Aziz, Sultan of Turkey	1876
Hussein Avin, his Grand Vizier	1876
Prince D. N. Kropotkin, Governor of Kharkov	1879
Alexander II, Tsar of Russia	1881
James A. Garfield, President of USA	1881
Lord Frederick Cavendish, Chief Secretary for Ireland	1882
Thomas Henry Burke, Under-Secretary for Ireland	1882

Awolowo, Obafemi

James Wallace Quinton, British Commissioner, Assam | 1891
Carter Harrison, Mayor of Chicago | 1893
M. F. Sadi Carnot, President of France | 1894
Nasr-ed-Din, Shah of Persia | 1896
Idiarte Borda, President of Uruguay | 1896
Antonio Canovas del Castillo, Prime Minister of Spain | 1897
Jose Maria Barrios, President of Guatemala | 1898
Empress Elizabeth of Austria | 1898
Ulisses Heureux, President of Dominican Republic | 1899
James Lyall, British Consul in Bolivia | 1900
King Umberto of Italy | 1900
William McKinley, President of USA | 1901

This list is far from being exhaustive; although Dora Kaplan's bullet did not kill ⟡ Lenin outright, it contributed to his death not long afterwards. The innumerable judicial murders committed by Hitler, Stalin, Mussolini, Franco were, of course, anti-revolutionary. The assassinations of President John Kennedy of the USA and his brother Robert have not been shown to be revolutionary killings and that of Doctor Martin Luther King, although political, was not revolutionary but reactionary.

Assassination tends to be used by revolutionaries chiefly when no other means of overthrowing the Establishment seems open to them: it was favoured by anarchists and ⟡ nihilists but, as a rule, repudiated by socialists and communists.

Awolowo, Obafemi (1910–) Nigerian nationalist political leader: *see* African power transfers.

Azania. The name by which some South African black revolutionaries know their country: *see* South Africa and Rhodesia, revolution in.

Azev, Ievno (1869–1918) Russian-Jewish Social Revolutionary terrorist and police informer, b. Lyskovo, Nizhny Novgorod, father a tailor. Primary education only. In 1887 while working as a commercial traveller, he was distributing revolutionary pamphlets. Denounced by an informer he robbed his employer of 800 roubles and escaped to Germany and for a year attended Karlsruhe University among other Russian socialist emigrés.

20

Soon destitute he was approached by an Okhrana agent and agreed to act as an informer on revolutionary exile activities. At the Okhrana's suggestion he later joined the ▷ Social Revolutionary Party. He won the confidence of his comrades in Germany, France and Switzerland and was so successful in enabling the Okhrana to make arrests by supplying them with information about SR activities inside Russia that he was called to Moscow and given the task of penetrating the top ranks of the Party. He did so, learned of a plot to assassinate Spyagin, Minister of the Interior, and to move the Party's secret press to Tomsk in Siberia. He informed the Okhrana of this move, thus causing the arrest of the militant SR leaders who headed 'Organization' (originally 'Organization for Combat'), the Party's terrorist wing. As a result Azev was entrusted with command of 'Organization' and successfully organized the ▷ assassination of Spyagin and of Prince Obolensky, Governor of Kharkov. At the same time his information was enabling the Okhrana to make numerous arrests of SR militants and Azev was made directly responsible to the new Minister of the Interior, Plehve, whose assassination he master-minded successfully. He was instructed by the SR Party's 1904 Congress (Paris) to organize the assassination of the Tsar's uncles, the Grand Dukes Sergei and Vladimir. He succeeded in the case of Sergei, Governor of Moscow, but failed in that of Vladimir. In April 1905 he defeated an attempt by the Party's leading ideologist, Chernov, to persuade the SR Party to abandon the policy of ▷ terrorism. He also talked his way out of an anonymous denunciation of himself, 'Comrade Valentine', as a police spy, and when arrested as a terrorist by a new Chief of Police in St Petersburg, talked his way out of that by invoking his record as a successful counter-revolutionary agent and by revealing the names of the assassins of Father Gapon who, following the Winter Palace massacre of demonstrators on 9 January 1905, had turned police informer. Azev himself had organized that assassination.

When called on to procure the assassination of the Prime Minister, Stolypin (1905) Azev informed the Okhrana of the plot and had all the conspirators ostentatiously 'tailed'. He used this state of affairs to suspend terrorist activities for the time being but when the Social-Democratic 'Maximalists' blew up Stolypin's house, Azev was relieved of his job as head of 'Organization'. His successor, Zilberberg, however, consulted him as an expert, on a plan to assassinate both Stolypin and the St Petersburg Chief of Police, von der Launitz. Azev warned the Okhrana; Stolypin

Azikiwi, Nnamdi

changed his plans and was saved; von der Launitz ignored the warning and was killed. Azev received a bonus of 9000 roubles from the Okhrana in the same week as his election to the Central Committee of the SR Party.

In 1908 Azev fell in love with a young dancer, and deserted his wife and children to live with her. This lost him the confidence of both the SR Party and the Okhrana. For years he had had control of the Organization's very considerable funds and as he had always managed his assassinations and other terrorist activities economically, he had a large amount in hand. With this and his savings from his Okhrana salary and bonuses, he took his mistress abroad. They lived a hunted life, moving from one country to another, for the SR Party had discovered his treachery and were bent on assassinating him. His money ran out, his mistress deserted him and he died, destitute, of a kidney disease in a Berlin hospital (April 1918).

Azikiwi, Nnamdi (1904–   ) Nigerian nationalist political leader: *see* African power transfers.

B

Bakunin, Mikhail (1814–76) Anarchist philosopher and militant revolutionary, b. Tver, Russia, s. of a rich and noble landowner. He began life as a Guards officer but, revolted by the cruelty with which Polish rebels were treated, resigned his commission and went to Berlin to read philosophy under the same masters as ⟡ Marx. He became a Hegelian and a revolutionary dedicated, at first, to the destruction of Russian absolutism, subsequently to international revolution. In 1848 ⟡ he tried but failed to spread the revolution into Russia. In 1849 he took part in an insurrection in Dresden, was arrested, tried and condemned to death, but, after months in chains in the condemned cell, was handed over to the Russians who kept him for five years in solitary confinement and, when he seemed to be dying of scurvy, sent him to Siberia. After another five years there he escaped and, by way of Japan and America, reached Europe, where his eloquence and writings, and above all his sufferings, had made him a revolutionary legend. But the views he had arrived at made sustained harmony between him and the one effective revolutionary organization, the First ⟡ International, impossible. The International, dominated by ⟡ Marx's and ⟡ Engels' thinking, was for open, planned advance towards socialism by all possible means excepting secret violent conspiracy. Bakunin believed in working through secret revolutionary societies dedicated to the use of violence; furthermore he believed that existing society and its physical structure must be totally destroyed: the whole past was evil, libraries and museums just as pernicious as law courts and prisons. Bakunin was, in short, the arch-anarchist for whom the future just society must be one in which there would be no authority of any kind. Thus, when he became a member of the First International it was because he thought he could infiltrate and change it, not because he agreed with its aims and methods.

His most nearly successful foundation was the International Social-Democratic Alliance. Almost as soon as its conspiratorial foundation was known it was publicly disowned and repudiated by Marx speaking for the

23

International. But Bakunin had a large following in many countries, was able to 'pack' the Basle meetings of the International Congress in 1869 and win some successes against the Marxists, and he continued to work for armed insurrection as the only possible revolutionary method regardless of whether or not a revolutionary situation existed. In 1870, when Napoleon III suppressed the International in France, the political police exposed the conspiratorial and violent nature of the Bakunist network; and despite Marx's repudiations – he had even attacked Bakunin as a Tsarist agent, although he retracted later – its enemies were able to tar the International with the Alliance brush.

The outbreak of the Franco-Prussian war seemed to Bakunin to be his chance. At Lyons in September 1870 he managed to raise an insurrection and to control the city for a few hours, announcing that 'formal government is now abolished'. The authorities soon got the upper hand, as they did in similar cases in Marseilles and Brest. Bakunin announced that he had lost faith in the French revolutionary spirit: 'The people have shown themselves incapable of their own salvation.' But the ⟡Commune restored his faith and he again began to work for control of the International. He succeeded in raising a strong opposition from the various national sections against central control of the organization, i.e. against Marx; and in imbuing some, notably the French Swiss, Italians and Spaniards, with his own anarchist ideas. But his involvement in the ⟡ Nechayev scandal did much to discredit him with international socialism, again forcing the Central Committee of the International to repudiate him and all his works. At its Congress in The Hague, September 1872, Bakunin and all his Alliance adherents were expelled.

His writings in translation include: *Confession* (Paris 1932); *God and State* (Boston 1893); *Marxism, Freedom and the State* (London 1950); *Œuvres*, 6 vols (Paris 1914).

Banda, Hastings (1905–) Malawi nationalist political leader: *see* African power transfers.

Bay of Pigs, Cochinos Bay (1961): the name by which is known a United States counter-revolutionary attempt, planned by the Eisenhower administration but carried out by President Kennedy, to overthrow the Cuban Communist revolution of Dr Fidel ⟡ Castro. A force of Cuban Right-wing exiles under American control was landed at Cochinos Bay to launch a counter-revolution. The US administration tried to give the impression that it was not involved, the ◊ CIA even going to the length of having a Cuban exile fly a B-26 bomber from Nicaragua to Miami, where he claimed to be a defector from Cuban communism who had been bombing Castro's airfields. The counter revolution invasion was defeated by Cuban communist forces, who killed sixty men of the Force and captured 1,200.

Bebel, August (1840–1913). The 'father' of parliamentary ◊ Social Democracy, the movement which transferred the revolutionary struggle to install ◊ socialism from the streets into the national assemblies. German socialism had two founders: ◊ Lassalle, founder of the General German Workers' Union (1863); and Marx, whose disciples, led by Bebel, founded the Social Democratic Workers' Party in 1869. Bebel was a wood-turner by trade but he had set up in business on his own and become a successful manufacturer. In 1871 he was one of the first two socialists to be elected to the Reichstag. In 1875 he succeeded in uniting the two German socialist parties into the Socialist Workers' Party, which became commonly known as the Social Democratic Party. And in 1891, at a Party congress in Erfurt, he succeeded in having the whole Marxist programme adopted as the Party's policy. At the elections in 1912, a year before his death, he appeared to be well on the way to accomplishing his aim of establishing socialism in Germany by parliamentary means. With 110 seats, the Social Democrats were the largest single Party in the Reichstag. But *see* Social Democracy.

Bejar, Hector Peruvian communist and ◊ guerrilla leader, author of *Peru 1965; apuntes sobre una experiencia guerillera* (Havana 1969). He was one of the young revolutionary intellectuals who, having been in Cuba to study Fidel ◊ Castro's successful revolution, returned to Peru with the poet revolutionary Javier ◊ Heraud, May 1963, with the aim of joining the guerrilla movement of Hugo Blanco ◊ Galdos. Bejar became leader of a guerrilla band which was first known as the '15 May Movement' to commemorate the date of Heraud's death at the hands of the police and a posse of landowners; and later as the 'Javier Heraud' guerrilla. For two years this group worked among the peasants of Huanta province, forming the nucleus of the National Liberation Army which, in September 1965, went prematurely into action against the army and police, in support of Luis de

Ben Barka, El Mehdi

la Puente ⟡ Unceda's appeal for solidarity among the revolutionary guerrillas. Bejar's group fought a number of actions against army detachments
between September and December 1965, suffered a series of defeats, and
in January 1966 Bejar was captured, tried and imprisoned. Later released,
he is now head of the Peruvian government's Youth organization.

Ben Barka, El Mehdi (1920–1965) Moroccan revolutionary, b. Rabat, s.
of a policeman. Originally a Nationalist agitator, co-founder of the Istiglal
Party, an independence movement aiming to establish a constitutional
monarchy or liberal republic in Morocco, he was repeatedly imprisoned by
the French for his political activities. Following the granting of independence to the monarchy, Ben Barka faced the fact that no revolution had
been accomplished, and moved Left to form the Union of Popular Forces,
(UNFP) to campaign for major agrarian reforms. He was one of the
twenty-nine members of the Union to be elected to the National Assembly
in 1963. Condemned to death for plotting the overthrow of the monarchy,
in the same year, he escaped into exile. Several attempts at his assassination
by the Moroccan Political Police directed by the Minister of the Interior,
Mohammed Oufkir, failed. At the 1965 Afro-Asian Conference in Tanzania, Ben Barka emerged as a passionate anti-capitalist revolutionary,
proclaiming that 'all wars, aggressions and interventions of imperialism, its
maintenance of military bases in foreign lands, and its support for cruel and
corrupt dictatorships spring from and are dictated by economic exploitation'. His aim became, like that of Franz ⟡ Fanon, coordination of the
struggle of all the exploited peoples against what he identified as the arch-
enemy, US imperialism. Out of this policy came the Organization of
Solidarity of the Peoples of Africa, Asia and Latin America (OSPAAAL)
better known as the Tricontinental. Ben Barka was elected Chairman of its
Preparatory Committee but did not live to attend a single meeting: in
Paris on Tricontinental business, he was arrested while seated on a café
terrace, by the French political police operating in collaboration with their
Moroccan colleagues, taken to a house in the suburbs where Mohammed
Oufkir was waiting, murdered, and his body thrown into the river Essone.
Oufkir and his chief of political police Ahmed Dlimi were charged with the
murder but as nobody could be produced, the charges were dropped.

Bernstein, Edouard: *see* Revisionism.

Black Panther Party. An all-black political party in the U S A founded by Huey P. ⇨ Newton and Bobby ⇨ Seale with, originally, limited 'liberationist' purposes but which has since become revolutionary. Known first as the Lowndes County Freedom Organization, it adopted the Black Panther as its symbol and then became known as the Black Panther Party for Self-Defence. It was in March 1965 that Newton, Seale and some other ⇨ SNCC workers moved into Lowndes County, Alabama, to set up a political operation as part of the Civil Rights campaign. The place was deliberately chosen as exceptionally difficult, for it has an atrocious record of both personal and institutional racism and the withholding of civil rights from blacks; it had long been run as what Stokeley Carmichael called 'a totalitarian police state' by the white minority's leaders. The SNCC's objective was to create a ⇨ Black Power base in the county and thereby make the black vote effective, for the first time, in the county elections of November 1966. The county had a large black majority but had always had all-white government. In theory an elected official in the U S administration represents all the citizens, so that his colour is irrelevant; but it has long been found in practice (*see* Black Power), especially in the South, that white officials and judges use their power to prevent their black fellow citizens from receiving their due share of political power, decision-making, education facilities, welfare, etc. The only way to change this situation was to elect black officials and judges, etc. Black grievances in the county were such as to create a revolutionary situation: e.g. average income of black households, $985; black houses had no running water or sanitation; 90 per cent of the community's farmland was owned by eighty-six white families with the result that a majority of the black population, although *de jure* full citizens, were *de facto* still little better than plantation slaves. The SNCC persuaded black citizens to overcome the fears induced by a long tradition of brutal intimidation and to register as voters; then steered them past the psychological and physical obstacles erected by white officials to prevent them from doing so; then tried to ensure that those registered did, in fact, vote – 3,900 registrations were achieved, but black candidates had then to be found and to that end the SNCC workers founded their political party, as Alabaman law entitled them to do. At every stage, from the organization of Primaries to the final poll, the Black Panthers had to deal with angry white obstructionism in a county where blacks had more than once been murdered for trying to assert their rights. In the event the new Party did

not win a single office: to ensure this the Democrat and Republican whites
split their vote, casting it for the white candidate regardless of Party; and
the white plantation owners motored their 'niggers' into town and terrified
them into voting for white candidates. But 40 per cent of the votes were
cast for black candidates and the whole operation was the first important
practical expression of Black Power theory.

H. P. Newton, known as the Party's Minister of Defence has thus
expressed the Party's attitude to the use of violence: 'A Panther will not
attack anyone but will back up first. But if the assailant is persistent then
the Black Panther will strike out and wipe out his aggressor thoroughly,
wholly, absolutely and completely.' That was the theory of counterviolence,
but following Newton's arrest for killing a policeman in 1968, the words
'self-defence' were dropped from the Party's title and the Party became
militantly aggressive, taking the violent vanguard in the Black Power movement; at about the same time it became social revolutionary and allied
itself with white and Chicano (Mexican-American) revolutionary groups.
Newton is serving a prison sentence but he remains the acknowledged
leader of the Party: he has given, as its aims and programme:

... to weld ourselves into a viable people; to gain economic strength by
forming all-Black cooperatives; to work for the total destruction of the
capitalist system ultimately by nationalization of the means of production,
etc., meanwhile by advocating the formation by all ethnic minority groups,
of business and industrial cooperatives – that is, not only by Blacks, but by
the Indians, Chicanos, Chinese, Irish and even Italians. Such cooperatives
must be controlled 'From the bottom up, not from the top down'. We fight
for our freedom in our own terrain, but in alliance with everyone who fights
our enemy, not just because we need each other tactically but because we are
brothers. As internationalists, then, it is our duty to create, as Che said,
many Vietnams.

The Black Panther movement has been crippled, if not quite smashed,
by two counter-revolutionary means: ruthless police violence; and penetration of the movement by *agents provocateurs* who were successful in
provoking internecine disputes which fatally weakened the Panthers. Their
principal achievement has been to give to American blacks confidence
in the possibilities of fighting back; at the time of writing they are
casting about for new tactics, e.g. Newton's plans for black community
projects.

Black Power. These words describe not a movement but what can best be described as a specifically Negro revolutionary state of mind, the context in which both militant and reformist movements among the 22 million American blacks exist. Its original intention was to obtain that share of political power and economic prosperity for the black population of America, proportional to its numbers, to which it is by law entitled. But it has become increasingly social revolutionary. The Black Power state of mind originates, perhaps, with the National Association for the Advancement of Coloured People (NAACP), but certainly with ◊ SNCC, originally led by Stokeley Carmichael. A long history of frustration of all black attempts to become assimilated into US society at large and obtain full civil and social rights under law, is the cause of the spread of the Black Power state of mind. The supporting argument is as follows: since the blacks have repeatedly failed, in the face of white opposition and obstruction, to advance their economic and political standing to full equality with the whites simply as American citizens, then they must advance to that objective specifically as blacks. The only way to do so is from Black Power bases: American blacks must learn to regard themselves, *vis-à-vis* the whites, as being in precisely the same situation as a black African people under the dominion of a colonial power. The setting up of such Black Power bases, e.g. the ◊ Black Panther Party, the ◊ League of Black Revolutionary Workers etc. means, in practice, the formation and organization of specifically black political parties; withdrawal of the black vote from white candidates for political or juridical office and concentration of that vote on black candidates; the new parties should have programmes of black advancement to political and economic power; organization of the blacks by black leaders to resist gerrymandering and manipulation of institutions and laws to exclude blacks from their fair share of power; elimination from the black American psyche of the inferiority feeling inculcated by the history of the blacks in America, that slave mentality which weakens them in their struggle for full citizenship; deliberate use of the only economic power they wield, i.e. purchasing power, by the boycott of white business, as initiated by the NAACP in Montgomery, Alabama under the leadership of Martin Luther King, to enforce the reinvestment of the profits of white commerce in black communities, in those communities. These were the original aims, but the arguments of the American black leaders now lead on to something more revolutionary than this; the younger leaders are fundamentally revolutionary. In so far as they find American institutions 'Anglo' – orientated and ineffectual in procuring the good life even for the poor white citizen, they have the right to set about changing those institutions which, they argue, are only expedients for living and in no way sacred. The failure of those institutions is such that the blacks are by no means alone in their predicament. On the other hand the solidarity which the colour of their skins forces on the blacks (excepting the spiritually 'white' blacks of the small, prosperous black bourgeoisie), their exclusion from full civil rights, their history of relegation to second-class citizenship, confronts them far more starkly than the poor whites with the realities of capitalism; they are, therefore, called upon, and peculiarly fitted to be the leading revolutionary class in American society. Black Power is not a manifestation of Marxism, but its intellectuals' analysis of its place in the Great Society is very reminiscent of the Marxist analysis of the place and revolutionary destiny of the working class in capitalist society; it is as if the whole working class just happened to be black; and it is certainly true that the American blacks are at least 90 per cent working class. This has become apparent to Black Power leaders, with a resultant shift towards a Marxist-Leninist ideology and cooperation with such international revolutionary organizations as ⟡ OLAS and the Tricontinental (⟡ OSPAAAL). But by no means all the Black Power leaders favour such cooperation and it is sometimes possible to detect a slight taint of Pan-American arrogance towards European, Asian, African and Latin American fellow-revolutionaries. The older, moderate leaders of the American blacks hoped to bring about the required changes and establish a fair measure of Black Power by peaceful means and organized their movements in that sense: even so, their warning to the whites was clearly uttered and might be summed up in the famous phrase: 'This animal is wicked; when attacked, it defends itself.' So that even those leaders, excepting such devout Christian pacifists as Martin Luther King, did not exclude recourse to the use of violence, if it was forced on them by white recalcitrance.

Black September: *see* PFLP.

Blanc, Louis (1811–82) French socialist revolutionary theorist and politician; b. Madrid where his father was administrator of the treasury during the Napoleonic occupation of Spain. As a law student in Paris he suffered poverty which could have been but was not alleviated by his mother's rich family. Partly as a result of personal bitterness against the establishment, partly from genuine compassion and partly from his reading of the socialist Saint-Simon, he developed revolutionary socialist theories of his own, and in 1839 published one of the key books of socialism, *L'Organisation du travail*. It advocated the right of every man to work; the establishment of cooperative workshops to be capitalized by the State but run by the workers themselves; equal pay for all regardless of industrial rank; and the famous principle 'to each according to his needs; from each according to his capacity'. Some light is thrown on his personal character by the fact that he was an admirer of Robespierre and tried to rehabilitate him as the friend of the working man. His pamphlet *Histoire des dix ans*, a savage and biting attack on the bourgeois Orleanist monarchy, contributed to the overthrow of Louis-Philippe and his government in the Revolution of 1848 which, by instituting manhood suffrage in France, put a measure of power into the hands of the working class for the first time. Blanc became a member of the revolutionary Provisional Government (February to May 1848) and Chairman of the 'Luxembourg Commission' charged with the task of eliminating unemployment. That seemed to be his chance to apply his theories in practice and he tried to establish ⟡ syndicalist-type workshops which would take over industry so that the workers could run it. The government did establish 'nationalized' workshops: but the workers assembled in them were of an assortment of trades, and were given no useful work to do. This botching of Blanc's ideas failed, as it was bound to do; the hungry and furious workers rose in insurrection; Blanc was made the scapegoat and was forced to take refuge in England. The Second Empire dictatorship made it dangerous for him to return, and he remained in England until 1871. He then returned to France to become a socialist deputy for Marseilles in the Third Republic. The fact that he had originated some of the ideas later attributed to ⟡ Marx seemed to offend the Marxists, and as they never trusted Blanc he remained a political outsider for the rest of his life.

Blanqui, Auguste (1805–81) French socialist revolutionary, b. Pujet-Theniers, s. of a Sousprefet. Ed. for law and medicine, he fought in the 1830 Revolution which sent Charles X into exile, but soon turned against the 'bourgeois monarchy' and was imprisoned in 1831 and again in 1836 for implication in republican conspiracies. In 1838 he organized the clandestine revolutionary Society of the Seasons which led an insurrection in 1839. Blanqui was arrested and sentenced to death, but the sentence was commuted to life imprisonment. In 1848 he was officially reported dying and released. This seems to have cured him instantly, for he set about organizing a political club, the Société Republicaine Centrale which he used to put pressure on the new republican government to force it to the Left. Implicated against his better judgement in the armed assault (15 May 1848) on the Assembly, he was sent to prison for ten years and there worked out his political philosophy. Communist *syndicats* (trade unions) were to be organized and used to break the bourgeoisie by strikes including the ◇ general strike, followed by an armed revolution; the revolution would be succeeded by a dictatorship of the proletariat managing a fully communist economic and social regime. When Blanqui was released from prison in 1859, he again organized secret political societies, was again caught and imprisoned (1861). He escaped to Belgium (1865) and from there resumed his work so effectively that when France's defeat by the Prussians (1870) created a revolutionary situation in Paris, he was able to raise a force of 4,000 trained and armed communist revolutionaries to overthrow the Imperial administration. Blanqui became head of a provisional revolutionary government in opposition to the bourgeois Versailles regime (*see* Commune 1871). But Blanqui was exhausted and Thiers persuaded him to stand down in the name of unity in the face of the Prussian enemy – he was always an ardent patriot. When he went to the country to recuperate, Thiers had him seized and imprisoned, so that he could not take the seat in the Commune to which his followers had elected him. While still in prison he stood for the Chambre des Deputés for Bordeaux. A long public agitation resulted in his release in 1879 and he spent the last three years of his life in making communist propaganda. Of his several published works the most important is *Critique Sociale* (2 vols., 1885). His Blanquist Party was absorbed into the French Socialist Party in 1905.

Bloody Sunday. The event which sparked off the ◇ Russian Revolution 1905. Georgy Gapon, an ambitious priest of magnificent presence making a career as a demagogue, had applied himself to improving the atrocious conditions of the St Petersburg workers. The Tsarist authorities, believing that it would be wiser to use than to suppress him, authorized him to organize the Assembly of Russian Factory Workers, a sort of trade union, on condition that he should confine himself to struggling with the employers for better wages and conditions, and keep clear of politics. But his Assembly became by far the biggest and most powerful working-class movement in Russia, independent of and even hostile to the Social Revolutionary ◊ and Social Democratic (◊ Bolshevik and Menshevik) Parties. In December 1904 four workmen were arbitrarily dismissed from the Putilov works. Gapon called a strike and the entire work force of 13,000 men responded. The strike soon became general throughout the capital, with an estimated 120,000 men (Nicholas II's diary) out; the government moved Guards regiments into the city and occupied all key institutions, and Gapon decided on a march of workers, their wives and children to the Winter Palace to present a petition to the Tsar.

The petitioners' march took place on the morning of 9 January 1905; 200,000 people took part, led by Gapon. But a military ambush had been prepared by the government near the Narva Gate, the procession was charged from the front by Cossacks using sabres to cut down the marchers, while a division of Guards opened fire from the sides. No casualty figures were published but it seems that about a thousand people were killed or badly wounded. Gapon escaped unhurt and went to join other Russian political exiles in Germany where he declared himself to be a Social-Democrat, a declaration which Lenin received with dour scepticism. The scepticism was justified: Gapon had been paid 50,000 roubles by the Okhrana to act as an informer among the revolutionary *emigrés*. This fact was known to the double-agent Azev, who was both an Okhrana agent and head of 'Organization', the terrorist wing of the Socialist Revolutionary Party. As a result, when Gapon returned to Russia, he was lured to an empty building and there hanged by Azev's SR assassins.

Bolivia: ◊ **Guerrilla movement.** The revolutionary guerrilla 'episode' in Bolivia (1967) was not a native movement. Ernesto (Che) ◊ Guevara, its leader, proposed to create, in mainland Latin America, the conditions in which mass revolution would become possible, by a guerrilla war of attrition against the establishments in Latin American countries. Bolivia was chosen as a centre and focus of this general action for what seemed to be sound reasons. Its mountainous terrain is such as to enable small groups of trained *guerrilleros* to pin down large regular army forces; frontiers with

c

five other republics favour the revolutionary forces' interior communications, while absence of roads make regular troop movements difficult; and
the extreme poverty of the illiterate peasant population might be expected
to prove fertile soil for revolution. (Guevara's theory, based on that of ◊
Mao Tse-tung and supported by the writings of Regis ◊ Debray, was that
in Latin American conditions the country must bring the revolution to the
cities.)

Guevara entered Bolivia early in 1967 disguised as a Uruguayan businessman and set up a secret HQ in a lonely farmhouse, where he was joined by
seventeen Cuban volunteers. But it proved very difficult to recruit Boli-
vians, partly because the politically conscious ones were under the influence
of the Communist Party whose Central Committee in La Paz, hamstrung
by the Sino-Soviet quarrel, was very reluctant to provide support. While
Che Guevara was out on a recruiting expedition north of the Rio Grande,
Regis Debray arrived (March 1967) at his HQ, ostensibly to interview him
as a journalist, actually to try to join him. He remained with the guerrilla
band for some time, moved with them when they went into action,
and was betrayed and arrested on his way out of the country charged
with the task of making propaganda for the revolutionary cause in Latin
America.

Meanwhile Che operated successfully for some months. Abandoning his
original base (betrayed by the deserter who denounced Debray to the
police) and operating from a cave, he ambushed and defeated the vanguard
of the military force sent against him. He was joined by a few more
peasants, and by some miner recruits belonging to a dissident, more or less
◊ Maoist communist group led by Moises Guevara (no relation). He hung
on in expectation of reinforcements from Havana, and from another
guerrilla group operating in the frontier country. His National Liberation
Army (NLA), as he called his group, operated with sufficient éclat to force
the Bolivian government, under CIA pressure, to suppress all left-wing
parties and, following another guerrilla victory over the army at Iripiti (10
April), to set up an anti-guerrilla training school under CIA command.
But the real weakness of the NLA was perfectly clear to Che and another
attempt was made to gain CP support, two members of the Central
Committee going to Cuba to discuss the matter with ◊ Castro. Eventually
the Bolivian government, using very large numbers of troops and American
helicopters, found and surrounded Guevara's band in the Quebrada del Yuro,

a narrow heavily wooded gorge in the mountainous heart of Bolivia. In trying to slip out of this trap with half his men while the other half (who eventually escaped) gave covering fire, Che was wounded in the leg, captured and, on orders from La Paz, shot. Since his death the guerrilla movement in Bolivia, although by no means extinct, has been ineffectual.

Bolshevik, Bolshevism, from the Russian *bolshintsvo*, majority. In 1903 the Russian Social Democratic Party split over the question of the organization of the party. The revolutionary faction led by ◊ Lenin was given a majority of the votes by the party congress, and thus became known as *bolsheviki*, 'majoritists'. The word was formerly used as synonymous with communists and occasionally still is. Among the West European and American ◊ bourgeoisie the word *bolshevik*, shortened in the English vernacular to *bolshy*, became a term to describe any left-wing radical, by extension, a term of abuse, or even a loose synonym of 'bloody-minded', i.e. discontented, subversive. The Russian for minority is *menshintsvo*: the minority of the congress voters in the Russian Social Democratic Party thus became known as *mensheviki*, or, in English, Mensheviks.

Borodin, Mikhail Markovich (real name Grusenberg: 1884–1951) b. Yanovich, Vitebsk, Russia. He joined the Jewish Social Democratic Bund in his teens, switched to the Bolshevik Party in 1903 and three years later was arrested and exiled for revolutionary activities. He emigrated to the US and after some terms at the University of Valparaiso (Ind.) set up a school for immigrants in Chicago. He returned to Russia in 1917 and acted as Bolshevik agent in Mexico, Scandinavia and Britain where, Glasgow 1922, he was sent to prison for six months for inciting to revolution, and then deported. The principal revolutionary work of his life was done as the Soviet Commissar serving with the Chinese Communists 1923–27, with the job of directing their revolutionary activities along orthodox Marxist lines, that is towards helping the 'bourgeois' revolution of ◊ Chiang Kai-shek and the Kuomintang: a policy seen at the time as prerequisite to a subsequent proletarian revolution. Since Borodin was acting on the strict orders of the Executive Committee of the CP of the USSR he cannot fairly be held responsible for the disastrous outcome of this policy, Chiang's massacre of his communist allies; nor was he blamed,

35

for he returned to the USSR to become People's Commissar for Labour. However, he was steadily demoted and from 1932 had the comparatively unimportant job of editing the English language *Moscow Daily News*. His relative obscurity enabled him to escape the Stalinist purges of the 1930s, but in 1949 he was arrested in one of the dictator's antisemitic, anti-intellectual drives, and died in a Siberian labour camp two years later.

Boumédienne, Houari, Colonel (Mohammed Bourkharouba, 1925–) s. of an Algerian farmhand, ed. universities of Tunis and El Azhar, Cairo. He became a school-teacher in Cairo where he met Ben Bella, founder of the ▷ FLN which he joined. With nine companions he returned to Algeria, landing secretly near Oran, joined the guerrilla bands fighting the French and a year later was one of the principal and most successful leaders. At a date not on record he crossed into Tunis and there undertook the training of an FLN army of 60,000 men, well armed with Soviet weapons and supported by President ▷ Nasser of Egypt. After France had been forced by the FLN to concede independence (1962) the first Algerian President of the new Republic, Ben Kedda, was far too moderate in his political attitude to suit Boumédienne, who had become a Marxist, and who used threats of a military coup to force the Government to the Left: threats failing, Boumédienne marched on Algiers, deposed the President and put Mohammed Ben Bella in his place and kept him there for three years by using the army to crush all signs of opposition. But, dissatisfied with the speed and measure of socialization of the Ben Bella government, and inspired by the examples of Nasser and Fidel ▷ Castro, in 1965 he used his control of the army to depose Ben Bella and the government, and to install, as government, a Council of the Revolution, with himself as President, and a policy of international socialism and the declared intention of extending the revolution to Tunis and Morocco.

Bourgeois, bourgeoisie. From (French) *bourg*, town. Literally in English, *burgess*, i.e. an urban householder (*cf* in demotic French, *ma bourgeoise*, 'my goodwife'). A term of abuse among left revolutionaries. As an adjective its literal meaning is 'belonging to the urban middle-class'. But in Marxist revolutionary parlance, although, used objectively, it simply means the capital-owning class which the revolutionary proletariat must overthrow and replace in economic and political power, it tends to become more or less pejorative according to context: thus, for the revolutionary artist or intellectual, *bourgeois* has come to mean 'having basely selfish, materialistic, conformist ideas'; and for the Marxist-trained militant, it means the class enemy. In socialist propaganda the word may mean a wicked person inspired by greed and animated by a cruel hatred of the workers, usually depicted in caricature as dressed in a frock-coat and silk hat and with a vicious, brutal face – thus, by extension, the Enemy of Mankind, or Devil; though in this usage, it has largely been replaced by ◊ 'Fascist'.

'Bourgeoisie' means, in Marxist parlance, the capitalist class as a whole. It is sometimes divided, usually by French theorists, into *petite bourgeoisie* (Eng. petty-bourgeois), the class of shopkeepers and other small business-men; and *haute bourgeoisie*, the plutocracy of bankers and monopoly capitalist industrialists. At least among artist and writers the pejorative usage antedates Marxism: a *bourgeois* was the antithesis of a *bohemian*.

Bourguiba, Habib (1904–) Tunisian Nationalist politician, leader of the Destourian Socialist Party. This is a reformist rather than a revolutionary party; and although Bourguiba suffered ten years of exile, some of them in prison, at French hands, for advocating Tunisian independence, he did not attain this object by revolution, but by concession, being released by the French to become President of the Republic of Tunis when they had decided to concede sovereignty (July 1957). *See* African power transfers.

Boycott. About 1880, at the suggestion of Charles Stewart ◊ Parnell, Irish farmers began to use a new method of fighting the Land League case for revolutionary changes in the laws of land tenure in Ireland. Oppressive or grasping landlords and land agents, e.g. those who evicted old tenants with a view to getting higher rents from new ones, were ostracized: not only did farmers refrain from making bids for the farms which they offered, but they refused all dealings, commercial or social with them. The first victim of this ostracism was the notoriously unjust and cruel agent of the Erne estate, Captain Charles Boycott. Parnell was imprisoned for inciting to boycott in 1881. Boycotting has since been used by revolutionaries and reformers, in some cases effectively, notably by ◊ Gandhi in India (1920–39) and by Martin Luther King in Alabama. Since it does not involve any breach of law it is extremely difficult to counter.

Bravo, Douglas

Bravo, Douglas (1933–) Venezuelan Communist and guerrilla leader, and last commander of the ◊ FALN. *See* ◊ Venezuela.

Bukharin, Nikita Ivanovich (1888–1938) b. Moscow, joined the Social Democrat, later Communist Party at eighteen and at twenty was serving on its Moscow Central Committee. Arrested and deported to Siberia 1911, he escaped to Germany. First met ◊ Lenin at Cracow 1912 and was, thereafter, one of the founding fathers of the October Revolution. Spent World War I in Switzerland, Scandinavia and the USA, where he edited the revolutionary newspaper *Novy Mir*. Returned to Russia on the outbreak of the ◊ Russian Revolution February 1917; elected Central Committee of the CP; edited *Pravda*. Executive Committee, ◊ Comintern, from 1919 and as such was principally engaged in the task of spreading the Bolshevik revolution beyond Russia. Published, 1920, *The Economy of the Transitional Period*, the first postwar work of communist scholasticism, and stigmatized as such by Lenin who nevertheless called Bukharin 'our Party's most valuable and greatest theorist', a reputation which he justified by a series of theoretical works during the next few years. He became a member of the Politbureau in 1924, supporting Stalin against Trotsky, who regarded him as unreliable. Bukharin changed sides over Stalin's crash industrialization policy which he disapproved (1928) and as a result was stripped of all his offices (1929). He tried but failed to restore his position by recanting, but was kept in obscurity. This did not save him from ◊ Stalin's pathological distrust and in 1937 he was judicially murdered by Stalin's courts in one of the infamous 'purge' trials of 'counter-revolutionaries'.

Bureaucracy. In his later writings ◊ Lenin distinguished bureaucracy as the mortal enemy of ◊ socialism and this view of CP bureaucracy has become for the ◊ New (Marxist- ◊ Leninist) Left a stick with which to beat the government of the USSR which ◊ Stalin made into bureaucratic tyranny, thus denying Russians the chance to make their country Socialist. A controversy between ◊ Trotsky and Lenin at the Eleventh Congress of the Bolshevik Party in 1920 brought out Lenin's fears of 'bureaucratic deformity' to which he was to revert in his *Cooperation* (1923) and other writings during the next three years. Trotsky was for rigorous centralization of power: 'the toiling masses must be set in motion and commanded like an army'; and at the 8th Congress of Soviets later that same year he called for 'unity of command of all the economic commissariats' and a virtual militarization of the trade unions which were to become simply instruments of the central planning authority. Lenin, while accepting the need for a unified national plan, opposed administrative centralization: realization of the plan must be accomplished by participation of 'large masses of the workers, not members of a political party, through their trade unions'. (For the significance of that 'not members of a political party' *see* Cultural Revolution.) The principal task of the trade unions, he said, was to check the growth of the Party bureaucracy's power and ensure that real power remained in the workers' hands; in particular, the trade unions must, each in its own industry, retain firm control over those administrators in whom personal power had been vested. 'Our State,' he wrote, 'is a worker State suffering from bureaucratic deformity.' Still more specifically: 'Such is our State today that the organized proletariat must now defend itself and we must make use of the workers' organizations to defend the workers against the State.' (Works xxxii, 17.)

Again, in *The Trade Unions Again* (1921), he wrote that a principal task of the trade unions was 'the struggle against bureaucratic deformation of the Soviet apparatus', and in a letter to Krijijanovsky (*ibid*, xxxiii, 489), one of the directors of the national economic plan: 'The greatest danger is excessive bureaucratization of the national economic plan. It is an enormous danger.'

The danger continued to preoccupy him until his death just before which he wrote: 'Our worst internal enemy is the bureaucrat, the Communist occupying a responsible post in our Soviet institutions' (*ibid*, xxxiii, 288).

Lenin's antibureaucratic feeling and thinking was not entirely original but was inspired by ◇ Marx's *Critique of Hegel's Philosophy of the State*, in which Marx describes bureaucracy as a concentrated manifestation of the alienation between the general and the particular interest; that was why bureaucracy was characteristic of any class regime founded on the exploitation and domination of the majority of the people by a minority: for it gives such exploitation and domination 'an anonymous face'. Marx continues: (*Oeuvres philosophiques*, iv, 102): 'The spirit of bureaucracy is secretiveness', it demands, 'passive obedience, faith in authority, automatic, mechanical response', for, 'the bureaucrat sees in the world of men only an *object* of his activity'.

What Lenin perceived with such alarm and warned of so repeatedly was

39

that the return of bureaucracy to the Soviet State reintroduced that alienation between the workers and what was supposed to be their own State, which made the worker once again an object, instead of a subject, of history. The *only* way to put an end to this very dangerous state of affairs was to ensure that every worker played a part in the management of both the economy, by giving power to his trade union and teaching him to run that union democratically; and in the management of the state apparatus. (Hence the association between his writings against bureaucracy and those on the cultural revolution: only an educated proletariat with access to the whole pre-revolution culture, could stand up to the bureaucracy.) When, *but only when*, that had been brought about in the condition of 'State monopoly capitalism' which had been achieved by the socialization of the means of production, distribution and exchange, would socialism have been accomplished.

Thus, bureaucracy is seen by both Marx and Lenin as the principal obstacle in the way of the achievement of socialism. It is probable that before he died Lenin had even spotted the arch-bureaucrat who represented the greatest danger to the hopes of making the USSR socialist: 'Comrade Stalin,' he said in the testament which he wrote when he had realized that he had not long to live, 'having become Secretary General [of the Party's Central Committee] has concentrated unlimited power in his own hands, and I am not satisfied that he can make use of it with sufficient circumspection'; and in the same document he urged that the Central Committee be increased to one hundred members, which would make it much more difficult for Stalin, or any other one man, to keep real power in his own hands.

As we know to our great cost, Lenin's warnings went unheeded; or, rather, Trotsky, becoming Stalin's principal opponent, was neither strong (he was seriously ill at the critical time), nor adroit enough to muster an effective opposition to Stalin. As a result, the revolution was betrayed, and the USSR fossilized at the state monopoly capitalist stage.

It is worthwhile adding that in the still capitalist countries, where the bourgeoisie has retained control, the loss of all liberty is implicit in the growth of 'managerial' power i.e. of the bureaucracy of the great monopoly capitalist industrial and commercial groups.

Burma, revolution in: *see* Thakin Than Tun.

C

Cabral, Amilcar (1921–73) b. Verde Islands; ed. Gil Eanes High School, Sao Vicente and Instituto superior de Agronomica, Lisbon. Portuguese Guinean revolutionary leader, and one of only four blacks from his country to obtain a university degree before 1950. In 1956 he helped found the African Independence Party of Guinea and Cape Verde (PAIGG) and made its first task a thorough study of his country's revolutionary potential. This enabled him to modify the Chinese, Algerian and Cuban theories of how to fight for Marxism- ◊ Leninism to suit Guinean conditions: in the virtual absence of a ◊ proletariat and with an illiterate and politically very backward 'peasantry', Cabral decided that the 'petty ◊ bourgeois' class to which he himself, by his own account, belonged, must be drawn into the vanguard of the struggle and his Party's propaganda to that end was so successful that in 1956 and 1959 the Portuguese government steadily stepped up the violence of the repressive measures taken against the Party. Meanwhile recruits were being trained in the neighbouring Republic of Guinea to form the FARP (People's Revolutionary Armed Forces) and with this instrument Cabral was able to react to government use of force by counterviolence on ◊ Maoist lines, applying a suitably modified version of the so-called ◊ Lin-Piao Theory of Revolution. In the absence of classically suitable ◊ guerrilla terrain (jungles, mountains) and in keeping with Cabral's often quoted maxim that 'rice cannot be boiled outside the pot', PAIGG forces have depended on their relationship with the local people to protect them from detection and obliteration by Portuguese forces and by 1969 had reduced the government's effective control over the territory to a tiny enclave around Bissau. Cabral's revolutionary aim can be conveyed briefly by quoting one of his speeches to his guerrillas before leading them into action: 'If we wage this war just to drive out the Portuguese, the struggle is not worth it. We fight for that, yes, but also so that nobody can exploit anybody else, white or black . . . we fight to build.'

His speeches in various parts of the ◊ New Left world indicated that what he hoped to build was African unity, a new Socialist society, but he

Cadres

had to carefully avoid identification with either 'Soviet' or 'Chinese' ideologies. He was assassinated in January 1973 by a small group of traitors. His main political publication in English is *Revolution in Guinea; Selected texts*, 1971.

Cadres, from the French *cadre*, Latin *quadrus*, a square or, by extension, frame or framework. First used in its present sense by the French army to mean the permanent, professional nucleus of officers of a military unit round which the full unit could be quickly built at need, it was adopted by Socialist revolutionaries to signify a hard core of revolutionary militants, trained for their work, about which larger revolutionary action units can be built when the time comes for action.

Capitalism, the principal target of all modern leftist revolutionary militant action is the economic system under which the means of production, distribution and exchange are privately owned by individuals or, more commonly, by more or less numerous groups of shareholders, and operated for profit; this contrasts with socialism in which they are owned by the state and operated for public service; or, e.g. ◊ syndicalism under which each industry's trade union would own it and operate it for wages and service costs. Capitalism was formerly a liberal system of competition between small or medium-sized units, competition tending to keep prices (but also, to some extent, wages), low. But socialists, notably ◊ Marx, argued that as the larger and stronger units must tend to eliminate or absorb the smaller and weaker, larger and larger concentrations of capital would occur, competition be eliminated, and the economic life of society be controlled by fewer and fewer huge combines, trusts or groups of companies. This forecast has been vindicated, and the process has thus produced and increasingly tends to produce monopoly capitalism. Attempts on the part of the state to protect its power, in the name of the people, e.g. by such devices as the USA anti-trust legislation or the British Monopolies Commission are rarely successful. Since very large economic units can only, like states, be managed by bureaucracies, power in monopoly capitalism passes out of the hands of the shareholders into those of the managers (cf. 'the managerial revolution'). In this respect monopoly capitalism tends to foreshadow socialism which it also resembles in some other respects, e.g. in replacing the control of prices by 'the market' with price-fixing; in the use of short-

and long-term planning; and in the transcending of political frontiers by an increasing measure of internationalism.

Although Karl Marx and Friedrich ⟡ Engels in *Das Kapital* (3 vols, 1867, 1885, 1894) described the history and functioning of capitalism objectively, including its flaws and inherent weaknesses, nevertheless, under the influence of strong revolutionary emotion and as a consequence of the human need to see one's enemy as wicked, it has in communist and to some extent also in socialist and other eyes acquired the attributes of a popular myth. No longer simply an economic system, it looms sombrely as the fount of all evil, replacing the devil, the great whore, the great enemy of the human race, in the popular revolutionary pantheon of demons. For the objections to it deriving from such respectable emotions as compassion and charity, and from rational arguments based on equity and the passion for justice, *see* socialism. For a complete critique of the system, refer to *Das Kapital*, available in all major languages.

For the final phase of capitalism, *see* Imperialism

Carmichael, Stokeley (1941–   ): *see* Black Panther Party, Black Power.

Castro, Fidel Ruz (1926–   ) Cuban Communist leader; b. Cuba, s. of an immigrant Galician farmer, Castro was educated at the Roman Catholic boarding school, Santiago, the Jesuit College, Belen, and Havana University. His first revolutionary action was as a partisan in a raid on the Dominican Republic (1947). In 1953 he and his brother Raül, in revolt against the corrupt dictatorship (nominally, presidency) of Batista, organized and took part in an attack on a Santiago army barracks in an attempt to obtain arms for the revolution. Caught, Fidel was sent to prison for fifteen years, his brother for thirteen. Released by Batista's 1955 amnesty for political prisoners, they went to Mexico to recruit and organize a revolutionary force to overthrow Batista and establish a Socialist government in Cuba. They returned to the island in December 1956 with a small force including Ernesto 'Che' ⟡ Guevara, which Castro led into the Sierra Maestre mountains. From there Castro launched his attack, and waged revolutionary war on Batista's forces, using ⟡ guerrilla tactics devised by Guevara. For three years his forces grew by recruitment from the peasantry and his successes grew until, on 1 January 1959 he marched into Havana and Batista was forced to flee the country.

Castro, Fidel Ruz

Castro suspended the American-style constitution and, as Prime Minister and Minister for the Armed Forces, with Raül as his Deputy, began to rule by decree of the collective leadership, his policies being shaped by Marxist-▷Leninist ideology, and his political instruments being a one-hundred-strong Central Committee of the Cuban Communist Party which emerged only after the revolution was over, with an eight-man ▷ Politbureau and a six-man Secretariat. Castro's government has been firmly established for twelve years.

He is far from being a conservative, USSR-type communist; his position is much nearer to that of ▷Mao Tse-tung, as was that of Che Guevara who was put in charge of the Cuban agrarian reforms, acted as principal envoy for foreign trade, and became president of the National Bank. In Maoist or Guevarist Communism, much less weight is given than in the USSR to a ruling party élite, and much more weight to the people, or at least to the peasant guerrillas or freedom fighters. Thus, great efforts have been made to involve the people in decision-making, and to educate them in the spirit of ▷ cultural revolution for that work.

Castro's positive achievements following the success of his communist revolution have been chiefly in land reform and education. The education programme, absorbing about 16 per cent of the national revenue, is designed to eliminate illiteracy as quickly as possible. The land, nearly all of which was held by a very small class of rich proprietors, has been redistributed in holdings of not more than 67 hectares (166 acres) for ordinary farms, not more than 1,340 hectares (3,300 acres) for sugar and rice plantation, and cattle ranches. Seventy per cent of the cultivable land is worked by 1,400 cooperative farms.

Before the revolution nearly 80 per cent of Cuban trade was with the United States. But following the ▷ Bay of Pigs affair, Castro saw the USA as his most dangerous enemy and looked for aid and trade to the Communist countries. Eighty per cent of his trade is now with those countries who supply Cuba with oil and manufactured goods, chiefly capital goods, in exchange for sugar, tobacco and nickel. There is, however, some trade with Western European countries, and Britain has supplied Cuba with buses and trucks.

Castro's was the first completely successful Marxist–Leninist revolution in the western hemisphere. But his attempts to spread it to other Central and South American countries and his agreement to allow Khruschev to

44

Chernyshevsky, N. G.

establish USSR missile-launching sites in Cuba have made the revolution some very powerful enemies.

Catechism, Revolutionary: *see* Revolutionary catechism; Nechayev; Bakunin.

Charro Negro, *nom de guerre* of Fermin Charry Rincon; *nom de plume* Jacobo Frias Alape. Colombian ◊ guerrilla leader, member of the Colombian CP, Central Committee, founder of Marquetalia (*see* Colombia). Killed in action January 1960.

Chernyshevsky, N. G. (1828–89) Russian revolutionary socialist theorist, important in the history of revolution for his inspiration of ◊ populist movements and of ◊ Nihilism. b. Saratov, Lower Volga, in recently colonized Cossack country; s. of an enlightened priest. A remarkable linguist, as a boy he learnt Latin, Greek, Hebrew, French, English, German and Polish, and despite theological studies read such profane authors as Dickens, George Sand, Byron, Pushkin and Gogol; and such revolutionary ones as ◊ Herzen. Since he was always at odds with his superiors at seminary, his father decided that he should not take holy orders and sent him to St Petersburg University (1848) where he mixed with revolutionary students, read German philosophy, notably ◊ Hegel and Feuerbach and, after a great moral struggle, lost his religious faith. Having concluded that, compared with Western European thought and art, Russia had contributed little of worth to the world, he sought, in socialism, the freedom to enable Russian culture to flourish. Disgusted with the selfishness of the upper class and the liberal dilettantism of the small middle class, he believed that the revolution which would install socialism would have to be made by the only uncorrupted class, the poor peasants and the workers. But, having studied Fourier, ◊ Blanc, ◊ Proudhon and other socialist writers, he believed that the resultant socialist regime would have to be administered by a benevolent dictatorship. Further study, notably of J. S. Mill, led him to give up his idea in favour of a form of direct democracy and cooperation between peasants, artisans and industrial workers, rather on the lines suggested by Proudhon. Meanwhile so evil were the consequences of absolute government, that any kind of revolution, however disruptive, painful and inconclusive at first, would be better than no revolution at all.

45

Chernyshevsky, N. G.

During 1851–53 he taught at a school in Saratov, was accused of subversive teaching and returned to St Petersburg to earn his living as a journalist and tutor, and to write his first book, *Aesthetic Relations between Art and Reality* (1855) which, under a pseudonym, he himself reviewed, by no means favourably, in order to enlarge his arguments against 'ivory tower' aestheticism and for his conviction that the writer must be politically 'committed'.

During the following years he developed his ideas on internationalism, decrying folk and nationalist traditions in art and letters; and went deeper into the details of his socialist ideas. When the emancipation of the serfs was promised (1857) he was among those who urged that the peasants be given land when they were freed; but also that they work it collectively in *obshchiny* (agrarian communes), an idea which he borrowed from ◇ Herzen and the Decembrists. From this he developed analagous ideas for collectivization in industry on roughly ◇ syndicalist lines. From J. S. Mill he learnt to see the fashionable doctrine of *laissez-faire* as no natural law but a mere economic hangover, and the State as the agency which would take power from the capitalist and hand it to the people, thereafter fading out as the workers learnt to work and exchange the product of their labour for the pleasure of creation and a sense of duty to each other. Yet strong feeling that although these changes were desirable and, perhaps, ultimately inevitable, they were far from imminent, led him to write with an irony and scepticism that subsequently justified the use of the epithet nihilist. The principal medium of his political and literary writings was the periodical *Sovremennik* of which he became managing editor, and in which he published works by Turgenev, Ostrovsky and the young Tolstoy. In July 1862 the paper was suppressed as subversive and Chernyshevsky arrested. In the Peter-and-Paul fortress until 1864, without trial, he did much writing; *Sovremennik*, restarted by his friends, published his political novel *What is to be done?* (1863), which, despite its literary poverty, had an enormous influence on a whole generation of young revolutionaries, on the populist movements and notably the nihilists. Among its practical proposals were student 'communes' of the kind revived in our own time by the quietest wing of the New Left; and workers' cooperatives for the running of industry. The Chernyshevsky hero had to be implacably and high-mindedly opposed to all forms of despotism, but he distrusted all forms of positivism, was anti-Comte, anti-Spencer and sceptical of the whole notion

46

of 'progress'. In 1864 Chernyshevsky was tried, convicted of subversion and treason, underwent 'civil execution' in public, and was condemned to seven years' forced labour in Siberia. When he had done his time, Alexander II refused to liberate him and from 1870–81 he was confined to remote Siberian settlements where he did some writing but eschewed politics. When, in exchange for his liberty, the revolutionary Narodnaya Volya movement (the assassins of Alexander II) promised to refrain from acts of terrorism during the coronation of Alexander III, he was allowed (1883) to move to Astrakhan; and, six years later, to return home to Saratov where, his health broken, he died within a few months.

Chiang Kai-shek (1886–) Chinese nationalist leader. He became an officer of the Imperial Chinese army and was in Japan, seconded to the Japanese army for training, when, in 1911, the Chinese revolution organized by the ◊ Kuomintang and led by Dr ◊ Sun Yat-sen broke out. Chiang deserted the army to join it and after long service was sent to Moscow to study advanced military methods, returning to become Sun's chief-of-staff. Although he was opposed to Sun's policy of welcoming a Communist faction into the Kuomintang, he succeeded Sun as Kuomintang leader and head of the national republican government in its capital, Nanking (1928). For the next decade he was continuously at war with various local warlord rulers, with the Japanese imperialist invaders, and with the Chinese Communists led by, among others, ◊ Mao Tse-tung, who captured Chiang in 1936 but released him to continue the war against Japan. He continued as Kuomintang leader, head of the Chinese Government, and C-in-C of its armed forces throughout World War II. The civil war between the communists and Kuomintang was resumed following the defeat of Japan – it had never really been suspended – and in 1948, following a decisive communist victory, Chiang was forced to retire to the island of Formosa (Taiwan), where he has since remained as head of the so-called Chinese National Republic, with United States support. Chiang's repeatedly declared intention to reinvade the mainland and overthrow the Chinese People's Republic had been reduced to the level of private fantasy, even before US recognition of the CPR.

Chicago May Day, 1886. In the 1880s Chicago was the stronghold of revolutionary anarchism in the USA, the influence of ◊ Bakunin's

Chicago May Day, 1886

International Social Democratic Alliance being powerful among both native and immigrant workers (*see* IWW). Almost all the German and Czech immigrant workers were either socialists or anarchists. There were five anarchist newspapers – one daily and four periodicals – with a total circulation of 30,000, i.e. a readership of probably quarter of a million. Most of the revolutionary workers were also influenced by the International Working People's Association, or Black International. And the fireball of this movement was Jacob ⟡ Most the German anarchist with his creed of all-out violence against the establishment. In the spring of 1885 the powerful Central Labour union (associated with the Black International) called a strike in its campaign to win an eight-hour day, and 60,000 workers responded. When by arrangement between industrial managements and the City Hall, strikers and demonstrators were savagely mauled by both police and gunmen hired from the Pinkerton agency, the Black International demanded counterviolence from the strikers; and the union responded by passing a resolution, proposed by an anarchist member, calling on the wage-earning class to 'arm itself in order to be able to put forth against its exploiters such an argument as alone can be effective – violence'. Soon the socialist and anarchist press was exhorting the workers to prepare for bloody revolution.

Thus a state of extreme tension existed when in the spring of 1886 the McCormick Harvester Corporation dealt with the Union demand for an eight-hour day by locking out the workers, engaging blacklegs, and hiring 300 gunmen from Pinkerton to protect them. The McCormick workers reacted by holding meetings outside the plant, and on 3 May the police and Pinkertons opened fire on a meeting and killed a number of the demonstrators. A protest meeting was held in Haymarket Square the following day, and while 200 police were trying to break it up, a bomb which was thrown from an alley into the square, killed some of them. The police lost their heads and opened fire wildly, hitting men of their own force as well as the demonstrators, and some of the workers who were armed returned their fire. Seven policemen and an unknown number of workers, but certainly more than twenty, were killed. As a result all known anarchists were rounded up and a 'show trial' was laid on. Nothing but their revolutionary sentiments was proved against any of the accused; the probability is that the bomb was thrown by an *agent provocateur* paid by McCormick, and a subsequent judicial

48

enquiry revealed that all the anarchists charged were, in fact, innocent. Nevertheless, four of them were condemned to death and judicially murdered by hanging.

Chinese Revolution 1911–27. The movement towards a ◊ bourgeois democratic revolution in the Chinese Empire began in the last quarter of the nineteenth century but did not gain impetus until the first decade of the twentieth. Like the Russian revolution, it was largely the work of intellectuals living in exile. Their reasons were much the same: a worn-out imperial dynasty clinging to absolute power was denying the middle class the profits of progress, and all classes the benefits and enlightenment of modern civilizations; and keeping the people in misery and subjection. But there was an additional motive – anti-imperialism: the seizure, following the Boxer Rising in the 1890s, of parts of China by Britain, France, the USA, Germany and Japan, aroused a new spirit of nationalism in the Chinese middle class. Even the Dowager Empress secretly encouraged the antiforeign 'Harmonious Fists' up to the point at which they threatened her own power.

In 1911, when its Pekin HQ were discovered by the Manchu authorities, the revolutionary movement was virtually forced into the open, to find that it had far more popular support than anyone had realized, and that the Manchu Dynasty, which in any case had always been disliked as alien, far less. There was little effective resistance from the authorities to the calling of a National Assembly in Peking, and the Assembly nominated a soldier, General Yuan Shih-kai as Prime Minister. Dr ◊ Sun Yat-sen returned from New York when he received news of the revolution, and a Revolutionary Assembly in Nanking hailed him as leader and appointed him Provisional President of a Republic of China. Sun realized the importance of unity, and in 1912, having joined with Yuan in persuading the boy-Emperor Pu-I to abdicate, yielded his office as President to Yuan who was to govern with a bicameral parliament (Nanking Constitution 1912). The parliament remained a cypher. Yuan soon made himself virtual dictator, while Sun and his party continued to govern in Nanking. In 1915 Yuan proclaimed himself emperor, but died six months later, whereupon China broke up into a number of provinces each ruled by a warlord frequently at war with his neighbours. The one steadily revolutionary, genuinely idealistic and purposeful movement remained Sun Yat-sen's Kuomintang

(Nationalist) movement which had been founded in 1894 (some authorities give different dates), to introduce democratic government, social and economic reforms, and a measure of moderate socialism, into China. For ten years, however, the new Republic controlled only a small part of the country and Sun could barely hold his own. But in 1922 he began to receive aid in his revolution from the young U S S R. This entailed modifying the statutes of the Kuomintang so that it became open to communists to join it. Thus Sun's successor and brother-in-law ◇ Chiang Kai-shek was able, in 1925, to move effectively against the warlords, with native communist and Russian aid.

The Communist Party of China accepted the Soviet Party's view that there was as yet no basis for a communist revolution in China, since there was only a small ◇ proletariat and ◇ Marxist revolution could not possibly be based on a peasantry. The Party therefore saw its task as that of helping to accomplish the ◇ bourgeois revolution, rather than that of attempting to install socialism in China. In 1926–27 Chiang made rapid progress in the work of bringing China under Kuomintang authority and in 1927 in Shanghai was strong enough to turn on his communist allies, massacre those he could get his hands on, and force the others to fly for their lives or 'go underground'. This completed the bourgeois stage of the revolution; it accomplished some sensible reforms and built new railways, but did nothing for the great mass of the people, the peasants; and Chiang began to move in a social and political direction which was more or less ◇ Fascist in style, soon becoming dictator. Moreover, the Kuomintang made only the feeblest resistance to the beginnings of the great Japanese imperial adventure, first in Manchuria, then in China proper.

Chinese Revolution 1927–49, Communist. The slaughter of communists by ◇ Chiang-Kai-shek in 1927 (*see* Chinese Revolution 1911) forced the Soviet CP to reverse its policy of support for the Kuomintang, and to advise the Chinese Party to cease trying to collaborate with the Nationalists and to fight back. Chiang's business should have been the defence of the republic against the ◇ imperialist Japanese, who were extending their activities, soon to be their conquests in Manchuria, and China; but he neglected this in his obstinate attempts to exterminate the communists. Since orthodox ◇ Marxism insisted that communist revolution could be based only on a ◇ proletariat, peasantries not being of the revolutionary class, the Comintern dogmatists instructed the commanders of Chinese revolutionary forces to capture cities. Among those who tried to carry out this idiotic policy which took no account of the special conditions in China was ⟡ Chu Teh, commanding the communist element of the Fourth Army. His forces were cut to pieces by the nationalists and he was forced to fall back on the mountains where, at Chingkangshan, he joined another beaten communist leader, ⟡ Mao-Tse-tung.

Mao was one of the few communist leaders who insisted on doing his own thinking; this led him to conclude that whatever might be the case in advanced industrial countries, in China the only hope for socialist revolution lay in the peasants, the great mass of the Chinese people. He and Chu set out to convert the peasants to communism, to abolish rent, dispossess the landlords, redistribute the land to the peasants, and suppress the moneylenders who were the bane of the Chinese peasants; in short to establish a rural communist regime in that part of the country which they controlled. Moreover, they carefully avoided positional warfare with the nationalist armies, developing that system of ⟡ guerrilla tactics which has since become famous; and left the great urban centres severely alone until they should be strong enough to 'bring the revolution from the country to the cities'. Although this policy was demonstrably successful, it was so heretical that the ⟡ Comintern and the Central Committee of the Chinese CP anathematised and solemnly expelled Mao Tse-tung. However, they could not actually get at him, which left him free to make the revolution in his own way. His pro-peasant and peasant-based policy won him the support of a wider and wider countryside in his fight with the Kuomintang, which was identified, fairly enough, as the landlords' and moneylenders' party. By 1930 the Maoist communists had rural Soviets governing in Kiangsi, Hunan, Hupeh and Kuangtung, rapidly winning respect from the hitherto reserved intellectuals for their austere integrity and purposeful-ness – and, incidentally, patriotism – in striking contrast with the growing corruption, self-indulgence and internecine strife of the Kuomintang. Nevertheless, Chiang still commanded the big battalions, foreign loans and aid; and, almost ignoring the stepped-up Japanese encroachment on Chinese territory and sovereignty, concentrated on wiping out the Chinese Soviets. This enabled him to blockade the entire region under communist government and to begin closing in on it, and in 1934 Mao was forced to lead the famous Long March of the whole communist community, military and civil, 3,000 miles into Shensi, on the Manchurian border, there to continue his rural communist revolution. Before leaving Kiangsi Mao had formally declared war on Japan; in Shensi he called for a union of all classes and parties against the imperialist enemy, thereby winning massive support from millions of ordinary Chinese, whereas Chiang continued in his obstinate dedication to the civil war. He went to Sian, capital of Shensi, to direct operations against the communists in person, was captured by his own, largely Manchurian, army, whose officers and men demanded that he make an alliance with the communists and start fighting the Japanese. He was forced against his will to negotiate with the communist envoy, ⟡ Chou-En-lai, and under threat of death, gave way. He was released to command the national Chinese army, in which the Chinese Red Army became the Eighth Route Army, against the invader.

From 1937 Kuomintang and communists fought the Japanese, the nationalists using formal positional warfare, and the Maoists guerrilla warfare. The latter did most of the serious fighting, and on occasion, when the communists were led by their successes to extend their field of operations, they had to fight the nationalists as well as the Japanese armies. The situation is curiously like that which developed in Yugoslavia on a much smaller scale a few years later: for Chiang read Mihailovic; for Kuomintang read Cetniks; for Mao read ⟡ Tito; and for Japanese read Germans. This state of affairs continued until the defeat of the Japanese by atom bomb in 1945. By that time the situation was broadly as follows: China south of the Yang-tse river, and nearly all the cities, were controlled by the Kuomintang. The whole countryside north of the Yang-tse, but not the cities, was controlled by the communists. The communists were trusted and supported by the peasants who, indeed, composed their enormous guerrilla armies; and, increasingly, by the intellectuals of the universities, for their integrity and their respect for the traditional Chinese qualities and virtues (unlike the intellectuals of other cultures in revolution, the Chinese were not confused by considerations of transcendental religion, since they had none). The Kuomintang, on the other hand, had become corrupt, its leaders were trusted by nobody; it was notorious that the Chiangs, Soongs, K'ungs and Ch'ens had enormously enriched themselves at the country's expense, and their incompetence was responsible for the galloping inflation which had ruined the currency. But it had the armour, the air force, trained formal armies, and the backing of the USA. In 1946 the USA tried to bring the two sides to terms but was forced to recognize that it could not be done; and that Chiang was determined to launch an all-out attack on the communists and exterminate them. In 1947 he committed the best of his forces to attempts to conquer Shantung and to get full control of Manchuria; he suffered total defeat in both campaigns and was cut off from his huge Manchurian army which found itself isolated in Mukden and Chungshan, while the communists began to advance southwards to the Yang-tse.

It was clear to Mao and his followers that the moment had come to pass over to the attack. ⋄ Stalin (through Liu Shao-ch'i), did his best to dissuade them: the very last thing he wanted in China as in Europe, was a triumphant communist regime owing nothing to the USSR. Chou En-lai took the lead in opposing the Russian arguments, Mao Tse-tung agreed with him, the communists took the initiative, and between July and October 1948 swept the North almost clear of nationalists, captured Shantung and Tsianfu and advanced towards the Yang-tse. In October/November Chiang tried to fight his way through to his beleaguered troops in the Manchurian cities, he was again defeated, so decisively that he had to remove himself and his HQ from Pekin, while in their southward advance the communists wiped out another Kuomintang army at the battle of Hsu Chou. By this time a schism divided the Kuomintang, with Chiang leading the ⋄ 'Fascist' wing, and General Vice-President Li Tsung-jen the liberals. Li opened secret negotiations for a compromise solution with the communists and agreement had probably been reached when a foreign press 'leak' forced both sides to repudiate the story. The plan, as did a later and similar one, involved expelling Chiang and his faction from the Kuomintang and forming a liberal-communist coalition government. Meanwhile, military action was resumed and (13 December 1948) the communists began the siege of Pekin. They refrained from using their artillery (neither side had aircraft) as they had no wish to damage the city or alienate the citizens. A plan for taking the place by storm was given up when the distinguished archaeologist Professor Liang Ssu-ch'eng pointed out to the communist command that to breach the mighty walls with their artillery at the only suitable spot for their purpose, would entail destroying the one remaining example of unrestored Ming military architecture. On the other hand, as there was a bitter personal quarrel between ⋄ Lin Piao commanding the communists, and Fu Tso-yi, his old Military Academy comrade, commanding the garrison, negotiations were impossible. Lin was therefore replaced by the brilliant guerrilla general Nieh Jung-chen and on 22 January 1949 Peking was surrendered without a fight.

From that moment the story is of communist victorious advance through the whole of China, with defeat after defeat for Chiang's generals. In April the communists published terms on which they would allow the Kuomintang to surrender; they were, in the circumstances, not bad terms, the Kuomintang would have retained some political offices and a measure of power. But Chiang must go; and Chiang would not go. He was therefore driven out, to take refuge with the rump of his army in Formosa there to live as an American puppet and pensioner for the rest of his life. By mid-1949 there was only one authority, one government and one army in all China – those of the Jen Min Kung Ho Kuo, the Chinese People's Republic.

Choseards. A pejorative term used by French right-wing royalist militants of the ◊ Action Française to describe their opponents, supporters of democratic institutions and therefore of the *Chose Publique* (*res publica* = public thing), i.e. the (Third) Republic.

Chou En-lai (1898–   ) Born of Mandarin stock, in Central Kiangsi. Ed. Nankai University and the Sorbonne. He began his revolutionary career in Paris where he became a Marxist and organized a cell of communists among Chinese students and workers there. Back in China in 1923, he was sent by the Party, at that time only two years old, as organizer and secretary for the southern half of the country which was dominated by the Kuomintang military dictatorship of ◊ Chiang-Kai-shek. Returning north, he became political head of the Whampoa Military Academy, Canton. When Chiang attacked the communists who had set up Soviets in the Yangtse Valley, in 1927, Chou fought against the Kuomintang forces but when in the 1930s China had to face the Japanese invasion, he was influential in arranging cooperation with the Kuomintang against the Japanese (see ◊ Chinese Revolutions); and in having Chiang Kai-shek who had been captured by the communists released to continue leading the struggle against the common enemy (1936). A member of the Communist Party Central Committee in the 1940s, in 1949 he became chief of the State Council. He supported ◊ Mao Tse-tung's Cultural Revolution, 1965–68,

CIA

becoming a 'Red Guard' and retaining his seat on the Central Committee when heads were falling.

Chu Teh (1886–) b. Szechuan, s. of a rich farmer; ed. Yunan Military Academy, graduated as an officer and later joined ◊ Sun Yat-sen's Kuomintang revolution which overthrew the Imperial Manchu dynasty in 1911 and instituted a Republic (*see* Chinese Revolution 1911). Chu visited Europe, studied Marxism and, Berlin 1922, joined the Communist Party. In 1927 the uneasy alliance of the Chinese Communist Party with the Kuomintang was ended in Chu's Nanchang revolt, and he then joined ◊ Mao Tse-tung in organizing a Red Army in Kiangsi and setting up Soviets to redistribute the land among the poor peasants. Following the defeat of the communists in the Soviet provinces by ◊ Chiang Kai-shek, Chu made the Long March (1939): *see* Chinese Revolution (1927–49) with Mao Tse-tung from Kiangsi to Shensi. He later held high command in the war to oppose the Japanese invasion of China, and still later played an important part in the final defeat of the Kuomintang which ended the civil war and established the rule of the Chinese People's Republic throughout China. Chu is Commander-in-Chief of the Republic's armed forces.

CIA, Central Intelligence Agency of the USA. The most powerful and militant counterrevolutionary organization in the world. The US, being the richest and most powerful capitalist country and the leading practitioner of ◊ imperialism (in the ◊ Leninist sense) has been forced into a militantly counterrevolutionary attitude in a period when 'revolution' has almost always meant anticapitalist and anti-imperialist, revolution; so its principal intelligence agency, the CIA, has become the militant instrument of counterrevolution. It was established in 1947 under the National Security Council, a body chiefly concerned with the detection and suppression of anticapitalist, i.e. in newspeak, 'anti-Democratic', subversion in the US, to control all military and political intelligence (i.e. espionage, counterespionage, 'security' and international propaganda) both in the US and wherever US capital has interests (i.e. throughout the world). Ostensibly the functions of the CIA are to advise the National Security Council on security; to coordinate the intelligence of all government departments and the fighting services; to correlate, evaluate and distribute intelligence

55

to government agencies; and to undertake various other 'security' tasks which are defined in official terms of reference so vaguely worded as to cover virtually any kind of activity protective of US and capitalist imperialist interests or damaging to socialism, from the financing and management of propaganda agencies like Radio Free Europe, to the training of anticommunist ◊ guerrilla forces in Latin America, provision of specialists to control antirevolutionary agencies of dependent foreign governments, or the provision of trained gunmen and killers in the counterrevolutionary struggle.

Like the Cheka and the KGB in the USSR or the Gestapo in Nazi Germany, the CIA has tended to become a law unto itself; with the result that its activities have several times seriously embarrassed US Presidents and Secretaries of State who have from time to time been confronted at critical moments in negotiations with foreign statesmen with angry complaints about CIA espionage activities in their countries – activities for which the US Government has been forced to take responsibility, although apparently not informed of them.

In the communist, and especially the ◊ New Left mythology, the CIA has assumed a monstrous avatar, and has become one of the manifestations of the devil, the eternal Enemy of Mankind. Although there is good evidence that its agents do not stop short of what in common law would be crime, including murder, it is probable that this demonification has resulted in exaggeration of the Agency's power, wealth, ubiquity and general wickedness. But its successes in imposing US sponsored governments in, e.g. Dominica, and in destroying such revolutionaries as, e.g. ◊ Sandino and ◊ Guevara, and the now notorious role played by it in Vietnam, do show the CIA to be a power within a power and a law unto itself.

Civil disobedience: *see* Passive resistance.

Class war. The originators of the class war as an intellectual concept were ◊ Hegel, Feuerbach, Pierre Leroux and ◊ Marx. It is a matter of history that classes within a single society have very frequently been at war with each other. The slave revolt led by the gladiator Spartacus against the Roman state 73–1 BC was a manifestation of class war, and so were the numerous *jacqueries* of the Middle Ages. But we are dealing with a formal concept. Hegel interpreted history as a process of evolution carried on by the resolution of two opposed ideas into a new one. Feuerbach and Marx argued that ideas do not exist in a vacuum: there have to be minds to conceive them, which are themselves conditioned by economic and social forces. Marx thus turned the Hegelian dialectic on its head, seeing the fundamental conflict as that between material forces in the form of economic classes. Thus history is seen as a continuous struggle between classes, i.e. a class war. A feudal aristocracy is challenged by a rising capitalist ⟡ bourgeoisie, and the bourgeoisie in turn gives rise to, and is challenged by, an industrial ⟡ proletariat (Marx borrowed the terminology 'bourgeoisie' and 'proletariat' from Pierre Leroux). It is this last struggle, the final battle between the two protagonists remaining at the end of a long history of class struggle, that is usually meant by contemporary use of the term 'class war', and its resolution will result in the classless society.

Cleaver, Eldridge (1936–) American black revolutionary leader, Minister of Information of the ⟡ Black Panther Party. Although, unlike some of his colleagues, he does not reject cooperation with white revolutionaries, he believes that world revolution must now be led by the people with black or brown skins. He served his first prison term in his 'teens for being in possession of marihuana, and has served further terms for assaults on the police and for a 'demonstration' rape of a white girl: in all, about twelve years. He has been one of the three leading militants of his Party and unlike ⟡ Newton has still, despite the shattering of the Panthers by police action, not repudiated violence as a revolutionary means. He was the original cause of the disturbances at Berkeley University when, at the invitation of the student body and in the teeth of opposition from the university authorities, he lectured there on Racism, calling the USA establishment the direct heirs of the Nazis, and the American way of life 'a fossil of history'. Hounded by the Federal Bureau of Investigation, he took refuge in Algiers and in 1970 led a Black Panther delegation to North Korea where he was received with apparent and perhaps real enthusiasm and promoted a 'program of people's diplomacy' against the USA in the land where, in his own words, 'US imperialism first bit the dust'. His much acclaimed book *Soul on Ice* is a badly written and confused but passionately sincere statement of the Afro-American cause, marred by overwriting and too indiscriminate hatred of the whites.

Codreanu, Corneliu Zelea

Codreanu, Corneliu Zelea (1899–1938) Romanian ◊ Fascist revolutionary terrorist, b. Iasi; mother, German; father, Polish Ukrainian. His social philosophy was based on Austrian Christian-Fascism, and a fanatical antisemitism acquired at university from his professor of moral philosophy. In 1923 Codreanu founded the National Christian League dedicated to the use of extreme terrorism against Jews, socialists and liberals and to the establishment of government on a basis of medieval chivalry. Arrested for preaching violence in 1924, he was released on the intervention of a powerful faction who saw in him a useful instrument against movements for social and economic reform, whereupon he personally murdered the Prefect of Police who had been responsible for his arrest. In 1927 he refounded his movement as the League of the Archangel Michael and a year later united it with Stelescu's very similar Brothers of the Cross movement to form the Iron Guard. It won five seats in the 1932 elections but was declared an illegal association by the Liberal prime minister Duea (1933). Duea was murdered by Iron Guard men a few months later. Codreanu strongly supported ◊ Hitler and the Nazi Party; his lieutenant, Stelescu, opposed the Nazis on the grounds that the Iron Guard was a Christian order of chivalry; as a result he was murdered by Codreanu. In 1937 the Iron Guard won 16 per cent of all the votes cast in the national elections but following the establishment of a personal dictatorship by King Carol later in the year Codreanu was first imprisoned and later (1938) conveniently 'shot while trying to escape' together with a score of his followers.

Cohn-Bendit, Daniel (1945–) German-born ◊ Marxist-◊Leninist revolutionary student who, while studying at Nanterre University, France, became the best known leader of the ◊ French Student revolt 1968, and popular student hero affectionately known in Britain as Danny-the-Red, as much for the flaming colour of his hair as for his political persuasion. A member of the Sozialistischer Deutscher Studentbund (SDS), he introduced its revolutionary ideas into France and an attempt to silence him made by the Rector and disciplinary council of the Sorbonne sparked off the revolt. He defined his revolutionary philosophy in an interview with J-P. Sartre (*Nouvel Observateur*) 20 May 1968: it was not feasible to overthrow the bourgeoisie at one blow; but a militant minority well grounded in revolutionary theory could, by a series of shocks, initiate an irreversible movement of change; this minority could not and should not try to control the movement which they initiated. The student revolution should provide the element of high-spirited spontaneity to inspire the workers. There are echoes, here, of Che ◊ Guevara's theories, although in a very different context. Hostile to Moscow-style 'establishment communism' which he stigmatized as 'Stalinist filth', and influenced by ◊ Maoism and Guevarism (see Guevara) Cohn-Bendit can best be described as an anarchist-communist who took advantage of the fact that the only way to get grievances attended to in a French university is to stage a riot, to spread his ideas far beyond the university limits. He became the focus and spokesman almost despite himself, of the Students' Revolution, but never effectively of the sympathetic workers' revolt which it inspired; yet it was Cohn-Bendit who, in direct negotiations with the Rector of the Sorbonne and the Minister of Education, broadened a student revolt into a national revolution with the words: 'We told him that what is happening in the street tonight is a whole generation rising against a certain sort of society'. The talents which brought him to the front were those of a comedian, which does not imply that he was anything but sincere: he had a quick and brilliant wit in debate, and a remarkable gift for sharp-pointed revolutionary clowning, for overcoming the opposition by exposing it as ridiculous. As soon as he realized that he had become the object of a 'personality cult', he withdrew from leadership while continuing active, a rare case of adherence to principles.

Collins, Michael (1890–1922) b. Cork, Ireland, s. of a farmer. He was one of the organizers of the 1916 Easter Rising, served two prison terms for nationalist revolutionary militancy, and was elected to the Dail Eireann in 1918. He was one of the Irish delegates to the negotiations with the British government which led to the Irish Free State settlement (1921), and in 1922 became Prime Minister of the Free State. The hard-liners of the ◊ Fenian and ◊ Sinn Fein movements rejected the Free State solution and, led by Eamon ◊ De Valera, waged revolutionary war on the Free State government with the ◊ IRA. Collins was assassinated (1922) by IRA men while inspecting a detachment of the Free State army.

Colombia ◊ Guerrilla Movements. In 1946 the election of a Conservative to the Presidency of Colombia, only a small minority of the people

Colombia

having cast their votes, led to outbreaks of violence. Following the murder
of the Liberal (and liberal) leader, Jorge Eliecen Gaitan, these built up
slowly into a state of indiscriminate civil war between 'Liberals' and
'Conservatives'. It lasted for six years and became known simply and
significantly as 'La Violencia'. It was carried on with atrocious ferocity,
both sides committing acts of grotesque sadistic cruelty unprecedented
even in this century of violence; and it was without direction or purpose,
Gaitan, the only man who might have restored order and instituted
reforms, being dead. At first the Communist Party, which might also have
given direction to the war, did nothing, the Central Committee failing to
recognize a Marxist-▷Leninist 'revolutionary situation' although, in the
1930s, the Party had led rebellious peasants in land seizures. But in 1949
the CP, or members of it, began to assemble and organize survivors of the
Violencia into disciplined groups in order to 'oppose the organized
violence of the masses to reactionary violence'. By 1952 the peasants under
CP leadership had secured control of a number of rural districts, and had
set up independent republics beyond the control of the central government
in Bogata. One of the most successful of these was Marquetalia, on the
borders of Tolima and Huila provinces, founded in 1949 by the communist
▷ 'Charro Negro', who had been a member of the CP Central Committee.
For some years there was a tacit truce between these republics and the
central government.

This first phase of what looked like being a nationwide guerrilla revolution ended when the reactionary President Gomez was deposed by a
military *coup* led by General Rojas Pinilla who made himself Dictator,
stopped all military action against the communist peasant republics and
declared a total amnesty. Despite attempts by such leaders as Marulunda
Velez (or Pedro Antonio Marin) who had succeeded Charro Negro in
Marquetalia, and Juan de la Cruz Varela of the republic of Sumapaz, to
hold the movement together, thousands of peasants took advantage of the
amnesty and the guerrilla movement was greatly weakened. Pinilla then
resumed military action against the guerrillas. Meanwhile leaders of the
old Conservative and Liberal parties in exile were negotiating a coalition,
formed a National Front, agreed to have alternate Conservative and Liberal
Presidents regardless of election results, forced Pinilla to resign (1958) and
installed Alberto Lleras Camargo as President. In January 1959 came Fidel
▷ Castro's spectacular revolutionary success in Cuba: this stimulated fresh

60

revolutionary activity all over Latin America, and in Colombia the formation of a *Movimento de Obreros Estudiantes y Campesinos* (MOEC); it had a short and ineffectual life but is significant in having been *Fidelista*, i.e. opposed to the official CP which had again become ◊ revisionist. Next came the *Frente Unido de Accion Revolucionaria* which was led by Gaitan's daughter Gloria Gaitan and her husband Luis Valencia. Students and intellectuals belonging to these movements tried to reorganize the rural guerrillas, believing that a revolution starting in the countryside could then be carried into the cities.

In 1962 the government sent an army brigade trained in guerrilla warfare with US help, to reconquer Marquetalia; the little republic put up a fierce fight, was supported by demonstrations in Bogota and other cities, and forced the government troops to withdraw. In the following year the government resumed the attack with 16,000 men, and by 1965 all the communist peasant republics had been exterminated. But their militants re-formed guerrilla bands in more remote country, all loosely linked together in the *Fuerzas Armadas Revolucionarias* (FARC) which had some CP support. Meanwhile a new guerrilla movement, the *Ejercito de Liberacion Nacional* (ELN), was started by Fabio Vasquez Castano with a view to fomenting armed insurrection among the masses and seizing power for the poor peasants and urban workers. The rebel priest and trained sociologist Father Camilo ◊ Torres tried to unite all the revolutionary groups and movements in a single popular front, the 'Platform for a Movement of Popular Unity', but he failed. He joined a guerrilla band and was killed in action (1966).

In January 1968 yet another guerrilla movement was started in Colombia, the *Ejercito Popular de Liberacion,* or People's Liberation Army: this was the first ◊ Maoist guerrilla in South America, and seemed as intent on fighting the orthodox CP, and also the *Fidelista* communists, as the Establishment. It operated with some success in the Alto Sinu region of Cordoba province and is one of the three surviving guerrillas still active in Colombia.

Comandante Chena: *see* Saher, Manuel.

Comintern. Newspeak word for the Communist or Third International (*see* also, ◊ International, First and Second). It was founded at Petrograd

Commune

in 1919 at the instance of ◊ Trotsky at an international conference chaired by ◊ Lenin himself, and attended by other leading ◊ Bolsheviks and by Communist Party (CP) delegations from the USA, the UK, Poland, Sweden and a number of Balkan states. It provided militant communists all over the world with a rallying organization to the left of the Second International which was too Menshevik for the Bolsheviks; and was intended to become an arm of Soviet foreign policy, supporting and fomenting communist revolution wherever appropriate; and to provide instruction, and issue orders and funds, to foreign CPs. Among its paid officials at various times were President ◊ Tito of Yugoslavia, Earl Browder, subsequently leader of the USA CP, Togliatti, later Chief Secretary of the powerful Italian CP, and ◊ Dimitrov, the Bulgarian hero of the Nazi Reichstag Fire trial. The Comintern continued its work, with varying success and no spectacular achievements until 1943 when, the USSR finding itself an ally of the USA and UK in World War II, ◊ Stalin dissolved it as a gesture of good faith, replacing it four years later with COMINFORM, ostensibly an information bureau for international communism, though it was used by Stalin as an instrument of control over foreign CPs. It was wound up three years after his death.

Commune. The Paris Commune of 1870–1. Faced with defeat in the Franco-Prussian war of 1870, socialist, anarchist and other revolutionaries rose in armed insurrection against the tottering regime of Napoleon III, and after France's fall, set up a more or less proletarian government in Paris, which they called the Commune. Short-lived as it was, the Commune is remembered as one of the first modern exercises in people's power, and it continues to intrigue revolutionaries. The leadership was diverse: French revolutionary émigrés who had been living in London and were or claimed to be connected with the International of ◊ Marx and ◊ Engels (who repudiated them), played a considerable part. ◊ Bakunin and his communist-anarchists, whose hope was that Prussia would defeat Napoleon III, and a revolutionary France then defeat Prussia and inaugurate revolution all over Europe, were busy from the outbreak of war organizing militant groups and working for the armed insurrection of the workers. ◊ Blanqui, who was for immediate insurrection, personally led the first act of revolutionary violence in Paris when he and a handful of followers tried to seize a gendarmerie on 14 August 1870. From London, Marx and Engels were trying to ensure that the obviously coming revolution would be led by the serious French section of the ⟡ International, and not by the London émigrés, French 'neo-Jacobins' whose political and tactical sense was felt to be thoroughly unreliable; and that, until the war was finally over and the Prussians out of the country, the proletariat would support the new ⟡ bourgeois Republic of Versailles (later Bordeaux) led by Thiers and not rise in arms prematurely. The disciples of ⟡ Proudhon (who had died in 1865) believed on the other hand that it did not matter which side won the war – nation-states were anachronisms anyway – but that an international revolution might now be started in Paris.

A sound revolutionary example was actually set in Lyon where the Marxist 'Internationalists' proclaimed the Republic without hesitation, but installed a commune as its representative, the executive being composed in part of revolutionary socialist working-men, in part of middle-class Republican radicals. It abolished the *octroi* – the municipal 'customs' which taxed incoming goods including foodstuffs – and set about arming the people for revolutionary resistance to the Prussians. It might have accomplished something had not Bakunin and his followers arrived, and led the extreme Left wing into immediate all-out war against the bourgeoisie, demanding the total abolition of the state, and thus wrecking the Lyon Commune within a few days. Meanwhile, in Paris, the admonitory voices of Marx and Engels went unheard, and when in the spring of 1871 a Central Committee for revolution was formed, it was composed of Jacobins, Blanquists and Bakunists, the Internationalist Socialists playing no part in the leadership, although many were to die for the cause when the fighting started. The original ostensible cause of the rising was the government's 'shameful' acceptance of Bismarck's harsh and humiliating peace terms. Paris refused to accept them; and the masses rose in the conviction that the city had been betrayed, that it had not been defended as it should have been, and that Thiers had accepted the Prussian terms in order to have Bismarck's help in putting down threatened insurrection in the capital. Of the 256 battalions of the National Guard 215 voted to support the Central Committee and formed a Central Committee of their own in support.

Apart from Blanqui's abortive and premature attempt to attack a

Commune

gendarmerie, there was no fighting until the government sent troops from Versailles to disarm the National Guard and confiscate the capital's artillery. The Guard resisted, and having arrested the two generals, Thomas and Lecompte, in command of the Versailles troops, hanged them as 'traitors'. Thiers withdrew his forces and waited for the Prussians to march into Paris; Bismarck made no move, and the Central Committee proclaimed the Commune as the revolutionary government of France, its members still being composed of Jacobins, Blanquists and Bakunists. As Engels wrote later, 'the International did not raise a finger towards the making of the Commune'. This meant that this first proletariat government had no experienced, trained socialist or communist politicians in its leadership although, as Engels added, 'it was the spiritual child of the International' that is, it represented the first major engagement in the class war of ◊ proletariat against ◊ bourgeoisie.

From the revolutionary point of view the Commune was too easygoing, despite outbreaks of murderous hysteria; was too slow to act; hesitated to declare and wage the necessary civil war; failed to grasp its chance of controlling the economy by seizing the Bank of France which lay at its mercy; failed to prepare for the inevitable attack by the government's armed forces; and failed to mobilize the considerable support which it had in the provinces. Less queasy about waging civil war, Thiers, with Prussian concurrence, sent a strong force into Paris, commanded by Marshal MacMahon and General Gallifet, with orders to put down the revolution at whatever cost. For a week there was savage street fighting, which is said to have caused more material damage than the Prussian war and to have cost more lives than Robespierre's terror. Twenty thousand Communards – socialists, communists, anarchists of all degrees – died on the barricades, in the streets, or in massacres of prisoners. Both sides were ruthless, shooting hostages and killing prisoners.

The crushing of the Commune is said by historians to have retarded the development of French socialism by quarter-of-a-century. But, from its events, Marx and Engels drew a number of lessons, and described it as 'the first incorporation of political power in society itself, constituting its life force, whereas it had hitherto been the instrument which controlled and dominated it; embodied in the masses of the people, political power became their strength, instead of being the organized form of their suppression'. (Manifesto of the General Council of the First International,

64

by Karl Marx, April 1871.) On the other hand the Commune also served, from the practical point of view, as an object lesson in how not to do it.

Communism. This word has a number of meanings: it may, e.g. be used to define the kind of society in which all property except intimate personal articles is common, each person contributing his work to, and receiving his needs from, the community through its instrument, the bureaucracy. Thus the Inca Empire was, in this sense, communistic. The word also designates that revolutionary movement whose object is to overthrow capitalism and the ⟡ bourgeois state, in order to establish first socialism, then communism, and ultimately the stateless and classless society. The distinction here, between socialism and communism, leads to another definition of communism, the one most commonly implied by the use of the word in any but a pejorative sense, and which should nowadays be equated with Marxism-⟡ Leninism.

Marxism-Leninism, then, more commonly known as communism in common usage, is a product of ⟡ Lenin's reinterpretation of ⟡ Marxism in the light of changes which had occurred in capitalism since Marx's time but had been foreseen by Marx. It concedes that the most skilled workers are likely to be bought over into the bourgeoisie by high wages, thus becoming the enemies of the poorly paid workers who remain the true ⟡ proletariat. The business of this proletariat, led by the Communist Party, is to become the ruling class – hence 'dictatorship of the proletariat' – by seizing the instrument of government, the state, and modifying its working to communist ends. This it will be forced to do by means of violent revolution; the moderate socialist's theory that it can be done 'constitutionally', by using the franchise machinery of the bourgeois state, is the heresy called ⟡ revisionism.

The first task of the proletariat once it has control of the state, is to establish socialism in which the principle 'from each according to his ability, to each according to his work', will be given effect: but, of course, this implies inequality, since some work will still be better paid than other work, some private property will be accumulated, and there will, consequently, still be some class distinction. However, having achieved socialism, the dictator-proletariat must then advance to communism, at which stage Louis ⟡ Blanc's principle, adopted by Marx – 'From each according to his ability, to each according to his needs' – will be given effect. This

Communist League

means that all distinctions between classes of labour and property categories will disappear. The presumption is either that all men, being virtuous (at this point anarchist theory becomes operative), will be content with simple necessities and, above all, be without differentials; or that the community's wealth, accumulated by socialist industry and paying no tribute to a bourgeois capitalist class, will be so considerable that all men will have what, under capitalism, only the rich can enjoy.

Given continuing technological progress and, a necessity which Lenin did not clearly foresee, adequate population control, the second prospect is at least technically realizable; most thinkers will hold that the first never was and that it does more credit to the hearts than to the heads of socialist and communist theorists. In the final stage of the Marxist-Leninist process, the anarchist dream is attained; the state withers away because the machinery of government and judiciary are no longer necessary since all men, having what they need, behave with full social responsibility and are, therefore, capable of cooperation without compulsion.

It is, perhaps, unfortunate, that the first country in which socialism was attempted was the technologically backward Russia of 1917, whereas Marx had expected it to be in one of the most advanced industrial countries. As it is, the grotesque and ugly tryanny of ◊ Stalin – a resumption and aggravation of the Tsarist tyranny – has intervened to vindicate, at all events for the time being, the cynicism of those who hold that, man being what he, apparently, is, the nobility of a theory does nothing towards making it practicable.

Communist League: *see* Karl ◊ Marx.

Communist Manifesto: *see* Friedrich ◊ Engels.

Congo: *see* Zaire.

Cultural revolution. The concept of a specific cultural revolution is ◊ Leninist. It was first expressed in a speech which Lenin made to the 3rd Congress of Soviets in Moscow in 1918: 'All the marvels of technique, all the achievements of culture will become the common heritage and henceforth never again will the human mind or human kind be transformed into

66

means of violence or exploitation.' Later, he wrote: 'We must take the whole culture left to us by capitalism and with it build Socialism. We must take all science, all technique, all knowledge and all the arts, for without them we cannot animate our building of a Socialist society' (*Works*, xxix, 67).

Lenin considered the worst enemy of the cultural revolution to be communist complacency; it was doubtless this judgement which ⇨ Mao Tse-tung had in mind when, in the 1960s, he launched the 'cultural revolution' in China, but Mao was probably even more influenced by Lenin's view that no cultural revolution could be valid without involving the mass of the people from its inception, a teaching which can be used against one faction of CP hierarchy by another, or against one CP by another, when that is politically expedient, since it enables one leader to unleash the people against another with 'holy writ' as his justification.

So dangerous for the revolution did Lenin consider communist complacency that he placed it above even illiteracy as the enemy of revolutionary culture. In *The Role of Militant Materialism* (1922), he wrote: 'One of the greatest and most dangerous mistakes which Communists commit . . . is the idea that revolutions can be made by the hands of revolutionaries alone.' The cultural revolution can be made only by an alliance with non-communists in the cultural field; and by what he describes as 'critical assimilation and integration of the achievements of materialism', meaning, in this context, pre-communist materialism, i.e. in the arts, sciences and in letters. To this Lenin added, as equally important, 'a systematic study of Hegel's dialectic from the materialist point of view', that is to say excluding, after Feuerbach's and ⇨ Marx's example, Hegelian 'idealism'.

It is clear that towards the end of his life Lenin was preoccupied with the subject of the cultural revolution, for he returned to it time and again. Thus, in an article on *Cooperation* (*Works*, xxxiii, 230 ff.) he writes: 'Our whole point of view of Socialism has changed radically' . . . i.e. as a result of the successful Bolshevik revolution. Emphasis had, rightly, hitherto been on politics and economics but 'Now the centre of gravity of our work must be educational action. . . In our case the political and economic revolution has preceded the cultural revolution which now becomes imperative. Today we have only to accomplish the cultural revolution to become a completely Socialist country.' Socialism thus does not consist merely in public ownership of the means of production, distribution and exchange: to that must be added assimilation of the materialist part, i.e. the concrete achievements in art, science and technology, of pre-socialist culture; and such an organization of the state as shall enable every 'worker' (i.e. in the post-revolutionary phase, every citizen) to take part in the management of society and make the fullest use of his natural gifts and abilities.

In communist scholasticism, Lenin's use of the word 'materialism' which no neo-Hegelian could avoid, unfortunately, provides bureaucratic hierarchs of the CP with a licence to pass dogmatic doctrinaire judgements on non-communist works of art and literature (and, under Stalin, even of science), by nineteenth-century positivist standards – a picture must tell a story (a story must have a moral purpose of the very kind which Lenin condemned as dangerous to the revolution – without laying themselves open to being convicted of heresy: a striking example of the importance assumed by semantics in modern communist theology.

D

Davis, Angela (1944–) Negro communist revolutionary. b. in Birmingham, Alabama. As Assistant Professor of Philosophy at the University of California, Los Angeles in 1969, she gave her lectures a revolutionary tone, holding 'education itself is inherently political. Its goal ought to be political', and that 'academic freedom is a concept which many professors seek to use to guarantee their right to work undisturbed by the real world, undisturbed by the real problems of society'. Her lectures attracted large numbers of students with ▷ New Left inclinations and the left wing of the ▷ Black Power movement, and drew record attendances of up to 1,500. These lectures were monitored by the University Board of Regents at the instance of the notoriously reactionary Governor Ronald Reagan of the State of California. Accused by the Regents of being a communist, i.e. not simply a member of a political party but of a subversive organization, she replied that she was indeed; and that she would not use the Fifth Amendment (protection of accused persons against self-incrimination) because her political faith incriminated not her, but 'the Nixons, Agnews and Reagans'. In June 1970 she was dismissed from her post on the grounds that having proclaimed that 'the first condition of freedom is an open act of resistance – violent resistance', and 'it is necessary to unveil the predominant oppressive ideas and acts of this country', she was unfit to teach. She became a leader in the mass movement of the blacks to save the ▷ Soledad Brothers, a symbolic leader figure of the Black Power movement, and of the New Left revolutionary movement in general. In August 1970, while a Negro, James McClain, was being retried in Marin County Court, Cal., after a mistrial on a charge of assaulting a prison officer during a San Quentin prison rebellion, Jonathan Jackson, seventeen-year-old brother of George Jackson, one of the so-called Soledad Brothers, entered the court, carrying guns, with a view to the rescue of the accused and of his witness and fellow-convict, Ruchell Magee. He armed both of them, and together they kidnapped Judge Haley, Deputy District Attorney Garry Thomas, and three women jurors, taking them out to a waiting van. Police and San

69

Debray, Jules Régis

Quentin guards opened fire as the van was driven away, and killed Judge Haley, McClain, Jackson and the driver, Christmas; seriously wounding Thomas and Magee; and slightly wounding a juror. In the subsequent investigation the Federal Bureau of Investigation (FBI) claimed that the guns used by Jonathan Jackson had been bought by Angela Davis and, as she had gone to New York, she was billed as 'Wanted' for inter-state flight, murder and kidnapping, under a law of 1872, Section 31 of the Californian Penal Code, touching the aiding and abetting of a criminal act. It was also charged that the kidnapping had been planned by her to obtain hostages to be used to secure the release of the Soledad Brothers. Davis was arrested by FBI officers in New York in October 1970. Her lawyers fought the requisition by the State of California for extradition through to the Supreme Court but their efforts were defeated by Governor Reagan's use of a Grand Jury indictment for murder and kidnapping and she was extradited to Marin County, Cal. Skilful abuse of legal procedures enabled the State of California to hold her in prison in the absence of hard evidence which would have enabled them to bring her to trial and thereby to transform her into a martyr sacrificed to capitalist-imperialist-racist oppression, for New Left revolutionaries all over the world. That this should have been so is curious since she is a firm supporter of Moscow-style orthodox communism stigmatized by the New Left as Stalinist and anti-socialist. In February 1972 Angela Davis was released on bail, to which she surrendered in due course and was acquitted by an all-white jury, whether on the facts of the case or because she had become a national – and international – symbol of oppression of black by white which it was expedient to repudiate, is by no means clear.

Debray, Jules Régis (1940–   ) French ▷ Marxist thinker and militant revolutionary, s. of a lawyer father and a well-known conservative politician mother. Ed. Lycée Louis le Grand; *Concours Général*, philosophy prize, 1956. Passed first into Ecole Normale, 1959 and paid his first visit to Cuba. In 1961 he spent some months travelling in Latin America. Ph.D. Ecole Normale, 1963. He went (1963) to Venezuela to make a film of ▷ guerrilla life for French TV and by one account helped to train guerrilla recruits. He travelled all over Latin America during 1963–64, returning to Paris to write *Castroism: the Long March of Latin America* (1965). In January 1966 he returned to Cuba as Professor of History, University of

Havana, where he wrote *Revolution in the Revolution*, the first Western work to give expression to that Marxist-◊ Leninist dissatisfaction with the orthodox communist parties which now separates the whole of the ◊ New Left from Moscow communism, stigmatized as state capitalism. In March 1967 Debray went to Bolivia to meet and interview Che ◊ Guevara for a French publisher and a Mexican magazine. Debray worked as a camp orderly and accompanied the guerrilla group when it went into action (*see* ◊ Bolivia, guerrilla movements). He urged 'Che' to enrol him as a combatant, but was refused on the grounds that he was of more use to the movement as a publicist. On his way out of the country to undertake this work he was betrayed to the police by a guerrilla defector, and arrested. He was tortured by Cuban exiles, officers of the US Central Intelligence Agency, kept in handcuffs for two months, tried, and sentenced to thirty years in prison. On the repeated intervention of the French government he was amnestied by the third Bolivian administration since his arrest and returned to France in December 1970.

Debs, Eugene Victor (1855–1926) United States socialist. b. Terre Haute, Indiana, at fourteen he went to work for the Vandalia Railroad. He became an organizer for the Brotherhood of Locomotive Firemen and (1880) one of its national officers, City Clerk, Terre Haute, and (1888) a member of the State Legislature. His personal efforts to federate the railroad craft unions failed, but when, in 1893, a nationwide industrial union, the American Railway Union, was formed, Debs became its president. In the same year the Pullman Car Company which paid notoriously low wages, cut wages by 25 per cent, so that many workers had less than $1 a week after deductions for rent, water and gas, all the service industries in the town of Pullman being owned by the Company. Debs and his fellow union organizers called a strike and busied themselves persuading workers to join it. In retaliation the employers 'persuaded' both State and Federal governments to 'persuade' judges to grant injunctions preventing union propaganda. Debs defied the injunction served on him, was sent to prison, without a trial, for contempt of court, and as a result became a national working-class hero. His experience with the railroad bosses and with the Pullman Company convinced Debs that capitalism was an evil system but he could not bring himself to advocate violent revolution. Instead he gave his support to the People's Party of the USA, known as the ◊ Populists

Democracy, democratic

and campaigned for William Jennings Bryan for President, a curious way of trying to attain his aims of nationalization of the railroads, repossession of public land given to the railroads and the steeply graded income tax advocated by Karl ⟡ Marx. He belatedly discovered his mistake and in 1898 founded the Socialist Party of the USA and, on a moderately Marxist ticket, ran for President in 1900, 1904, 1908, 1912. In 1918 he was arrested and imprisoned for preaching pacifism, but again ran for president in 1920, obtaining 6 per cent of the popular vote. Meanwhile, in 1905, he had founded, with W. D. Haywood and others, the ⟡ Industrial Workers of the World, known as the I.W.W. or 'Wobblies', an international socialist and ⟡ syndicalist movement. However, his distaste for violence forced him to leave this movement too, when its extreme faction concluded, with Marx and ⟡ Bakunin that the revolution would not succeed without the use of force.

Debs was neither a reader nor a thinker, though he educated himself by his own efforts. His positive qualities were gentleness, a warm affection for his fellows, transparent honesty and complete sincerity, all serious handicaps in political life.

Democracy, democratic, originally from *demos* (Gr. people) and *kratos* (Gr. power), meaning rule by the people. The only possibly authentic known cases of democracy in practice – if the non-enfranchisement of women and slaves be overlooked and tribal democracy in primitive, and probably in prehistoric, society – are from the history of Greece between the 8th and 3rd centuries B C, the Athenian government being taken as the model case, with its rule by all the citizens equally joined in public assembly, which assembly even received, heard and answered foreign embassies. Near-democracies were, at various times, briefly established in some small Italian states, and modified versions of democracy can be found in German and early Russian history. It is probable that democracy is one of the oldest, as it is the nearest to just, forms of government. But it has invariably been destroyed by growth of the state entailing an increase of citizen population such that democratic assemblies became impossibly unwieldy and were, by force of circumstances, corrupted by the introduction of representational systems which are themselves peculiarly liable to further corruption. The US republic, commonly referred to as a democracy, was never intended to be, and has never become, a democracy. Based, by

72

founders with good English classical educations, on.an idealization of the Roman Republic, it was, like that Republic, first an aristocracy and later a plutocracy.

As currently used in both capitalist and communist states, the words *democracy, democratic* must be regarded as merely 'newspeak', i.e. words or locutions which have a recognized *purpose* in social, political and commercial propaganda, but are meaningless in that they are not, in the general understanding, intended to designate an actual state of affairs or practice. A measure of meaning may, however, be restored to the words by the use of a qualifying adverb or adjective of special intention. Thus, e.g. when British or US or USSR government agencies refer to the systems obtaining in their countries as *democratic* the word has no specific meaning and is used only to convey a more or less vague impression that government is, in those countries, being carried on for the benefit of the mass of the people; in such a context no man in his senses would take the word to mean, or to be even intended to mean, what the dictionary says it means. But, e.g. *social democracy, direct democracy* still retain specific meanings.

In established communist states (*see* Communism) the words are used to convey or reinforce the impression, although everyone knows that in practice rule is exercised solely by the executive committee of the CP, that the committee is giving expression to the 'dictatorship of the proletariat'. They are, in short, used poetically and not scientifically or didactically. Similarly, in capitalist states which are not under Fascist or military dictatorships in which the two words are now pejorative, systems of representational democracy have been developed whereby political parties, i.e. oligarchical machines for political and economic manipulation, actually rule (or, rather, their executive minorities do so) but the illusion 'democracy' is created by allowing the people to vote for representatives to a national assembly at more or less considerable intervals of time. The real political power is in the hands either of a plutocracy, or, more recently, of a managerial élite, but is in any case not wielded by the people.

One of the ostensible aims, in communist theory, of the ▷ cultural revolution, is to bring about a condition in which the socialist state (*see* Socialism) is managed directly by all the people, thus becoming communist. Such a state would, of course, be a democracy: no socialist state has, as yet, accomplished this miracle. Cultural revolution is a ▷ Leninist

De Valera, Eamon

concept and both the Leninist and Trotskyist ◊ New Left whether in advanced industrial countries or in the industrially backward countries castigates both the established capitalist and communist systems as shamefully undemocratic. It has had to use the expression 'direct democracy' to designate its own aims, as a consequence of the word democracy losing its meaning. An example of that loss of meaning will be found in the use of the word to describe the two-party parliamentary oligarchy of, e.g. the U K and the U S A, in which the electorate are given a choice between Tweedledum and Tweedledee. This farce was exposed by Aristophanes in Athens in his satirical treatment of Kleon, the democratic leader, c. 400 B C, but has nevertheless been taken seriously for another 2,000 years.

The last genuine attempt to establish a democracy was made, in Russia during the two 1917 ◊ Revolutions, with the cry of 'All power to the Soviets', i.e. Councils of the common people. But owing to the size of modern populations even the Soviets had to resort to systems of representation and like all representational bodies these were easily turned into instruments for denying political power to the people and concentrating it in the hands of the executive committee of the Soviets, and, finally, of the militantly effective and ruthless Bolshevik élite.

In short, given the size of modern populations, the fact must be faced that democracy is a physical impossibility and it might be as well if this were realized. But despite degradation by long abuse the word still retains so much glamour that it will doubtless continue to be used by propagandists to glorify systems which are increasingly undemocratic.

De Valera, Eamon (1882–   ) b. New York, father Spanish, mother Irish; ed. Blackrock College, Dublin. Irish Nationalist revolutionary. He held his first revolutionary military command under Pearse (◊ Fenian) and Connolly (◊ Sinn Fein) in the Easter Rising of 1916. Captured by the British he, together with other leaders, was condemned to death, but because of his U S citizenship was one of the few not executed. From 1917 to 1926 he led the Sinn Fein in fighting the British (1919–20); and, when its moderate wing led by Arthur Griffith accepted the Irish Free State agreement with the British government, he led the extremist wing in the Civil War against the Free Staters, forming the Irish Republican Army (◊ I R A) and later the Fianna Fail political party. In the 1932 elections Fianna Fail emerged victorious and De Valera became Prime Minister of what was still the Irish Free State, but was evolving, under a British policy of non-interference, first into 'Eire' (1936) and finally, but not officially until the proclamation of 1949, into the Republic of Ireland. During his 1932–48 term of office, De Valera completely dissociated Ireland from the U K, and refused to declare war on Nazi Germany in 1939, or to allow the U K or the U S A to use Irish ports for naval operations against Germany. Fianna Fail lost the election of 1948 but De Valera was again Prime Minister 1951–54 and 1957–59. In 1959 he became the President of the Republic, an office which he still holds.

Dialectic. Marxism is based on a philosophy of history which Marx elaborated on ⟡ Hegel's Law of the Dialectic. The inspiration of this Law (the resolution of thesis and antithesis in synthesis) was the doctrine of the unity of opposites which he found in Heracleitos of Ephesus (*c.* 540–475 B C), whose philosophy also had considerable influence on ⟡ Lenin's thought.

Dimitrov, Georgi Mihailov (1882–1949) Bulgarian communist revolutionary. b. Kovachevtsi, became a socialist in his teens, joined the Social Democratic Party of Bulgaria and led its extreme left wing which (1919) he separated from the S D Party, to form the Bulgarian Communist Party. He did all in his power to keep Bulgaria out of World War I and in 1918 was imprisoned for subversive pacifist activities. When released he went to the U S S R and by 1921 was serving on the Executive Committee of the ⟡ Comintern. He returned to Bulgaria in 1923 to lead a number of armed risings designed to overthrow the ⟡ Stambolisky (peasant) government. These failing, Dimitrov escaped from the country, was condemned to death in his absence, and for ten years worked as a communist agent in various parts of Europe, including Germany where (1932) he suddenly became world famous for his brilliant and courageous defence when he was 'framed' with the charge of burning down the Reichstag, a crime actually perpetrated by the Nazis themselves. Following his acquittal, he returned to the U S S R and was given Soviet citizenship (1933). From 1935 to 1943 he was General Secretary, Executive Committee of the Comintern in which office he was able to protect ⟡ Tito and one or two other foreign communists from being judicially murdered in ⟡ Stalin's purge trials; he was also a Deputy in the Supreme Soviet of the U S S R. He organized

Dimitrov, Georgi Mihailov

communist resistance to the Nazis in Bulgaria in World War II and in 1945 resumed Bulgarian citizenship, to become the first Prime Minister of the Bulgarian People's Republic whose Constitution he wrote. He lost favour with Stalin when, with Tito, he discussed a possible Federation of Bulgaria and Yugoslavia, but remained Prime Minister of Bulgaria until his death.

E

Eighteen-forty-eight. The roots of many twentieth-century revolutions will be found in the year 1848, *annus mirabilis* of revolutions, when the European ⟡ bourgeoisie, often in alliance with the ⟡ proletariat, and led by intellectuals, mostly French, rose against the dead conservative authoritarianism or absolutism of Metternich's Continental System; against poverty and misery produced by bad harvests and economic depression; against the strains produced by rapid industrial evolution: – and tried to overthrow absolute monarchies and aristocratic or plutocratic oligarchies all over Europe, in order to replace them with parliamentary democracies.

The movement began in Switzerland in November 1847: the Federal Council expelled the Jesuits; a group of reactionary clericalist cantons, the Sonderbund, rose in arms against this decision; Austria, supported by Prussia and France, threatened to intervene on their side. Oxenbein, Swiss radical leader, replied that if they did, he would invade north Italy with 20,000 men and liberate it from Austria. The Austrians lost their nerve and in three weeks the Sonderbund was beaten. Austria's loss of nerve encouraged the Italians, open revolts broke out against her in the north, and against the Bourbons in Naples and Sicily: Naples, Turin and Florence proclaimed a constitution and King Ferdinand of Naples had to run for it.

In Belgium, where massive unemployment had produced starvation, the Democratic Association, created by Karl ⟡ Marx, organized risings against the liberal government. But it was to France that all European revolutionaries looked for a lead; the tension there was extreme and when, 23 February 1848, troops opened fire on a peaceful demonstration, revolution flared, barricades went up all over Paris, the Republic was declared, the Palais Royal seized and Louis Philippe forced to flee for his life. The throne was publicly burnt and a provisional government installed. Meanwhile, the Belgian government had mobilized its armed forces, was strong enough to arrest or expel the chiefly German leaders of the Democratic Association, including Marx who went to Paris, where the right wing of the revolution and the provisional government were led by Lamartine, the left

77

by the socialist Louis ⟡ Blanc, while the followers of the socialist ⟡ Blanqui were calling for war to carry the revolution to the rest of Europe. The German émigré revolutionists were organizing a legion to invade Prussia and calling on the French to give them arms. Marx tried desperately to prevent this folly. Meanwhile the government's failure to organize the national industrial workshops started by Blanc, led to a second, wholly proletarian, insurrection which split the bourgeois–proletariat alliance.

In Austria, Metternich was turned out of power by riots in Vienna and demands for a parliamentary democracy. Emperor Ferdinand bolted for the frontier, but recovered his nerve at Innsbruck, or at all events halted there when it became clear that revolution seemed to be breaking out all over the continent. He agreed to summon a Constituent Assembly, which sat in Vienna from July until October. Its only permanent achievement was the emancipation of the peasantry from the payment of feudal dues to landowners. Elsewhere in the Empire the Czechs rose in Prague, accidentally killing the Princess Windischgraetz, thus so provoking Windischgraetz, the Military Governor, that he bombarded Prague, set up a military dictatorship, extended it to Vienna, and, with other aristocratic leaders, forced the abdication of Ferdinand and the accession and coronation of his nephew Franz Josef.

Before this abdication Ferdinand had been forced to concede autonomy to Hungary, led by the patriot Kossuth and the Hungarian Diet. The Croats then demanded independence of Hungary, were refused and with Austrian backing, started a war on Hungary. The Hungarian army defeated both the Croats and Prince Windischgraetz, and Kossuth was elected Regent of Hungary. Next to rise in arms demanding independence and a constitution were the Serbs and the Romanians, both of them minorities within Hungary. Meanwhile Franz Josef called upon the Tsar of Russia for help, the Russian army defeated the Hungarian army at Tenesvan, and following the peace of Vilagos, abandoned them to the savage revenge of the Austrians. There were no revolutionary gains.

In Germany there were two, linked, movements: one for parliamentary democratic government in the various kingdoms and principalities; the other for a united Germany. Riots in Berlin forced King Frederick William of Prussia to call a Constituent Assembly, and other German princes followed his example; as they did when, encouraged by the triumph of counter-revolution in the Austrian Empire, he felt strong enough to reassert the royal authority, claiming the divine right of kings. But a first All-German Parliament sat at Frankfurt (May 1848 to April 1849), drew up a federal constitution for all the Germanies, and elected Frederick William Emperor of Germany. On the grounds that his kingly right was from God, he refused to accept an imperial crown from the hands of a constitutional assembly; the parliamentarians went home. The most revolutionary part of Prussia was the Rhineland: Marx had gone from Paris to Cologne and, leading the Workers' Association, later the Democratic Association, and the Communist League, fought hard to prevent the revolutionary extremists from refusing alliance with the bourgeoisie against the absolute monarchy, boycotting the election to the first all-German parliament won by the revolution, and trying to fight both class enemies at once.

In Britain the Chartists made their final and futile attempt to get the constitution reformed, and there was a peasant nationalist insurrection in Tipperary which was easily crushed.

The Danes secured a democratic parliamentary constitution from their king, Frederick VII.

When the tumult and the shouting died, it was widely if tacitly recognized that the rule of kings, princes, archdukes, counts and prince-bishops was coming to an end, despite the almost universal victory of the counter-revolution. Power was shifting into the hands of the class of industrial and commercial capitalists and their bankers, i.e. the high bourgeoisie. But, already, their ultimate loss of it was forecast, for, in the opening phrase of the ◊ Marx- ◊ Engels *Communist Manifesto*, published in the same year, 'A spectre is haunting Europe; it is the spectre of Communism . . .'

Eisner, Kurt (1867–1919) German socialist revolutionary; b. Berlin. Read philosophy and published a number of philosophical works and at the same time became a political journalist, editor of the Social Democratic Party's newspaper *Vorwärts*. Although an orthodox Marxist he believed that deviant opinions should be respected, and when two of his colleagues on the paper were dismissed for ◊ revisionism, he resigned the editorship. He went to Munich, working as a freelance socialist journalist, and took out papers as a Bavarian citizen. He held firmly to the Second International resolution that socialists must oppose war by all means in their power, and

79

Engels, Friedrich

in 1917 he was imprisoned for making pacifist propaganda, but released on the intervention of the Social Democratic members of the Reichstag. He continued his socialist and pacifist propaganda and in November 1918 was at the head of the movement of workers in Munich which proclaimed a Bavarian Republic. Eisner was its prime minister during its short and precarious existence and was assassinated in February 1919 during the rightist military *coup* which abolished it.

Engels, Friedrich (1820–95) German communist revolutionary theorist and co-founder with Karl ⟡ Marx of modern socialism. b. Barmen in the Wupper industrial valley, s. of a textile manufacturer with factories in Barmen and Manchester, England. Engels was reared in a strict and gloomy Calvinist atmosphere and, unlike Marx, was in close contact with the miseries of the industrial workers from his childhood. At high school he began to react against the narrow obscurantism of his home and his father's circle: he read the revolutionary young poets, Heine and Börner, wrote poetry, and resolved to escape into a broader world. Excelling in languages, all the great literatures were open to him. His father, whom Engels hated, contained his revolt by putting him to work in the factory a year before he had finished school and then sending him to work for a Bremen cloth merchant with whom he had business relations. But reading the poets had made Engels a radical; reading Strauss's *Life of Jesus* relieved him, after a painful struggle with the fundamentalism he had been taught, of the burden of his father's gloomy religion; reading ⟡ Hegel made him a Hegelian; and finally, reading Feuerbach made him a communist. When the time came for his military service, only one year because he was a volunteer, he was posted to Berlin (1841) and soon gravitated into the circle of the Young Hegelian revolutionaries, the *Freigelassene*. He began to write for the radical press, and to write anti-'idealist' pamphlets, soon winning a literary reputation. When his father sent him (1842) to Manchester he made the journey by way of Cologne, where Marx was editing the *Rhenish Gazette*. But this first meeting was cold because Marx did not trust the head-in-air radicalism of the *Freigelassene*, though it was arranged that Engels would send him articles for the paper from England. Their brilliance when they arrived converted him to a respect and admiration for Engels's talent which he never lost, and he welcomed Engels's *Umrisse zu einer Kritik der Nationalökonomie* (Paris 1844) as a work of genius.

Engels joined forces with the Chartist leaders, wrote for Robert Owen's *The New Moral World* in which bourgeois institutions including marriage were analysed and condemned, and studied, at close quarter, for he was a man who could make friends regardless of social station, the atrocious lives of the Manchester millhands and their families. Out of this, and his loathing of the cruelty of capitalism, came (1845) his *Die Lage der Arbeitbenden Klasse in England (The Situation of the Working Class in England)*. In 1844 he visited Paris and met Marx again, and so was formed a friendship based on ideological accord, mutual admiration and trust, which lasted the rest of their lives. Agreeing to work together, they wrote their first pamphlet in common (the satirical *Die Heilige Familie, oder Kritik der kritischen Kritik*, 1845). From Paris Engels went to Germany where he joined enthusiastically in the movement of intellectuals and educated working-men who believed that the communist revolution was just round the corner, and he even found communism spreading through the Wupper valley among the wretched workers employed by his father. On Marx's insistence he rejoined his new friend, this time in Brussels, where together they worked on Marx's theory of historical materialism and on the long *German Ideology* (not published until 1932), in which those theories were first applied. Together, too, they worked for the 'League of the Just', later the Communist League, the only secret revolutionary society Marx ever joined. Engels returned to England to attend the London Congress of the League as delegate of the Paris Communists (1847). It was during that Congress that, at the White Hart Inn in Drury Lane, was adopted an 'order of the day' which was to strike terror into the bourgeoisie for a century: *Proletarians of all countries, Unite!* Marx suggested it; Engels proclaimed it: nothing could be more characteristic of their long relationship. Engels's next task for the revolution was the drafting of that document (for the Communist League Congress of 1848 which never took place, because of the outbreak of European revolution) which became known as *The Communist Manifesto*, and which he and Marx worked over together later. He took part in the 1848 revolution, first in Cologne, with Marx, then in Baden. After the triumph of the counterrevolution, Engels returned to Manchester as a clerk in his father's firm, at a salary which was by no means generous, for the father had no more love for the son than the son for the father. But when Marx, his lovely wife Jenny von Westphalen, and their children, arrived in London as hunted and penniless exiles

(August 1848), he sent them money as often as he could, did his best to help Marx to newspaper work, and as often as not wrote his friend's articles for him so that Marx himself could get on with his major work, research for the writing of *Das Kapital*. He also wrote articles for the *New Rhenish Gazette* which Marx edited in exile (1850). If he was not able to do as much for the Marx family as he would have wished to do, it was not only because he was kept on short commons by his father, but because with what money he did have he had to keep up a decent appearance, as the son of the firm of Ermen and Engels. He also had to meet responsibilities (which he took seriously) towards his adored mistress (he was far too consistent in his rejection of bourgeois institutions ever to marry), Mary Burns, an Irish working-girl who reciprocated his love, and her parents, whom he helped to support. The truth is that for twenty years Engels devoted his attention to a trade he hated, and neglected his own research work in social science, in order to keep the Marx family from starvation and to ensure for Marx at least a measure of freedom to continue his major work, which Engels regarded as far more important than anything he himself could contribute towards the revolution. In 1860 Engels senior took his son into partnership and within a few years he was in a better position to help Marx, but in 1863 their friendship was put to a severe strain when Engels wrote a heartbroken letter announcing Mary Burns's death and Marx, again in desperate financial straits, included a request for more money in his letter of rather offhand condolence. (Try as he would, Marx could never achieve his friend's emancipation from middle-class conventions.) Marx followed up his letter with an apology, but it took Engels several weeks to get over his pain: he had, in that year alone, given Marx £350. In 1870, when Engels inherited his father's business and became a comparatively rich man, he made Marx an annual allowance which freed him from financial anxiety for the rest of his life.

Engels played a considerable part in the foundation and running of the First ◊ International, and from *c.* 1865 worked hard with Marx to save it from being taken over by hotheaded idealists whose revolutionary theory was unsound (chiefly the French); and by ◊ Bakunin's anarchist conspiracy. From 1870 he devoted his life to working with Marx on revolutionary writings and international organizing activities aimed at the propagation of practical, properly educated, soundly based communism. After 1873, when Marx fell ill and seemed to lose the will for sustained, consistent work,

Engels did his best to 'stand-in' for him, without any question of acknowledgement or credits. Although Marx had started on the second volume of *Das Kapital* his repeated sickness, his shattering grief at the death of his wife and then of his favourite daughter, prevented him from finishing it. Engels did it for him and it was published in 1885. From such notes and annotated books as Marx had accumulated, he wrote the third volume and saw it published (1894) a year before his own death. Of the great nineteenth-century revolutionaries he had the warmest heart and the sweetest nature.

Enragés. Originally a group of extreme left, violent, *sans-culottes* revolutionaries led by Jacques Roux in the French Revolution 1789. The epithet was borrowed by the '22 March Movement' led by Daniel ◊ Cohn-Bendit in the ◊ French (Student) Revolution 1968.

EPL. Ejercito Popular de Liberacion. ◊ Maoist ◊ guerrilla group. *See* ◊ Colombia.

Establishment. Used by revolutionaries as a term of abuse to designate that complex of interests and people which is the fount of effective economic and therefore political power. The meaning given to the word is an extrapolation from the nonconformist's use of the expression 'established Church'. In common usage it designates not so much the body of office holders in the national institutions, as the rather vaguely defined complex of political, social, financial, industrial, academic, religious, literary and artistic groups whose members are linked by a common interest in preserving the *status quo* in which their own wealth and power are involved.

F

Falange, Falangists. The Falange Española was originally a Spanish version of Italian ⟡ Fascism founded, as a political movement, in 1933 by Jose Antonio Primo de Rivera, son of the Dictator of Spain 1923–31, who seized power at the instance of King Alphonso XIII, dissolved the *Cortes*, suspended trial by jury, introduced censorship of the press and threw leading democrats into prison, in order to destroy the growing revolutionary and nationalist movements such as anarchism and Catalan separatism. The elder Primo de Rivera's failure to establish a completely Fascist regime, probably due to a certain aristocratic squeamishness about torture and execution being used as freely as necessary to destroy liberty, led to the downfall of the Spanish monarchy, and the institution of the democratic Republic. His son's foundation did something to recover the initiative for the right wing, even though he was shot by the Republicans in 1936, for the Falange survived his death until, having shown some signs of social reformism of the kind anathema to true Fascists who recognize an ultimately implacable enemy in the working class, it was merged (1937) by Francisco ⟡ Franco into the Falange Española Tradicionalista y de las Juntas Ofensiva Nacional Sindicalistas, which has since been the only political body legal in Spain and has, on the whole, been submissive to the ⟡ Caudillo, although very occasionally the memory of Jose Antonio has stimulated miniscule gestures in the direction of liberalism. A curious by-product of the 'martyrdom' of the younger De Rivera was his political canonization by younger members of the Spanish ⟡ bourgeoisie whose distaste for the crudities of the Franco Fascist regime found an outlet in the illusion that things would have been less uncharitable under Jose Antonio.

FALN: Fuerzas Armadas de Liberacion Nacional, a Venezuelan revolutionary organization composed of seven ⟡ guerrilla groups, formed in December 1962. For its programme and activities: *see* ⟡ Venezuela.

Fanon, Franz (1925–1961) Black revolutionary theorist and propagandist, b. Fort-de-France, Martinique. He studied medicine at Lyon University and fought under De Lattre de Tassigny against the ◊ Nazis in World War II. Serving as a psychiatrist in Blida Hospital, Algeria (1952), he found himself treating both torturer and tortured, and required to reconcile both with their fate. He developed the theory that the mental disturbances he had to treat were a byproduct of colonialism produced in the colonized people and resolved that it was the system, not the individual, that had to be changed. He began to publish violent polemics against the French in Algeria and as a result was forced to take refuge from the French political police; he went to Tunis where he joined the Algerian National Liberation Front and became editor of *El Moujahid*, its official organ. He adopted a Pan-African revolutionary attitude and, as diplomatic representative of the Provisional Government of the Algerian Republic, travelled all over Africa on behalf of the Algerian struggle, continuing with this work after he had realized that he was dying of leukaemia. In 1961, working fast to cheat death, he wrote *The Wretched of the Earth* in which he analysed the world in terms of a vast exploitative pyramid, the controllers of capital in the rich countries at the top, and the poor peasants (the fellaheen – his theory was very much Algeria-based, and weakest when he tried to generalize too broadly) of the poor countries at the bottom. These, and not the industrial working classes of the world, he said, were now the true revolutionary force because they alone had nothing to lose but their chains. He called upon all the peoples of Africa, Asia and Latin America who were being exploited by US ◊ imperialism using neocolonialist means, to rise up and fight that evil. Of that imperialism (used in the ◊ Leninist sense) Fanon wrote that it 'is not a body endowed with reasoning faculties. It is naked violence and will yield only when confronted with greater violence'. Violence was therefore the duty of the revolutionary masses, for the cry for non-violence in the struggle is a fraud, and only to be heard when the victims are white. The violence inflicted on the exploited takes many forms, as hunger, poverty, disease and ignorance. The revolutionary violence to be used against it 'frees the native from his inferiority complex and from despair and inaction; it makes him fearless and restores his self-respect'.

Fanon's works have since been translated into English and other languages and in Africa and the Third World generally his unorthodox ◊ Marxism has had a profound influence on revolutionary thinking.

FAR

FAR: Fuerzas Armadas Rebeldes, i.e. Rebel Armed Forces, a revolutionary ◊ guerrilla movement in ◊ Guatemala.

FARC: Fuerzas Armadas Revolutionarias Colombianas. A Moscow-Communist association of guerrilla groups: *see* ◊ Colombia.

FARP: People's Revolutionary Armed Forces. The revolutionary guerrilla army of the African Independence Party of Guinea and Cape Verde: *see* ◊ Cabral.

Fascism, Fascist. Right wing revolutionary doctrine, from *fasci*, and hence *fasces*, the bundles of rods bound round an axe helve which were borne before the Roman Consuls by the Lictors, as the symbol of public power. As a revolutionary political movement it was founded in Italy by Benito ◊ Mussolini in 1919, by combining his *fasci* of workers, that is small groups organized to bring about revolutionary changes in the political and social structure of Italy, into the *Fascisti*. The party's doctrine was that of the corporate state, theoretically revolutionary since it was supposed to be anti-capitalist; it was certainly anti-democratic and anti-socialist, although its principal ideas were borrowed from the ◊ syndicalism of the socialist ◊ Sorel. Fascisti wore a uniform, the black shirt and, frequently, top boots, used the Roman military salute, and constituted a paramilitary force which, at its lowest level, was a gang of murderous hooligans, at its highest a semisecret police force.

In practice Fascism was closely allied with big capitalism, of which it became, to some extent, the militant instrument against socialism, at the expense of bourgeois parliamentary democracy. Thus, in Germany, the National Socialist ◊ (Nazi) Party, which borrowed ideas from Fascism, was generously financed by certain great industrialists, as a bulwark against communism. And in Italy, Germany, Spain, Portugal and elsewhere, by crushing the trade unions and imposing wage and salary scales by force, Fascism enabled industrialists to dictate instead of negotiating wages and conditions. In Fascist Italy, in theory, the labour force had a voice, since it was represented in the industrial and commercial corporations; but in practice the corporations were ruled by the employers. These corporations were combined in a National Council of Corporations to manage the country's economy, while politics became the business of the Fascist

86

Grand Council of ministers presided over by Mussolini as *Duce* (leader). He came to power in 1922 when invited by King Victor Emmanuel III to become prime minister.

In the UK a Fascist movement founded and led by Sir Oswald ▷ Mosley was based on the Italian model with a policy of suppressing freedom of the press, free speech and other democratic rights; it was strongly imperialistic and antisemitic, following the Nazi rather than the Fascist. It was repeatedly involved in violent hooliganism chiefly in the East End of London. It was suppressed during World War II, and Mosley imprisoned; in 1948 it was revived as the British Union, still under the nominal leadership of Mosley although he lived in France.

Since the defeat and subsequent democratization of the two leading Fascist powers in World War II, and the elimination of the Fascist and Nazi parties, neo-Fascist movements have repeatedly cropped up in both countries and a neo-Fascist Party has seats in the Italian Parliament. Fascist movements in Britain now tend to be confined to a lunatic fringe.

Fascism is the only revolutionary movement which has a strong appeal for the class of small businessmen, such as individual shopkeepers who feel their livelihood threatened on the one hand by socialism and on the other by monopoly capitalism, and who are in danger of proletarianization. But Fascist militia are also recruited in the subclass called by ▷ Marx the *lumpenproletariat*, the tradeless, rootless dregs of the working class without class loyalty or self-respect.

In Italy from 1922 to 1939 at least, Fascism did have a philosophy of the state and a social programme. But the word had come to mean, on the whole, any militant right-wing organization using armed force to hold down the working class and its intellectual allies.

The abuse of the words fascist and fascism when used by USSR propagandists and, in general, by all left-wing revolutionaries, as a term of abuse for all opponents to the right of the user's political position, has almost deprived them of specific sense, a common consequence of political ▷ propaganda and polemics; just as the abuse of the words communist and communism in right-wing propaganda and polemics has tended to degrade the correct meaning of those words. In both cases the words now tend to be used to invoke a myth – the Enemy of Mankind; i.e. 'Fascist' used pejoratively invokes not so much a political-economic opponent, as the Devil, the implacable and it would seem unkillable opponent of the good; in other words, the very principle and essence of evil. Nevertheless, there is a strong element of Fascism in the government of Portugal; it survives in the governments of Spain and Brazil; it has been revived by military dictators in Greece, Brazil and elsewhere; and is implicit in such recurrent phenomena as Poujadism in France and Powellism in the UK.

Fenian Society. The use of revolutionary violence by secret societies dedicated to particular causes has a fairly long history in Ireland. In 1772 the Peep O'Day Boys society was formed in Ulster with a view to the extermination, by murder, of Catholic farmers. The 'Orangemen', another Protestant secret society, derived from the Belfast Orange Lodge of Freemasons, was less ruthless in its methods, although later connected with the originally anti-Catholic, later anti-Negro, violently reactionary Ku-Klux-Klan, in America. The Carders, Threshers, Oak Boys, Ribbon Society and others were Roman Catholic groups using terrorism to persuade farmers not to pay tithes to the alien and hated Church of Ireland clergy. They were ancestral to the Fenian Society or Irish Republican Brotherhood (Fenian is from *Fiann*, a legendary band of warriors), founded in New York 1857, Dublin 1858, to liberate Ireland from the English yoke and found an Irish Republic. Its activities during its first ten years are obscure, but in 1867–70 it became active, blowing up Clerkenwell Prison, London, attempting an invasion of Canada, and trying to seize and hold Chester Castle. It is probable, though it was never clearly established, that Irish-American Fenians were behind the assassination by the Invincibles, another secret society, of Mr Burke, Permanent Secretary for Ireland, and (more or less incidentally), Lord Frederick Cavendish, Chief Secretary of State, in Phoenix Park, Dublin, 1882. The Fenians were ancestral to ◊ *Sinn Fein* (Ourselves Alone) from which derived the Irish Republican Army (◊ IRA) whose revolutionary guerrilla warfare forced the British government to concede Ireland a measure of freedom (1921), and which, waging Civil War on the government of the Irish Free State, ensured the establishment of the Irish Republic. The Fenians used an original and witty method of raising funds: they sold to their non-militant adherents Republic of Ireland banknotes, in dollar denominations, which 'promised to pay' six months 'after the acknowledgement'. It has proved impossible to discover whether any were ever presented.

Fifth Column, fifth columnist, the latter being a traitor to his country or, in class war, his class, working inside that country or class in the interest of a national or class enemy, often by means of ⟡ sabotage. It is derived from a saying attributed to Francisco ⟡ Franco who, when attacking Madrid in the 1935–9 Spanish Civil War with four columns, is said to have referred to his active and militant adherents inside the city as his 'fifth column'.

FIR: Frente de Izquierda Revolucionaria, a 'Front' of guerrilla bands organized for Socialist revolution by Hugo Blanco ⟡ Galdos in Peru.

FLN (1): Frente de Liberacion Nacional. Venezuelan revolutionary political organization, the political side of the ⟡ FALN, comprised of seven guerrilla groups: *see* ⟡ Venezuela.

FLN (2): Front de Liberation Nationale. A militant nationalist and originally only moderately Socialist movement founded (1954) by Mahommed Ben Bella to expel the French from Algeria. Its parental organizations were the Democratic Union of the Algerian Manifesto (UDMA) and the more militant Movement for the Triumph of Democratic Liberties (MLTD). In November 1954 the FLN declared war on France in the name of the Algerian people and at once went over to the attack. Guerrilla warfare was waged with persistence and great bitterness, becoming a model for revolutionary civil war for the New Left in several parts of the world. The Algerian guerrilla was led at first by Ben Bella and, when he was captured by the French in 1956, by Ferhat Abbas and Krim Belkacem. But in 1960 Colonel Houari ⟡ Boumedienne, with 60,000 men armed by the USSR through Egypt, highly trained by himself in Tunis, became the supreme militant leader. As a result the FLN moved to the left. After eight years of warfare in which the French troops were convicted of using torture to extract military information from their prisoners, the FLN achieved its first military purpose by forcing the French government to concede independence and even to enforce this decision which was savagely resisted by the *Pieds Noirs*, the Algerian-born Europeans, French and Spanish. The FLN was then transformed into a political party of the left and it remains the only legal party in Algeria today. It is, in

Forman, James

essence, New Marxist-Leninist with strong sympathy with Cuban Castro-Guevarist communism (*see* ◊ Castro *and* ◊ Guevara). It has expropriated the large estates, limited landholdings to 30 hectares and nationalized the oil industry, the only industrial undertaking of any importance. But its revolutionary importance is limited by the country's underdeveloped state and consequent poverty and unemployment.

Forman, James. Foundation member of ◊ SNCC, dedicated to 'Liberation' of American blacks. He has become a revolutionary in the full sense of the word, that is a social revolutionary, by identifying the cause of the American blacks with the worldwide cause of the 'neocolonized' peoples of Asia, Africa and Latin America. See USA, Revolution in, and the cross references under that head.

Frelimo. Mozambique Liberation Front: *see* Portuguese Africa, revolution in, and Mondlane.

French Student Revolution, May 1968. Important as the only attempted revolution in a Western industrial postwar society to date. On 18 March 1968 a group of student and schoolboy members of militant anti-American (anti-Vietnam War, anti-imperialism) movements bombed a number of US establishments in Paris; five were later arrested. On 22 March students at the huge Nanterre annexe of Paris University called a meeting protesting against these arrests. From this meeting emerged the '22 March Movement' of student revolutionaries led by the Franco-German student Daniel ◊ Cohn-Bendit. In the subsequent events this Movement was supported by a large number of small political groups, the most important being the Jeunesses Communistes Revolutionaires, a ◊ Trotskyist group; the Union des Jeunesses Communistes Marxistes-Leninistes, a ◊ Maoist group; the Comité d'Action Lycéen (CAL), a widespread extreme ◊ New Left movement of secondary schoolboys and girls; the Mouvement d'Action Universitaire, a group of revolutionary Marxist postgraduate students; the Union Nationale des Etudiants de France, the New Left-dominated French students union; the Syndicat Nationale de l'Enseignement Supérieur, and the Fourth ◊ International. Cohn-Bendit and his 22 March Movement called themselves the ◊ *Enragés*. The original movement of protest behind which lay deep dissatisfaction with the gross overcrowding of universities, antiquated methods of teaching, examination-idolatry, outworn centralist bureaucratic control of higher education, archaic moral rules in university halls of residence, and educational elitism, was transformed into a rebellion against the bourgeois-capitalist-imperialist-affluent-inequitable society, by University and Ministry of Education tactlessness in calling in police to repress student protest instead of dealing with it reasonably at Faculty, or individual University level. Protest and skirmishing hardened into revolution in May by which time the students were organized, the principal leaders being Cohn-Bendit (22 March), Alain Krivine, Marc Kravets, Jean-Louis Peninon, and Michel Recamati – average age 23·5, Recamati being only 17. The first show of strength came after the Easter holidays when the *Enragés* announced a ⟡ boycott of the examinations and the Dean riposted that examinations would be held under police protection. The first actual fighting was started by a raid on Left wing student organizations by the Right wing 'Occident' movement. The *Enragés* provoked the Dean by showing a filmed life of Che ⟡ Guevara in a lecture-hall required for normal work; and the Dean provoked the students by calling in armed police to clear 500 students from the central court of the Sorbonne, thereby rallying tens of thousands of uncommitted students to the militants' cause. Within twenty-four hours of the first clash between students and police the revolution had spread to a score of provincial universities, and professors and lecturers were joining the students. From 6 to 13 May there were demonstrations involving tens of thousands of students, riots and heavy street fighting with the police and security forces armed with clubs, shields and CS gas, while the students built barricades with overturned cars and paving blocks. By 10 May the revolution had ceased to be simply about university grievances and had become, under ⟡ Trotskyist guidance, a generalized, New Left politically conscious attempt to overthrow the Gaullist government and the ⟡ capitalist system. Italian, Belgian and Spanish students joined in, and the German SDS sent a contingent. Peyrefitte, Minister of Education, and the Dean of the University between them made every possible tactical mistake and the student leadership showed brilliance in taking advantage of their ineptitude. The only two politicians capable of dealing with the revolt, de Gaulle and Georges Pompidou, were out of the country. The most violent street battles occurred on the Night of the Barricades, 10–11 May, when there were several hundred casualties though only one death. The battle began when 5,000 secondary school children led by the CAL leaders who showed themselves rousing orators, demonstrated for more freedom and participation in school management. About 20,000 students rallied to them, and as news of the battle spread, by radio, many thousands of young workers from the factories joined in. The hitherto neutral elitist Sciences Politiques School and the medical students now joined the students.

On the night of 11 May Pompidou returned to France, reversed Peyrefitte's policy, and conceded the students' principal demands for university reform and release of arrested students. But this was too little too late; the revolution had, by then, its own momentum. Sparked off by the students' success in defying the government, strikes broke out in factories and offices all over France. The French CP, and the communist-controlled trade unions, respectable ⟡ establishment organizations about as revolutionary as the British Labour Party, had opposed the revolution as firmly as the Government. But, terrified of being outflanked by the Trotskyist-Maoist-Guevarist New Left as soon as strikes began to spread, they were forced to take the lead at least in demands for huge pay increase and improved conditions. On 13 May 800,000 students and strikers demonstrated in Paris, workers seized, occupied and, in some cases, began to operate, their factories. The students seized university buildings, held a daily General Assembly and appointed action committees by way of an executive, with a clear command structure beginning to emerge, and a rigorous respect for the idea of direct democracy, which was to replace representative democracy. This student Soviet was, however, weakened by a schism between the Trotskyist and other New Left extreme revolutionaries, among them the leaders; and the reformist moderates. But by 22 May, with 9 million workers on strike and the student revolution under firm leadership, it looked as if power really might shift from parliament and the Palais Matignon, into the streets. The Government lost control of a powerful medium when the broadcasting services went on strike and TV ceased operating. And in Nantes the workers set up a Soviet which for six days, 26–31 May, effectively ruled the city and district. At this point de Gaulle began to fight back and drove a wedge between the students and the workers by conceding almost all the trade union demands. The revolution at once began to fizzle out.

Although the May Revolution gained some university reforms for the students, and very large benefits for the workers (pay increases of the legal minimums from 35 per cent to over 70 per cent, improved conditions, workers participation in management, etc.), it was a political failure for a number of reasons: de Gaulle's hold on the middle class, confirmed by his fighting speech of 29 May ('I will not withdraw; I have a mandate from the people; I will fulfil it'); the steady refusal of the CP leaders to recognize a revolutionary situation and throw their weight behind the revolution; insufficient preparation for the control of events which nobody had anticipated and which could not be managed by improvised controls however brilliant; inability of the several Left parties to agree on a common policy and course of action and so present the French people with a credibile alternative government. Nevertheless, the revolution roused France from the Gaullist dream and gave the New Left a first and salutory opportunity to know its strength – and weakness – and to flex its growing muscles.

Frente de Izquierda Revolucionaria: *see* FIR.

Frente de Liberacion Nacional: *see* FLN.

Front de Libération Nationale: *see* FLN.

Fuerzas Armadas de Liberacion Nacional: *see* FALN.

Fuerzas Armadas Rebeldas: *see* FAR.

Fuerzas Armadas Revolutionarias Colombianas: *see* FARC.

G

Galdos (Hugo Blanco, 1933–   ) Peruvian ◊ Trotskyist revolutionary, b. Cuzco, s. of a lawyer. Refusing parental aid he worked his way through the University of La Plata, Argentina, by manual labour. He there joined Professor Bressano's Trotskyist Palabra Obrera. Returning to Peru 1956 he joined the clandestine, Trotskyist Partido Obrero Revolucionario (POR), and went to live in the La Convencion valley in Cuzco province, working, dressing and eating as a poor peasant, and learning the peasants' language, Quetchua. His revolutionary work consisted in organizing the peasants into unions, of which he formed in all 142, and those unions into a federation. By calling 'strikes', in which the peasants refused their labour by which they paid the rent for smallholdings, on the great haciendas, he obtained improvements in conditions and in 'wages'. And by his persistent educational work he put down the abuse of alcohol and the drug *coca* among the peasantry. His name became famous among reformers and revolutionaries all over South America, and anathema to the small oligarchy of Peruvian rich and their dictatorship. In 1960 his party, POR, decided to advance to insurrectionary action in support of a programme of socialism. The decision was deplored by the Moscow-style CP whose Central Committee did not believe that a 'revolutionary situation', as defined by ◊ Lenin, existed in Peru. But Galdos appealed to the Secretariado Latinamericano de Trotskismo Orthodoxo (SLATO), the Buenos Aires bureau of the Fourth ◊ International, for help and funds. ◊ Cadres were forthcoming, but no money, although a big subsidy was promised. A Revolutionary Front of guerrillas, the Frente de Izquiera Revolucionaria (◊ FIR) was set up and Galdos himself came to Lima. The movement split on the questions of how far they should go in militancy, Bressano being unwilling to go beyond supporting the peasants in land expropriation; and on the question of funds. Some money was obtained by 'expropriating' a bank, but not nearly enough. The FIR group in Lima obtained a large sum, 3 million *soles* (about $120,000) by another bank robbery, but were captured by the police with the money still on them. Galdos ended

94

his connection with the Fourth International, but that left him isolated from other Left movements. After trying to raid a police post to get arms for his guerrilla band, he became a hunted man, hounded by communist propaganda which represented him as a criminal, abandoned by 'his' peasants when they suffered savage police persecution on his account. He was captured in May 1963 and sent to prison for twenty years, but his work had directed the attention of all Peruvian revolutionaries to the possibilities inherent in first educating and then arming the peasants – i.e. to the fact that in a country like Peru, as in Cuba, the revolution must start in the countryside and not in the cities. (*See* ◊ Peru, guerrilla movements.)

Gandhi, Mohandas Karamchand (1969–1948) Indian nationalist politician. Read law in London, was called to the bar, and practised in Bombay. The transfer of political power by the British Government to India and Pakistan, largely Gandhi's work, was not, of course, a revolution. But Mahatma ('saint') Gandhi conceived, perfected and used an important method of forcing revolutionary changes on a ruling Establishment, which has proved of great value to pacifist revolutionaries: ◊ Passive Resistance. He first used and elaborated the technique between 1907 and 1914 in South Africa, in his successful struggle to win some civil rights for Indian immigrants to that country, first from the Boer government of the Transvaal, later from the Union Government of General Smuts. And he again used it in India, from 1920, to win first more political power for Indians, and later independence for his country, while he was leader of the Indian Congress Party. For various acts of passive resistance he served four prison terms between 1922 and 1942, meanwhile attaining international status for the 'saintliness' of a nationalist leader who refused his followers the right to use violence in any form. His long campaign persuaded the British government to concede independence in 1947; but his acceptance of the policy of the partition of British India into two sovereign states, Muslim Pakistan and Hindu India, was deeply resented by Hindu extremists who had always regarded the Muslims as being as much alien, and formerly imperialist, invaders of their country, as the British. It was one of these pan-Hindu extremists who shot Gandhi dead on 30 January 1948.

Gapon, Georgy: *see* Bloody Sunday.

Garibaldi, Giuseppe

Garibaldi, Giuseppe (1807–82) Italian nationalist revolutionary. b. Nizza, Piedmont (now Nice, France). As a result of his revolutionary militancy in ⟡ Mazzini's Young Italy movement he had to escape as a voluntary exile to Uruguay where he won worldwide fame as a soldier by his defence of Montevideo against the Argentine army. The 1848 ⟡ Revolution enabled him to return to Italy and with Mazzini he seized Rome from the Pope and established a Roman Republic (1849). Napoleon III sent a French army to recover his property for the Pope and Garibaldi withstood a siege of two months before being forced to retreat again into exile. Ten years later he was back, commanding a guerrilla force against the Austrians in the Italian lake district, and in 1860 he invaded the kingdom of Naples and Sicily with his one thousand Red Shirts, defeating the Bourbon army at Calatafimi and again on the Volturno. Against the wishes of Mazzini, who wanted an Italian republic, not Victor Emmanuel's Piedmontese monarchy governed by Cavour, he relinquished his conquered kingdom to the Piedmontese, thus unifying all Italy and Sicily, bar Rome which remained a papal temporality. In 1862 Garibaldi tried to take Rome from its French garrison, but the Italian army intervened and he was wounded and captured. But when, late in 1866, Napoleon III thought it safe to withdraw his garrison, Garibaldi made another attempt to take the city, the French hastily returned, and he was captured at Mentana (November 1867). The great revolutionary's last campaign was against the Prussians, as a volunteer in the French Republican army following the flight of Napoleon III (1870) in the Franco-Prussian war. Garibaldi and Mazzini were the last of the romantic, flamboyant revolutionaries inspired by the (imaginary) virtues of the ancient Roman Republic, and the belief that a Republic was necessarily juster than a monarchy.

Geismar, Alain (1939–   ) French ⟡ New Left Marxist revolutionary, Secretary of the Syndicat National de l' Enseignement Supérieur, the trade union of French university teachers which he rallied to the ⟡ French Student Revolution 1968. His intervention on 6 May brought him into national prominence, to some extent seeming to obscure the student leaders. He showed remarkable firmness and coolness in controlling tens of thousands of turbulent young revolutionaries. On the Night of the Barricades (10–11 May), it was he who conducted, over a radio link provided by Radio Luxembourg transmitter vans covering the revolution for the station's news, negotiations between the revolutionaries and the Rector of Paris University, and demanded that imprisoned student revolutionaries be released before any peace talks could begin, refusing to yield to the threat, which soon became a reality, of force. With ⟩ Cohn-Bendit, he led the 800,000 students and striking workers who marched and demonstrated through Paris on 13 May, and it was largely the impression of substance and serious purpose which he imparted to the leadership that persuaded the workers to strike in support of the students. When, on 16 May, Prime Minister Pompidou decided to 'expose' the ineptitude of the revolutionary leaders by putting them on T V, opposed by three experienced publicists, Geismar and Cohn-Bendit made fools of their opponents. After the collapse of the revolution, he resigned his trade union office to devote himself full time to politics, as a ⟩ Maoist.

General Strike. A simultaneous strike by all the workers in all the industries of a country. It is favoured by ⟩ syndicalists and anarcho-syndicalists as a means of overthrowing ⟩ capitalism, in preference to political and insurrectionary means *or* as a preliminary to insurrection. The concept is due to the English Owenite Socialist William Benbow, and the Owenite Grand National Consolidated Trades Union which (1833) advocated what was charmingly called a Grand National Holiday of the Working Class, as a means of bringing an end to capitalism and a beginning to the management of industry by the workers for the community. The anarcho-syndicalist trade unions, chiefly French, of the 1880s were the next to take up the general strike as a revolutionary tactic: it had the advantage, over revolutionary insurrection, of being unobjectionable to the many pacifists in the anarchist and socialist movements; and of avoiding the lapse into dictatorship which, according to the anarchists, invariably follows revolution accomplished by political means.

That the general strike never has been successfully used to accomplish a revolution does not mean that it must fail: it has never been thoroughly tried. In the late nineteenth and early twentieth centuries the anticapitalist revolutionary movement was split between Marxist socialists and anarcho-syndicalists: the anarchists and their allies refused to use political means to revolution, on the grounds that they would only lead to yet another tyrant state; and history has vindicated them. The Marxists, on the other hand, refused to admit to the major revolutionary organizations those who repudiated political means. And the Marxists, organized in the social democratic parties, were the stronger. Consequently, the general strike unaccompanied by insurrection and long sustained has never been used. *See also* General Strike, Britain 1926.

General Strike, Britain 1926. In May 1926 the British coal miners were threatened with wage cuts which would further reduce their already miserable standard of living. They had long been struggling with the coal-owners for higher wages and the 1925 meeting of the Trades Union Congress (TUC) had passed a resolution to support them. They struck, under the militant leadership of A. J. Cook, and called on the TUC to fulfil its pledge. The TUC did so by calling a general strike of all its members – transport workers, builders, printers, all workers in heavy industry and the engineering workers (4 May). The Conservative government of Stanley Baldwin was, however, well prepared for this confrontation and some of its members, notably Winston Churchill, welcomed it as a means of breaking the power of the trade unions, then at a zenith, and forcing down wages. The easy and even servile temper of the strikers and the timidity of their leaders excepting Cook, prevented the situation from becoming revolutionary. The Government were able to recruit volunteers from the middle class to run essential services and likewise special constables to keep order, and although many of these behaved in a provocative manner the strikers were too dispirited to react and there were few violent clashes. The Government used troops to ensure food supplies into the cities, and by its absolute command over the only one of the mass media still working, the radio, was able to give an impression of being in control of the situation. On 12 May the TUC called off the strike without obtaining anything substantial for the miners, who, betrayed and embittered, continued the strike alone until August when their children's hunger drove them back to work at the cut wage. The Baldwin government celebrated this triumph of the ◊ bourgeoisie over the workers by passing the Trade Disputes Act 1927 making the general strike illegal: this Act was repealed by the Labour Government of 1946. The 1926 General Strike was the last occasion on which the British ruling establishment was in serious danger from what might have been a revolutionary movement, but turned out to be a paper tiger.

Goldman, Emma (1869–1940) b. Kovno, Lithuania; d. of a theatre manager; ed. Königsberg and St Petersburg. In 1885 she emigrated to the USA and obtained work in a garment factory where she became a militant socialist. Moving to similar work in New Haven, Conn. she fell in with a group of Russian anarchist immigrants, and became an ardent anarchist, removing to New York where she lectured in anarchist theory, and was arrested and imprisoned for inciting to riot. She had long been living with the German anarchist Alexander Berkmann and when (1906) he was released from a prison term served for an attempted assassination during a strike of steel-workers Goldman rejoined him, and until 1917 they worked together, propagating anarchist revolution. In 1917 they were arrested for obstructing the draft and on release from prison in 1919, deported to Russia. Anarchists were far from *persona grata* with the ▷ Bolsheviks, nor were the Bolsheviks acceptable to Emma. She moved to England and there wrote *My Disillusionment in Russia* (1923); then went to Spain where the anarchists were strong, and thereafter to Canada where she wrote *Living My Life* (1932) and where she died.

Guatemala: guerrilla movements. Revolutionary guerrilla movements in Guatemala grew out of resentment at the USA's ▷ imperialist interference in the government of the country and specifically at the overthrow of the liberal elected government of President Jacobo Arbenz Guzman, known as Arbenz, by the ▷ CIA in July 1954. Arbenz was driven from office for his toleration of legal communist movements in Latin America; for buying arms in Eastern Europe when denied them by the US and her NATO allies; and for refusing to reverse land reform legislation which inconvenienced the powerful United Fruit Company of the US. Despairing of liberal reforms by means of parliament, certain radical groups, not all of them socialists, had recourse to armed insurrection and 'armed propaganda' among the peasants, in emulation of ▷ Castro and ▷ Guevara.

The movement was started by two young army officers, Yon Sosa and Turcios Lima, who had been trained at the US Guerrilla Warfare Training School in the Panama Canal Zone. Surviving the crushing of a reformist military revolt, they aimed to restore the basic democratic rights raped by the virtual dictatorship of General Ydigoras Fuentes (known as Ydigoras), who succeeded Arbenz. They attacked army posts, and built up a fund by

Guatemala

robbing offices of the United Fruit Company. Their movement, carried on largely among the peasants, with support in the city from university students—but not, as a rule from the organized Communist Party (⟡ PGT) – inspired the formation by Colonel Paz Tejada of a second guerrilla group, '20 October Front', quickly crushed by the army. The activities of both groups gave rise to insurrections and riots among the students and peasants, which were crushed in their turn.

Turcios Lima and Yon Sosa separated. Turcios Lima to form the FAR *Fuerzas Rebeldes Armas*, as an executive branch of the PGT Communists with whom he had patched up an uneasy alliance. He set about trying to organize the peasants of the Sierra de las Minas for revolution; and when Ydigoras was replaced in the presidency by the still more reactionary Peralta Axurdia, known as Peralta, more guerrilla groups joined him, to overthrow the regime. Yon Sosa and his ⟡ MR 13 group, which had Trotskyist (Fourth ⟡ International) sympathies, however, remained independent. He issued a 'Declaration of the Sierra de las Minas', calling for armed socialist revolution, rejection of the 'pacifist and conciliatory' Moscow line, and recognition of US imperialism as the arch-enemy. More peasants and students were recruited to the cause, army and police officers notorious for torturing political prisoners marked down and shot dead. FAR, anti-Trotskyist but breaking with the PGT, worked on similar lines, and later MR 13 also broke with the Fourth International. The PGT, too, anxious to get on the guerrilla bandwagon but not quite sure that its wheels would not fall off, briefly recombined with FAR to issue a call for armed revolution on orthodox communist lines. This combination did not last.

Guerrilleros assassinated the Chief of the US Military Mission (February 1965) and Minister of Defence Arreaga (May 1965); and raised more funds for the revolution by kidnapping and ransoming rich businessmen and landowners. In March 1966 when elections were held, FAR ⟡ boycotted them, but PGT decided to vote against the military candidates, for the liberal Montenegro. The army and CIA assassinated him and arrested communist leaders; but his brother Mendez Montenegro was elected. The Montenegro government received, as a legacy of the Peralta government, responsibility for guerrilla and other political prisoners who, in fact, had been secretly done to death. FAR mounted a campaign to force the government to release their prisoners, and to ensure their safety from torture and execution, kidnapped as hostages Presidential Press Secretary Cruz, Chief Justice Augusto de Leon and Vice-President of Congress Mendez de la Riva. Montenegro was forced to admit that Peralta had had the prisoners murdered; FAR then released their prisoners in exchange for the one guerrilla prisoner still held by the government.

On 2 October 1966 Turcios Lima was killed in what may have been a mere accident in a motor-car, and was succeeded by his lieutenant Cesar Montes. Meanwhile, under pressure from the US, the Guatemalan government gave the army a free hand to try to exterminate the guerrillas, assisted by US troops and air strikes, and by two groups of right-wing terrorists for which junior army officers were allowed to 'volunteer'. The guerrillas suffered a series of defeats, forcing the principal revolutionary movements, much weakened by internecine quarrels, to combine for a time under Yon Sosa's leadership. In January 1968 they shot dead the head of the US Military Mission and the US Naval Attaché, as the start of a deliberate policy of 'executing' US military 'advisers'. When the authorities captured Camilo Sanchez, one of Montes's lieutenants, they tried to kidnap, and, in the struggle, killed, the US Ambassador.

The role of the US was placed in an embarrassing light by Father Thomas Melville, an American RC missionary, in a letter to Senator William Fulbright, stating that the ordinary people of Guatemala had been intolerably provoked by the torture and execution of 2,800 political prisoners; that the guerrilla cause was at least more Christian than that of the Guatemalan government and its CIA allies; and that the presence of US forces in the country was largely responsible for a state of civil war.

The alliance of Guatemalan government forces and the US forces has, since 1968, been sufficient to hold the revolutionaries in check. But not, probably, for long, especially as the guerrilleros have a new and very powerful ally in the younger clergy of the Roman Catholic Church: about half of these preach the incompatibility of capitalism in its imperialist phase with Christianity. The Marxist movement among the young priests, supported by one or two of the bishops, is organized as the COSDEGUA (Confederation of Diocesan Priests of Guatemala) which is dedicated to the struggle against 'capitalist materialism'.

Guerrilla. Diminutive of *guerra*, Sp. *war*, hence means 'little war'. During the Peninsular War small bands of Spanish irregulars carried out raiding, harassing and sabotage operations against Napoleon's armies, disappearing into the inaccessible mountain strongholds after each operation and living off the country with the help of the peasantry. This type of warfare became known as *guerrilla*, and one who wages it is, correctly, a *guerrillero*; but, surviving into modern usage in most European languages, *guerrilla* is now commonly used to mean the warrior rather than the warfare, or both. *Guerrilla* bands, if they are cleverly coordinated and inspired by a charismatic leader able to command absolute obedience and loyalty, can, in suitable terrain, pin down regular troops much more numerous and better armed than themselves, and, in the long term, prove virtually invincible. This technique of warfare is, therefore, of particular interest to revolutionaries, and has been put to effective use notably, by ◊ Mao Tse-tung in his long war against the Kuomintang in China; by ◊ Tito in Yugoslavia during World War II, when his irregulars, ill-armed, ill-clad and half-starved, pinned down as many as ten German divisions at a time; by the Russians, whose guerrillas operated behind the German lines during World War II; by Fidel ◊ Castro and Che ◊ Guevara to defeat the army of Batista in Cuba; and by the ◊ Vietcong in their struggle with the USA. Left-wing revolutionary guerrillas are operating in a number of Latin American republics against the armies of the ruling dictators and their ◊ CIA allies. A modern development is the urban guerrilla, whose 'mountain stronghold' is the slum quarters of a city where the population protects him from the police and military, and whose operations vary from the bombing of public buildings and robbing of banks to obtain funds for the cause, to the kidnapping of prominent foreigners, usually diplomats, to constrain governments to release political prisoners or make some other concession to the revolution. The two principal textbooks on guerrilla warfare available in European languages are, Che Guevara, *La guerra de Guerrillas* (Havana 1960); and Alberto Bayo *Ciento cinquenta preguntas a un guerrillero* (Havana 1959).

Guerrilla movements. In Latin America: *see* Guevara; Debray; *and under* Bolivia, Guatemala, Peru, Venezuela.

In the USA: *see* Weathermen.

Guevara, Che (Ernesto Guevara Lynch de la Serna, 1928–67) Argentine ◊ Marxist revolutionary ◊ guerrilla leader. b. Misiones, s. of landowning aristocrats on both sides. At two years old he developed asthma from which he suffered all his life, and his family moved to the drier climate of Alta Gracia (Cordoba) where his health did not improve. Primary education at home, mostly by his mother, Celia de la Serna. He early became a voracious reader and as ◊ Marx, ◊ Engels and Freud were all available in his father's library, it is probable that he had read some of their works before he went to secondary school (1941), the Colegio Nacional Dean Funes, Cordoba, where he excelled only in literature and sports. At home he was impressed by the Spanish Civil War refugees and by the long series of squalid political crises in Argentina which culminated in the 'Left Fascist' dictatorship of Juan ◊ Peron, to whom the Guevara de la Sernas were opposed. These events and influences inculcated in the young Guevara a contempt for the pantomime of parliamentary democracy, and a hatred of military politicians and the army, the capitalist oligarchy, and above all of US dollar ◊ imperialism. Yet although his parents, notably his mother, were anti-Peronist activists, he took no part in revolutionary student movements and showed little interest in politics at Buenos Aires University (1947) where he studied medicine, first with a view to understanding his own disease, later becoming more interested in leprosy. In 1949 he made the first of his long journeys, exploring northern Argentina on a bicycle, and for the first time coming into contact with the very poor and the remnants of the Indian tribes. In 1951, after taking his penultimate exams, he made a much longer journey, accompanied by a friend, and earning his living by casual labour as he went: he visited southern Argentina, Chile, where he met Salvador Allende, Peru, where he worked for some weeks in the San Pablo leprosarium, Colombia at the time of *La Violencia* (*see* Colombia, guerrilla movements), and where he was arrested but soon released, Venezuela, and Miami. He returned home for his finals sure of only one thing, that he did not want to become a middle-class general practitioner. He qualified, specializing in dermatology, and went to La Paz, Bolivia, during the National Revolution which he condemned as opportunist. From there he went to Guatemala (*see* Guatemala, guerrilla movements), earning his living by writing travel-cum-archaeological articles about Inca and Maya ruins. He reached Guatemala during the socialist Arbenz presidency; although he was by now a Marxist, well read in ◊ Lenin, he refused to join the Communist Party, though this meant losing the chance of a government medical appointment, and he was penniless and in rags. He lived with Hilda Gadea, a Marxist of Indian stock who forwarded his political education, looked after him, and introduced him to Nico Lopez, one of Fidel ◊ Castro's lieutenants. In Guatemala he saw the ◊ CIA at work as the principal agents of counterrevolution and was confirmed in his view that the Revolution could be made only by armed insurrection. When Arbenz fell, Guevara went to Mexico City (September 1954) where he worked in the General Hospital. Hilda Gadea and Nico Lopez joined him, and he met and was charmed by Raul and Fidel Castro, then political émigrés, and realized that in Fidel he had found the leader he was seeking.

He joined other Castro followers at the farm where the Cuban revolutionaries were being given a tough commando course of professional training in guerrilla warfare by the Spanish Republican Army captain, Alberto Bayo, author of *Ciento cincuento preguntas a un guerrillero* (Havana 1959). Bayo drew not only on his own experience but on the guerrilla teachings of ◊ Mao Tse-tung, and 'Che', as he was now called (it means 'chum' or 'buddy' and is Italian in origin), became his star pupil and was made leader of the class. The war games at the farm attracted police attention, all the Cubans and Che were arrested, but released a month later (June 1956). When they invaded Cuba, Che went with them, first as doctor, soon as a Comandante of the revolutionary army of *barbutos* (*see* ◊ Castro). He was the most aggressive, clever and successful of the guerrilla officers, and the most earnest in giving his men a ◊ Leninist education; he was also a ruthless disciplinarian who unhesitatingly shot defectors, as later he got a reputation for cold-blooded cruelty in the mass execution of recalcitrant supporters of the defeated president Batista. At the triumph of the Revolution Guevara became second only to Fidel Castro in the new government of Cuba, and the man chiefly responsible for pushing Castro towards communism, but a communism which was independent of the orthodox, Moscow-style communism of some of their colleagues. Che organized and directed the Instituto Nacional de la Reforma Agraria to administer the new agrarian laws expropriating the *latifundios* (large landholders); ran its Department of Industries; was appointed President of the National Bank of Cuba; forced non-communists out of the government and key posts and, acting obstinately against the advice of two eminent French Marxist economists who were called in by Fidel Castro and who wanted Che to advance much more slowly, and of the Soviet advisers, he pushed the Cuban economy so fast into total Communism, and into crop and production diversification, that he temporarily ruined it.

In 1959 he married Aleida March and together they visited Egypt, India, Japan, Indonesia, Pakistan and Yugoslavia. Back in Cuba, as Minister for Industry he signed (February 1960) a trade pact with the USSR which freed the Cuban sugar industry from dependence on the US market; intensified the nationalization programme in the teeth of strong opposition and expert advice; and signed trade pacts with China and the DDR. In May he published his *Guerrilla Warfare: a Method* (Havana): in it is foreshadowed his failure in the Congo and Bolivia, in an axiom which proved to be hopelessly misleading: 'It is not always necessary to wait until the conditions for revolution exist; the insurrectional focus can create them.' And, with Mao Tse-tung, he believed that the countryside must bring the revolution to the town in predominantly peasant countries. Also, at this time, he glorified his own kind of communist philosophy (published later in e.g. *Socialism and Man in Cuba, Marcha,* 12 March 1965). It can be summed up in his 'Man really attains the state of complete humanity when he produces, without being forced by physical need to sell himself as a commodity.' He was moving away from 'Moscow', towards Mao, and beyond into what is essentially the old idealistic ◊ Anarchism. His formal breach with the Soviet Communists came when, addressing the Organization for Afro-Asian Solidarity at Algiers (February 1965), he charged the USSR with being a 'tacit accomplice of imperialism' by not trading exclusively within the Communist bloc and by not giving the underdeveloped socialist countries aid without any thought of return. He also attacked the Soviet government for its policy of coexistence; and for ◊ Revisionism. He initiated the Tricontinental (◊ OSPAAAL) Conference (Havana) to realize a programme of revolutionary, insurrectionary, guerrilla cooperation in Africa, Asia and South America. On the other hand, after a halfhearted attempt to come to some kind of terms with the USA, he was also attacking the North Americans, at the UN as Cuba's representative there, for their greedy and merciless imperialist activity in Latin America.

Che's intransigence towards both capitalist and communist establishments forced Castro to drop him (about mid-1965), not officially, but in practice. For some months even his whereabouts were a secret and his death was widely rumoured: he was in various African countries, notably the Congo surveying the possibilities of turning the Kinshasa rebellion

Guillaume, James

into a Communist revolution, by Cuban-style guerrilla tactics. He returned to Cuba to train volunteers for that project, and took a force of 120
Cubans to the Congo. His men fought well, but the Kinshasa rebels did
not, they were useless against the Belgian mercenaries and by autumn
1965 Che had to advise Castro to withdraw Cuban aid.

Che's final revolutionary adventure was in Bolivia: he grossly misjudged
the revolutionary potential of that country with disastrous consequences
(*see* ◊ Bolivia, guerrilla movements). The attempt ended in his being
captured by a Bolivian army unit and shot a day later.

Because of his wild, romantic appearance, his dashing style, his intransigence in refusing to kowtow to any kind of establishment however communist, his contempt for mere reformism, and his dedication to violent,
flamboyant action, Che became a legend and an idol for the revolutionary –
and even the merely discontented – youth of the late 1960s and early 70s, a
focus for the kind of desperate revolutionary action which seemed to
millions of young people the only hope of destroying the world of ◊
bourgeois industrial capitalism and communism.

Guillaume, James (1840–) Swiss schoolmaster and libertarian socialist
theorist and revolutionary who led the Socialist watch-maker/farmers of
the Jura villages out of the Marxist Fédération Romande to form the
Bakunist Fédération Jurasienne which became the principal centre of
European Anarchism, its *Bulletin*, edited by Guillaume, being the leading
Anarchist periodical between 1870 and 1878. An enthusiastic disciple of ◊
Bakunin, Guillaume was expelled, with Bakunin and other Anarchist
leaders, from the First International at the Hague Congress (1872) on a ◊
Marxist motion that Bakunin's undertaking to discontinue the activities of
his conspiratorial *Alliance* (see Bakunin) had not been kept. Guillaume's
principal achievement as an Anarchist evangelist was the conversion of ◊
Kropotkin (1872) and following Bakunin's death he was for about a year
one of the chief propagandists of the libertarian brand of Socialism. But
the failure of the many Congresses which he attended to accomplish anything substantial caused him to lose heart and in 1878 he moved to Paris
and sank into political obscurity until, twenty years later, he came forward
as an Anarcho-Syndicalist.

Guinea and Cape Verde: *see* Cabral.

106

H

Habbad, Wadi: *see* PFLP.

Habbash, George: *see* PFLP.

Hawatmeh, Nayaf: *see* PDF.

Haymarket Square Massacre: *see* Chicago May Day 1886.

Hebert, Mathieu: *see* Quebec, revolution in.

Hegel, Georg Wilhelm Friedrich (1770–1831) German philosopher whose work inspired the philosophy of ◊ Marx and many other leading socialists of the nineteenth century. b. Stuttgart and ed. Tübingen, he was successively professor of philosophy at the universities of Jena, Nuremberg, Heidelberg and Berlin. In his lectures and such writings as *The Philosophy of Right* (1821) he taught a theory of Idealism, conceived of as a spiritual force or forces by which he supposed the historical process to be motivated; and a Law of the Dialectic whereby the same process is interpreted as an evolution carried on by the resolution of two opposed ideas into a new one, those ideas embodying the motivating ideals. Marx rejected, as did many of the so-called neo-Hegelians, the idealist metaphysic but he borrowed the dialectic, substituting for opposed ideas, opposed social classes using Pierre Leroux's terminology of ◊ 'bourgeoisie' and ◊ 'proletariat' to designate them. These classes were not moved by ideals but by material interests; thus the process of history becomes the class war and the study of it becomes the study of dialectical materialism. Another of Hegel's themes had a powerful effect on Marx's thinking: Hegel had all the Prussian's reverence for the State which, using the law of the dialectic, he saw as the transcendental *synthesis* of the individual as *thesis* and the crowd as *antithesis*. As a consequence an excessive state-worship became an integral part of orthodox communist doctrine, or rather dogma, with the result that liberty, which had been one of the principal aspirations of the pre-Marxist socialisms, became a casualty of the revolution. This need not, of course, have happened: it is a question of interpretation; but the dogma is permissive of evil and the chief interpretor happened to be ⟡ Stalin whose overwhelming power corrupted him into a tyrant.

Heraud, Javier (Javier Heraud Perez, 1942–63) Peruvian poet and ⟡ guerrilla 'martyr'. s. of rich parents, he was educated at Markham, the English 'public school' in Lima, and at the Catholic university where he began to make a name as a poet (see *The River*, his prize-winning book of poems), and, sickened by the condition of the great majority of his country-men, the poor peasants, turned to socialism. He was in Cuba, probably studying ⟡ Marxism, when, in May 1963, it became known that Hugo Blanco (⟡ Galdos), organizer of peasant unions and guerrilla leader, was very hardpressed by the police. Heraud led a group of young Marxist intellectuals in an attempt to go to his aid. About forty of them landed from two boats in Bolivia, and were taken across the frontier into Peru by communist guides. Heraud and some companions were arrested by the police when passing through Puerto Maldonado. They resisted and a policeman was killed. Hunted down by a detachment of police armed with machine pistols helped by a posse of local landowners with sporting rifles, the poet was wounded and then killed, his body being riddled with bullets. This made him a guerrilla martyr, and his name was given to a guerrilla group led by Hector ⟡ Bejar.

Herzen, Alexander Ivanovich (1812–70) Russian liberal-socialist revolutionary thinker and writer. ed. Moscow University. Civil service 1835–42. His liberalism brought him under suspicion and he was denied normal promotion in the service. When (1847) he inherited a considerable fortune, he exiled himself so that he would be able to write freely, living part of the time in London and part in Geneva, mixing with revolutionary exiles in both cities and in Paris, where he observed the 1848 revolution, appalled at the revolutionaries' romantic blundering. His principal contribution to revolution was a brilliant series of essays published in several periodicals which were printed in London or Switzerland for illicit distribution inside Russia. In them he argued that revolutionaries must rise above merely romantic feelings to a cool study of the social, economic and political facts of life, upon which alone an effective plan for the desired changes could be based. As a socialist of ⬦ Proudhon's school, he was not approved of by ⬦ Marx, yet there is no doubt that he did much to prepare the ground and educate the middle class for the coming Russian revolutions. Herzen's London house became a European centre for revolutionaries in exile, many of whom he supported with subsidies, among them ⬦ Bakunin whose total commitment to violence and anarchy Herzen seems not to have appreciated. In at least one respect Herzen showed foresight, when he argued that the simple rural communes of Russia were a sounder basis for socialism than any west European institution and that consequently Russia was best suited to be the first socialist country; by the same token he might have foreseen Stalinist tsarism.

Herzl, Theodor (1860–1904) Hungarian Jewish journalist who inspired and launched ⬦ Zionism.

Hitler, Adolf (1889–1945) Austrian National Socialist revolutionary leader whose revolution was, in his own words, against the Revolution and whose aim was to exterminate both Marxism and Democracy. b. Linz, s. of a customs officer. ed. 1895–1900, primary school; 1900–1904, Linz *Realschule* from which he was dismissed as unteachably stupid. His father having died 1903 he lived on his mother, who had a pension, calling himself an art student though his first attempt to enter Vienna's academy of Fine Arts was not made until 1907 when he was rejected at the entrance exam as unable to draw. A year later his mother died, and he then lived on his orphan's pension, loafing, listening to Wagner and trying, in occasional outbursts of excited energy to write and draw. From 1909 to 1913 he lived in Vienna as a casual labourer and also painted postcard views of the city for sale by his only friend, a tramp named Hanisch. His pleasures were newspaper-reading, reading history in the public library, and street-corner politics, over which he was apt to become noisily excited. His virulent antisemitism, his belief that politics is the art of playing on fear, greed, lust and envy by lies, and his Pan-German radicalism, all date from this period, as does his political philosophy which was a syncretism of borrowings from social-democracy, pan-German nationalism, and the Christian Socialist policy of exploiting the fears and envy of the lower middle class. In 1913 he moved into Bavaria to avoid military service, but was caught by the police and forced to report for a medical exam, which he failed. He returned to Munich, living by peddling his postcards and drawing advertisements. In World War I he fought in a Bavarian regiment on several fronts, was wounded, badly gassed, twice decorated with the Iron Cross for conspicuous bravery, and much disliked by his fellow-soldiers; he attained the rank of corporal. Still in the army and stationed in Munich after the war, he acted as an informer against communists and on army orders infiltrated the Nationalist German Workers Party with a view to making use of it against the Social-Democrats. Having at last discovered his real talent as a demagogue, he left the army for politics and built up his National Socialist Party with the support of the army, of Röhm's conspiratorial *Freikorps* (which provided the strong-arm element) and of the big industrialists led by Thyssen of *Vereinigte Stahlwerke*. He turned it into a mass party to compete with and finally exterminate the left-wing movements. In 1923 the Nazis tried to seize power in Bavaria by a *putsch*, an armed show of strength in the streets (8–9 November) combined with a backroom deal with the ruling Bavarian triumvirate. The latter sold them, and the former was easily crushed, Hitler bolting ignominiously from the front of the procession when the police opened fire. Tried for high treason, he turned the trial into an indictment of the Government, won the admiration of court and public, and was given the minimum of five years in prison where he lived in comfort, dictated *Mein Kampf*, and was paroled after one year. He then had to reunite the Party, riven by quarrels among his lieutenants; to fight for control against the socialist wing led by the Strasser brothers, whose genuine radicalism was endangering Hitler's subsidies from heavy industry; and to dominate Röhm and his private SA army. He steadily increased the party's numbers, but as National Socialism could thrive only in conditions of public discontent the Government's success (1925–29), in restoring the economy and political stability made the going difficult. From 1930 however, he won massive new support by exploiting nationalist resentment of the Young (Reparations) Plan. His chance was eventually made for him by the World Depression following the New York financial collapse of 1929. Before the 1930 elections Hitler repudiated the socialist element in the Party and expelled Otto Strasser; and openly declared that the Nazis would 'defeat democracy with democracy's weapons'. To his amazement the Nazis won 107 Reichstag seats (the communists won 77). Later he made an alliance with the German National Party (44 seats). In the 1932 presidential election although Hindenburg was returned with 53 per cent of the votes, Hitler received 13½ million votes. An attempt was made to check his growing power by making the two private Nazis armies, the 400,000 strong SA and SS, illegal. Röhm, their commander, wanted to defy this order and resort at once to insurrection; Hitler had other ideas: let them simply discard their uniforms for the time being. From 1932 – when the Nazis won 37·3 per cent of the votes in the general election and 230 seats in the Reichstag – until January 1933 – when, by brilliantly exploiting the conflicting lusts for power of such politicians as von Papen, such politico-soldiers as von Streicher, the greed of the great industrialists, and the fears and envy of little burgesses who voted his ticket – Hitler manoeuvred his way to the Chancellorship of the Reich. It was then, January 1933, *after* attaining power instead of before, that the Nazis made their revolution. Gregor Strasser and the socialist wing had already been crushed, largely as a result of Strasser's inability to match Hitler in a battle of wills, for Strasser had been offered the vice-chancellorship if he would (as he could have) detach the socialist wing of the National Socialist Party, from Hitler; Röhm and his principal lieutenants were disposed of by murder on 'the night of the Long Knives'; parliamentary and all democratic institutions were totally destroyed and the Reichstag burned to the ground. Trade unions and, of course, all other political parties were destroyed, communist and social-democrats persecuted, as well as the Jews.

The success with which this street-corner loafer and gutter demagogue chose and ruled the right men to make Germany economically and militarily able to conquer Europe (1939–40); nearly overthrew both the communist and capitalist establishments of Europe, America and Russia by precisely those base means which he describes in his writings; and won the adherence of a very considerable section of the bourgeoisie all over the world, makes it probable that he might, but for the single blunder of attacking the USSR prematurely, have succeeded in extending his revolution permanently to the whole of Europe; and founded that Thousand Year Reich which was his aim.

In at least one respect Adolf Hitler was a great revolutionary: according to conventional capitalist economists and financiers, it was impossible for Hitler's Germany to achieve her aims because the necessary money would not be forthcoming. Hitler, however, realized that money is not a commodity, a profoundly revolutionary discovery; in that respect, he was a disciple of ◊ Proudhon; with the aid of the banker Schacht, he was able to isolate the German economy from global capitalist economy, and thus to give the German people a measure of stable prosperity by cutting Germany off from the highly stylized and unrealistic economies of the rest of the capitalist world. From the 'socialist' component of his political philosophy he retained enough to ensure an expedient regard for social welfare, which persuaded millions of working-class and lower middleclass Germans to support him.

Ho Chi Minh (1890–1968) Vietnamese Marxist- ◊ Leninist revolutionary leader, s. of a civil servant b. under French colonial rule which his father was penalized for opposing. Self-educated, from 1911 to 1914 he served as deck-hand in merchant ships, learning a number of languages. He learnt English while working (from 1915) as a hotel servant in London; and perfected his French while living in France (from 1918), where he worked for the communist revolution among the Vietnamese community in Paris. He represented Vietnamese Communists at the 1922 Congress of the French CP. Worked (1922–25) at the Comintern in Moscow and was then sent to Canton as an aide to the Bolshevik adviser to the Chinese CP, ◊ Borodin. From there Ho organized a SE Asia branch of the Comintern and directed Communist cooperation with Nationalist rebel movements in French Indo-China. For fifteen years he worked to build up communist strength in Indo-China, and in 1941 when the Vichy French agreed to share colonial rule with the Japanese, he formed the Viet-Minh, an armed resistance movement of communists and nationalists to fight the two imperial powers. In this movement were formed the cadres and traditions which were the backbone of the Lien Viet Front (1951) and its formidable fighting strength. In 1945 the Viet-Minh received the Japanese surrender in Annam and Tonkin. Ho proclaimed the foundation of the Democratic Republic of Vietnam, with himself as President, and made it clear that he would resist any attempt to restore French rule. Strengthened by official recognition from the USSR and China, when negotiations with the French over the future status of the three countries which had composed French Indo-China broke down, he attacked Hanoi and waged an eight-year war on the French which ended in victory at Dien Bien Phu (1954).

An international conference at Geneva, presided over by the UK and the USSR alternately, fixed a cease-fire line between the communist North and the non-communist South, but the peace broke down in 1961 when the peace-keeping guarantor powers, drawn from both political camps, fell out over the South Vietnamese complaint of North Vietnamese 'subversion, sabotage and terrorism', i.e. against the organization of communist revolution in their territory. The inability of South Vietnam to resist the revolutionary advance of the communist guerrilla forces (Vietcong) supported by Ho Chi Minh's government, led to the intervention of United States 'advisers' to the South Vietnamese forces, ultimately by the hundred thousand. In plain language, Ho Chi Minh, masked as the Vietcong, was trying to carry the revolution to the whole country; and the United States, masked as the South Vietnamese, was trying to contain the revolutionary advance on behalf of Western capitalism. This swiftly escalated into the major war from which the US was forced by public opinion to withdraw in 1973; Ho Chi Minh died, therefore, before completing his revolutionary work; but since the forces he inspired show no signs of flagging in their revolutionary zeal after thirty years of almost continuous warfare while their Chinese allies have grown steadily stronger, the final outcome is hardly in doubt. Ho Chi Minh means 'He Who Enlightens'.

HUKS. A ◊ guerrilla revolutionary force recruited and trained by the Moscow-orientated Philippines Communist Party (PKP), originally to fight the Japanese in World War II. The force was used after the war to fight the 'neo-colonialist' (*see* ◊ Imperialism). Philippine government and was still doing so in 1956. In the great communist schism between the People's Republic of China and the USSR, the HUKS took the Chinese side, repudiated the PKP and adopted Mao's analysis of the revolutionary situation and ◊ Lin Piao's Theory of Revolution. That is to say that they are Marxist ◊ Leninists but not institutional communists.

Hungarian Revolution, 1956. At the end of the Russian Revolution Militant came the Revolution Triumphant which was soon transformed in the USSR and its East European satellite states into a rigorously conservative ◊ establishment. As such, and especially as reform can come only from within the establishment CP itself, it cannot fail to be attacked by revolutionaries, true heirs of the socialist struggle for a just society, however hopeless their task may seem to be. As the grip of the Party is not quite so firm outside the frontiers of the USSR as within them, revolutionary movement is more likely to originate in the satellite states: this has already happened twice, in Hungary (1956) and in Czechoslovakia (1968); and has appeared embryonically in E. Germany and Poland. The first USSR satrap to secure absolute power for the Party in Hungary (1949) was Matyas Rakosi (1892–1963). Following his forced admission of both agricultural and industrial failure (1953), he retained his place as First Secretary of the Hungarian CP but resigned the premiership to the more liberal Imre Nagy whose policies of modest liberalization had two dangerous effects: they went to the heads of the people, who began to dream that they might be free and prosperous; and they badly frightened the Stalinist hard-line Party conservatives, who therefore contrived his dismissal and replacement by a Rakosi henchman, Andras Hegedus. By then, however, the revolutionary ferment was at work in the people and, moreover, an anti-Rakosi faction within the Party had grown strong. Rakosi's dismissal from office as First Secretary coincided with an insurrection of the people of Budapest; Nagy was hastily restored to the premiership (1956) and under popular anti-Soviet pressure announced Hungary's withdrawal from the Warsaw pact (the communist NATO). The Russians at once took over the work of crushing the revolution and Soviet forces stationed in Hungary were reinforced from outside. Budapest was attacked with armour, and by 6 November the fighting was over and the streets quiet. The insurrection was attributed to ▷ imperialist plots and Nagy, who had taken refuge in the Yugoslav Embassy, was replaced by the 'reliable' Janos Kadar whose government lured Nagy out of Yugoslav protection with a safe-conduct, and judicially murdered him. Subsequently, Kadar resigned the premiership while retaining the more powerful office of First Secretary of the renamed Socialist Workers (Communist) Party. Although the revolution was a failure, it did result in some gains: Kadar, and two successive prime ministers, Gyula Kallai and Jeno Fock, have had slowly to concede some relaxation of Stalinist rigidity: measures of economic decentralization and social freedom have resulted in an improved standard of living and a less precarious political stability.

I

Ilič Danilo: *see* Princip, Gavrilo.

Imperialism, Imperialist. One of the definitions under this head in the *Concise Oxford English Dictionary* is 'extension of the British Empire where trade required the protection of the flag'. This is a fair introduction to the sense in which the word is used by Marxist -◊ Leninist revolutionaries to describe the practice of modern monopoly Capitalism; but their usage derives from ◊ Lenin's *Imperialism, the Final Stage of Capitalism* published in 1916 to supplement ◊ Marx's *Capital* with a chapter on the post-Marx/◊Engels development of capitalism: monopoly or 'imperial' capitalism. In that work Lenin, as philosopher, followed Marx's example in distinguishing the dialectical characteristic in the development of capitalism; but the essay also has political and social aspects. Lenin argued that in World War I, which was then in progress and which he was trying to stop by calling on the working class to turn the imperialist war into a civil war, both sides were fraudulently obtaining working-class support by using 'defence of king-and-country, hearth-and-home' slogans to mask the reality, i.e. the attempt of the imperialist-monopolist capitalists of the two rival groups to establish world hegemony.

The social-democrat theorist Kautsky was arguing at this time that the logical development of imperialist monopoly capitalism, if one strictly followed the Marxist (◊ dialectic ◊ Kautsky was the father of the sterile and pestilential Marxist scholasticism which, coupled with bureaucracy, has been the bane of socialism) must be the ultimate installation of a single and universal monopoly; and that this was desirable in that it would make possible a worldwide planned economy in a world freed from contradictions and conflict; the theory is called 'ultra-imperialism'. This simplistic 'economic determinism' as Lenin called it (fundamentalism is the word I should prefer), byproduct of a misinterpretation of the dialectic and underestimation of the historical role of the masses, led Kautsky and the Second International – according to Lenin – straight into the counterrevolutionary imperialist camp. Lenin's refutation of the attempt to reconcile socialism and ultra-imperialism, *The Proletarian Revolution and the Renegade Kautsky*, appeared in 1918. In it he analysed the theoretical basis of what he stigmatized as the social-democrats' treason; and compared the 'formal' (parliamentary) democracy of the imperialist powers, with what a real socialist democracy would or should be.

So when Lenin uses the word 'imperialism' it has nothing much to do with the classical meaning of the word – the politico-military rule of an emperor over an empire or *imperium* either metropolitan or colonial or both: his usage foreshadows the post-World War II 'dollar imperialism'. So that when revolutionaries in one of the successor states to the old European empires overseas accuse Britain, or France, or Belgium, or America, of 'imperialism' and still declare that their struggle is with the 'imperialists', it is no answer to point to the emancipation of the old colonies: native ◊ bourgeois regimes welcoming foreign investment are 'neocolonialist'. Imperialism means the Union Minière du Haut Katanga using a Moise Tshombe in an attempt to retain political as well as economic control of the most profitable part of the old Congo; it means the military intervention on behalf of imperialist monopoly capitalism of the USA in the former Japanese colony of Korea and the former French colonies of Indo-China. Those are self-evident, even glaring examples. But the 'imperialism' stigmatized by Marxist-Leninists is not always, or usually, so obvious: the capital invested by any bourgeois monopoly capitalist enterprise, be it American, Japanese or European, in an 'emergent' country is necessarily and inevitably 'exploitative' since, given the nature of capitalism and its primary motive, that investment is made in expectation of a profit for the shareholders, i.e., export from the exploited country of the surplus value of its workers' labour; this is one of the famous internal contradictions of capitalism. Moreover, since capitalism must, of its nature again, seek constantly to extend its field of investment, modern capitalism is necessarily 'imperialist': the more successful the foreign capitalist in his investments, the more dependent on him do the native workers become, and the more powerful the capitalist's *imperium*. Thus US capital investment in Latin America is 'imperialist' or what a wit of the French left called '*cocacolanization*'.

Oddly enough the most succinct and immediately apprehensible definition of 'imperialism' as used by Marxist-Leninist revolutionaries is implicit in a witticism uttered by a Member of the British House of Commons when he was attacking the operations of the Birmingham firm of Chamberlain, two of whose members became leading Conservative politicians, the second, Neville Chamberlain, being the man who in the interests of bourgeois capitalist solidarity (code word 'Peace') kowtowed to the Nazis in 1938: 'Mr Speaker, it is a striking fact that the more the Chamberlain family contracts the more the British Empire expands.'

The 'Chamberlains' of the 1970s are the military–industrial complexes of America, Japan and West Europe; but also, it should be added, that of the USSR which, as well as backsliding from socialism into state mono-poly capitalist bureaucracy, has backslid into 'imperialism' very much on American lines.

Neocolonialism is a phase of imperialism when direct rule of colonial countries by the imperial power is replaced by manipulation of indigenous puppet governments; or of world economic forces to put pressure on recalcitrant Third World countries.

In New Left revolutionary parlance persons, groups or nations engaged in indirect domination of exploited nations by the manipulation of puppet governments of native bourgeoisie (South Vietnam, South Korea, Philip-pines), or by the abuse of economic power (Latin America, Morocco) are described as neocolonialist. The term is often used also to describe the native bourgeois allies of Capitalism in countries involved in revolution; e.g. the Saigon government of South Vietnam, or Pacheo's government in Uruguay would be so described.

India, Revolution in. The inertia of thousands of years of resignation to their miserable condition, the apparent hopelessness of solving the problem of poverty on so gigantic a scale, and the influence of Mahatma ⟡ Gandhi in persuading the Hindu masses of the merit of indifference to material wellbeing, combine to make the Indians disinclined to revolution and satisfied with the achievement of substituting a native bourgeois-nationalist government for the British Raj, presumably on the grounds that it is better to be oppressed and exploited by one's own people than by foreigners. There are two Communist parties, the CP of India-(R) (R is for Right) which follows the Moscow line and opposes all acts of revolutionary violence; and the more or less Maoist CPI(M) – M is for Marxist – which, in the programme adopted at its Seventh All-India Congress (1964) included armed revolution as one of its aims. But when, at Naxalbari in West Bengal (1967) the rebellious peasantry of Terai procured arms and killed Bengal government officers and a number of rich landlords and then took to the hills to wage guerrilla war on the authorities, the CPI(M), having two of its members, B. T. Ranadive and Promode Das Gupta in the United Front Government of West Bengal, condemned the revolt on the grounds that India was not yet ripe for armed revolution. The Terai peasant revolutionaries are led by a group of revolutionary Marxist- ▷ Leninists of the ▷ Maoist or ▷ Guevarist persuasion who believe that revolution is made by revolting and that in the rising of the Terai peasants is the germ of a People's War.

Indonesia, Revolution in. Revolutionary action began with the formation (1920) of the Partai Kommunis Indonesia (PKI) led by Dipa Musantara Aidit. It was natural enough for the new Party to follow, at that time, directives of the USSR CP, but the habit of doing so slavishly was disastrous in the event. On Stalin's orders Aidit placed the communist ▷ guerrilla bands formed to fight the Japanese invaders in World War II, under the command of the Dutch colonialists; and after the war, at the disposal of Sukarno's Nationalist Party in the struggle to expel the Dutch and British. Aidit, following the Stalin line and ignoring Chinese experience although it was much more relevant to Indonesian conditions, envisaged a two-stage revolution, the bourgeois nationalist phase to be followed by the final, socialist, phase. The Party thus, unlike the Chinese CP, did nothing to 'politicize' the peasants (65 per cent of the population) and had no geographical territory under its control to use as a base or refuge when the inevitable split with the nationalists came. With such blind persistence did Chairman Aidit follow the Stalinist book, that following Indonesian independence (1947) he surrendered all PKI arms to the nationalist government, leaving the communists helpless when, 1948, General Nasution launched his first campaign of extermination against them. That campaign was stepped up immediately following the *coup d'état* of 1965 in which Nasution seized dictatorial power from Sukarno, and between half a million and one million communists (PKI was about 3 million), including Aidit and other leaders, were massacred. PKI leaders took refuge in Pekin but still maintained their former line. It is ignored by the younger, ex-PKI men who are now preparing for a '◊ Guevarist' type revolution, i.e. a prolonged 'people's war' to be carried on by increasingly numerous guerrilla bands until revolutionary strength is sufficient to make revolution on a national scale possible.

Industrial Workers of the World, known as the IWW or Wobblies. This revolutionary movement was founded in Chicago in 1905. The US labour unions which organized skilled workers and were grouped under the conservative American Federation of Labour, were indifferent to the miserable plight of the great mass of unskilled, chiefly immigrant labour which poured into the US in the last decades of the nineteenth and first decades of the twentieth centuries. Responding to this indifference, the IWW was founded by William D. Haywood, President of the Western Federation of Miners; Daniel De Leon, founder and leader of the US Socialist Labour Party; and Eugene V. ◊ Debs, leader of the US Socialist Party who, however, took little part in its activities. Early in its career the new movement split on the issue of whether to use constitutional methods, i.e. propaganda and the vote, favoured by De Leon; or direct action, to gain control of the state and the means of production for the working class, favoured by Haywood. The 'constitutionalists' were absorbed into the socialist parties, and Haywood was left sole leader of the IWW proper.

Its theoretical doctrine was ◊ syndicalist and (from 1908) even anarcho-syndicalist. It therefore rejected political means and action entirely and proposed to achieve its aims – 'the organization of the workers of the world as a class to take possession of the earth and of the machinery of production and abolish the wage system' – by social and industrial action, its two principal weapons being, in theory, the ◊ general strike and mass ◊ sabotage; in practice, local strikes and sabotage, but it rejected anarcho-syndicalist doctrine when it came to violence against the person.

In its earlier activities the movement, which was never numerous but saw itself as a revolutionary *élite* leading the toiling masses to economic and social salvation, had a number of successes in organizing and winning big strikes. But it was hampered in the business of following-up and consolidating such victories by inability or disinclination for the work of actually running labour unions, and by its refusal to countenance 'class collaboration', which excessive purism barred it from signing wage-and-conditions contracts with employers.

Industrial Workers of the World

The IWW attempted to help, and organize, the masses of wretched immigrants and ruined small farmers reduced to the kind of seasonal migratory labour described in John Steinbeck's *The Grapes of Wrath*, who were ruthlessly exploited by industrial and agricultural capitalists. It was the inability of those people to afford the contributions to union fighting funds or strike funds which led to the use by the Wobblies of sabotage, in the form of acts which damaged plant and so slowed-down or otherwise hampered production – a revolutionary method in which they were pioneers, since earliest movements of machine-wrecking, like that of the English frame breakers, were aimed at preventing mechanized production, and were not acts of class war.

These methods of direct action were anathema to the Social-Democratic Party of America which split over the issue again, and in 1912 Haywood and those who thought like him and his IWW followers, were expelled from the party.

The IWW was also a pioneer in a form of passive resistance with which it had some success in its campaign for free speech. The method was to begin a programme of revolutionary street oratory in a chosen town, with a large team of speakers in reserve: as soon as the speaker was arrested, another took his place and so on until the town gaol was full, or the police tired of the game and allowed the speaker to continue.

The IWW vigorously opposed US participation in World War I, whereupon their leaders were arrested and their press confiscated. The authorities' attack on the movement may be said to have begun in 1917 when its successful organization of a copper miners' strike at Bisbee, Arizona, led to the forcible 'deportation' of 1,250 Wobblies to Columbus, NM. In 1919, at the beginning of the ruling and bourgeois classes, 'Red Menace' panic sparked off by the ⟡ Russian Revolution, many states passed laws against what was called 'criminal syndicalism', and the IWW became illegal. Its members were hunted down and beaten up by gangs of self-styled 'vigilantes' often in fact criminals recruited by big corporations which had considerable experience of strike breaking by violence, took the class war seriously, and could afford to wage it. But curiously enough it was the rise of orthodox communism in the US which more or less destroyed the Wobblies, many members defecting to the new party in the 1920s, and much of the movement's energy being dissipated in rows with the communists. But there were still enough members left – about 1,500 –

for the IWW to be placed on a Federal Bureau of Investigation list of 'subversive' organizations in 1949.

The IWW had little international impact: it was fairly firmly established in Australia from 1906 into the 1920s and it gained a footing in Glasgow for a few years.

International, First. In 1863 an insurrection in Poland against Russian dominion roused liberals and politically conscious workers all over the world to solidarity with the Polish rebels. Organizations of the French working class petitioned Napoleon III to intervene, but were told that although the emperor was sympathetic, France could do nothing for fear of offending Great Britain. Meanwhile Palmerston, petitioned by English workers, replied that British undertakings to France prevented him from acting against Russia. French and English workers' organizations got together and the fraud was exposed. A Franco-British demonstration in favour of Polish freedom was held in London 22 July 1863. It did not help the Poles; but before separating the two delegations agreed to form an International Working Men's Association to promote a union of the working class in their struggle for economic and social betterment and political power. Before the inaugural meeting a French delegate, Le Lubez, called on Karl ◊ Marx, then living in London, and asked him to sit on the platform as representative of the German workers: Marx suggested that his friend Eccarius should attend as German representative, while he himself would sit on the platform only as an observer. The meeting formally founded the Association, with HQ in London, and a committee, of which Marx was a coopted member, was appointed to write rules and a programme of action. Marx, deeply committed to other work, at first took little part, but when Italian and British drafts were rejected as unsatisfactory, Marx was called on to produce better ones. He wrote a Constitution for the International based on the propositions: 'The emancipation of the working class must be accomplished by the workers themselves'; and 'The conquest of political power has become the principal task of the working class.' It was adopted unanimously.

The International won early success as working-class political parties were founded in Italy, France, Belgium, Germany and elsewhere, and linked with trade union and other working-class organizations in the UK and USA. It was soon seen as so potentially powerful, that revolutionaries of various different doctrines began to fight for control of its administration. At the Lausanne Congress (1867) for example, there was a struggle between ◊ Proudhon-inspired 'collectivists' and the moderate anarchists known as 'mutualists'. Marx managed to retain control of policy and aims by keeping the really major controversial matters off the agenda. In 1867, a year of strikes all over the industrial world, the International was successful in getting joint action across frontiers, so that, e.g. employers were unable to bring in foreign strike-breakers. Conservative newspapers were attributing a membership of 7 million (a gross exaggeration) to the organization, and ◊ bourgeois governments and their paymasters watched with growing alarm. As it happened, they need not have worried: the anarchist ◊ Bakunin and his Social-Democratic Alliance, an organization with an 'open' and also a 'secret' wing, made a long and determined effort to win the International over to its programme – immediate revolution by the most violent means, destruction of existing institutions, and triumph of international anarchism. He was opposed by Marx, leading the scientific Social-democrats with their much more realistic assessment of what was possible. This strife, carried on at Congress after Congress and in between Congresses, wasted the strength, destroyed the unity and confused the purpose of the International: it culminated, 1872, with the expulsion of Bakunin and the removal of the HQ to the less contentious atmosphere of New York. Although Marx continued to work for it, its administrative centre was too far away for him to inspire it, and, cut off from the roots of working class growth in Europe, it withered into insignificance and in 1876 it was dissolved.

International, Second. The dissolution (1875) of the First International left the working-class organizations of the industrial nations without any international linking body; and since all the various socialist doctrines had working-class international solidarity in common, this was felt to be unsatisfactory. The Second International Working Man's Association was founded in Paris 1889 and its secretariat a year later. The German Social-Democrats played a much greater part in it than the German workers had done in the first International; it was much more loosely organized, had less genuinely working-class support and was very much in the hands of Social-Democrat intellectuals. Its early Congresses were bedevilled by the controversy over Revisionism – dominated by the German socialist theorist

Karl ⬦ Kautsky – to the quasi-exclusion of other business. The 1905 Congress, Amsterdam, was important for establishing the resolution that social-democratic parties should not permit their leaders to accept office in bourgeois coalition governments, a rule which was respected even by such dissident socialists as ⬦ Jaurez: but the trial of strength came after the 1910 Congress, Copenhagen, at which it was resolved that the workers of all affiliated national socialist parties and movements would join in international action to prevent their countries from going to war with each other. When the chance came, in 1914, the German Social-Democrat Party, the most powerful in the world, was the first to rat on this agreement, by failing to oppose mobilization and the voting of war supplies in the Reichstag, and refusing to call a strike against the war. The Second International thus proved ineffectual, collapsed and was finished off by World War I.

International, Third: *see* Comintern.

International Fourth. Founded in the 1930s by ⬦ Trotsky to organize his followers, the opposition to Stalinism, in all countries for worldwide ⬦ Marxist-Leninist revolution which was betrayed by Stalin's 'Socialism in one country'. Strong in intellectuals but weak in contact with and following in the working class, the movement was further weakened in 1953 by a split in the leadership, and today the most militant Trotskyist groups, e.g. the Socialist Labour League in Britain and the Lutte Ouvrière in France remain outside the International. One of the leaders at the time of the split was Michel Pablo: the Pablists have concentrated their attention on Third World revolution, cooperating, notably in Algeria, with New Left movements with which they have much in common, notably respect for 'pure', anti-bureaucratic ⬦ Leninism and socialist internationalism.

International Alliance of Social Democracy. In September 1867 an international committee of liberals including John Bright, J. S. Mill and ⬦ Garibaldi held a Congress in Geneva to discuss means for 'the maintenance of liberty, justice and peace'. ⬦ Bakunin, who was by then a revered revolutionary hero, appeared at the Congress, was given a standing ovation, and elected to its executive committee. His advocacy of violence to destroy centralized states, of the organization of mankind in a federation of free communes, and of socialism based on labour as the sole title to goods or rights, alienated the more conventionally liberal delegates, but he was elected to the League of Peace and Freedom founded by the Congress. He wrote a programme for it, partly ◊ Proudhonian anarchist, partly socialist – *Federalism, Socialism and Anti-Theologism*. It was rejected by a large majority at the 1868 Congress of the League in Berne. Bakunin and seventeen followers withdrew from the League and formed the International Alliance of Social Democracy which more or less absorbed Bakunin's earlier foundation, the ◊ International Brotherhood. Revolutionary anarcho-communist groups in each country were to be loosely federated under national bureaux which together would comprise the International. Its policy was to work for the destruction of national states and their replacement by an international 'union of free associations agricultural and industrial'; abolition of inheritance; and workers' control of the land, all capital, and the means of production. The International's HQ were in Geneva and branches were promptly set up in Madrid, Barcelona, Paris, Marseilles, Naples and Palermo. Bakunin tried to affiliate his International Alliance to the First ◊ International, which he aimed to take over by overwhelming it with anarchist recruits. But Karl ◊ Marx disliked and distrusted Bakunin and detested his ideas, and he persuaded the Council of the International to reject the application. Bakunin accepted this decision with apparent good grace, dissolved the International Alliance and in 1869 allowed its branches to become part of the First International.

International Brigade. When, in 1936, General Francisco Franco took command of a Fascist revolt to overthrow the Republican Government of Spain, which resulted in the Spanish Civil War (1936–39), he immediately received massive support in armies and weapons from Fascist Italy and ◊ Nazi Germany. This provoked, a worldwide spontaneous movement of sympathy with the Spanish people and their government among anti-Fascist liberals, socialist and communists. Thousands of young men in a score of countries were anxious to volunteer to fight for the left in Spain. Organization of this movement was undertaken by the ◊ Comintern which used the national CPs as its agents, so that it was the CP which transported the volunteers into Spain, was responsible for their military training, and dominated the Brigade's political life. One of the most successful IB organizers was the Yugoslav Comintern executive, Josip Broz, later known as ⟡ Tito. The Brigade's greatest victory was on the Guadalajara where, covering Madrid, it routed a superior force of Italian Army regulars. It also played an important part in the year-long defence of Madrid besieged (1938) by Fascist armies, Spanish, Moorish and Italian, and bombed by the German airforce. From 1936–39 the International Brigade was more than a volunteer fighting force in Spain: it became, for the revolutionary left all over the world, the focus and symbol of the revolution. But, like the Spanish government itself, like the social-democratic, anarchist and other Spanish left movements and parties, it was betrayed by the CP of the USSR, then under Stalin's heel, when at a moment when the Nazis and Fascists were stepping up supplies from Germany and Italy, the USSR cut off supplies to the Spanish Republicans and thus ensured their defeat. This was shortly before Stalin signed his pact with Nazi Germany.

International Brotherhood. An international revolutionary anarchist association founded by ⟡ Bakunin in 1864 in Florence. This first foundation came to nothing, and the Brotherhood was refounded by him in Naples in 1868. Its guiding theory was expressed in the ⟡ *Revolutionary Catechism,* drafted by the terrorist ⟡ Nechayev and rewritten or edited by Bakunin. The Brotherhood opposed religion, the state and all authority. It held that the sole title to rights and to control of the economic organization of society must be labour. The social unit was to be the commune, the communes to be linked in a loose federation. The revolution which would bring in this new form of society was to be accomplished by the only effective means – violence. The Brotherhood was to be managed by the International Family, a body composed of experienced and mettlesome revolutionary anarchists of different nationalities; under that would come the National Families; and under them, owing absolute and unquestioning obedience to the Family, the rank and file. In a letter to ⟡ Herzen who supported him financially, Bakunin claimed support for the Brotherhood in eleven countries. There is little evidence that it had any real existence outside Bakunin's imagination anywhere but in southern Italy where, in due course, it gave rise to a popular and potentially powerful anarchist movement.

International Marxist Group. A British Trotskyist revolutionary group which publishes the journal *Red Mole* is affiliated to the Fourth ⟡

125

International, and was formerly led by the Pakistani student Tariq Ali. *See* ◊ New Left.

International Socialism Group. A British Trotskyist-oriented, but not officially Fourth ◊ International, revolutionary group also known as the 'Cliffeites' after its leader (1971) Tony Cliffe. *See* ◊ New Left.

International Working-Men's Association (anarchist). A revolutionary Anarcho-Syndicalist association of libertarian trade unions founded, Berlin 1923, by the Revolutionary Syndicalist Congress 1922–23. The Congress was attended by delegates from the Union Sindicale Italiana (500,000 members); the Federacion Obrera Regional Argentina (200,000 members); the Federacao General de Trabalho (Portugal, 150,000 members); the Freie Arbeiter Union (Germany, 120,000 members); and from smaller but very considerable unions in Chile, Denmark, Norway, Mexico, Holland, Sweden and France; there were also some Russian anarchists exiled by the ◊ Bolshevik Government. The Association, in its manifesto *Principles of Revolutionary Syndicalism,* rejected nationalism in any form; condemned and rejected militarism; rejected political action as a means to revolution; and aimed to use industrial action to establish a regime of 'free communism' (*see* ◊ Kropotkin). In 1924 the Spanish Confederacion Nacional del Trabajo joined the Association, with 1 million members and in the next few years so did anarcho-syndicalist unions in nearly all the Latin American countries. By 1928 the Association had 3 million members. It was destroyed by the rise of Fascist regimes and military dictatorships all over the world.

IRA. The Irish Republican Army came into being as such, composed of one Republican Socialist and several different Republican Nationalist movements and forces which took part in the Easter Rising (1916) – although it is usually considered to have started as the military wing of the ◊ Sinn Fein group which fought under the command of Eamon ◊ De Valera during that week of warfare with the British army in Dublin. When, following the brilliantly successful terrorist campaign conducted by Michael ◊ Collins the British Government was forced to come to terms with the Irish revolutionaries (throughout most of this time, 1917–20, De Valera was interned) and recognize all Ireland excepting six Ulster counties as the Irish Free State within the Commonwealth, Sinn Fein, again led by De Valera, regarded the acceptance of that half-measure as a betrayal. The IRA declared and waged war on the Free State government, chiefly by terrorism, including the assassination of Michael Collins. The formation of De Valera's Fianna Fail party represented an abandonment of what had been an IRA principle, not to stand for elections to the Free State parliament. This split the Republican movement. The British tacitly conceded sovereign independence to Ireland although the Republic of Ireland was not formally recognized by the British Parliament until 1949. Meanwhile a terrorist organization, calling itself the IRA but outlawed by the Irish Government, had carried out a short campaign of bomb outrages, chiefly by planting bombs in letter boxes and post offices in London, a sort of token revolutionary war for the liberation of the Six Counties in Ulster and their incorporation in the Republic. This campaign was unrealistic if only because the strongest opponents of the policy were the Protestant majority of the Northern Irish population.

In 1969 the Ulster Catholics began a campaign of peaceful demonstrations and marches to claim full civic rights, denied them by the Protestant Unionist government in Stormont. Protestant hostile reaction, and Catholic response to it, led to civil strife reminiscent of the communal warfare in British India. The Royal Ulster Constabulary, suspected of partiality in favour of the Protestant Unionists, were disarmed in an attempt to reduce tension. But meanwhile the IRA had intervened to protect the Catholic enclaves. That led to the Stormont government's request to the British Government for troops. This military intervention, and adoption of a policy of internment without trial of suspects, resulted in the IRA waging outright war on the British army and using terrorist tactics, such as the bombing of buildings and shooting of Unionists, in an effort to bring down the Stormont government.

The most spectacular acts of terrorism, and the most ruthless, were carried out by a new wing of the IRA known as the Provisionals, or Provos for short. It came into being as follows: a consortium of Irish Republican businessmen, British businessmen in the Republic, and Republican politicians, offered financial aid and supplies of arms to the IRA on condition that they confine their revolutionary activities to the North. Cathal Goulding, the IRA Commandant, refused the offer; he believed it was made with the object of splitting the IRA and so weakening it in its opposition to the Government of Prime Minister Jack Lynch, some of whose Ministers were subsequently implicated in a plot to supply the IRA with arms. But another IRA officer, Sean Mac Stiofan (real name Stevens, an Englishman), believed that the offer should be accepted; and the breakaway wing which he led became the Provos.

The ideological spectrum within the IRA and its political wing, Sinn Fein, is remarkably wide, extending from Catholic Republicans on the Right to ▷ Marxists and ▷ Maoists on the Left. Those IRA men who are not merely nationalists but social revolutionaries and Marxist- ▷ Leninists see the solution to Ireland's problems in the rousing of a revolutionary working class as hostile to the RC hierarchy as to the Ulster Orangemen, which will sweep away all these evil vestiges of feudalism and ▷ bourgeoisie, together with the capitalist system, and unite all Ireland in a fully democratic socialist state.

At the time of writing the IRA terrorist campaign has been very successful: it has brought down the Unionist government at Stormont and forced the British Government to assume direct rule in the province. It has also forced the Government to begin a programme of relaxing internment. But it has produced a violent Protestant reaction and the prospect is now one of open civil war.

Iraq, Revolution in. The revolutionary movement in Iraq was hamstrung by the Stalinist line – peaceful coexistence with capitalism, and cooperation with the ▷ bourgeois nationalist, albeit anti- ▷ imperialist movements such as Nasserism and the Syrian Ba'ath – which was rigorously adhered to by the Iraq Communist Party. Thus the communist revolutionaries helped the national revolutionaries to win control of the country; but disarmed and subservient to the nationalists, who were making some social reforms, the communists were helpless (cf. ▷ Indonesia) when the Ba'athists, helped by the peasants whom the CP had neglected, overthrew (1963) the rule of the CP's ally Abdul Karim Qassem and set about arresting, torturing and slaughtering communists. Some genuine revolutionaries among the survivors, who did not regard Arab nationalism sustained by anti- ▷ Zionism as the be-all and end-all of revolution, split the ICP to form ▷ New Left-style, Marxist- ▷ Leninist urban and rural ▷ guerrilla forces. This led to a major schism in the ICP and the more revolutionary schismatics formed the mildly militant ICP Central Command to take charge of guerrilla forces. The ICPCC accepted the proposition that 'subjective conditions for achieving victory do not all ripen simultaneously but crystallize through direct and resolute revolutionary struggle', which might be described as sub-Guevarist (*see* Guevara). The guerrillas were formed into the Front for Popular Armed Struggle (FPAS) led by Khaled Ahmed Zaki, former President of the Iraqui Students' Organization in Britain. In an action against government forces using helicopters, in the Al-Ahwar marshes in June 1968, Zaki was killed and the FPAS more or less exterminated. There has since been no effective revolutionary action in Iraq.

Irgun Zvan Leumi: *see* Stern, Abraham.

Irish Republican Army: *see* IRA.

Iron Guard. Romanian Christian- ◊ Fascist terrorist movement 1923–38. *See* Codreanu.

Iskra: *see* Trotsky, Leon.

Israeli Socialist Group, founded 1962: *see* Palestine (Israel), revolution in.

IWW: *see* Industrial Workers of the World.

J

Jabotinsky, Vladimir (186?–1940) Russian Jewish militant ⟡ Zionist, organizer and Commanding Officer of the Jewish Legion to fight with the Allied Powers against the Turks in Palestine in World War I.

Jackson, George (1941–71) American Negro revolutionary, b. and reared in a black ghetto, became a petty criminal. Sentenced to from one year to life for a minor offence by a Soledad, California, court he met Marxist-Leninist fellow-prisoners and was, in his own word 'redeemed' by Marx, Lenin, Trotsky, Engels and Mao. Becoming politically conscious and articulate he was consequently repeatedly refused parole. He had served seven years in atrocious conditions and mostly in solitary when (January 1970) he was charged, with others, of killing a white warder in revenge for the shooting of three Blacks by the guards. By the treatment of black prisoners and conduct of the trial the Soledad prison authorities and justiciary rendered themselves infamous and Jackson became a potent symbol for social revolutionaries all over the world. Two things made Jackson world-famous: his prison letters to ⟡ Angela Davis and others (*Soledad Brothers, 1970*), his *Letters to Jonathan (1971)*, his young brother and his *Towards a United Front*, published in Angela Davis's *If they come in the morning*; and ⟡ Jonathan Jackson's attempt to rescue him by force, while he awaited trial. Following that attempt he was shot (August 1971) in the back by warders; the official version, for which there is no reliable evidence, is that he had attempted, armed with a gun smuggled in to him and with which he had shot two guards, to escape from San Quentin prison where he was being held. Since US and world public opinion had been aroused in his favour and acquittal was probable, his death was very convenient for the Californian authorities. See also ⟡ Soledad Brothers.

Jackson, Jonathan (1953–70). American Negro youth who on 7 August 1970 invaded a courtroom in San Rafael, California, carrying a bag full of guns, armed three Black convicts on trial for killing a prison guard, seized five hostages including the judge, and demanded the release of his brother George ◊ Jackson. His getaway van was machine-gunned in defiance of orders by court guards. Jonathan, the judge and two of the convicts were killed. *See* Soledad Brothers; Jackson, George; Davis Angela.

Janatha Vimukthi Peramuna, People's Liberation Front. Ceylonese revolutionary movement founded in 1966 by Rohan Wijeweera (b. 1944) to pursue extra parliamentary methods of struggle. The main leadership of the Front is Marxist ◊ Leninist, but it is unaligned with the Soviet or Chinese Communist Parties. It organizes mainly among students, agricultural workers and peasants, but claims some support from sections of the membership of the traditional ◊ Marxist parties which are part of the Government.

In April 1971 the JVP launched ◊ guerrilla actions throughout the country, in what it regarded as a legitimate defence of the 'people's rights' against attack by government. A state of emergency declared at the time is still (1973) in force, over 16,000 people are still held in Ceylon prisons, and in all some 50,000 people are believed to have lost their lives in the fighting and consequent repression. According to government reports, JVP forces have withdrawn to the jungle and continue to work clandestinely.

Jaurès, Jean (1859–1914) French philosophy teacher who became a socialist leader. b. Castres into the middle class; ed. Ecole Normale. He became Lecturer in Philosophy, Toulouse University. His first theoretical contribution towards the revolution was his doctoral thesis (*Origins of German Socialism in Luther, Kant, Fichte and Hegel*). He was a socialist deputé 1885–86, 1893–98 and 1902–4, but he was continuously at odds with the orthodox Marxists, his spiritual ancestors being ◊ Proudhon, ◊ Blanc and other French socialist thinkers. He was more than once offered office in coalition administrations but respected the ruling of the Second ◊ International that socialists should refuse office in ◊ bourgeois governments. In 1904 he founded the socialist, now communist, newspaper *L'Humanité*. Despite the French roots of his socialism, Jaurès was a true internationalist, detesting chauvinism, and particularly the sort of military chauvinism which had disgraced the French army during the Dreyfus case.

131

Juarez, Benito

In July 1914 he went to meet German Social-Democratic leaders in Brussels in a desperate attempt to persuade them to prevent the coming war by calling a general strike against mobilization and refusing to vote war credits in the Reichstag. Failing, he returned to Paris where (31 July) he was assassinated by a rightist 'patriot'.

Juarez, Benito (1806–72) Mexican (Amerindian) republican revolutionary leader. He led (1854) a liberal insurrection against the conservative-clerical government of great landowners and their clerical allies, became prime minister 1855–57), and introduced a series of radical reforms to improve the conditions of the poor peasants, purge and modernize the judiciary and curb the overweening power of the very reactionary Church. These measures provoked a violent reaction, in the civil war of 1857–60, during which, while the conservative-clericals ran one government from Mexico City, Juarez and the liberals ran another from Vera Cruz. The conservative-clericals were supported by European powers with large loans; and when Juarez's forces reestablished their leader as chief minister in Mexico City, Juarez repudiated this debt, since it had been incurred without the consent of the people. This gave that great capitalist adventurer, Napoleon III of the French, his chance – the United States being busy with their own civil war – to invade Mexico with a powerful army under the command of Marshal Bazaine, ostensibly to collect the Mexican debt for French moneylenders, actually to set up a puppet Mexican Empire (following the precedent of the 'emperor' Iturbide, 1824), under the Hapsburg Archduke Maximilian as 'emperor'. Juarez was forced to take to the mountains to wage ◊ guerrilla warfare on the French and their conservative-clerical allies, which he did, with some US help, for six years (1861–67). He finally forced the French to withdraw in despair, leaving their unfortunate puppet Maximilian, a man of good-will who had taken his responsibility to the Mexican people seriously, to be captured and shot out of hand by Juarez (June 1867). Juarez became President of the Republic of Mexico and retained that office until his death: he failed to implement the greater part of the reforms which had been his aim, but nevertheless became the Grand Old Man of revolution to the liberals and even revolutionaries of Europe. The French aftermath of their adventure is remarkable for the frankest defence of a failed soldier ever offered by an advocate at a court martial: infuriated by his failure, Napoleon III had Bazaine charged with treason and tried: at a critical point in the trial Bazaine's advocate urged the judges: '*Mais regardez-moi cet homme, messieurs! Ce n'est pas un traitre, voyons! C'est un imbécile!*' The Marshal was acquitted.

Jura Federation (1867) An organization of revolutionary anarchists, Jura mountain villagers who combined watch-making with smallholding farming and were, under the leadership of ◊ James Guillaume, followers of ◊ Bakunin and members of his Social-Democratic Alliance. They were expelled, with Bakunin, from the First ◊ International, at the instance of Karl ◊ Marx, because the Alliance was a conspiratorial organization whereas only open revolution was approved by the Marxists. The Federation became the effective centre for the dissemination of anarchist doctrine and action all over the world in the 1880s. Guillaume, and in general the Federation, were instrumental in making an anarchist of ◊ Kropotkin.

K

Kanafani, Ghassan: *see* PFLP.

Kapp Putsch. In 1920 the German Government headed by Ebert, was far too inclined to the ⸱ social democratic left, and seemed far too accommodatingly subservient to the victorious Allied Powers, for the taste of the German counterrevolutionary right, for whom Ebert was no better than a ⸱ Bolshevik. A plot was made to overthrow his government and to seize power for the Right wing. Its leader was a German-American publicist, Wolfgang Kapp (1868–1922), but its active executive was General von Lüttwitz who had at his disposal *Freikorps* (military irregulars) troops who had been fighting communists in the Baltic Provinces and who, wearing the swastika sign on their helmets, were forerunners of the Nazis. Lüttwitz seized Berlin and installed Kapp as Chancellor of the Reich. Ebert and his government fled the capital, but called for resistance. They received a wholehearted response from the German workers, who were for the most part social democrat or communist, and who called a general strike. The country was paralysed and Kapp, helpless, bolted after five days in power, whereupon Ebert returned and resumed the government of Germany.

Kautsky, Karl (1854–1938) b. Prague which made him Austrian by law; he later became a Czechoslovak citizen. A leading revolutionary social democrat theorist, as a delegate to the Second ⸱ International 1901 Congress in Lübeck he led the opposition to the ⸱ Revisionists. In World War I he led the pacifist movement among those socialists determined to carry out the Second International resolution that the social democratic parties in all countries must refuse to support wars between ⸱ bourgeois governments. Despite his opposition to revisionism Kautsky was hostile to the Bolsheviks, and did not support the October Revolution (1917), being opposed to the implications of 'direct democracy' in Lenin's 'dictatorship of the ⸱ pfoletariat'. Lenin denounced him as a renegade.

Kemal, Mustapha (1880–1938) Known as Kemal Ataturk, Turkish nationalist revolutionary and creator of the modern Turkish republic. A professional army officer who distinguished himself in a number of campaigns (Libya 1911; the Balkan Wars 1912–13; O.C. Turkish forces, Gallipoli 1915), he joined the ▷ Young Turk movement in 1908 but broke with it following a personal and political quarrel with Enver Pasha, its leader and the effective ruler of Turkey following the deposition of the Sultan Abdul Hamid in 1909. Posted to Samsun, Anatolia, following Turkey's defeat in World War I, in 1919 he decided to take miliary action to block the Greek attempt to annex the city and province of Smyrna. This initiative sparked off a national revolution motivated by resentment of Allied plans to dismember Turkey, and by 1920 Kemal was able to establish a Revolutionary Provisional Government in Ankara. By 1922 he had decisively defeated the Greeks and driven them from Smyrna. In the Treaty of Lausanne with the Allied Powers, he obtained better peace terms for his country than those which had been signed by the Young Turk government, but they entailed one of the greatest and most harrowing population migrations in modern history, over 350,000 Turks being forced to quit Greece, and over a million Greeks being moved into Greece proper from Eastern Thrace. Kemal abolished the Sultanate (November 1922); proclaimed the Republic of Turkey with himself as president (October 1923); abolished the Caliphate (March 1924) and was virtual dictator until his death in 1938. He destroyed the political power of the Muslim clergy, secularized the whole apparatus of the state, and forced the Turks to dress as Europeans, emancipate their women, use the Latin alphabet, and undertake the establishment of modern industries. It is doubtful whether even the ▷ Bolsheviks in Russia wrought such a total change in the lives of a whole people as Kemal Ataturk did in Turkey.

Kenyatta, Jomo (1893–) *see* Mau Mau.

Khrushchev, Nikita Sergeyevich (1894–1971) Revolutions, like the Church, have, if they succeed, two manifestations: the revolution militant is succeeded by the revolution triumphant. Nikita Sergevevich Khrushchev was never a revolutionary; on the contrary, he was the complete ▷ establishment politician; he appears here, however, as the first heir, as ruler of the USSR, of the revolution triumphant – and corrupt; the consolidator of a rigorously conservative, chauvinistic state-capitalist empire which must itself become the target of new revolutionaries. Khrushchev was the son of a very poor peasant and coalminer living on the Great Russia–Ukraine border. He had no formal education, worked in the fields till fifteen, then in the foreign concessionaires' pits and factories at Yuzovka in the industrial Donbas, becoming a winding-gear foreman at twenty. Married 1915: two children. He took no part in the prerevolutionary political ferment but in 1918, seeing the ▷ Bolshevik Party in charge in the Donbas, joined it. He fought in the Red Army in the Civil War, proved a reliable party man, returned in 1920, during the famine, to Yuzovka, as mine manager, did good work getting the mines and industries going again and had his first formal education at the new Donets Mining School where he held his first party office. From that base, and protected by the local party boss, Kaganovich, and by being more Stalinist than ▷ Stalin, he rose through the hierarchy in the provinces. In 1929 he was sent to the Stalin Industrial Academy, Moscow, to purge it of anti-Stalinists, among whom was Stalin's beautiful wife, Nadezhda Alliluyeva. His success in this dirty work got him the party secretaryship of one of the Moscow districts, and once again he rose steadily, by using Stalin-style shock-tactics and brutal repression, until he became, in succession to his protector Kaganovich who had moved up, and whom he was later to destroy, Secretary of the Moscow District Committee of the Party. He was responsible for the building of the Moscow Underground in which thousands of forced labourers, former communists lured to Moscow, were used and many died. In the mid-1930s, by discretion, cunning, exact timing of calculated outbursts of apparent boldness, ruthless self-regard, calculated treachery, expedient subservience – in short, all the usual basenesses of an accomplished politician – he avoided the dangers of Stalin's 'purges' and by 1939 was a member of the Politburo and First Secretary (i.e. complete boss) of the Ukraine (pop. 40 million), in which capacity, following the Soviet invasion of Poland (September 1939), he personally oversaw the deportation of over one million Poles, Jews, and others to Siberia in the process of Sovietizing the Polish Ukraine. During World War II he was the only Party boss to spend his whole time with the armies, as a sort of commissar supremo, but taking real risks and knowing just what the Russian soldiers were suffering. On at least one occasion he tried to save one of the armies from the certain massacre in which Stalin's military interference, ineptitude and malice against his own people was always involving them. He may have had something to do with organizing the evacuation of industry to the Urals, and with organizing the partisans who harassed the German armies on their flanks and rear. He was present at the siege of Stalingrad. In 1944 he was reappointed First Secretary of the Ukraine and in addition Chairman of the (Ukrainian) Council of People's Commissars, i.e. prime minister, and thus became responsible for the physical and moral rehabilitation of the utterly devastated Republic. This he achieved by a mixture of terrorism and cajoling, courage, shrewdness and hard work. He suffered partial demotion in 1947 following the Ukrainian famine resulting from a serious drought, but blamed on the slow progress of his collectivization policy; but was fully reinstated a year later and by 1950 was back in Moscow as Secretary of the All-Union Central Committee. There followed a long and bitter power struggle with the most brilliant of the heirs apparent, Malenkov, in the course of which Khrushchev made remarkable recoveries from such mistakes as yet another disastrous agricultural adventure. When Stalin died, he lay low and waited for the successor, Malenkov, to reveal that he had neither the will to persist in his 'thaw' policy against hardline opposition among the top bosses, nor the 'apparatus' to manipulate the leading men as Khrushchev himself was doing. When Malenkov resigned the First Secretaryship, retaining the prime ministry, no new First Secretary was nominated, but Khrushchev was *primus inter pares* of the six-man Party Secretariat, and used his power to purge the top ranks of the Party of Malenkov men and promote his own. He was strong enough to take the title of First Secretary in 1953 and when, in 1954, Malenkov resigned as prime minister, Khrushchev contrived the appointment of his stooge, Bulganin, to that office. At sixty-one he thus became the supreme ruler, just short of Stalin's absolute autocracy, of the USSR, and set to work to transform it, as fast as he could, into an affluent society nation based on state capitalism, on the (from an idealistic revolutionary's point of view) squalid and repulsive United States model. Stalin had betrayed the Revolution; Khrushchev tried to consolidate the new conservative establishment. He had denounced Stalin for, among other crimes, fostering a personality cult; for the same crime, and for his wildly intuitive and usually disastrous policy decisions he was brought down by a collective of CP bosses. But it has proved impossible to re-Stalinize, and Khrushchev's work may be regarded as sound enough to ensure that nothing

Kim Il Sung

short of another revolution could purge the great power which is heir to the October Revolution, of its gross failure to achieve more than a few of the socialist ideals.

Kim Il Sung (1912–) b. North Korea; real name Kim Sung Chu (Kim Il Sung was originally the name of a legendary ◊ guerrilla fighter against the Japanese Occupation). He fought in China with the communist ◊ guerrillas until 1941 when he went to the USSR, returning as a major in the Red Army when the USSR invaded Korea to drive out the Japanese in 1945. He soon became the dominant personality in the Korean CP and by 1948 had succeeded in negotiating a merger with the ◊ Maoist New People's Party, the new, joint Party being called the Korean Workers Party with Kim as Chairman. An original thinker of independent character despite his use of the most tedious jargon of Soviet communism (in which he is strikingly inferior to ◊ Mao Tse-tung, whose use of plain, powerful language is one of his virtues), Kim purged his party of both Soviet and Chinese partisans, denounced the USSR leadership for the crime of ◊ revisionism and the Chinese leaders for interfering arrogance. He supported Che ◊ Guevara's line of national communist independence combined with internationalism, and he denies that any one country is or can be the centre of world revolution. The very striking success of his economic policy in the late 1950s and 1960s, which brought both socialism and a respectable measure of prosperity to North Korea in a remarkably short time, enormously strengthened his hand among Far Eastern revolutionaries. *See* ◊ Korea, Revolution in.

King, Martin Luther: *see* Passive resistance.

Korea, Revolution in. A tributary of the Chinese Empire from 1637, before which it had been independent, Korea was restored, nominally, to independence, but was placed under Japanese 'protection', following the Sino-Japanese war of 1894–95, and was annexed as a province by Japan in 1910. For the next thirty-five years Korean ◊ guerrillas waged sporadic war on the Japanese authorities and on Japanese settlers round Seoul. In 1945, towards the end of World War II, the USSR invaded Korea to drive out the Japanese and ensured control of the country by the Korean Communist Party, founded about 1920; and more specifically by its ablest leader, ◊ Kim Il Sung, at that time a major in the Red Army and in whom, had they but known it, they had caught a Tartar. Meanwhile the USA had taken control of South Korea using as their instrument a ◊ bourgeois-nationalist government of the kind stigmatized by Marxist- ◊ Leninist revolutionaries as 'neocolonialist'. By 1948 Kim had formed the Korean Workers' Party which was independent of the USSR and Chinese CPs and which directed the conduct of the war with the South, or rather with the United States and her allies and the ruling class of the South, which broke out in 1950 and ended in 1953 with Korea still divided along the 38th parallel. The North Koreans received massive help from China but little from the USSR. During the following fifteen years the Workers' Party were strikingly successful in the economic field, raising industrial and agricultural production far above the prewar level while proceeding with economic socialization so fast that by 1958 it was complete.

In this economic success, vouched for by expert Western observers, North Korea became the model Far Eastern socialist state. This success was almost certainly due to the application of the principle known as *Juche* which is defined by Kim Il Sung as: 'Abiding by the principle of solving all problems of the revolution and construction independently in accordance with the actual conditions in one's own country and primarily by one's own efforts. This implies a creative application of Marxism-Leninism and the experience of the international revolutionary movement, in keeping with the true conditions and national peculiarities of one's own country. It also signifies independent solution of one's own problems in the revolutionary struggle and construction by displaying the spirit of self-reliance.' It was *Juche* which led Kim to expel pro-USSR and pro-China comrades from the Workers' Party and it cost North Korea almost the whole of Soviet aid; but it made the country nearly self-sufficient in, for example, such essentials as machine production by 1964. Another principle insisted on by Kim and his chief colleagues had been Lenin's rule for ◊ cultural revolution, that is, 'helping the functionaries rid themselves of bureaucracy and acquire a revolutionary method of work by relying on the masses'. This has been accomplished by a method called *Chongsan-ri*: a *ri* is the basic, lowest administrative unit; all Party officials, including Kim himself, are obliged, from time to time, to spend a season, which may be only weeks but may be months, working in one of the remoter rural *ri*, so that they always have personal experience of conditions at the grass roots. At the same time the system spreads knowledge and control of the Party, and humanizes it, so that the people have come to trust their government and to work enthusiastically for the new system. One competent Western observer has said that North Korea has eliminated poverty entirely without imposing the burden of excessive toil.

In South Korea as in the North there is a militant communist movement which became active following the Japanese surrender at the end of World War II, when there was rioting and revolutionary action, including a general strike, among both industrial workers and peasants and at least one army mutiny. US support of the nationalist government was not the only reason for the failure of the revolution in the South – at least according to Kim Il Sung who attributed it in part to the weakening of the Communist Party there by factional strife due to the rival influences of the two great communist powers, and to faulty analysis of the revolutionary situation. The CP apparatus in the South was more or less destroyed by 1949. But not, apparently, the revolutionary spirit, for it was a popular rising which finally overthrew the notoriously corrupt Syngman Rhee administration in 1960. Kim sees a long and 'torturous' People's War as now necessary for the achievement of revolution in South Korea, and has pledged the Workers' Party to support it.

Kropotkin, Prince Pyotr Alexeyevich (1842–1921) Russian anarchist philosopher and revolutionary. Reared by his father's serfs whose condition he deplored and ed. by a series of tutors who introduced him to advanced ideas, he passed with distinction through the elite Corps of Pages, but on leaving it (1862) refused the brilliant future offered him and went to serve among the mounted Cossacks in eastern Siberia. His efforts to obtain penal reforms on behalf of the grossly maltreated convicts were frustrated by reactionary officials, and he turned to science, exploring widely in the Far East, travelling 50,000 miles, refusing to carry arms even in the wildest country, and becoming a distinguished geographer. Resigning from the service in disgust at the harsh treatment of some political prisoners, he was disowned by his father. He enrolled at St Petersburg University, earned a pittance as clerk to the Russian Geographical Society, and lived as a poor workman in one room. Meanwhile he had been reading political philosophy, notably ◊ Proudhon, and had become a libertarian socialist. Offered (1871) the secretaryship of the Geographical Society

Kropotkin, Prince Pyotr Alexeyevich

which meant a career in the science he loved, he rejected the offer and went to Western Europe to seek a means to help the Russian peasants in revolutionary philosophies. He met ♢ Marxists, anarchists and other socialists in Zurich and Geneva, studied the anarchism of the ♢ Jura Federation of village artisans led by James ♢ Guillaume, was captivated by it, and returned to St Petersburg to preach it as a Chaykovskyist ♢ Narodnik. Arrested and imprisoned in the Peter-and-Paul fortress (1874), his health collapsed (scurvy) and he was moved (1876) to the military hospital whence he made a spectacular escape to England, returned to Switzerland, visited Belgium for a Socialist conference, fled to England again when harassed by the police, spent a year working on anarchist theory in the British Museum Reading Room, went thence to Paris to found anarchist cells, and to found (1878) the anarchist newspaper *La Révolte*, most of which he wrote himself. Published in Switzerland, it was revolutionary in matter but moderate in manner. Under pressure from Russia, the Swiss expelled Kropotkin but he continued to edit the paper from Thonon in France until he moved back to Paris and refounded *La Révolte*. There, following violent disturbances among workers, attributed to anarchists, he was arrested, charged, with fifty others (although he was not implicated in the riots) with being a member of an illegal organization, the ♢ International, and imprisoned. From prison he published articles in scientific journals and wrote some entries for the *Encyclopaedia Brittanica*. He fell seriously ill with malaria: when international attempts by men of letters and science to have him amnestied revealed that the French Government was only holding him under Russian pressures, there was such an outcry that he was released. He went to England (1886) and lived there for the next thirty years, working as a geographer and scholar, as a theorist of anarchism, contributing articles to *The Times*, and becoming a famous gardener. He never ceased to propagate his gentle doctrine of the evils of capitalism and of all government, and of mutual aid as the only sound foundation for society, but he urged peaceful methods and deplored the use of assassination by anarchists. He conceded that the struggle for existence was a reality, but saw it not as a struggle of man against man, but of cooperation, mutual aid, and loving men against adverse circumstances.

He welcomed the ♢ Russian Revolution, and in April 1917 returned to St Petersburg after an absence of forty years, was given a royal welcome by the Provisional Government and offered office in it, which he refused. Following the October Revolution, much of which he approved, he became isolated, being associated with the Provisional Government in the eyes of the ◊ Bolsheviks. He repeatedly protested to ◊ Lenin against Bolshevik acts of oppression and in November 1920 published a *Letter to the Workers of the World* praising Bolshevik economic and social egalitarian measures and the institutions of workers' Soviets, while pointing out their mistakes and calling on the world's workers to put a stop to the iniquitous interventionist war. But by this time he was quite isolated; his anarchist friends were all in Bolshevik prisons. Sad and sick, he worked until the day of his death on finishing his last book.

Kropotkin's revolutionary doctrine was simple: if, on the morrow of revolution, it is found that we have done nothing but change persons and formulae, then nothing has been accomplished. What must at all costs be avoided is the institution of that absurdity, a 'revolutionary government'. What must be achieved *at once* is social and economic equality so complete that there can be no going back. All the means of production must at once revert to their only true owners – everybody, and the controlling organ should be the *commune*, by which he meant both the local municipality composed of representatives of all social interests, and the natural, mutually aiding collective of all the people of the locality. The state disappears as, being evil, it must; in its place we have a network of co-operating communes without central authority. There must be no wages: if wages are paid, then the wage receiver seems subservient and becomes so to the wage payer. Instead, goods and services are to be distributed according to need. The capitalist use of necessity as a spur to work is not only evil, it is unnecessary, for men, once equal, will work because it is natural and pleasant to do so and consciousness of useful achievement is enjoyable. Leisure will be filled with crafts, arts, study and science. The key to his system is his firm belief that men were naturally good and naturally social animals – the absolute antithesis of Stirnerism (*see* ◊ Stirner, Max). Of course, there are antisocial or at least asocial men; the only pressure we can properly use to make them work like the rest is that of public reprobation, and such men, persisting in their wickedness, will be pariahs.

Kropotkin produced a large number of books. The three most important are *Mutual Aid: a Factor in Evolution* (London 1902); *The*

Conquest of Bread (London 1906); *Ethics: Origin and Development* (New York 1924).

Kun, Bela (1886–1937) Hungarian Communist revolutionary. Captured by the Russians while serving as an NCO in the Austro-Hungarian army in World War I, he was converted to communism when the revolutions of 1917 released war prisoners. After some training in Moscow he was sent to Budapest to ferment a ⊳ Bolshevik revolution in Hungary. By then, late 1918, Hungary had been declared an independent republic with Count Karolyi as Provisional President. His government was liberal but weak, and Bela Kun was able to do to Karolyi's ⊳ bourgeois revolution what ⊳ Lenin did to Kerensky's – take it over and force it far to the left. Kun and his Hungarian Bolsheviks raised the workers and after a feeble resistance Karolyi was forced to resign and go into exile and Kun became effective ruler of about half Hungary. His Bolshevik government at once introduced a number of extreme socialist measures, on Russian lines. These were welcomed by very large numbers of the people; but the brutality with which certain of the Bolsheviks abused their power soon aroused a sullen reaction against them. Moreover Kun's government was threatened with counterrevolutionary reaction from Romania and from the Czechs, and by the military government of Admiral Horthy centred on Szeged. In August 1919 a Romanian army invaded Hungary with a view to annexing a part of it, and occupied Budapest; and in November Horthy marched on the capital and after some months of confused conflict, became (March 1920) Regent of Hungary. Bela Kun, after 4½ months of power, fled to Vienna where the authorities returned him to Moscow in exchange for some Austrian banners seized by the Russian army which had helped the Habsburgs put down the revolution of 1848 (⊳Eighteen forty-eight). In Moscow Kun was appointed head of the Balkan Secretariat of the ⊳ Comintern, an office which he seems to have held into the 1930s when, probably falling out of favour with ⊳ Stalin, he was superseded by a German communist, Wilhelm Pieck. But he was still on the foreign staff of the Comintern when ⊳ Tito was also working there in 1935. It was not until 1937 that he was arrested and, presumably, judicially murdered, like so many other foreign communists.

L

Land and Liberty. Two different movements bore this name in Russian revolutionary history. The first was a political secret society formed after the emancipation of the serfs in 1861. It was inspired chiefly by the writings of the nihilist ⟡ Chernyshevsky, and notably by his *Aesthetic Relations of Art and Reality* (1855), a work expressing the classic nihilist view that a sound pair of boots is worth all the poetry in the world. The movement sought to free the peasants from the oppressive burden of redemption payment for their land, imposed on them with emancipation; to win the fundamental human rights and freedoms; and to obtain the right of secession from the Empire for minority nationalities. Aristocratic, romantic and ineffectual (one of its adherents tried to convert the Tsar to socialism in a half-hour personal interview), the society collapsed in 1863.

The second Land and Liberty movement took that name only in 1878, having been known since its formation in 1876 first as the *Troglodytes,* and then as the *Revolutionary-Populist Group of the North.* From early in its career it was split into two factions, one dedicated to the peaceful propagation of socialism, the other to the same end but by the use of terrorism. At a meeting in Voronezh in August 1879 this split was made formal, the moderates, led by ⟡ Plekhanov calling themselves *Black Partition,* and the terrorists, led by Andrei Zhelyabov, calling themselves *The ⟡ People's Will.* At the same meeting the adherents of Zhelyabov solemnly and formally condemned the Tsar, Alexander II, to death as an enemy of the people, a sentence which they carried out.

Lassalle, Ferdinand (1825–64) German-Jewish socialist theorist and militant organizer, b. Breslau; ed. Berlin where he became a Hegelian but, unlike ⟡ Marx, did not reject ⟡ Hegel's 'idealism'. Beginning, as a Left democrat, in the 1848 revolution he was imprisoned for 'issuing a call to arms against the King's sovereignty'. This, and a meeting with Marx the same year, turned him into a communist, but never a Marxist. He and

Marx corresponded copiously, but Marx soon came to consider him intolerably conceited and dangerously ambitious, hardly surprising when he was receiving from this youth of twenty letters containing such stuff as: 'I am the servant and master of an idea, the priest of a god, myself. I have made of myself both actor and plastic artist, all my being is a manifestation of my will, expressing whatever meaning I wish to give it. The shaking of my voice, the flashing brilliance of my eye, the least quiver of my face, all must slavishly convey the dictate of my will.' (*Works*, F. Lassalle, ed. Hirsch 1963). A brilliant orator, born demagogue and clever politician, his flamboyance and self-dramatization offended Marx and aroused his distrust. But from 1861 Lassalle enjoyed extraordinary success in recruiting and organizing a German workers' political party, which no other socialist had yet been able to do. His new party was formally founded, May 1863, as the Association General of German Workers, and it swiftly became so influential that Bismarck was forced to take account of it. Lassalle's ideas were in the economic rather than the political field: he wanted to form workers' industrial cooperatives (pioneered in England) and needed state subsidies to finance them. Bismarck was much more afraid of the ◊ bourgeois progressive parties which aimed at political power and with which Lassalle, against Marx's advice, refused to cooperate. So Bismarck and Lassalle engaged in secret negotiations (not revealed until 1927 when a cache of letters between them was found in an old cupboard), for an alliance between right and left against the centre, of *Junkers* and workers against burgesses. Marx knew nothing of this negotiation but, from Lassalle's pamphlets, he seems to have suspected some such 'treachery' and his dislike of Lassalle turned to hatred; in a letter to Engels (30 July 1862) he describes him as 'that Jewish nigger'. ('Jew' in workers' parlance = capitalist). Lassalle was the dictator of his party; he held that the workers were best governed by a personal dictatorship, provided the dictator was working in their interests; if the Prussian State would subsidise his Association, its members would accept the king as their 'social dictator'. But whatever his shortcomings, it was Lassalle who gave the German workers, and notably the Berlin workers who adored him, political awareness; and in his Association he founded what evolved into the German Social-Democratic Party (*see* ◊ Liebnecht; Bebel) which, for some time, made German workers and their intellectual mentors leaders of the soberer element in revolutionary Europe. Lassalle would no doubt have accomplished more, had he not been shot dead in a duel over a personal quarrel in August 1864.

League of Black Revolutionary Workers. American militant revolutionary organization centred on Detroit and the automobile industry. It has cells in a number of factories and about twenty groups of young revolutionaries in the schools are affiliated to it. It has a collegiate system of leadership, among its leaders being the jurist and barrister Ken Cockrel and the automobile worker John Watson, one of the founders of the League who, in 1970, visited Italy and gave a showing of the film *Finally Got the News*, made by the League, about its own activities in American factories. The League has a Marxist- ⬦ Leninist ideology and believes that the black Americans must be armed, and prepared to use their arms now and not in some speculative and eventual revolutionary situation in the future. It holds that an exclusively black Marxist movement is necessary because the white workers, having a privileged position *vis à vis* the black workers, tend to defend their privileges at the expense of the blacks at least until the revolution is much further advanced. But as the revolution makes headway, alliance with the white workers will become possible and ultimately inevitable, since the white workers, realizing that they are being exploited, will begin to fight racism, capitalism and ⬦ imperialism. Moreover the blacks must be the most conscious and advanced revolutionaries because they are 'super-exploited', their factory working conditions being much worse than those of the whites, because the bosses use them as pace-setters and neglect their safety rules. The strikes organized by the League, in defiance of the unions as well as management, have nearly all been for better working conditions rather than higher wages. The League publishes its own newspaper and plans to make it a daily, *The Inner City Voice*, printed on its own rotary presses entirely by League labour. It also owns the film unit which made *Finally Got the News* and a publishing house, the Black Star Publishing Corporation, which publishes books and pamphlets for circulation in the factories, and some books for general distribution, e.g. *The Political Thought of James Forman*.

John Watson has expressed the League's aims as follows: 'Our short-term objective is to seize political power by putting control of the means of production into the hands of the workers guided by the most advanced sector of the ⬦ proletariat, that is to say the vanguard of Black Workers.'

Left Book Club

That was, of course, the role assigned by ⟡ Lenin to the ⟡ Bolsheviks. He continues: 'Our long-term objective is to bring to birth a society free from all oppression whether racial, sexual, class, or nationalist, based on the principle: 'To each according to his needs', and no longer on the principle 'From each according to his capacity'. (translated from an interview with Don Georgakas in *Quaderni Piacenti*).

Left Book Club (1936–48) The near collapse of the capitalist system in 1929, resulting in massive unemployment and economic misery throughout the Western world; the brutal militarist and police excesses of bourgeois reaction in its Fascist form in Italy; the rise of ⟡ Hitler and the ⟡ Nazis in Germany; the successes and excesses of Japanese imperial militarism in the Far East; the failure of the League of Nations; and the jealously fostered illusions of Western socialists touching the nature and role of the USSR which misled them into seeing the dictator Joseph ⟡ Stalin as the white hope of socialist civilization, gave rise in the Western democracies (1930–39) to a mood which was intellectually revolutionary, although the left was either too timid or too committed to parliamentary reform (or not physically wretched enough) to advance to revolutionary action. This mood gave rise e.g. in France, to the political Popular Front of socialists and communists, a huddling together of frightened sheep confronted by the bourgeois wolf turned rabidly savage; and to the ⟡ International Brigade which fought in the Spanish Civil War. One of its manifestations in Britain was the Left Book Club, founded May 1936 by the publisher Victor Gollanz, a sentimental idealist of outstanding commercial shrewdness and drive, aided by the socialist theorist Professor Harold Laski and the former Oswald ⟡ Mosley, later left socialist theorist and politician, John Strachey. Those who joined the Club received, for the low price of half-a-crown (12½ pence today) per month, a book dealing with some aspect of political economy, science, art or history from the socialist point of view; and a magazine entitled *Left News*. The books published for the Club were written by authors of exceptional talent or ability in their field and deeply committed to the cause of the Left: they were either didactic or polemical, and expressed the 'Popular Front' mystique in their internationalism and in their authors' varying degrees of leftism. The first to be published was *France Today and the People's Front* by the French Communist leader, Maurice Thorez; among the more lasting were André

147

Lenin

Malraux's *Days of Contempt* (1936); John Strachey's *The Theory and Practice of Socialism* (1936); George Orwell's *The Road to Wigan Pier* (1937); Tom Harrison's *Savage Civilization* (1937); R. H. Tawney's *The Acquisitive Society* (1937). Later publications were more remarkable for educational worthiness than for brilliance. The Club gave rise to discussion groups, of which there were about 1,500 by 1939 and at that point might, given different leadership, have turned into a militant left socialist revolutionary movement. But that year, with a membership of 57,000, was its zenith; the political confusion consequent on the outbreak of a war in which Nazi Germany and the USSR were parties to a non-aggression pact, infected it with a debility which became manifest in a decline which continued until 1948 when, with only 7,000 members remaining, the Club ended its existence. As an instrument of revolutionary propaganda the Club was a failure, possibly because it could not divorce itself from sentimental subservience to the idea that the USSR must be accepted as the leader of world socialism, manifest in, e.g. its publication *The Socialist Sixth World*, an illusion which also affected the editorial policy of *The New Statesman*, at the same time. But the hundreds of books which it published educated a whole generation of liberal left intellectuals and their followers; the monument to that achievement was the radical reformist British Labour Government between 1945 and 1952, whose great achievement was the creation of the Welfare State.

Lenin (Vladimir Ilyich Ulyanov, 1870–1924) b. Simbirsk, Russia, s. of an inspector of primary schools. He had a normal middle-class boyhood; at school he was apparently studious and biddable (the Soviet biography has made him into a prig, but is not good evidence). In 1887 he went to Kazan university to read law. It has been suggested that he turned revolutionary as a result of the execution of his elder brother at nineteen for implication in a plot to assassinate the Tsar, but no doubt he had imbibed some of his brother's ideas before then. He was suspended from university for a year for his revolutionary activities among the students, but on his return joined a ⊳ Marxist club and made a study of Marx's *Das Kapital*. Transferred to the University of Samara under surveillance, he organized a Marxist study group there, and finally took his degree by correspondence at the university of St Petersburg. He went there from Samara to work with proletarian revolutionary movements, and write his first book, a refutation of the economic and philosophical ideas of the ⬦ Populists, *Who are the People's Friends?* (1894). Arrested, released and again arrested, he was sent to Siberia (1897) where he continued to plan for revolution and wrote his *The Development of Capitalism in Russia* (1899). Being under police surveillance he was unable to attend the foundation meeting of the Russian Social-Democratic Party in Minsk (1899).

Released in 1900 he went to Switzerland where he met and worked with ⬦ Plekhanov and other revolutionary exiles, then to England where he spent most of his time reading and writing in the British Museum library. He also paid visits to revolutionary exiles in Germany and France. He was one of the founders of *Iskra* (The Spark), which he edited, in which he and other Marxist *émigrés* propagated their ideas for revolution, and which was regularly smuggled into Russia. His principal work in this period was the pamphlet *What is to be Done?* (1902), in which he laid down what should be the theory and practice of a revolutionary Marxist party. He stuck firmly to these ideas until the revolution was accomplished.

The Russian Social-Democratic Party's 2nd Congress was held in London in 1903: the Congress split over the question of the organization of the party. Lenin won a majority of the votes and became a leader of the 'majoritists', i.e. ⬦ Bolsheviks. A year later he published *One Step Forward, Two Steps Back*, castigating the 'opportunism' of the 'minoritists' i.e. Mensheviks.

Lenin returned to Russia to take part in the 1905 revolution (*see* ⬦ Russian Revolution 1905) but following its failure was obliged to go into exile again, in Switzerland, Austria and France. He continued his work of producing a whole literature of Marxist revolutionary textbooks with *Two Social-Democratic Tactics in Democratic Revolution*, in which he discussed the role of the proletariat in a bourgeois parliamentary revolution, and showed how, by recruiting the poor peasants and other 'semi-proletarian' classes, the bourgeois revolution could be taken over and turned into a dictatorship of the proletariat. At the same time he was writing *Materialism and Empiriocriticism* (*see* Leninism).

In 1912 he succeeded in having the Mensheviks barred from the Social-Democratic congress in Prague, and established the Bolsheviks as a separate party. He had a hand in the founding of *Pravda* which was to be published (legally) in St Petersburg. He could still not enter Russia safely but settled near the border in Cracow until, arrested by the Austrian police and ordered to leave the country immediately (1914), he returned to Switzerland and for some time concentrated on polemical writing against the 2nd (Socialist) International which was 'opportunist', the legal German Social-Democratic Party, which had been created by ▷ Lassalle and ▷ Bebel, having fulfilled his gloomy prognostications by voting in the Reichstag for war. He convened a meeting of all the European socialists he could muster, at Zimmerwald (1915), to denounce the war, which he saw as a power struggle between rival bourgeois capitalist powers from which the working class could gain nothing. Although his own theory contained the blueprint for turning such a war into a revolutionary class war, he did not consider that the conditions for revolution (*see* ▷ Leninism) existed; nor does he, at that time, seem to have foreseen that it would create the opportunity he was waiting for.

Meanwhile he was making an intensive study of ▷ Hegel, making notes for his *Philosophic Notebooks* (1915); and reading in preparation for his *Imperialism, the Last Phase of Capitalism* (1916); and for his *The Right of Nations to Self-Determination* (1916). He was still (1916) trying to organize European socialism to stop the war, convening a conference to that end in Kienthal, which had no useful results.

Following the outbreak of the February revolution in 1917 (*see* ▷ Russian Revolutions), he returned to Petrograd with the help of the German High Command, who hoped that once in Russia he would disrupt the Russian war effort; he is supposed to have been taken across Germany into Russia in a 'sealed train'. There, while agitating for the transformation of the bourgeois revolution into a proletarian one, he found time to write his next textbook of revolution, the *April Theses*. The slogan with which he and his Bolsheviks went to the workers and mutinous soldiers was 'All power to the Soviets', i.e. the revolutionary councils of workers and soldiers. The Provisional Government, already half-intimidated, put up with this until July, when it ordered his arrest; he escaped into Finland, there wrote *The State and the Revolution* (1917), slipped back into Petrograd on 7 October and persuaded the Party Central Committee to call for armed insurrection. He directed this from Bolshevik HQ in the Smolny Institute (*see* ▷ Russian Revolutions). With victory over the moderates and other socialist groups, he became Chairman of the People's Council of Commissars (the title 'Ministers' was rejected as being tainted with bourgeois corruption), with an initial policy of Peace, Land and Bread.

His government secured peace by the Treaty of Brest-Litovsk, brilliantly negotiated by ◊ Trotsky. The land was redistributed to the peasants. But bread was another matter and Russia was soon starving. Lenin nationalized the banks and all means of industrial production; but this attempt to install a completely socialist economy while fighting a civil war on a dozen or more fronts, facing British and Japanese seizures of Russian territory in support of the counter-revolution, and trying to create both a civil and military state apparatus out of the wreckage of the old, led to the total collapse of the Russian economy in 1920. Lenin then showed his flexibility by introducing the New Economic Policy, known as NEP, in which a measure of private enterprise was legalized. Meanwhile he found time to write *The Immediate Tasks of Soviet Power* (1918), and the polemical *Proletarian Revolution and the Renegade Kautsky* (1919), and to move the whole apparatus of his revolutionary government to the Moscow Kremlin.

He had to face not only war from the Right but also violent opposition from some other socialist groups, notably the ◊ Social Revolutionary Party, which in 1918 began a campaign of assassinating Bolshevik leaders. This had the effect of greatly hardening the Bolshevik line with the opposition, but claimed some victims, Lenin for one: the bullet fired at him by the Social Revolutionist Dora Kaplan in August 1918 did not kill him, but, severely wounded, his health steadily declined. In 1919 he founded the Communist (Third) International, i.e. ◊ Comintern. And he still presided over a government coping not only with war, an increasingly victorious one, but famine, plague and sabotage. He continued to write, producing *Communism's Infantile Malady* (1920), a pamphlet against sectarianism and inflexible dogmatism, which he saw as a dangerous sickness of the revolution; *The Importance of Militant Materialism* (1922), and a number of works in 1923 including *On Cooperation*, and the interestingly empirical *Better Less but Better*. In his last year he was deeply disturbed by the growth of a Party bureaucracy which he considered to be the revolution's most dangerous enemy, and ◊ Stalin was among those whom he reproved for letting it 'mutilate' socialist democracy, in his *Political Testament*. He died, chiefly, in all probability, of exhaustion, on 21 January 1924 at the age of fifty-three.

Leninism

If Lenin had any private life at all, it is of no importance: he married; he is said to have been warm-hearted with his closest friends, and by Trotsky's account he had a shrewd sense of humour. But his work to bring about the revolution and establish socialism was all his life. He was the one socialist revolutionary of his epoch who knew absolutely that he was right, whereas others were apt to be weakened in their purpose by being open to argument; this gave him a formidable strength of will. His writings, wholly devoted to the philosophy, interpretation, techniques, strategy, tactics and purposes of Marxist socialist revolution and government by proletarian dictatorship fill 38 printed volumes. His monument, despite the hideous damage done to it by Stalin, is the USSR where, preserved as a mummy in his Red Square mausoleum, a place of unending pilgrimage, he is virtually deified. For his philosophy and revolutionary thought *see* Leninism.

Leninism. Nowadays more commonly called Marxism-Leninism, is the revolutionary philosophy contained in the body of ⟡ Lenin's writings, in which he interpreted and extended Marxist thinking in the light of the conditions obtaining half a century after ⟡ Marx's death, from his *Who are the people's friends?* (1894) down to his later major works, *Imperialism, the Final Stage of Capitalism* (1916); *The State and the Revolution* (1917); and *The Role of Militant Materialism* (1922). Owing to the intervention of Stalinism and the necessity which ⟡ Stalin was under of pretending to derive his political thought and acts from Leninism, the most commonly accepted image of Leninism is seriously distorted; thus, the USSR is very far from being Leninist; and both the Chinese and ⟡ New Left views of Communism are nearer to Leninism than is that of Moscow. In so far as Leninism is embodied in Lenin's definitions of socialism, it can be briefly summarized as follows:

Economics. 'Social' (public) ownership of the means of production, distribution and exchange. 'Such is the dialectic of history that war which has strikingly accelerated the transformation of monopoly capitalism into State monopoly capitalism has, by the same token, brought humanity much nearer to Socialism ... State monopoly capitalism is the most thorough material preparation for Socialism... Socialism is State mono-

152

poly capitalism placed at the service of the entire people' (*Works*, xxvi, 107).

Up to that point we have what might pass for Stalinism as living generations have seen it, although in practice Stalinist socialism was not equally 'at the service of the entire people' any more than it is today in the USSR. But Lenin goes on to say that it is not enough that the economic apparatus be managed *for* the people, it must be managed *by* the people.

In practice this means workers' control of industry for: 'The man only is a Socialist in practice ... who relies upon the experience and instincts of the toiling masses ... The intelligence of tens of millions of creators provides us with something infinitely more valuable than the most extensive and brilliant theoretical forecasts' (*Works*, xxv, 389 ff, and 496).

That is the Leninist licence for the 'direct democracy', now preached by the communists of the New Left and ultra-Left.

Politics. Marx, while he was precise enough in defining the nature of and conditions for the socialist revolution which would demolish the ◊ bourgeois capitalist state, was unsatisfactorily vague when it came to defining what would replace it. Lenin points out that Marx did little more than indicate what the problems of construction would be and went no further towards solving them than to say that the demolished State apparatus would be replaced by 'the organization of the proletariat as the dominant class'. Here Lenin extended Marxism in the direction of a more positive solution: 'We are not utopians; we know that the first labourer or housewife to hand are not immediately capable of taking part in the management of the State ... [But] we demand that workers and soldiers enter without delay on their apprenticeship in State management' (*Works*, xxv, 109). He had in mind the ◊ Soviets and their executive committees. By this means a state apparatus of millions could be recruited; and they must be, because the real strength of the socialist state was to be found in those proletarian millions and nowhere else. So that, here again, we have Lenin's emphasis on 'direct democracy', his effort to make the dictatorship of the proletariat a reality. He says: 'For us, a State is strong only by virtue of the masses' political awareness. It is strong when the masses are informed of everything so that they can form their own judgments and go into action fully aware of what they are doing' (*Works*, xxvi, 263).

Leninism

In the building of a socialist society by far the worst and most dangerous enemy is bureaucracy. The danger is described in Marx's own language here, as 'enormous'. (Cf. Marx in *Critique of the Philosophy of the Hegelian State.*) Consequently the new proletarian democracy must be alert to destroy bureaucracy root and branch, and the task of correcting the state's tendency to 'bureaucratize', a never-ending one, will fall to the trade unions. Here, once again, is one of the sources of the New Left's emphasis on Marxism-Leninism as the source of its philosophy; and of its hostility to Moscow communism which is one of the most hardened, almost fossilized bureaucracies in the world. And these New Left attitudes are reinforced by Lenin's insistence that the bureaucracy can and must be replaced by a 'popular democracy' (*The State and the Revolution*, p. 520). Lenin was aware that Stalin, in 1920, was building a bureaucratic apparatus and this, as much as the man's rebarbative character, was what led him to warn the Party in his 'Will', of the danger to the revolution which Stalin represented. Again and again he laid heavy emphasis on the revolutionary importance of involving the masses and keeping them permanently involved. Thus, in 1917: 'If the power of the Soviets, the will of the Soviets is victorious, it is because they have, from the beginning, applied the principles long since laid down by Socialism . . . have striven to arouse the most oppressed and burdened classes of society to life, and led them into taking the Socialist initiative' (*The State and the Revolution*, p. 483).

In other words, Socialism is meaningless without the autonomous, conscious and active participation of the masses. In this sense, then, whereas today ⟡ Maoism is orthodox Marxism-Leninism, those New Left revolutionary groups which insist on the value of immediate violent small-scale ⟡ guerrilla action, are not: they are, in fact, in the situation of the late nineteenth century ⟡ Populist groups in Russia which were castigated by Lenin in *Who are the People's Friends?* (1894). Strict Marxism-Leninism would almost certainly not have room for the ⟡ Guevarist theory of guerrilla terrorism as a means of recruiting the mass support requisite for effective revolution.

Cultural revolution. Lenin wrote: 'All the wonders of technology and all the triumphs of culture must become the common heritage; and henceforth the mind and kind of man must never again become the means of

154

Leninism

violence and exploitation' (*The State and the Revolution*, p. 503). It should
be borne in mind that the Russian masses had been kept outside the culture of their own country by want of education; and that in the same essay
Lenin deals with illiteracy as one of the enemies of the revolution. This
theme therefore is not now relevant in the advanced, industrial countries,
but is still very relevant in e.g. China, or Latin America. Even here reservations must be made: one could, e.g. see commercial advertising, the
dominance of the media by capitalism, in advanced industrial countries, as
an 'exploitive' abuse of culture. Lenin said that the whole culture created
by capitalism must be taken over and used to build socialism and in view
of what he added to this it would seem that the distrust and maltreatment
of *ci-devant* bourgeois intellectuals in the post-Lenin Stalinist period of
USSR history ran counter to Leninism. Lenin was, indeed, specific about
this danger: the cultural revolution had its enemies and the worst and
most dangerous was communist 'complacency', implicit in the belief that
the Party leadership was entitled to impose cultural decrees. The 1930s
and 40s produced some outrageous examples of its doing just that, e.g. in
official support for the charlatan biologist Lysenko who obligingly made
nature submit to a narrow and doctrinaire Marxist rule, just as the Roman
Catholic Church had formerly tried to force nature to agree with its own
image of the universe. The same anti-Leninist crime is committed, of
course, by the present Soviet government when it persecutes non-con-
formist writers and other artists. 'We have to learn to educate politically;
but we have not yet learnt how to do it and have still to find a correct
method of undertaking the work' (*Works*, xxxiii, 72).

The theme recurs in *The Role of Militant Materialism* (1923) and highly
particular interpretation of it has given rise to some of the most abominable
crimes of thought repression in history. And yet the Leninist lesson is
clear: for communists there is no greater mistake than to believe that in
the cultural or any other aspect, revolution which is worth anything can be
made without the cooperation of non-revolutionaries: in the cultural
revolution there must be alliance with non-communists in every cultural
field, critical assimilation of the product of pre-communist materialism,
integration of savants and scientists into the new socialist culture and, as a
catalyst, systematic study of ◊ Hegel's dialectic from the materialist point
of view: 'In our case political and social revolution have preceded
the cultural revolution (*Cooperation* 1923), which is what we must now

155

Liebnecht, Karl

undertake. Today we have only to accomplish this cultural revolution
to become a completely Socialist country' (*Works*, xxxiii, 488).

Leninism, or Marxism-Leninism, is, then Lenin's continuation of
Marxism beyond the point reached by Marx. For Lenin, basing himself
on Marx but taking the economic, social and political developments of his
own times into account, socialism consists not merely in the public
ownership of the means of production, distribution and exchange, but in
all that *plus* an organization of the State such that every worker can and
must take part in its management; and a cultural revolution giving every
man access to the whole pre-socialist culture and ensuring for all men
and women the opportunity to develop their gifts to the limit of their
capacities.

Liebnecht, Karl (1871–1919) s. of Wilhelm Liebnecht, cofounder with
August Bebel of the German Social-Democratic Party. He became a lawyer
and joined his father's party but early asserted his independence of judgement by criticising the Party's bureaucracy. He made his name by defending revolutionaries on trial in German courts, notably in the trial of
Russian revolutionaries in 1904. He took part in the Second ◊ International Congresses and in 1907 founded the first Socialist Youth movement.
In the same year he published his antimilitarist *Militarismus und Anti-
militarismus*, for which he was arrested, tried and sent to prison for
eighteen months. Elected to the Reichstag in 1912, a year later he exposed
a number of high officials in the Ministry of War for accepting bribes
from Krupp, the armaments manufacturer. On the outbreak of war he
took the same line as ◊ Jaurès, that the Second International resolution
requiring Social Democrats to boycott imperialist war must be taken
seriously, and in December 1914 was the only Reichstag member to refuse
to vote war credits. With Rosa ◊ Luxemburg he fought a long battle with
the SD Party leaders over their support for the war, with her formed the
extreme Left *Gruppe Internationale* in the party, later transforming it into
the ◊ *Spartakusbund*. His revolutionary attitude led to his expulsion from
the SD Party (January 1916). For a few months he served as a private in a
labour battalion, and in May led a demonstration of his followers through
Berlin, protesting against continuance of the imperialist war. Arrested, he
was sentenced to four years hard labour, but was released 22 October 1918.
He had reluctantly concluded that socialism could only be accomplished

by violent revolution: with Luxemburg he transformed the *Spartakusbund* into the German Communist Party and proclaimed (November 1918) a German Socialist Republic in Berlin. Some weeks later he and Luxemburg were murdered by *Freikorps* (ex-army officer right-wing strong arm band) thugs, so that their Republic died at birth. Liebnecht's most important contribution to the body of Marxist literature is *Studies of the Laws of Motion in the Development of Society* (1920).

Lin Piao (1910–71) ed. Whampoa Military Academy, Canton, graduating officer-cadet at sixteen. He fought under ◊ Chou En-lai in defence of the Communist Soviets of the Yangtse Valley when they were attacked by ◊ Chiang-Kai-shek in 1927, and took part in ◊ Mao Tse-tung's Long March (*see* Chinese Revolution 1927–49). He commanded Chinese Red Army troops against the Japanese in Manchuria, and was the organizer of victory over the Kuomintang in the civil war (1945). During the Korean War he commanded the Chinese Red Army 'volunteers' sent to help North Korea against South Korea and its American and European allies. In 1959 he became Minister of Defence of the government of the Chinese People's Republic, and in 1965 backed Mao Tse-tung's cultural revolution, placing the army at its disposal, introducing ◊ guerrilla training, and abolishing all titles of rank. He was subsequently said to be second only to Mao Tse-tung in the hierarchy of the Chinese Communist Party.

In September 1965 he contributed to *The People's Daily* an article in which he first expounded the 'Lin Piao theory of revolution', giving militant expression to ◊ Maoism: 'The countryside and the countryside alone can provide the revolutionary basis from which the revolutionaries can go forward to final victory. Taking the entire globe, if North America and Western Europe can be called the cities of the World, then Asia, Africa and Latin America constitute its rural areas . . . In this stage of the revolution, imperialism and its lackeys are the principal enemy; it is necessary to rally all anti-imperialist patriotic forces including the national bourgeoisie. . . . It is harmful to confuse the two stages, that is the national democratic and the Socialist revolution.' This doctrine has become the rule for all the Asian, African, Latin American Marxist-Leninist movements and ◊ guerrillas. In 1971 Lin Piao died in an aircraft crash in the course of a power struggle in the CCP hierarchy; it is likely that the accident was contrived.

Liquidation

Liquidation. Newspeak for murder of political opponents whether judicial or by means of hired assassins. Derived from the commercial usage – to pay or settle a debt, or to wind-up a company and so terminate its activities. It is not clear whether this word was first used as a euphemism by apologists for ◊ Nazi political murder, by extension from, e.g. 'to liquidate the Jewish question', i.e. by killing all the Jews; or by apologists for Stalinism during the 1936–38 judicial murders of anti-Stalin communists. It has become a common usage for the murderous activities of such political police forces as the Russian GPU, the Gestapo, and the ◊ CIA.

Liu Shao-Chi (1905–   ) b. Hunan, s. of a peasant. A scholarship took him to Moscow at the age of fifteen. At sixteen he became an active revolutionary by joining the Socialist Youth Organization and at seventeen he was a member of the China Labour Union secretariat, and communist trade union organizer for urban areas. Elected to the Central Committee of the Communist Party in 1927, he worked 'underground' for five years. In 1932 he was boss of the Revolutionary Trades Union movement in the Yangtse Valley where ◊ Mao-Tse-tung had established Soviets. From 1936 to 1942 he was again working 'underground', organizing communist cells in Shanghai, Tientsin and Peking. He has held various CP offices – including Vice-Chairman, People's Revolutionary Military Council; Chairman, International Labour Federation; Vice-Chairman, People's Political Consultative Council; and finally, Chairman of the Republic. But in 1966 his attitude to Mao Tse-tung's Cultural Revolution led to an accusation of (Soviet) ◊ Revisionism, and two years later he was removed from his offices excepting his Chairmanship of the Republic, which he lost in 1969.

Lockout. A means used by industrial managements to force workers to accept lower wages and worse conditions than they demand, that is to say of lowering the price of the only commodity which the workers have to offer, their labour. The factory is either closed down or operated by 'blackleg' labour and the workers thus 'locked out'. The lockout was vividly defined by the late H. M. Tomlinson as follows: 'The boss sits down on the stomach of the worker's baby; the outcome depends on which tires first, the boss's bottom or the baby's stomach.' Growth in the strength

158

of the trade union and labour movements has made it very difficult if not impossible to use the lockout, at least in Britain, but it is occasionally still used in continental Europe.

Lumumba, Patrice (1925–61) Congolese patriot whose martyrdom has made him a symbol of African revolution. b. Wembonyana, Kasai province, Belgian Congo (Zaire); ed. for teaching, he felt no vocation for it and entered the civil service as a post office clerk. As a result of covering up for some colleagues, he was sent to prison for two years for embezzlement of post office funds. He joined the Congolese Nationalist Movement and was its President when, in the 1960 elections wrung from the Belgian government by mass demonstrations in which the police killed about fifty people, it won thirty-five seats and thus became the largest party in the Chamber, though a minority. Lumumba negotiated a coalition – he was a brilliant talker – and when independence was conceded, became first prime minister of the Congo Republic. Lumumba was not, by conviction or temperament, a revolutionary, a fact which is very clear from his book, *Congo, My Country*, published posthumously in 1962: he was a moderate nationalist who had originally called for a slow, planned handing over of political and economic responsibility to the Africans and close cooperation with the Belgian authorities and European capital. But the secession of Katanga, contrived by the big money interests behind the Union Minière du Haut Katanga and backed with the force of a mercenary army, resulting in a bloody civil war, pushed him into an increasingly revolutionary attitude (*see* Zaire, Revolution in). His murder at the hands of Moise Tshombe, the Union Minière's ruler of Katanga, with the connivance of Lumumba's chief rival for power, General Mobutu, turned him, ironically, into a martyr of the ◊ New Left revolution.

Luxemburg, Rosa (1870–1919) Polish ◊ Marxist revolutionary, b. Zamoc into a middle-class Jewish trading family. Ed. Warsaw *Gymnazium*, she became a socialist while still at school, and later joined the ◊ 'Proletariat' Marxist party. Threatened with imprisonment for her recruiting activities, she had to leave the country (1889) to join ◊ Plekhanov, Vera Zasulich, Axelrod and other Russian revolutionary exiles in Zürich, where she studied science and received a doctorate for a thesis entitled *Die Industrielle Entwicklung Polens* (1898). She became one of the leaders of the Polish Social-Democratic Party, but although Polish nationalism was a popular cause with Marxists and had, indeed, been the immediate cause of the founding of the First ▷ International, she would have nothing to do with it or with any other nationalism, one of the principal points of socialism being its freedom from such unbrotherly and contemptibly bourgeois shibboleths. This opinion was to bring her into conflict with Lenin over his policy of national self-determination. Deciding that she could be more useful working for the most powerful of all the social-democrat parties, the German, she acquired German citizenship by an expedient marriage, and sprang into international prominence with her eloquent opposition to the ▷ Revisionist doctrine which, like Kautsky, she regarded as a dangerous heresy. When the ▷ Russian Revolution 1905 broke out, she returned to Warsaw to take part in it, was arrested, and spent part of 1906 in prison. Released when her health broke, she returned to Berlin and while teaching in the Social Democratic Party's school, wrote *Die Akkumulation des Kapitals* (1913), one of the most important works of Marxist theory. With Karl ▷ Liebnecht she became leader of the extreme left wing of her party, but there also took her own firm line, first as an advocate of the ▷ general strike as a political weapon, secondly as a forceful opponent of ▷ Lenin's doctrine of the Bolshevik Party as the sovereign agent of the 'dictatorship of the proletariat', which would, in her view, be death to that 'direct democracy' which alone could enable the proletariat to rule. She unhesitatingly denounced the Bolshevik terror of 1918–19. When the ultra-Left of the German S–D Party broke away under her leadership and Liebnecht's to become the ▷ *Spartakusbund*, she wrote its manifesto – *Die Krise der Sozialdemocratie* (1916). Twice imprisoned for openly preaching against the ▷ 'imperialist' war, she continued to write in prison, her articles being smuggled out to be published in the illicit *Spartakusbriefe*. When she was released in 1918 she and Liebnecht transformed *Spartakusbund* into the Communist Party of Germany and Rosa Luxemburg wrote its programme. Its swift growth from 1918 to 1933 would have placed at the disposal of this most brilliant and passionate of all women revolutionaries a very powerful political instrument; had she lived, and Liebnecht lived, it is even probable that the German, rather than the Russian, CP would have taken leadership of the world revolutionary movement, in which case it is unlikely that either Hitler or Stalin would ever have played leading parts in world affairs. But on 15 January

1919, only two months after Liebnecht's proclamation of a German Socialist Republic in Berlin, she and Liebnecht were seized, maltreated and murdered by a gang of the *Freikorps* (ex-army officer right-wing strong-arm band) thugs who were then infesting Germany, and their attempted revolution collapsed. In all the communist martyrology, Luxemburg's is the most attractive figure.

M

Malatesta, Errico (1850–1932) greatest of the Italian anarchist revolutionaries; no connection with the infamous Tyrant of Rimini. b. Naples into a family of landed gentry, he was educated as a physician at Naples University whence he was expelled for republicanism. He joined the anarchists and, on inheriting a family estate, gave it to the tenants while he trained as a skilled electrical fitter. The rest of his long life was devoted to the revolution; he led insurrections in Apulia, travelled as an anarchist agitator in Spain, and founded anarchist groups in Egypt, Syria, Turkey, Greece. He took a leading part in the London Anarchist Congress of 1881, and with another Italian anarchist founded and edited the journal *Insurrezione*. He also founded, Italy 1883, *La Questione Sociale* to counter the influence of the Socialist Party of whose *étatisme* he disapproved.

He was arrested (1884) for belonging to an illegal organization, the ⬦ International; given a three year sentence, but remanded pending appeal, he spent his remand time saving lives, at the risk of his own, in the cholera epidemic which was decimating the Neapolitans (1885). Meanwhile his sentence was confirmed, but he fled to Argentina where he joined the Italian *Circolo Communisto-anarchisto* and founded an Argentine edition of *La Questione Sociale*. To get funds for the revolution, he prospected for gold in Patagonia and found it, but was dispossessed of his claim by a conspiracy between a mining company and bribed officials. He returned to Europe, settled in Nice, was driven out of France by police persecution, and went to London (1889). He settled in Fulham and founded the journal *Associazone*. Two years later he risked attending an Anarchist Congress in Italy and founded the Anarchist-Socialist Revolutionary Party; but the socialist wing soon separated from the parent body, repudiating anarchism, and Malatesta returned to London.

Having all the civilized world for his revolutionary province he was working for the cause in both Spain and Italy in 1894 and 1895, but was back in London for the Congress of the Second International in 1896. When the anarchists were expelled from the International, he returned to

Italy, started another anarchist newspaper, was arrested for subversive activities among the Ancona workers, and sent to prison for six months. Although he was in prison when the anarchist Bresci, revenging the massacre of peacefully demonstrating anarchist workers in Tuscany and Lombardy, assassinated King Umberto, he was sent from prison to a five-year exile on the island of Lampedusa, escaped in a small boat, was picked up by a ship and landed in Malta and went from there to the US. There he was shot at and wounded by an extremist of his own persuasion, and returned to London (1900), where he remained twelve years, serving a prison term for libel for having called a police spy a police spy, returning to Italy in 1913 to settle in Ancona. In 1914 he led the Unione Sindicale Italiana in a general strike which spread into other provinces and, during 'Red Week' (June 1914), nearly developed into a mass revolution; but the Italian equivalent of the TUC predictably ratted, ordering its members back to work, and Malatesta was again forced into exile in London, returning to Italy only in 1919 to found the first anarchist daily, *Umanita Nova*. Again there were vast strikes and occupations of factories by their workers; again the CGL (TUC) lost its nerve and withdrew its support, and Malatesta was arrested. Thwarted and despairing, some of his associates resorted to terrorism; a lot of people were killed in bomb outrages and, as a consequence, Italian anarchism was discredited. What survived was rigorously suppressed by Mussolini's Fascist terror. But, as an untouchable hero of the Italian workers, Malatesta was left in peace until his death at the age of eighty-two.

Mandela, Nelson Rolihala (1918–) South African revolutionary leader, member of the Tembu royal house. ed. Witwatersrand University. Mandela and Oliver Tambu, acting President of the African National Congress (ANC), now in exile, were the first Africans to set up a law firm in South Africa. Joined the ANC, at that time a bourgeois-led reform movement, in 1944; using its militant Youth League he was instrumental in driving the leadership into the radical policies of the 1950s – the 1952 Defiance Campaign, and the 1955 Congress of the People whose Freedom Charter demanded equal political, economic and social rights for all South Africans and nationalization of the natural resources; it was branded as 'socialist' by the right wing. The Suppression of Communism Act enabled the Nationalist government to ban Mandela from normal public life. He was one of the accused in the 1956–61 Treason Trial. Following the banning of the ANC after the Sharpeville massacre in 1960 (*see* South Africa and Rhodesia, Revolution in), Mandela was one of the leaders responsible for the decision that freedom in South Africa could not be won by non-violent means, and the consequential founding of ⟡ *Umkhonto we Sizwe* which organized ⟡ sabotage of government installations from December 1961. In 1962 he went underground, travelling both inside and outside SA. He was arrested (1963) and accused at the so-called Rivonia trial of plotting to overthrow the State by force. In his defence he showed that in SA blacks had either to accept a permanent state of subservience or, after long and patient pacifism, to answer violence with violence. 'I have cherished the ideal of a democratic and free society in which all persons live together in harmony and with equal opportunities. It is an ideal which I hope to live for and achieve. But if need be it is an ideal for which I am prepared to die.' A worldwide outcry saved him from being sentenced to death but he was sent to life imprisonment in the fortress on Robben Island.

Mao Tse-tung (1893–) b. Shaoshanch'ung, Hunan, s. of a prosperous peasant and usurer. He began work on his father's land at five, was taught to read and write by a tutor at seven and became a passionate reader of romantic novels. Revolting against being called lazy by his father and beaten by his teacher, he ran away at ten, but was brought home after three days. At fourteen he was working full time on his father's farm and was married to a girl of eighteen, but later repudiated the marriage on the ground of non-consummation. In 1910 he went to primary school in Hsianghsiang, his mother's native town. It was a year of famine and he is said to have given away money and some of his clothes to the starving. He studied the classics, took against Confucianism, read geography and history, conceived an early distaste for the natural sciences, and read translations of biographies of Napoleon, Peter the Great, Wellington, Washington and Gladstone as well as the writings of the leading Chinese social reformers. Passed the examination into the Middle School in Chang'sha (1911) and when the ⟡ Chinese Revolution 1911 broke out, joined the Republican army led by Chao Heng-ti. When the Revolution triumphed, he left the army (1912), tried for six months to resume school, gave it up and, living on bread and water, spent his time in the Provincial Library reading Adam

Mao Tse-tung

Smith, Darwin, Huxley, Mill, Spencer, Montesquieu and Rousseau, and all the newspapers he could find. He was a student at the First Teachers' Training School in Chang'sha (1913–18).

Though not personally involved in the struggles between the war lords and the outlawed Kuomintang and other factions, whose warfare repeatedly interrupted his studies, he was led by them to conclude: 'If people are weak what is the use of perfecting their virtues? The most important thing is to be strong' (Siao Yu). His first radical thinking was inspired by Friedrich Paulsen's *A System of Ethics*: his copy of the book has 12,000 characters of his marginal notes, in many of which the germs of his future social and political philosophy can be found (Ch'en). In 1917 he formed his first political group, The New Citizens' Society, 'to work and make sacrifices for our country'; and he ran evening classes for workers and shopassistants. In 1918 he graduated and went to Peking, became an assistant in the library of Professor (Political Economy) Li Ta-chao, met most of the men who were to form the 1919 May 4 Movement (*see* below), read ◇ Bakunin, ◇ Kropotkin, ◇ Tolstoi, inclined to anarchism, had a love affair with Yang K'ai-hui, his old teacher's daughter, read and was enthused by Li Ta-chao's articles on the ◇ Bolshevik Revolution, and returned (1919) to Chang'sha as teacher in the Hsiu-yeh Primary School. In May came the 'intellectual revolution' known as the May 4 Movement: leading intellectuals and university students called for the breaking down of the barriers of Confucianism, tradition and superstition to let in modern science, modern humanism and modern technology; and for revolt against Japan's claim, ratified by the Paris Peace Conference, to the former German possessions in Shantung, support for which Japan had bought by huge 'loans' to some of the Chinese warlords in control of the country. On 4 May Peking students staged a gigantic patriotic demonstration, which spread to the whole country. Mao in Chang'sha used his New Citizens Society to form a Students' Union and then called all the students of Hunan out on strike. At the same time he founded and edited the *Hsiang River Review*, soon suppressed by the warlord Governor of Hunan, General Chang Ching-yao. Mao accepted the editorship of the Students' Union weekly, *Hsin Hunan*, and Chang promptly suppressed that. Mao founded a discussion group, and was sent as a delegate of the anti-Japanese (Chang was pro-Japanese) party to Peking to lobby for support of a campaign to get rid of Chang.

Mao Tse-tung

While in Peking he read (in translation; he was a bad linguist) Kirkup's *History of Socialism*; the *Communist Manifesto*; ▷ Engels's *Socialism; Utopian and Scientific*; and Kautsky's *Class Struggle*, and became confirmed in his communism. He went to Shanghai, selling his fur coat to pay the fare, and, working in a laundry, had his first experience as one of the proletariat. In July he returned to Chang'sha as teacher in his old college, during the confusing struggle between rival warlords which finally rid the province of General Chang. Mao took an active part in the movement to give Hunan a measure of autonomy and a democratic government; and at the suggestion of Ts'ai Ho-sen he took a series of steps, beginning with the setting up of numerous socialist bookstalls, towards the foundation of a Communist Party in Hunan. The foundation of a Chinese CP was accomplished in July 1921 by the coming together of a number of provincial foundations similar to his own, at a First Congress of which Mao was elected Secretary. Returned to Chang'sha, where he had by 1923 a group, including two of his brothers, organizing industrial labour unions; another forming a provincial Central Committee of the CP, a third running an association of peasants; and a Communist Youth Movement with 2,000 members. In 1921 he had married his old sweetheart Yang Kai-hui who bore him a son and a daughter. (In 1930 she and her son, and Mao's sister, were arrested by the Governor of Hunan, Ho Chien, and she was required to repudiate her marriage; when she refused both she and her sister-in-law were murdered by Ho's guards; the fate of the boy is uncertain.)

In 1922 the CCP had resolved on a revolutionary alliance with the Kuomintang, though reserving its independence of action, but a year later, under Soviet pressure, accepted a United Front with the Kuomintang which, in practice, meant the subordination of its forces to the supreme command of ▷ Chiang Kai-shek. With a warrant out for his arrest as a 'radical', Mao went to Shanghai, where he attended the Party's 3rd Congress and was elected to the Central Committee. In 1924 he attended the National Congress of the Kuomintang in Canton at which the communists and their Left allies were predominant; its Manifesto was drafted by ▷ Sun Yat-sen's Soviet adviser, ▷ Borodin. Mao was elected a member of the Central Executive Committee, and sent as secretary of the organizing branch of the CCP in Shanghai, where his job was to coordinate CCP and KMT policies; partly because he was despised by the KMT leaders for his humble origins, he failed, and falling ill, was sent (1924–25) to Hunan, where he concentrated on organizing revolution among the peasants.

A new warrant for Mao's arrest was issued by the Governor, again alarmed at Mao's successes among the peasants, and he was forced to leave Hunan for Canton, where he was given charge of a school to train political organizers for the peasant movement, and where he first made friends with ◊ Chou En-lai who was political Commissioner to the KMT First Army. Mao's own courses of lectures were *Problems of the Chinese Peasants*, and *Village Education*, while Chou lectured on *The Peasant Movement and Military Campaigns*. In 1926 Mao became head of a new Peasant Department of the CCP and, after Chiang Kai-shek's reconquest of Hunan from the warlord Chao Heng-ti, he returned to work among the peasants of his native province and published the first of a great many papers on the revolutionary peasant movement, *Analysis of the Classes in Peasant Society*, which he followed with *Report on an Investigation into the Peasant Movement* early in 1927, in which he listed 'Fourteen Deeds' which must be done to accomplish 'Revolution by the Peasants'. They were the blueprint for his political work during the next twenty-two years. Meanwhile the peasants of Hunan were already occupying and sharing the land of the rich landowners, despite the opposition of KMT troops; their movement was paralleled by increasing proletarian unrest in the cities, although the workers' loyalty was more to the socialist-inspired left wing of the Kuomintang than to the CCP.

During all this period the CCP, which by 1927 had 50,000 members, was taking its orders from the USSR, that is from ◊ Stalin who consistently misjudged and misunderstood Chinese conditions; under those orders, the Party exercised extraordinary restraint in submitting to humiliation by the Centre and Right groups of the Kuomintang. ◊ Trotsky, who had not yet been silenced, repeatedly pointed out Stalin's mistakes and called for a China policy which was more nearly what Mao himself envisaged, in his *Fourteen Deeds*. When in mid-1927 Chiang, victorious in the North and feeling his strength, turned on his CCP allies, outlawed the Party, and began that massacre of communists known as the White Terror, the Party was helpless and let itself be decimated. Now *see* ◊ Chinese Revolution 1911–27; and ◊ Chinese Revolution 1927–49 in which Mao Tse-tung and Chu-teh accomplished 'revolution by the peasants', Mao emerged as the virtual master of China, and founded (1949) the Chinese People's Republic: under those heads will be found his achievements as an original political thinker and a superlatively able man of action.

According to Dr Jerome Ch'en, who has published English translations of many of Mao's poems and other papers (*Mao and the Chinese Revolution* and *Mao Papers*, both Oxford University Press), Mao's talent as a poet would have earned him a place in contemporary Chinese literature even had he not been a great man in the political sphere, and that although he writes in the old classical style and does not understand modern poetry. But his prose style is, apparently, very different. He deliberately adopted the modern style as a result of the May 4 Movement in order to make his thinking accessible to as many people as possible, and to facilitate and encourage popular translations of great Western philosophers, economists, historians, novelists and playwrights. Mao has never allowed himself to write the ridiculous jargonized polemics of the second and third-rate Marxist journalists and publicists; perhaps partly because he owes much to his early studies of the classics and partly through the influence of the woman with whom he fell in love in 1939–40, Lan P'ing. She was a film actress who had followed other artists and writers to work in Yenan, and make it a cultural centre. Better known later as Chiang Ch'ing she was Mao's fourth wife (his third died on the Long March: *see* ◊ Chinese Revolution 1927–49), and she introduced him to modern Chinese poetry and the 'new prose' of Hsün. It was between about 1940 and 1945 that Mao Tse-tung formed that style which made his writings such enormously effective instruments of education not only in China, but, because of the directness, penetration and saltiness of his style, among revolutionaries all over the world.

There are considerable differences of opinion about Mao's worth as a political philosopher: a majority of critics regard him as a genuine original and for some of them Maoism is to ◊ Leninism what Leninism was to ◊ Marxism. Others, notably Professor K. A. Wittfogel, believe that while Mao's achievements as a militant revolutionary, a man of action, are of course undeniable, they were inspired by Marxism- ◊ Leninism and not by Mao's own and original interpretation of Marxism-Leninism. The argument turns on the value attributed to his reversal of the Marxist-Leninist axiom that socialist revolution necessarily begins in the cities and is spearheaded by the ◊ proletariat. According to Dr Ch'en, the historians

Hu Ch'iao-mu and Ho Kan-chih say that 'to start the revolution in the countryside by means of armed struggle, establishing bases and increasing their number and size, and then to encircle and subsequently seize the cities' is the 'law' of revolution in China; in other words, that in action as in his poetry Mao Tse-tung is a traditionalist, a classicist. But it could be argued that a revolutionary leader who brings the economic and social benefits of socialism; of relatively stable central government with a right measure of decentralization and democracy; of great power status; and of freedom from foreign domination, to hundreds of millions of people who are heirs to 3,000 years of feudalism, and to do all this in terms which link the revolution culturally to China's greatest traditions, is an achievement so remarkable that there can be no question that Mao Tse-tung must be counted among the half-dozen greatest revolutionaries in history.

The worldwide appeal, especially to the young, of the book of aphorisms known as *Mao's Thoughts*, is also a phenomenon so rare that their author earns a place among the score of men who, in the history of mankind have renewed faith, hope and charity in hundreds of millions.

Maoism. A word coined by Harvard scholars, notably Professors B. Schwartz, J. K. Fairbank and C. Brandt, to describe the theory and practice of revolution by ◇ Mao Tse-tung, Chairman of the Chinese Communist Party during the ◇ Chinese Revolution 1927–49. According to Dr J. Ch'en the term Maoism is not used by Chinese historians: the term they use, *Mao Tse-tung ssu-hsiang* suggests that 'the honour of suffixing *ism* (*chu-i*) to a personal name should be reserved for more original and systematic doctrines such as ◇ Marxism and ◇ Leninism'. A first expression of the theory appears in a letter by Mao from his stronghold between Hunan and Kiangsi to the Party leaders in 1930. Now known by the title *A Single Spark can start a Prairie Fire*, the letter forecast that the Chinese revolution would be accomplished only by 'long and tangled ◇ guerrilla warfare waged by peasant armies establishing Liberated Areas, small at first, but progressively more extensive', and explains how and why such armies, fighting on their home ground, could withstand assault long sustained by much more powerful enemy forces. In this same letter Mao outlined what later came to be known as the ◇ Lin Piao Theory. The important deviation from the orthodox communist theory of revolution contained in this document is the role given to the peasants which is central to Maoism. As now developed, Maoism is more Maoist than Mao, for in his *Revolution in Two Stages* (Foreign Languages Press 1966) he reverts to orthodoxy with: 'Unless it is led by the proletariat the Chinese revolution cannot possibly succeed.' But he does make the point that the Chinese proletariat is largely composed of bankrupted peasants so that it has natural ties with the peasant masses; it should be remembered that this pamphlet, originally entitled *The Chinese Revolution and the Chinese Communist Party* (Yenan 1939) was written with the help of other Central Committee members of the CCP and under Stalinist pressure. The theory expressed in the 1930 letter was put into practice by Mao and his brilliant military colleague ◊ Chu-Teh during the nineteen years of revolutionary warfare and from that experience has come the body of revolutionary rules which, expanded into a revolutionary philosophy in the *Thoughts of Mao Tse-tung*, constitute Maoism. The first rule is that no revolution can succeed without a People's War on the tenants of economic and political power; the war must be in two stages: a nationalist stage in which alliance with the national ◊ bourgeoisie against, e.g., feudal landlordism or foreign ◊ imperialist domination, must be accepted at whatever cost. (In the Chinese case it cost, e.g., the massacre in 1927 of about 50,000 communists by their Kuomintang allies led by ◊ Chiang Kai-shek.) The second stage is the socialist or class war stage. But according to Mao, the Party and the masses need not fear rebellion by the national bourgeoisie, since at the end of stage one they have a powerful state apparatus wholly or partly in their hands; this view, put forward in *Democratic Dictatorship* (1949) is not accepted by the Guevarist Communists (*see* ◊ Guevara) nor, in general, by any of the non-Chinese Marxist-Leninist ◊ New Left revolutionaries, and a too rigid adherence to it cost the Indonesian CP about half-a-million massacred. In the Maoist revolution the people's war must be waged from the countryside so as to isolate the cities, because the cities are controlled by the imperialist enemy and because the peasants, having a totally different economy, feel no kinship with the city way of life. On the other hand the Party, leading the peasants in this people's war, must have strong links with the revolutionary proletariat and intellectuals and, of course, with the city militants, e.g. urban guerrillas. It is a very important tenet of Maoism that a politically-conscious, dedicated and armed people *cannot be defeated*; wars are won by people, not machines; consequently the revolution has, in the long run, nothing to fear from even such mighty technologically advanced imperialist powers as the USA, which cannot possibly sustain innumerable people's wars all over the Third World, at the same time. This idea would appear to be the origin of Che ⬦ Guevara's call for 'many Vietnams'.

Maoism as a revolutionary practice would seem to be appropriate only for countries more or less comparable with China, e.g. some Latin American countries, and some parts of Africa. It is not clear that it can be modified to work in industrially advanced countries like the USA itself, although (*see* ⬦ USA, Revolution In), it is possible to cast the American blacks in the role of Mao's 'peasants'. But philosophical Maoism has a strong appeal for revolutionary students and intellectuals in general: by comparison with the conservative and oppressive state communism of the USSR it appears to be a much 'purer' ideology, and much nearer to humanism in its insistence on the importance of people rather than the Hegelian State (*see* ⬦ Hegel). Its insistence that machines, even H-bombs, cannot beat people offers a release from the frustration of helplessness against the massively armed state, imperialist or communist. In theory, too, it is nearer to the ideas of Lenin's ⬦ cultural revolution – that is to say it offers much less power to the Party bureaucracy than does Russian communism of the sub-Stalinist persuasion, and is therefore more democratic. It should not, however, be taken that official Chinese communism is as Maoist as Maoism: its degree of Maoism would seem to depend on which leader is in the ascendant at a given time and not all Chinese communists are Maoists. It is not even clear that Mao himself is consistently Maoist. For Mao's influence on students and intellectuals, both Chinese and foreign, due to such qualities as his knowledge of the classics, his work as a poet, and his clear and vivid literary style as a prose writer, and, in general his personality as a sympathetic sage, *see* ⬦ Mao Tse-tung.

The 'Cultural revolution' concept entails involving all the people in upgrading their own lives; in decentralization of decision-making and administration; in social and economic self-help and cooperation. This is reflected in the European brand of Maoism: the orthodox communist practice of going to the people as leaders of the ⬦ proletariat, with a fixed dogma, an inflexible means of social and economic analysis, and rigid rules for the means of accomplishing revolution, is rejected. Instead, the Maoist joins the people in their lives and work, at their own level; he listens to their ideas, joins in discussion throwing his weight of knowledge and

Marcuse, Herbert

argument always to the left, but not offering or trying to 'lead', only suggesting action appropriate to the local conditions. His role is that of detonator of the revolutionary bomb, as it were; but the explosion he detonates must be implicit in the revolutionary state of mind of the people at large, and he insists that every individual concerned understand and concur in what is being done.

Marcuse, Herbert (1898–) Marxist- ⟡ Leninist philosopher and teacher. b. Berlin; ed. universities of Berlin and Freiberg. In 1934 he emigrated to the USA and was granted citizenship in 1940, working during those years at the Institute of Social Research of Columbia University. During World War II he served in the Office of Strategic Service of the State Department and remained there until 1950. Russian Institute of Harvard and Columbia Universities, 1951–3; Professor of Philosophy, Brandeis University, 1954–65; Professor of Philosophy at University of California since 1965. His published works include *Reason and Revolution* (1941); *Soviet Marxism* (1958); *The Ethics of Revolution* (1966). He is not really an original revolutionary thinker but appears here as the favourite teacher of the young Marxist-Leninist ⟡ New Left, and such leaders of it as Angela ⟡ Davis, in the USA. His doctrine of the 'alienation' of classes of American society from their society and of individuals from their classes became fashionable in the 1960s.

Marquetalia. Independent 'communist' republic in Colombia (1949–65): *see* Colombia, guerrilla movements in.

Marx, Karl (1818–83) German socialist philosopher and militant revolutionary. b. Trier, Rhineland, s. of a prosperous Jewish lawyer turned Christian; ed. universities of Bonn and Berlin where he read law but also followed other courses including Greek mythology and the history of art. No bookworm, he joined a *Kneippvereine* (tavern club), occasionally got drunk, ran into debt, joined the Poets' Club, most of whose members were revolutionaries, wrote a lot of verse, fought a duel and was wounded. During the summer vacation before his move to Berlin he fell in love with the pretty girl next door, Jenny, daughter of his father's aristocratic German-Scottish friend Ludwig von Westphalen, and the young couple became secretly engaged (1837). At Berlin Marx read law and history under

Eduard Ganz, ♢ Hegel's most brilliant pupil and successor. Conceiving a taste for philosophy he began to read it, wrote a 300-page *Philosophy of Law*, studied English and Italian, conceived a lifelong love of Shakespeare, and continued to write poetry, damaging his health by working all night instead of sleeping. Romantically opposed to Hegelian philosophy, he tried to refute its tenets in a philosophical essay in dialogue (*Cleanthus, the Point of Departure and the Development necessary to Philosophy*): it led him straight into the arms of Hegel and he emerged a Hegelian but with reservations which led him to turn Hegelianism upside down (*see* Marxism). Meanwhile he was a member of the liberal-revolutionary *Doktorklub*, and an habitué of Bettina von Arnin's salon, where he met revolutionaries and reactionaries, artists, poets, soldiers, jurists and statesmen. He became a leading 'Young Hegelian', rejected the master's idealism but adopted his ♢ dialectic. He became locally famous as an aggressive and original thinker, perspicacious, very bold in stating and then answering problems, 'a young lion, a magazine of thoughts, a hive of ideas' (Nicolaievski).

Marx had expected to continue at Berlin or go to Bonn as a lecturer: the advent, with Frederick-William IV, of a reactionary government prevented the appointment but he got his certificate of studies from Berlin; and from Jena, notoriousness for its free-handedness with PhDs, his doctorate. In 1842 he went to Bonn and began a career in revolutionary journalism, with articles on the freedom of the press in the *Rheinische Zeitung*, meanwhile shocking the burgesses by driving in the Sunday carriage parade behind a team of donkeys. His passionate revolutionary zeal and growing erudition made a deep impression on all his acquaintances. He and his friends took over *The Cologne Gazette* and turned it, as *The Rhineish Gazette*, into a revolutionary socialist journal. He made a thorough study of English Chartism and French communism, became managing editor of the paper, began a series of articles attacking the 'romantic-absolutist' nature of the Prussian state, and made the paper an international socialist force to be reckoned with. The government tolerated it, first because its suppression would have raised an outcry among all the German intellectuals, secondly as an ally against Rhineland Roman Catholic clericalism. But on the angry intervention of the ultrareactionary Tsar Nicholas I of Russia, to whose government Prussia was then subservient, the paper was at last prohibited.

In 1843 Marx married Jenny von Westphalen and they moved to Paris where he was to write for and help edit a revolutionary review, the *Franco-German Annals*: only one number appeared; the Prussian government had Marx, the poet Heine, and others connected with the review, convicted *in absentia* for high treason; and their backer withdrew his support. Marx now undertook a thorough study of political economy, familiarized himself with revolutionary movements among the Paris workers, and met such socialist thinkers as ⟫ Blanc and ⟫ Prudhon, and the visiting ⟫ Engels. In 1845 he, with his wife and baby daughter, went to join Engels in Brussels where the two men formed a lifelong friendship of heart and head. He made an exhaustive study of the major political-economic revolutionary writers and, with Engels, wrote *German Ideology*, a critique of romantic revolutionary ideas, not published until 1932. It was in Brussels that he perfected his theory of historical materialism (*see* ⟫ Marxism) while organizing 'correspondence committees' to link Belgian, German, French and English socialists and communists. He wrote and spoke against the sentimental and romantic 'communism' of the kind he abhorred, perfecting a virulent polemic style; and he joined the German revolutionary secret society, the League of the Just, later the Communist League, with the intention of bringing it into the open and giving it a hard, thought-out policy under his new motto 'Proletarians of all countries, unite'. His writings in the *Brussels German Gazette* attacked pseudosentimental and romantic socialists as well as the bourgeois opposition. He had not lost his zest for enjoyment, and took Jenny dancing and to poetry readings and concerts. They were poor and ran into debt and Marx's mother, who never forgave him for not becoming 'my son, the lawyer', refused to hand over his share of what his father had left the family. At last she was forced to release over 6,000 marks (£300 gold pounds) of what she owed him, but he spent most of it on revolutionary activities or in supporting them.

He paid his first visit to London in 1847 as Belgian representative of the Continental Democratic Association at a congress of the British Fraternal Democrats; meanwhile he and Engels, who represented the French branch of the Association, were working on the ⟫ *Communist Manifesto* which was first published in London in ⟫ Eighteen-forty-eight, that year of revolutions sparked off by the civil war in Switzerland (November 1847). Marx took an active part in the Belgian manifestation of the revolution, was accused of using his 6,000 marks to buy arms for the workers of Brussels and, when the government got the upper hand again, expelled under pressure from the Prussian ambassador. He went to Paris where German revolutionary émigrés were raising an armed legion to carry the revolution by force into Germany. Marx condemned this venture as irresponsible and certain to fail. He was elected chairman of the new Anglo-French-German Central Committee of the Communist League whose strength began to grow all over western Europe.

The legion of German revolutionaries having, as Marx had foreseen, been wiped out as soon as it crossed the Rhine, Marx and other serious socialists slipped quietly into Germany, he and Engels making for Cologne. Germans were demanding that their governments introduce radical reforms, many of the demands and demonstrations being organized by the Communist League. In Prussia a democratic Parliamentary constitution was conceded; there was fighting in Cologne, led by the ultra-revolutionary Workers Association; Marx fought hard to prevent these extremists from boycotting the elections which had been granted; he had no use for the ultra-leftism of ▷ Blanqui and other revolutionary romantics and was willing to collaborate with the liberals for the time being. He helped to found a Democratic Association and became its leader; and *The New Rhineish Gazette*, becoming its editor. As soon as the government had gathered its forces, it attacked the revolutionaries, Cologne was besieged and Marx, in his newspaper, called for a boycott of taxes and an armed rising of the proletariat to resist the army, then realized that Germany was not yet ready for this, and urged those workers who had taken up arms to lay them down, and the rest to refrain from a violence which could not hope to succeed. As soon as the government felt strong enough, they took advantage of the fact that he had renounced Prussian citizenship while an émigré and ordered him to leave the country. He published a last, challenging, defiant number of the *Gazette*, printing it in red, and took Jenny (who was expecting her fourth child) and the children to Paris.

There he involved himself at once in the fight against the reaction from the revolution; but he was penniless, was cheated or disappointed in various projects to earn a living by writing, and, finally, ordered to leave France within twenty-four hours. He was refused permission to enter Belgium and Switzerland, for he was now world famous as a leading and formidable revolutionary militant. The Marx family went to England, not intending to remain long; they remained for thirty-four years, the rest of

Marx, Karl

his life. Marx's only income in England came from his regular contributions
as European correspondent to the *New York Tribune*; it was quite inadequate, his earnings from other sources were small and occasional, and
although Engels gave him what he could, often more than he could afford,
out of his salary as a clerk in his father's Manchester branch, the family
were reduced to the most grinding poverty, often starving, living in two
rooms in a slum, their few sticks of furniture seized for miserably small
debts to tradesmen. Nevertheless, Marx worked grimly on, keeping in
touch with the revolutionary movements, taking part in English working-
men's associations, and reading and writing at the British Museum where
he completed the first volume of his masterpiece, *Das Kapital*, and the
preparation of the enormous bulk of notes for the other two volumes
which Engels was to complete after his death. There were times of happiness despite poverty; Marx adored his children who called him 'Old Nick',
or 'the Moor', loved to walk them to Hampstead and play with them, read
with them, take them to see Shakespeare at the theatre where they had to
stand, not being able to afford seats. And he enjoyed sitting up half the
night, drinking and talking with friends, when there were a few shillings
in the house to spend on such luxuries.

His writing was not his only contribution to the coming revolution: he
helped the founders of the International Association of Working-men,
later known simply as the ⟡ International and worked for it, especially to
keep it out of the hands of the mere liberals, on the one hand, and of the
anarchists led by Bakunin on the other. Poverty and overwork took a
terrible toll of the whole family: two of the children died; Jenny's health
broke down, and Marx himself was often too ill to work. But when Engels
inherited the English branch of his father's firm in Manchester, he was
able to make the Marxes a substantial and regular allowance so that Marx
could get on with his real work; and Marx received another instalment of
his inheritance, when his mother died; this paid their debts and enabled
them to move into a decent small house.

His last great struggles in practical politics were with Bakunin for control
of the International; and to save the Paris ⟡ Commune from foundering in
chaos. In both he failed, knowing that he must. Near the end of his life he
gave a great deal of attention to Russia, forecasting the communist revolution but for a date much earlier than the event. He had come to understand
the English working class and British institutions, and believed that

Britain would be the only country which might attain communism without passing through a violent revolution. He took a great interest in his grandchildren, his daughter Jenny Longuet's children, and sometimes went to Paris to see them; he half-jokingly deplored that they were girls, for he foresaw clearly a century of war and revolution and knew that men would be needed. But the twilight of his life was grim: his wife had cancer, and he was repeatedly attacked by pleurisy or pneumonia. In 1881 Jenny Marx died, and he never recovered from his grief. He was in the Isle of Wight, suffering from another attack of pleurisy, when he received his deathblow: Jenny Longuet had died suddenly in Paris. He returned to London, took to his bed, refused to eat or speak, and on 14 March 1883 died of what was described as an abscess on the lungs.

Marx's influence and that of Marxism – not the same thing, for, as he himself once said, 'Whatever I may be, I am surely not a Marxist' – have been paramount on all the working-class and revolutionary movements of the twentieth century. They have been hardly less so on the development of capitalism, for their existence as an economic and political force have driven capitalists and capitalist states to concede not only higher and higher wages, but working conditions which go some way to meet socialist demands. For hundreds of millions of people he has become a myth, either an incarnation of Satan or the prophet of that ultimate social and political peace which is to follow the dictatorship of the proletariat which will make possible that withering away of the state which, like the anarchists, Marx saw as the final, if very remote, good.

Marxism. Particularly, the philosophy of history, economic theory and revolutionary programme of Karl ◊ Marx; generally, communist doctrine, based on those writings, but variously interpreted by such active communist revolutionary leaders as ◊ Lenin, ◊ Trotsky, ◊ Mao Tse-tung, Fidel ◊ Castro and others; and by pure theorists such as Karl ◊ Kautsky, Rosa ◊ Luxemburg and others. The basis of philosophical Marxism is dialectical materialism. ◊ Dialectic is the system of persuasive argument developed by ancient Greek philosophers and often given expression, e.g. by Plato, in the form of dialogue. It was used, in an historical context, by the nineteenth-century German philosopher ◊ Hegel who presented history as a process of evolving practical manifestations of developing 'ideas', thesis taking form as event and giving rise to antithesis, also taking form as event, until the emergence, from time to time, of synthesis, that synthesis resolving practical problems but giving rise to others. Marxism makes use of the dialectic concept but denies any positive role to ideals. Material events develop out of each other dialectically (hence 'dialectic materialism') and give rise to ideas; so that there is an analogue with that psychological process called 'rationalization'. In Marx's own words, his method is 'inclusion in the positive understanding of existing things, understanding of the negative implications of their necessary termination'. Applied to historical analysis ('historical materialism'), thesis and antithesis in the dialectic become event and anti-event, institution and anti-institution, establishment and anti-establishment. That is to say that all historical forces generate their opposites; e.g. a feudal society generates a ⟡ bourgeoisie ultimately hostile to it and obliged to overthrow it; and a capitalist society arising out of that bourgeoisie generates a ⟡ proletariat to serve it, but bound in the long run to destroy and replace it.

As a revolutionary theory, then, Marxism calls on the proletariat to recognize its 'historical necessity', arise and seize control of the state from the bourgeoisie, and establish the 'dictatorship of the proletariat'. But it must use sensible tactics. In Marx's own words, 'The proletariat must march forward with the great democratic army, as the extreme point of its left wing, but being careful always to maintain its connection with the main body of the army. It must be the most impetuous in attack and its fighting spirit animate the army assaulting the Bastille . . . The proletariat has no right to isolate itself.' Only when the bourgeoisie is already the tenant of political power, must the proletariat attack it, turning against it its own social and political conditions. Thus, in the earlier part of Marx's own lifetime, whereas in Germany and Russia the proletariat had to be the militant *ally* of the middle class against absolutism, in Britain and France its enemy was already the bourgeoisie whose own parliamentary institutions should be turned against it, and armed force resorted to only when a sufficiently considerable majority of the proletariat having been awakened to their destiny and historical duty by communist teaching and leadership, there was a real chance of the revolution succeeding against the armed force of the government in power.

Although Marxism holds the interest of the proletariat of all countries to be identical, the enemy being always the absolute monarch or the bourgeoisie, regardless of nationality, international war should be welcomed if it advances the revolutionary cause, e.g. if it be between an extreme reactionary country and a more liberal one.

The economic content of Marxism cannot be resumed in a short article: Marx sought to show, using historical materialism, that in any case, capitalism carried within itself the seeds of its own decay. Some socialists have argued that in that case the revolution is not necessary, one has only to wait. But Marxism holds the revolution to be necessary to forestall and prevent the appalling misery of the masses which must be entailed by that process of decay. For the only source of wealth is labour, but the 'surplus value' created by labour is appropriated by the bourgeoisie in the form of interest, rent and profit. Concentration of capital in fewer and fewer hands as the richer capitalists absorbed the less rich would diminish the number of 'haves' and increase that of the 'have nots'. Some of these aspects of Marxism had to be modified by Lenin (see Marxism- ▷ Leninism) because Marx foresaw a constant lowering of working class living standards as a result of this process; he underestimated the amount of 'surplus value' which highly mechanized, scientific industry would produce and which made higher and higher living standards possible.

In its original form Marxism called for the expropriation of the land and the application of rent to State expenditure; similar treatment of the means of production, distribution and exchange; abolition of the right to inheritance; nationalization of the banks to centralize the control of credit in the hands of the State; abolition of child labour and state education for all; and the duty of all to work: *see also* Anarchism; Communism; Leninism Socialism; Syndicalism; Marxism-Leninism.

Mau Mau. A secret revolutionary society which operated in Kenya 1952–59, using terrorism in an effort to overthrow the white government and establishment of Kenya and its black allies, and bring the country under independent native rule. Its members were predominantly Kikuyu, but also Meru and Embu tribesmen who were bound to secrecy and obedience by oaths administered with a barbarous but impressive ritual. The society maintained a campaign of terrorist murder accompanied by horrifying mutilation, the crushing of which involved a major operation by British military forces. In so far as most of its members had any positive aims whatever, they were no more than the ridding of the country of whites, restoration of the White Highlands, the best farmland in Kenya,

Mazzini, Giuseppe

to the blacks, and return to tribalism. The society had no social revolutionary content. But Mau Mau was made use of by more sophisticated black
politicians and its supposed leader was Jomo Kenyatta (b. 1893) who was
imprisoned 1953–59, became President of the Kenya African National
Union 1961, Prime Minister of Kenya 1963, and President of the Republic
of Kenya 1964.

Mazzini, Giuseppe (1805–72) Italian nationalist revolutionary. b. Genoa,
Italy, s. of a doctor. In the early 1820s he joined the Carbonari ('Charcoal-
burners': they used charcoal and coal shops as cover), a secret society
dedicated to overthrowing the Neapolitan Bourbons, and other princely
governments, and to uniting all Italy in a republic. The society managed
to provoke a number of insurrections which were shortlived and accomplished nothing, and Mazzini, disgusted with its ineptitude, formed his
own 'Young Italy' movement which absorbed the best elements of the
Carbonari. His object was a united republican Italy based firmly on the
highest Christian ethics, but completely secular. From this movement he
tried to develop a broader 'Young Europe' movement for a union of
sternly secular but highly moral European republics. In 1848 (⟡ Eighteen-
forty-eight) he led a rising which liberated Milan, and then, with ⟡
Garibaldi in command of the revolutionary force, set up the Roman
Republic (1848). But as Garibaldi and his ablest ally, Cavour, who proved
successful, favoured uniting Italy under the royal house of Savoy while
Mazzini remained obstinately a republican, the great Genoese revolutionary was forced to live in exile, although he did manage his wish to die in
Italy. A man of the noblest vision and highest principles, Mazzini was
nevertheless prepared to use and justify the assassination of kings and
tyrants: a letter which he wrote to Daniele Manin (1865), begins, 'Holy
in the hand of Judith is the sword which cut off the head of Holofernes ...'
It includes a passage in the form of an address to a tyrant in which will
be found his justification: 'You torture millions of my brothers, you
withhold from them that which God has decreed is theirs, you destroy their
bodies and corrupt their souls; through you my country is dying a lingering
death; you are the keystone of an entire edifice of slavery, dishonour and
vice; I overthrow the edifice by destroying you.'

Although Mazzini's life ended just before the hundred years with which
this book is concerned, such was his influence on the next generation of

revolutionaries, not only in Europe but in the USA, that it is impossible to exclude him.

Menshevik, Menshevism: *see* Bolshevik.

MIR: *Movimento de Izquierda Revolucionaria* (Movement of the Revolutionary Left). Two Latin American movements bear this name: it is (1) a socialist party founded from a leftist breakaway from the Venezuelan political party Accion Democratica and deeply involved with the militant ◊ guerrilla groups; and (2) a revolutionary group founded from the left-wing of the Peruvian APRA party by the ◊ guerrilla leader ◊ Unceda: *see also* Peru *and* Venezuela; guerrilla movements in.

MOEC: Movimento de Obreros, Estudiante, y Campesinos. Guerrilla movement: *see* Colombia.

Moleiro, Moses. Founder and first leader of the Venezuelan revolutionary party ◊ MIR.

Mondlane, Eduardo (1921–69) Mozambique revolutionary leader. ed. universities in South Africa, Portugal and USA. Professor of Sociology at Syracuse University NY; served as a UN official. He became President of the Mozambique Liberation Front, FRELIMO, formed Dar-es-Salaam 1962, which by 1967 had a fighting force of 15,000 and had liberated one-fifth of the country. Author of *The Struggle for Mozambique* (1969). He was assassinated, probably, by Portuguese secret police (PIDE) agents at Dar-es-Salaam 3 February 1969: *see* Portuguese Africa, revolution in.

Monimambu, Spartacus (193?–   ) Angolan revolutionary leader commanding the military wing of MPLA: *see* Portuguese Africa, revolution in.

Montes, Cesar (1942–   ): *see* Guatemala, guerrilla movements.

Montoneros. Argentine ◊ guerrilla revolutionary group comparable with the Uruguayan ◊ Tupamaros and the USA ◊ Weathermen. It is composed of young men and women chiefly of the middle class but with some militant trade unionist members, dedicated to the defeat of authoritarian and military government in Argentina, and of US 'imperialism'. The members are organized in cells of up to twelve *companeros* who, until they become known to the police, continue their ordinary work and lives, but at the same time receive political and military training for revolution. Funds for buying arms, and printing propaganda, are obtained by armed bank robberies, some of which have been spectacularly successful. The politics of the group can best be described as Peronism modified by communism, an idealized ⧫ Peron serving as a catalyst to enable orthodox ⧫ Marxists, ⧫ Trotskyists, ⧫ Maoists, Nationalists, etc., to work together. The most spectacular feat of the Montoneros to date was the arrest, trial before a People's Court, and execution of ex-President Pedro Eugenio Aramburu, on nine charges of 'murder', four of which they claim he admitted.

Morris, William (1834–96) English socialist, originator of Guild Socialism, ed. Marlborough and Oxford. He became a socialist by way of his own successful attempts to beautify the design of domestic furnishings and articles of daily use and in general the practice of manual craftsmanship. Consequently his socialism is tainted with an unrealistic medievalism. As a designer and printer he was admirable; his wallpapers, and his Kelmscott Press editions are excellent; as painter and poet he was merely competent. He believed that capitalism was evil because it condemned the workers to a sterile concentration on mere money. The solution was the means of production to be owned in common and all men to become worker-craftsmen whose production would replace that of machine industry. His principal socialist writings are *The Dream of John Ball* and *News from Nowhere, see* Utopia. His Guild Socialism was developed as a manifestation of Syndicalism by G. D. H. Cole.

Mosley, Sir Oswald (1896–   ) 6th baronet. Founder and leader of a Right-wing revolutionary movement based on the model of Italian ⧫ Fascism but with some ⧫ Nazi elements, e.g. antisemitism. It was originally called the British Fascist Party and its members wore the Italian blackshirt uniform. The movement was dedicated to the overthrow of democracy in Britain. Mosley spent World War II in prison under Regulation 18B, as a potential ally of Britain's enemies. He revived his movement in 1948 but it has had no popular success.

Most, Johann (*c.* 1848–?). German social-democratic member of the Reichstag whose inflammatory revolutionary speeches and anarchist propensities resulted in his expulsion from the party, and thereafter made it necessary for him to leave Germany. In 1879 he arrived in London where, until 1883, he published and edited the violently revolutionary *Die Freiheit*. Revolutionary violence became, for him, not a mere means but an end in itself, and in 1881 his editorial applauding the assassination of the Tsar Alexander II resulted in his imprisonment on a conviction of seditious libel. While he was serving his term his successor printed an editorial congratulating the Irish Invincibles for the assassination of T. H. Burke and Lord Frederick Cavendish – the notorious Phoenix Park murders – and the paper was suppressed. On release in 1883 Most went to New York and refounded *Die Freiheit* to advocate every kind of violence in the fight to overthrow capitalism and install an anarchist-communist regime in its place. He gained an enormous influence over both native American and immigrant revolutionary anarchists and was largely responsible for the call to violence culminating in ◊ Chicago May Day Massacre of 1886. His chief claim to immortality as a revolutionary is his pamphlet *Revolutionare Kriegswissenschaft*; in order to be able to write it he obtained work, under a false name, in a Jersey City explosives factory; the pamphlet is a handbook dealing with the making of bombs, the do-it-yourself confection of nitroglycerine, burglary, arson and the use of poisons, for the revolutionary cause. Of all the nineteenth-century revolutionaries, only ◊ Nechayev exceeded Most in the advocacy of destructive violence against the Establishment.

Movimento de Izquierda Revolucionaria: *see* MIR.

Movimento de Obreros, Estudiante, y Campesinos *see* MOEC

MPLA: *see* Portuguese Africa, revolution in.

MR 13: Movimento Revolucionario 13 de Noviembre. A ◊ guerrilla movement in Guatemala; at one time ◊ Trotskyist, it broke away from the Fourth (Trotskyist) ◊ International. Has sometimes operated alone, sometimes in alliance with ◊ FAR: *see* Guatemala: guerrilla movements.

Mussolini, Benito (1883–1945) Founder of ⋄ Fascism. b. near Forli in the Romagna, Italy, and named Benito after the Mexican liberator Benito ⋄ Juarez by his blacksmith father and schoolteacher mother, he taught school for a year after leaving school, then fled to Switzerland to evade military service. There he worked as a labourer, met socialist exiles, read socialist theory and was converted to the ⋄ syndicalism of ⋄ Sorel. Returning to Italy in 1904, he earned his living by socialist journalism and for eleven years was an active member of the Italian Socialist Party. But having ceased to be a pacifist, he rejected the party's pacifism, resigned, joined the army and was wounded in action on the Austrian front. After demobilization he went to Milan as editor of the socialist newspaper *Il Popolo d'Italia* and to organize *fasci* (from the Latin *fasces*, bundles; the rods and axe symbol of office of the Roman consuls) of workers to agitate for social and political reforms. But he had so changed his views on how to accomplish these reforms that when he united his *fasci* into the Fascist Party (1919), his policies for it were nationalistic-patriotic, anti-communist and anti-democratic; his aim became to make Italy a corporate state on syndicalist lines but authoritarian. He formed a Fascist militia who wore black shirts, breeches and boots, and behaved like hooligans, breaking up political meetings of their opponents and beating up communists and socialists. They used the ancient Roman military salute, glorified war, and used a flashy ritual devised for them by the poet D'Annunzio.

The state of semi-revolution and incipient war prevailing in Italy in 1921, and socialist successes in the industrial north where workers were taking over the factories, forming ⋄ Soviets, and running them without ⋄ bourgeois management, so terrified the ruling classes that King Victor Emmanuel III invited Mussolini to become prime minister of a Fascist and Nationalist government – the story of a heroic 'March on Rome' is a myth. Mussolini accepted, called himself *Duce*, leader, initiated a reign of terror against the left, dealt with opponents by having them beaten up, dosed with castor oil, banished to penal colonies, or, in the case of the socialist deputy Mattiotti who dared to defy him, murdered; and emerged as Dictator. He abolished parliamentary democracy, freedom of speech and of the press, ruling through a Fascist Grand Council of ministers, and a National Council of Corporations. His principal instruments were his Fascist militia and the secret police and his principal aim to make Italy a great military and imperial power. He invaded Ethiopia and annexed it in

1935, was forced out of the League of Nations, chiefly by Britain and France, as a result, and in 1936 formed the 'Rome-Berlin Axis' of mutual aid between Italy and ⟐ Hitler's Germany. In the same year he gave massive military support to ⟐ Franco in the Spanish Civil War. He annexed Albania in 1939 but held back from joining in World War II until sure that Germany would win; in June 1940 he declared war on France, following her defeat, and on Britain. That was his zenith: when he invaded Greece, October 1940, his armies were defeated, as they were by the British in Libya and East Africa. By mid-1941 he was kept in power only by ⟐ Nazi German support. Two years passed before the King and Badoglio, C-in-C Italian Armed Forces, supported by a majority of the Fascist Grand Council including Mussolini's son-in-law Count Ciano (whom he later had shot), arrested and imprisoned him.

Rescued by a German parachute commando, he was set up as head of a puppet republican Fascist government in northern Italy. Threatened by the Anglo-American advance up Italy, he made for refuge, with his mistress, in Switzerland, was caught on the way by Italian socialist partisans, shot, and his body hung by the feet in the Piazza Loreto in Milan, exposed to the hatred and derision of the mob he had cowed for twenty years.

Mussolini's positive achievements were in public works, including Europe's first motorways, and the Lateran treaty with the Vatican. His repudiation of his revolutionary past and success in suppressing left-wing working-class and intelligentsia movements made him the hero of the ⟐ bourgeoisie everywhere, including Britain. But his reckless bellicosity, ⟐ imperialist adventures, and chauvinistic bombast alienated their affections.

N

Narodnik movement. Russian revolutionary movement active from a little before 1873 to 1876. The name is derived from the nature of the activity of its early, mostly student, adherents (*narodniki*): 'going to the people', i.e. *khozhdeniye v narod*. Like other revolutionary movements in Russia before the rise of the ▷ Marxist parties (Bolshevik and Menshevik social-democrats), the Narodnik movement was a derivative of ▷ Nihilism, but at first a gentle one. Students and other intellectuals – the Russian word *intelligentsia* derives from this period – grew to feel that they were under an obligation to the Russian peasants who produced the nation's wealth and paid more than 90 per cent of its taxes. They must, therefore, do something for these miserably poor illiterates. What they did was to 'go to' them with teaching and preaching socialism as a means to a just society and better living. The first Narodniks were the Chaykovskyists, named after one of their leaders. From 1873 students of both sexes, alone or in small groups, went to live among the peasants, dressing, eating and sleeping as peasants, often practising some manual trade, and preaching socialism. The peasants failed to understand what they were talking about and usually mistrusted them, and the Narodniks made very little impression. After 1876 those Narodniks really dedicated to gentle means continued in their course under the name of Lavrovists, after a theorist of the movement; others turned to Bakunist anarchism (▷ Bakunin), that is to preaching and practising violent revolution including the use of assassination. In 1877 revolutionaries of the latter persuasion succeeded in provoking an armed rising of some thousands of peasants in the Chigirin region near Kiev. It was put down by the military with savage brutality. There were widespread arrests of Narodniks and anarchists, and the Narodnik movement ended with the 'trial of the 193' (St Petersburg 1877) which, however, the accused managed to convert into a forum for their ideas, one of their number, Ippolit Myshkin, earning fame by his denunciation of the court: 'This is no trial but a farce or something worse: more revolting and shameful than a brothel where a woman sells her body because she is poor.

Whereas here judges, out of base slavishness, for the sake of promotion and high pay, trade away other people's lives, truth and justice.' Some of the Narodniks were acquitted, among them the Chaykovskyist Sophia ◊ Perovskaya who became a terrorist, organizer of the assassination of the Tsar Alexander II.

Nasser, Gamal Abdul (1918–70) b. Cairo; ed. Cairo Military Academy, becoming a professional army officer. In his early twenties Nasser became a revolutionary, dedicated to the overthrow of the Egyptian monarchy, to the removal of British forces from the Suez Canal Zone, and to the establishment of a socialist administration in Egypt and, more ambitiously, throughout the Dar-al-Islam. His particular objections were to the concentration of the greater part of the Egyptian agricultural land in the hands of a very few rich men and the government's failure to develop the country's resources, so that the *fellahin* (peasants) were not much better off than they had been during the past four thousand years of Egyptian history. He did not, however, join any revolutionary movement but, in 1948, after fighting in the campaign in which Israel defeated an Egyptian invasion, a defeat for which he blamed the government's ineptitude, he formed the Free Officers Movement which co-opted General Mahomed Neguib, the only senior officer of any reputation in the Egyptian army, as leader. In 1952 the movement had become strong enough for Nasser to mount a coup d'état, force the abdication of King Farouk, install Neguib as chief of state, and make himself Deputy Prime Minister and Minister for the Armed Forces.

Neguib was no revolutionary: it is not clear whether he really wanted a return to parliamentary government, or to establish a ◊ bourgeois nationalist dictatorship. Nasser and his young leftist officers were determined to introduce socialist measures before returning to parliamentary government. They therefore removed Neguib from office and installed Nasser, first as Prime Minister, with a Committee acting as President; and, in 1956, as President with virtually dictatorial powers.

His social and economic reforms included abolition of titles; increase of taxes in order to balance the budget; redistribution of the agricultural land with a relatively low limit on the size of holdings; the setting up of a National Production Promotion Council to improve agricultural methods and establish industries; severe penalization of corruption in public life;

introduction of improved social welfare schemes; suppression of the extreme right-wing Muslim Brotherhood; emancipation of the Suez Canal from foreign control by nationalization (the subsequent closure of the canal was a byproduct of war with Israel, and beside the point in this context); and the building of the Nile High Dam to irrigate a vast area of land and to generate electrical energy. This dam was originally to have been built with the financial help of the World Bank, but that help depended on contributions to be made by the USA and the UK. When Nasser concluded a deal with Czechoslovakia to supply Egypt with arms those contributions were withdrawn; and the dam was built with the help of the USSR.

In 1956, following the nationalization of the Suez Canal, Britain, France and Israel attacked Egypt. These operations were halted by the intervention of the United Nations Organization, strongly supported by both the USA and the USSR; and thereafter, until its closure during a later phase of the Israeli–Egyptian war, the canal was operated by Egypt.

In 1958, after negotiations with Syria, Nasser united the two countries under his Presidency as the United Arab Republic, but following a coup d'état in Syria three years later, Syria withdrew from this union; the new name, however, was continued and remains the correct name for what, in history, is known as Egypt.

Despite aid, chiefly military, from the USSR, the state of almost perpetual war with Israel, punctuated by humiliating defeats, and conservative Muslim distrust of socialism and communism, greatly retarded Nasser's social revolution. Furthermore Nasser gravely handicapped himself in the work of introducing effective social and economic reforms in Egypt by expending energy and financial resources on waging war against the royalists in the Yemen, in support of the left-wing revolution there; and on unrealistic attempts to realize a Pan–Arab, socialist federation; these undertakings distracted his attention from domestic evils.

When he died suddenly of a heart attack in 1970 the grief of the Egyptian people was as spectacular as it was genuine. Just what his revolution effected is not yet clear, but very few revolutionary leaders accomplished so much with so little suffering to their own people.

Nationalism. Political doctrine which requires the political state and the 'nation' to be coextensive within recognized geographical frontiers; that is to say, the 'nation' must enjoy self-determination and self-government, and not be governed from outside its frontiers by, for example an imperial power, whether colonialist (e.g. Britain during her century of empire); military-political (e.g. the USSR today); 'feudal' (e.g. the Habsburg Empire or the Ottoman Empire until 1918); or imperial-capitalist (e.g. the USA today). In this context, which has also usually been the revolutionary context, 'nation' cannot be defined as the *Oxford English Dictionary* defines it for general practical purposes, since that definition, in order to cover such concepts as 'the British nation' allows for the coexistence of diverse 'races' within one nation, and is invalidated by the very existence of, e.g. 'Welsh nationalism' or 'Breton nationalism'. An acceptable modification of the *OED* definition might be: *A congeries of peoples, ethnically of like or common descent and having a distinctive language and history in common, living or aspiring to live within a defined and preferably recognized geographical limit.* But even if that be acceptable there are reservations so important that in modern times the problem has often been to define what is meant by 'nation'. The Serbs and Croats are of common descent but have mutually hostile 'nationalisms' based chiefly on religious differences, while in Africa common descent is often less important than tribal history; or, in Latin America, than political history. On the other hand, common descent and language (albeit dead until artificially reanimated) and religion have, in special cases, been of more weight than any other factor: e.g. in the 'nation' of Israel Europeans and Americans of the most sophisticated Western cultures are combined with illiterate Yemeni Bedouin.

The assertion, often by long-sustained violence entailing much suffering and self-sacrifice for the nationalist, of a particular 'nationalism' can be justified on purely rational grounds only where it is accompanied by a measure of social revolution: the separation of a national group from a larger political unit – e.g. the Greeks or Wallachians from the Ottoman Empire, the Czechs from the Austrian Empire, the Kenyans from the British Empire, may very well confer no economic advantage on the ordinary people of the new nation; since small economic units tend to be less efficient economically, or rather less viable, than large ones, these people may even be worse off. But there are other equally important considerations. In the relationship between an imperial power and its colonial dominions there is always a greater or less element of exploitation; transfer of power from the hands of the imperial power to those of the natives substitutes for this direct exploitation a contract between foreign capitalists and the new national government which, even though it does not entail the economic liberation of the people, is both less inequitable than direct exploitation and very much less humiliating. The former imperial (still ▷ 'imperialist') powers practising direct exploitation in their colonies could and did remove from the colony in question its wealth, e.g. in oil: since the establishment of the new 'emergent' nations of Asia and Africa as a result of the triumph of nationalist revolutions, the foreign capitalist's share of the oil revenues (or revenues from other sources of wealth) has been steadily reduced, that of the oil-producing nations steadily increased. And in some cases the ordinary people have benefited from this measure of redistribution, e.g. where the wealth from oil has been spent on welfare, and in general because more money is circulating, more goods being imported for workers with wages increased as a result of increased industrial investment and activity. 'Revolution', in the sense which this *Dictionary* has adopted, only occurs when nationalist and social revolution occur together; but at least a nationalist revolution, like bourgeois revolutions in the old European regime, are a step in the revolutionary direction.

Thus, nationalism has had an important role in the context of twentieth-century ▷ Marxist revolution. Although ▷ Marx himself, and all correct Marxists, inherited and valued the international, and, indeed, anti-national, traditions of socialist theory, as also did the anarchist and ▷ syndicalist revolutionaries, social democrats and communists.

Communists found it expedient to favour nationalist struggles for 'self-determination', first from the great 'feudal-type' empires within Europe, and later against the colonial empires, finally against 'dollar-imperialism'. There were a number of reasons for this: (1) Socialism was by long tradition committed to the idea of 'liberty'; and national self-determination, even if in practice it entail a ▷ Fascist dictatorship, is conceived of as a form of liberty. (2) Certain forms of socialism, e.g. anarchism, always favoured a loose, voluntary federation of 'national' groups rather than a strongly centralized socialist 'empire' (cf. Trotskyism as against Stalinism). (3) Nationalist struggles within a great bourgeois-capitalist or feudal-type empire weakened the imperial ruling classes both politically and economically, and so tended to produce a 'revolutionary' situation. (4) Assertions of national independence reduce the element of exploitation by capitalist imperialism.

On the triumph of the Russian (Bolshevik) Revolution (October 1917) there was, as a consequence of this Marxist approval of nationalism, much talk and parade of self-determination for the minority 'nationalities'; and, indeed, the Russian empire was divided by the communists into a number of theoretically autonomous Soviet Republics. But attempts made by those republics to assert their independence of the central Muscovite power were as ruthlessly suppressed as were those, a century ago, of the Southern States of the USA, by the central power in Washington, to secede.

Support for particular nationalism by revolutionaries remains, in our own time, a means of weakening the power of 'imperialism' (in its Leninist sense, the 'last phase of capitalism'); and it may also be used by the capitalist-imperialist as a weapon against communist-imperialism. What remains the only certainty is that, excepting in the very unlikely event of a final triumph of anarchist ideas over the other forms of revolutionary socialism and over industrial internationalism ('imperialism'), nationalism, even in its pure, ideal form is obsolescent.

Nazi. Vernacular and originally derisory contraction of the name Nazional Sozialist, the political party led by Adolf ⬦ Hitler which ruled Germany 1933–44. The first popular contraction was Nazi-Sozi. By the time this had been shortened to Nazi the Germans, and most other Europeans, were no longer laughing. Originally the party had, in its composition and policy, both nationalist and socialist elements.

Nechayev, Sergei (d. 1882) Russian anarchist revolutionary charlatan, s. of a house serf, self-educated. As member of a revolutionary students' group (1868) he gained ascendancy by boasting that he had been imprisoned in the Peter-and-Paul fortress and made a spectacular escape. Before these lies were exposed he had fled to Geneva where, with the same tale and a claim to be delegate of a secret revolutionary conspiracy in Russia, he gained the same ascendancy in revolutionary Russian émigrés circles and was taken up (1869) by ⬦ Bakunin, despite the fact that his stories were patently false. He helped Bakunin with his pamphleteering and wrote a remarkable pamphlet himself: *The* ⟡ *Revolutionary Catechism*. Bakunin sent him back to Russia (1869) as a delegate of the anarchist Alliance (*see* Bakunin), and he there represented himself among revolutionary students as the emissary of a vast secret revolutionary committee which must be obeyed without question. Challenged by one Ivanov as a liar and charlatan, Nechayev strangled the man and again fled to Switzerland where Bakunin, although informed of this atrocious story, welcomed him into his house. Bakunin was desperately short of money. Some Russian students trying to help him persuaded a publisher to commission from him a Russian translation of *Das Kapital*, the contract being made (Bakunin having no civil status), in the name of one of the students, Lyubavin. When Bakunin, bored with the work (he completed only thirty pages), wanted to get out of it without returning the fee, Nechayev, pretending to speak in the name of a secret revolutionary society, accused Lyubavin of deliberately exploiting Bakunin and taking him away from his really important work, and threatened 'less civilized' action should he require Bakunin to return the fee. Lyubavin complained to Bakunin who said he knew nothing about all this and promised to repay the money for which Lyubavin was legally liable: he never kept that promise. On parting with Bakunin Nechayev lived in London, Paris and Zürich, chiefly by blackmailing revolutionary exiles who had any money with the threat of denouncing them to the police; on at least one occasion he 'planted' compromising papers on an exile who had defied him, and caused his arrest, imprisonment and death. In 1872 while in Zürich Nechayev was himself denounced to the authorities by a Polish 'revolutionary' who was actually an informer. Arrested, he was extradited to Russia as a common law criminal and there sentenced to twenty years in the Siberian salt-mines. But while held in the Peter-and-Paul fortress he suborned his guards, got in touch with revolutionary groups, and elaborated a plan for seizing the fortress and releasing all the prisoners. Informed on by a fellow-prisoner, he was put into absolute solitary confinement on a diet which resulted in scurvy of which he died. His principle doctrines as a revolutionary were two: revolutionary ends are justified by absolutely any means whatsoever without exception; and (cf. Jean Genet in our own time) 'The worst are the best'.

Neocolonialism: *see* Imperialism.

Neto, Agostinho (1922–   ) Angolan revolutionary leader, physician and poet, President of the MPLA (*see* Portuguese Africa, revolution in). In 1962 he made a spectacular escape from prison in Lisbon.

New Citizens' Society: *see* Mao Tse-tung.

New Left. The Marxist- ◊ Leninist revolutionary movement which is in revolt not only against ◊ imperialism – Lenin's 'last phase of capitalism' – but also repudiates Moscow-style ◊ 'establishment'-communism as still Stalinist, obscurantist, ◊ revisionist, undemocratic, viciously bureaucratic and stupidly dogmatic; and, as such, a betrayal of Marxism-Leninism. The focus of New Left feeling was provided by the war in ◊ Vietnam in which the ◊ Vietcong guerrilla armies, supported by Marxist-Leninist North Vietnam, were engaged in driving out the Americans, the mightiest imperial power in history. The David and Goliath element in this struggle has given it exceptional power over the naturally decent feelings of the young.

Important elements in the composition of the short but rich New Left traditions are the triumph of the Chinese CP and establishment of the People's Republic of China followed by the ◊ Maoist cultural revolution; the militant social-revolutionary aspect of the struggle of the American blacks for civil rights – ◊ Black Power; the victory of the socialist-nationalist Algerian revolution over French imperialism; the triumph of the ◊ Castro- ◊ Guevara Marxist-Leninist revolution in Cuba; the revolutionary ◊ guerrilla operations in Latin America; the ◊ French students' revolution of May 1968; the Berkeley, California, Kent State and other university revolts, with their martyrs to police terrorism – ◊ Student power; the anti-apartheid movement in South Africa and Rhodesia. The charismatic leaders, and at the same time philosophers of the New Left are three: ◊ Mao Tse-tung, the only one who is still alive at the time of writing; Che Guevara, killed in revolutionary action by the principal counter-revolutionary agency of ◊ imperialism, the ◊ CIA by means of its Bolivian agents; and ◊ Ho Chi Minh, leader of the revolution in Vietnam.

Although the New Left is composed of many different groups, associations and parties, using diverse revolutionary methods and declaring aims and purposes which differ in detail, all have certain fundamental ideas and purposes in common. Their purposes are: the overthrow of imperialist-capitalist power by revolution; and the overthrow of Stalinist state capitalism as practised by the Moscow-style communist parties. Their ideas are those of Marxism-Leninism with a strong bias towards the ▷ cultural revolutionary aspect of that philosophy, so that they envisage a government based on direct democracy with a rigorous and critical democratic control of the minimum of bureaucracy, a minimum of dogma and a maximum of flexibility within the general limits of socialist philosophy.

There are in New Left feeling and thinking strong echoes of anarchist theory: perhaps few New Leftists envisage the complete and immediate abolition of the state apparatus; but most of them are very suspicious of, and hostile to both state and party apparatus. The workers are to manage their own industries; the students are to manage their own universities; and all the citizens take a hand in managing the nation's business. The practice of controlling and directing a bureaucracy, whether of industry (the management), of universities (the faculty), of municipalities (the council), or of the nation (the executive), by means of elected representatives is rejected as demonstrably unsatisfactory.

Perhaps the greatest strength of the New Left, as it matures and grows, will turn out to be the fact that in it virtually all the traditions and ideas of democracy and socialism come together: primitive communism; Hellenic direct democracy; socialism, from Hall and Mably through ▷ Marx and ▷ Engels to ▷ Lenin; the permanent revolution of ▷ Trotsky; the anarchism of Godwin, ▷ Proudhon and ▷ Kropotkin; the syndicalism of ▷ Sorel; Maoism and Castro-Guevarism based on modern experience.

Of the three most nearly 'formal' New Left disciplines, it seems likely that Maoism has a very important and long-term revolutionary future; that Trotskyism is of only temporary importance; and that Black Power will, when its power bases are restored after recent damage by police counterterrorism, make the most immediate impression. Trotskyism is at once too fragmented, too scholastic and too much inclined to dogmatism to have a future, and moreover its most important element, the permanent revolution, is virtually embodied in the Maoist version of the Leninist cultural revolution.

In France the Maoists are 'going to the people' – not to teach and lead, but to learn, to create flexible local revolutionary programmes out of what they learn, to suggest and persuade as they work side by side with the people in factories, offices and universities. Whereas most of the other New Left movements remain distinctly elitist.

In Britain the New Left movements have two major derivations: the CND (Committee for Nuclear Disarmament) movement; and the people, to the number of 10,000, who left the Communist Party in disgust at the 'imperialist' behaviour of the USSR in Hungary and Czechoslovakia; more generally, it is recruited also from the less formal anti-Vietnam War movement. About a score of New Left movements are Trotskyist, the most considerable being the Socialist Labour League which publishes the *Workers' Press*; the International Marxist Group; and the International Socialists. There are also some Maoist groups, notably the Marxist-Leninist Communist Party led by Reg Birch of the Amalgamated Union of Engineering Workers. In the US the New Left finds expression in the Student Power movement, in the violent ▷ Weathermen, and in Black Power. For France *see* French Student Revolution 1968; Latin American, African and Asian New Left movements are dealt with under the names of specific countries.

Newton, Huey P. (1942–   ) Black American revolutionary leader, b. in the deep South of very poor parents, raised in various black ghettoes. He took a prominent part in the black rebellion in the Watts (Los Angeles) ghetto in 1965. Joint founder with Bobby ▷ Seale of the ▷ Black Panther Party (1965). Arrested, Oaklands, 1968, for killing a policeman, he was convicted of 'voluntary manslaughter' and sentenced to from two to fifteen years. The sentence was quashed on appeal in 1970. Of America he said, in September 1970: 'The right to life, liberty and the pursuit of happiness has become the right to death, oppression and the pursuit of profit.' Since May 1971 he has repudiated violent revolution and now seems to favour a strategy of building black economic power through the encouragement of community projects and the growth of black capitalism: *see also* USA, Revolution in.

Nihilism, Nihilist. A native Russian manifestation of anarchism with which it was not identical. The name was first coined to describe what ▷ Marx stigmatized as the 'sterile negation' of the Prussian social revolutionaries of the 1840s. The coinage is usually attributed to the Russian novelist Turgenev who, however, learnt it when mixing with the revolutionary theorists in Berlin in the entourage of Bruno Bauer, the Hegelian philosopher. Twenty years later Turgenev, in *Fathers and Sons,* called nihilists those intellectuals who followed the teachings of a brilliant twenty-year-old political theorist called Pisarev. His writings began to appear in *Russkoe Slovo* in 1861, his theme being that scientific rationalism would, of itself, be a sufficient basis of social and political order; that both political and artistic life were anachronisms in an age of science; and that no authority but that of scientific thought was required. Pisarev's followers rather hastily concluded that all forms of religious, social and political authority should be destroyed by violence, and dedicated themselves to ridding Russia of these anachronisms by means of ⟡ assassination and bomb-throwing. Their principal success was the assassination, directed by ⟡ Perovskaya of ⟡ the People's Will branch of nihilism, and carried out by the nihilists Rysakov and Grimevetsky, of Tsar Alexander II in 1881.

Nkrumah, Kwame (1909–72) Ghanaian nationalist leader and former President of Ghana: *see* African power transfers.

Non-violence: *see* Passive resistance.

NOW. National Organization of Women. A moderate and reformist ⟡ Women's Liberation movement.

Nyerere, Julius (1922–) Tanzanian nationalist leader and President of Tanzania: *see* African power transfers.

O

Ojeda, Fabricio. Venezuelan ◊ guerrilla leader, captured by the military police in 1965 and murdered in his cell: *see* Venezuela; guerrilla movements.

OLAS. Organization for Latin American Solidarity, founded 18 January 1966 in Havana, is designed to coordinate the revolutionary activities of all Latin American Marxist- ◊ Leninist, and more specifically, Guevarist (*see* Guevara) movements. Some African, United States and Asian revolutionary New Left movements are affiliated with it, in the spirit of the Tricontinental (OSPAAAL). It was set up by the twenty-seven delegates from Latin American and Caribbean countries attending the inaugural Tricontinental meeting.

OSPAAAL. Organization of Solidarity of the Peoples of Africa, Asia and Latin America, also known as the Tricontinental or Tricon: *see* Ben Barka.

P

PAIGG. African Independence Party of Guinea and Cape Verde: *see* Cabral.

Palestine (*Israel*) revolution in. The existence of a genuine left socialist revolutionary movement centred on Palestine or Israel is masked and confused by the nationalist struggle of the Palestine Arabs against Israel, supported by the Arab and other Muslim states and by the socialist-type economy of the *Kibbuzim*. The fact that the Arabs are fighting to oust the Israeli 'colonialists' and reoccupy the country makes them appear to be the 'revolutionaries' in the case, especially since they tend to look to the communist block for support whereas the Israeli government looks to the capitalist block. On the other hand Israel is clearly more nearly socialist and democratic than most Muslim states. But that is a gross oversimplification. There are three revolutionary movements properly so-called in this area: (1) the Israeli Socialist Group, a Marxist- ▷ Leninist ▷ New Left Internationalist organization formed in 1962; (2) The Palestine Revolutionary Liberation Movement (Al-Fatah) and its military branch, Al-Assifa; and (3) The Popular Democratic Front. These three organizations have much ground in common: all make a clear distinction between *peoples* and states in the region; thus, e.g. Al-Fatah and the PDF certainly seek to overthrow the state of Israel, but they do not seek to drive out the Jews, as do the Arab Nationalists, but on the contrary to involve the Jewish with the Arab people in making a socialist revolution; and the ISG does not seek to defend the state of Israel but rather to unite the Jewish and Arab peoples in a joint struggle against ▷ 'imperialism' whether it be Jewish or Arab. All three movements regard the existing Arab states as being either feudal-fascist and as such just as allied with ▷ imperialism as Israel; or petty ▷ bourgeois nationalist and, since allied with foreign capital, neocolonialist (*see* imperialism). The revolution must, therefore, seek to destroy them. The most militant of these three organizations, and the one least confused or compromised by ideologies irrelevant to revolution (Nationalism, Islamism, Judaism, etc.) is the Arab Marxist-Leninist PDF which, in the manner of the New Left throughout the world, envisages a prolonged 'people's war' to overthrow all the 'feudal-fascist' and 'bourgeois nationalist' regimes in the Middle East and replace them by an international socialist direct democracy: *see also* PFLP.

Pan-African Congress (PAC): *see* South Africa and Rhodesia, Revolution in.

Pankhurst, Emmeline (née Goulden, 1858–1928) b. Manchester, she married women's rights campaigner Richard Pankhurst. She founded the Women's Franchise League in 1889 and in 1892 joined the Independent Labour Party, the only political party which paid even lip-service to the idea of votes for women. During her husband's lifetime she conducted her campaign of propaganda in a peaceful and law-abiding way which accomplished nothing. But in 1903 she founded the more militant Women's Social and Political Union, and following her failure after three years to obtain even a glimmer of hope of concession from the Liberal government, resorted to violence (1906), and to such passive resistance methods as the hunger strike. Violence included windowbreaking and arson, and from 1901–13 she served three prison sentences. She suspended operations during World War I, to help recruit women into war work. The franchise was conceded to women in 1918, whereupon Mrs Pankhurst proved she was no revolutionary, in any general sense, by quitting the ILP and joining the Conservative Party. But her work liberated the spirit of womankind almost all over the world, and its most recent consequence is the ▷ Women's Liberation Movement.

Parnell, Charles Stewart (1846–91) Irish Nationalist leader whose Home Rule for Ireland policy contained some revolutionary elements, notably in the matter of land tenure laws. An Anglo-Irish Protestant of the land-owning class, he was elected to the Westminster parliament in 1875 and became leader of the Home Rule Party in 1877. He used his control over the Irish members to put pressure on the government by repeatedly disrupting the business of the House. At the same time he used his great influence over the Irish peasantry to persuade them to ▷ boycott landlords rather than murder them. As a result of his imprisonment (1881)

Partido Obrevo Revolucionario

for inciting to boycott, violent disturbances, including murders, became much more frequent, and Gladstone was obliged to release Parnell and appeal to him for help to pacify the Irish people. Gladstone's Home Rule Bill more or less met Parnell's demands and he gave it his support. But he lost his influence with the people and his control of his party when he was cited as co-respondent in a suit for divorce.

Partido Obrero Revolucionario: *see* POR.

Passive resistance. A method, implicit in certain aspects of Buddhist and Christian quietism and repudiation of violence, but developed in our own time by M. K. ◊ Gandhi, of forcing a ruling ◊ establishment to concede reforms or revolutionary changes, without recourse to violence. It consists in the deliberate practice of civil disobedience to laws or regulations which the resisting party objects to, followed by passive obstruction of the police or military force attempting to enforce them. Gandhi's successful use of it in South Africa and India was followed by its use elsewhere, notably and successfully by Dr Martin Luther King (1929–68), leader of the (Negro) Southern Christian Fellowship in the US who, like Gandhi, was subsequently assassinated by an extremist who believed that repudiation of violent means compromises rather than forwards the cause. The means of resistance used may extend to boycott of the opponent's commerce, used, e.g. by King, against Montgomery, Alabama, public transport services to obtain a legal desegregration order; to deliberate, symbolic lawbreaking, e.g. Gandhi's salt-making against the salt-tax in British India; to obstruction by mass physical inertia, as when a body of resisters sit or lie down in a highway to impede traffic, refuse to move even when assaulted by the police, and have to be carried away; to hunger-strike to the point of death against an authority which would be politically embarrassed by that death, used, e.g. by the British Suffragettes in their struggle for votes for women – they were forcibly fed, an outrage which led to a public outcry and so forwarded their cause. The ultimate in passive resistance is self-immolation by fire, as used by the Czech student Palach in protest against oppression of his country by the USSR in 1968.

The obstruction by mass physical inertia method was used in Britain by unemployed Welsh miners and other industrial workers in the 1930s when they marched on London and lay down in its principal thoroughfares, impeding the movement of traffic, in protest against their miserable condition. Another form of passive resistance, in the context of social revolution, is the sit-in: the workers occupy their plant or students their university, and remain in it, doing no work since they are on strike, and denying access to the management. It is an element in presentday ⟡ Maoist revolutionary method, which has been used in France, but it is far from new, having been very widely used by striking French workers in the 1930s, during the decline of the Third Republic, and in the 1950s against the exploitation of labour under the Fourth Republic.

Demonstration marches are another means of passive resistance. They were developed into institutions of briefly national importance, in Britain, by the Committee for Nuclear Disarmament, CND, whose 'Aldermaston Marches' attracted a wide range of protestors from ⟡ bourgeois liberals on the Right, to the New ⟡ Leftists. They served to make the ordinary citizen aware of the hideous danger in which development of the A and H bombs had placed the entire human race.

Indian Maoists have developed, for use by striking Indian workers, an interesting variety of passive resistance – not quite 'passive' since it entails the use of constraint, and is comparable with the juridical practice of locking a jury into a room until they reach a verdict: the board of directors of a company whose workers are on strike are imprisoned in the board room until they concede the strikers' demands. This method has the merit of forcing the management to call in the police to rescue them, thus demonstrating clearly the role of the police and the law in bourgeois societies, i.e. the protection of the capitalist and his bureaucracy.

Passive resistance would seem to be effective only against governments which are themselves subject to the pressure of public opinion to which, indeed, it appeals over the heads of government. It cannot succeed against a dictatorship strong enough either to impose a censorship of news, or to ignore the ordinary humane feelings of its subjects. Gandhi himself conceded this fact when he supported the British war effort against the ⟡ Nazis.

PDF. Popular Democratic Front. A small splinter group of the ⟡ PFLP. It is an extreme left Marxist– ⟡ Leninist organization of Palestinian and Jordanian Arab revolutionaries led by the Jordanian ⟡ Marxist philosopher

People's Bank

Nayaf Hawatmeh, a former PFLP leader who took himself and about 200 followers out of the PFLP on the grounds that its leadership was not far enough to the left. The PDF is inspired by the ◊ Maoist and Cuban forms of communism. It has neither the numbers nor the means to be effective in direct action on its own account, but it is important as a fermenting political yeast in the Arab revolutionary movement at large.

People's Bank (1849). Under ◊ Proudhon's system of mutualist and federalist anarchism the working class was to contract peacefully out of the capitalist economic and ◊ bourgeois political systems and so leave them to die of inanition: agriculture, and manufacture, whether at artisan or industrial level, would be managed by the workers themselves, in voluntary associations of free individuals, those associations linked in a loose federation, exchanging their products mutually. To facilitate those exchanges, which would become the new economic system, Proudhon conceived a People's Bank which would link the producers' federation with the existing conventional money system, handling money for external business relations and advancing to members, at a nominal interest rate, money for administration costs and development. But the internal currency between members would be 'labour cheques' – the producer's labour being, in Proudhon's view, the only just basis of value – covering transactions between members. The Bank was founded in Paris January 1849 and very quickly had 27,000 'members'; but at the same time Proudhon was charged with sedition and forced to flee the country; consequently the Bank never operated and when Proudhon returned secretly to France he liquidated it to prevent it falling into the wrong hands.

The People's Will. A Russian revolutionary secret society formed from the terrorist wing of the ◊ Land and Liberty movement in 1879, and dedicated to the single purpose of 'executing' the Tsar Alexander II who, as autocrat of the Russian Empire, was seen as the principal enemy of the partly liberal, partly socialist reforms which the Land and Liberty movement had at heart. The People's Will was led by the nihilist Andrei ◊ Zelyabov, son of a serf, but with a university education; it numbered about 400 active adherents, most of them students. It is ironical that Alexander II had to pay for the sins of his fathers rather than his own: unknown to, but shortly after his condemnation to death by, the People's Will, he had

Perón, Juan Domingo

surrendered to liberal pressure and empowered his chief minister Loris-Melikov to set up a commission to produce a constitution as soon as possible. But it is not certain that had this been known it would have saved him, for the Tsar was the symbol of the principle of autocracy which the revolutionaries wished to destroy. During eighteen months they made repeated attempts on his life, by blowing up railway lines where his train was to pass, and even mining certain streets in St Petersburg where he might be expected to pass. A carefully laid plot to ambush him in St Petersburg and bomb his carriage was nearly prevented by the arrest of Zelyabov, but his second-in-command Sophia ⟡ Perovskaya, took over direction of the work and was present to signal to the two Nihilist students under her orders when to throw their bombs. The first bomb fell among the Tsar's Cossack escort; Alexander stopped his carriage and got out to help the wounded. The second bomb landed and exploded between his feet and he died of his wounds an hour and a half later. The five principal conspirators were caught, tried, convicted and publicly hanged. With them the movement petered out, but its terrorist work was taken up by the ⟡ Social Revolutionaries.

Perón, Juan Domingo (1895–   ). Argentine army officer who seized power in Argentina by a military *coup d'état* in 1946 and was dictator until 1955 when he was overthrown and exiled by another military *coup d'état*. From time to time revolutionary ideas are precipitated by a leader, especially one who is dead or in exile, who is not himself a revolutionary but who, for want of something better, acts as a catalystic agent. Perón was not a revolutionary: but because he saw the need for and was willing to concede a measure of social reform; because, for that reason, he won the support of the trade unions; because he seemed aggressively to assert Argentine independence of US 'dollar imperialism' so hated by Latin American revolutionaries and seemed to promise to make Argentina a great power (a delusion which led him into being hoaxed by a German 'scientist' who offered to make him an A-bomb); because, above all, his beautiful ex-dancer wife had a great following of her own in the working class – the *descamisados* ('shirtless ones', cf. *sans-culottes*); finally, because subsequent Argentine governments have been the dreariest kind of right-wing, military dictatorships without the slightest intention of making any of the necessary social or economic reforms, for all these reasons the 'image' of

Perón (actually a very rich exile in Spain) has become transformed in the popular imagination, with the result that the Argentine ⟡ New Left ⟡ 'guerrilla' movement is shot through with an idealized *Perónismo* very much more 'socialist' than either Perón himself, or Eva Perón, ever were.

Perovskaya, Sophia (1853–81) Russian ⟡ nihilist revolutionary. d. of a provincial governor, later governor of St Petersburg, she despised the frivolous life of her class, devoted herself to study, and 'went to the people', living as a poor worker. She joined the moderate Chaikovskyist group of the ⟡ populist movement, to which ⟡ Kropotkin also belonged, and was among the first of the anarchist intellectuals to make effective contact with St Petersburg factory workers (from 1873). As a result of increasingly repressive police measures against the propagators of revolutionary doctrines, the populist movement was divided into those who persisted in their moderate and peaceful methods, and those, notably the ⟡ People's Will who concluded that they must resort to violence and terrorism. Perovskaya joined the terrorists, in the 'cell' of ⟡ Zelyabov. A plan to assassinate Tsar Alexander II was worked out, but shortly before D-Day, 1 March 1881, Zelyabov, the chief organizer, was arrested. Perovskaya stepped into his place, was present to signal, with her handkerchief, to the two bomb-throwers the moment for throwing their bombs as the Tsar's sleigh was driven alongside the Catherine Canal, and escaped after the success of the plan. She was arrested ten days later; Zelyabov was already in custody and immediately declared to the authorities that he alone was responsible for the assassination. They and their comrades were tried (26–30 March) and Perovskaya bore herself with conspicuous bravery both during the trial and on the scaffold where, before surrendering her neck to the rope, she embraced her companions (3 April 1881).

Peru, ⟡ guerrilla movements. The origin of revolutionary movements in Peru is the impossibility of correcting the miserable condition of about nine-tenths of the population by any legal means. The principal source of wealth and the only means of living for 90 per cent of the people, is land; 83 per cent of it is owned by 3 per cent of the total number of landowners, so that 97 per cent of the people have to share 17 per cent of the land. The peasants pay rent in work for their smallholdings – so many days of work per year – to the great landowners, who thus have their land worked without paying money wages. A very large majority of the peasants speak no Spanish, but only one of the native tongues, either Quetchua or Aymara, the principal languages of the old Inca Empire. As all schooling is in Spanish only, and there are, in any case, schools for only about 60 per cent of the children, about 40 per cent of adults are illiterate. In rural areas there is one doctor per 50,000 inhabitants. Government is by military dictatorship representing the small and immensely rich oligarchy. Elections are held, but if a candidate with a liberal programme is returned the election is immediately nullified by a military coup. When a particularly outrageous case of military takeover of this kind led the U S Kennedy administration to withdraw aid in protest, a promise of amendment was made and, instead of takeover by coup, election-rigging was resorted to on the next occasion. To deal with this state of affairs there have been three revolutionary movements closely associated with three outstanding leaders: *see*, therefore, Bejar, Hector; Galdos (Hugo Blanco); Unceda (Luis de la Puente); *also*, Heraud, Javier.

Petkoff, Luben (1933–) Venezuelan communist and ⟡ guerrilla leader. In 1965 he landed at the head of a group of trained guerrillas from an island off Venezuela in what was known as 'Operation Bolivar' and after being attacked by the government airforce, took to the mountains, whence he has since operated: *see* Venezuela, guerrilla movements.

PFLP and PLO: Popular Front for the Liberation of Palestine and Palestine Liberation Organization. A Marxist- ⟡ Leninist militant revolutionary movement based on Jordan which developed out of the Arab Nationalist Movement, and which wages ⟡ guerrilla warfare by means of terrorism on Israel. Its objects are, first, the destruction of the 'imperialist' state of Israel; and second of capitalism throughout the Middle East, followed by the installation of communism throughout the Dar-al-Islam. The Front is manned chiefly by intellectuals and students but claims roots in the peasantry and is aware of the need to involve the people at large in its revolution. Among its principal leaders (1971) have been George ⟡ Habbash, its founder, as he was also of the ANM; Dr Wadi Habbad, chief administrator, and organizer of the sensational campaign of airliner hi-jackings in 1970; and the poet and novelist Ghassan Kanafani, who edits the movement's newspaper *Al-Hadaf*. The Front is organized as a guerrilla warfare movement using the methods of terrorism and not a political party; its political party associate is the Arab Workers Socialist Party, founded September 1970, which looks far beyond the Arab-Israel conflict over Palestine to the ultimate goal, an all-Arab Marxist-Leninist revolution. The PFLP and the AWSP have links with the CPs of both the USSR and China, both of which supply them with weapons and money subsidies. PFLP members receive training in guerrilla warfare techniques; until 1971 they operated out of the Palestine refugee camps on Jordan's west bank and through an extensive underground network. Driven out of Jordan by King Hussein, who was unwilling to suffer Israeli reprisals for its sake, the PFLP moved its principal base into the Lebanon. The principal PLO Group is that known as ◊ Al-Fatah, led by Halilal Wazir and Abu Ayad. This group has a militant terrorist wing, the so-called Black September group whose leaders are said to be Ali Hassan Salameh, Abdel Al-Kadar Husseini and Fahri El Omari. This group was responsible for the assassination of Jordan's prime minister Wasfi Tal in 1971; the assassination of eleven Israeli athletes at the Munich Olympic Games in 1972; the assassination (by letter-bomb) of the Counsellor of the Israeli embassy in London (1972) and other acts of terrorism: *see also* PDF.

PGT: Partido Guatemelteco de Trabago. Left wing political party in Guatemala, following the orthodox communist line, more or less pro-Moscow but occasionally veering towards Pekin. Has sometimes supported, sometimes opposed the armed activities of the ◊ guerrilla movements: *see* Guatemala: guerrilla movements.

Philippines, revolution in: *see* HUKS.

Pieck, William: *see* Kun, Bela.

Pinto, Tirso. Venezuelan communist and ◊ guerrilla leader: *see* Venezuela guerrilla movements.

Plekhanov, Giorgy Valentinovich (1856–1918) Russian ◊ Marxist theorist. b. Gudalovka, Tambov, into a family of landed gentry. He became a member of the Populist ◊ Land and Liberty movement in his late teens but, objecting to the use of terrorism, he led a faction out of the movement to form the Black Redistribution movement dedicated to revolution by peaceful means. In 1880 he went to west Europe, there first encountered and soon embraced Marxism, and in 1883 founded the Liberation of Labour society to propagate Marxist Socialism in Russia. He was the most rigidly orthodox of Marxists. He collaborated with ◊ Lenin in publishing and editing *Iskra* and supported him at the 1903 Congress of the Russian Social Democratic Party during which it was split into Mensheviks and ◊ Bolsheviks led by ◊ Lenin. But he distrusted Lenin as being apt to depart from strict Marxism by imposing a revolution from above on masses not yet prepared for it or themselves active in making it; and in October 1917 he openly denounced the Bolshevik Revolution as a *coup d'état* carried out by a minority. Threatened with lynching by a mob of revolutionary sailors from the Baltic Fleet, Trotsky's most militant activists, Plekhanov fled (1918) to Finland and there died shortly afterwards, an embittered man. His writings on aesthetics must be held partly responsible for the imposition on Soviet artists of ◊ Socialist Realism.

Popular Democratic Front: *see* PDF.

Popular Front for the Liberation of Palestine: *see* PFLP.

Populists. Name used to designate the several revolutionary groups active in Russia from the post- ◊ nihilist era, from *c.* 1870 to *c.* 1881 (*see* Narodniki movement; Land and Liberty; People's Will); they were succeeded by the Social Revolutionaries, who were succeeded and eliminated by the ◊ Bolsheviks.

POR: Partido Obrero Revolucionario. Peruvian Trotskyist party: *see* Galdos, Hugo Blanco.

Portuguese Africa, revolution in. A number of revolutionary movements, some purely nationalist, some Chinese-orientated communist, and still others more or less socialist, wage ◊ guerrilla warfare on the colonial government of Portuguese Africa and have kept large parts of the territory in a state of chronic civil war for about a decade. Three of these movements are substantial and important. In Angola rebellion broke out in 1961 and has continued ever since, conducted by the Popular Movement for the Liberation of Angola (MPLA) which has an orthodox communist ideology and controls about one-third of the country. In Mozambique the Mozambique Liberation Front, Frelimo, has about 12,000 men under arms pinning down about 60,000 government troops, controls 20 per cent of the territory and has already introduced agrarian reforms in the part of the country which it controls. For the situation in Portuguese Guinea, see ◊ Cabral. The original leader of Frelimo, Eduardo ◊ Mondlane, author of *The Struggle for Mozambique* was murdered in Tanzania in 1969. MPLA is led by Agostinho ◊ Neta and its military wing by Spartacus ◊ Monimambu. Their aim is not merely national independence, but what Monimambu calls 'the basic transformation of the people', by which he is taken to mean the restructuring of the whole society on socialist lines.

Potemkin, battleship. The ratings of the Imperial Russian battleship *Potemkin,* who mutinied during the Russo-Japanese War (1904–05) have an important place in the Russian Revolution hagiography, their shrine being the famous and architecturally remarkable Potemkin stairway in Odessa. Under the London Naval Convention of 1841 the Black Sea Fleet was unable to leave the Black Sea; its crews, bottled up and unable to take part in the fighting against Japan in the Far East, became restless, infected by the general social malaise. In June 1905 the crew of the *Potemkin,* which lay at Odessa, mutinied in sympathy with the general strike then paralysing the city. They were attacked by still 'reliable' units of the Fleet, fought back, took their ship to sea, steamed her to Constantsa in Romania and there surrendered to internment. The *Potemkin* mutiny was the subject of a remarkable film by Eisenstein.

Princip, Gavrilo (1894–1918) Revolutionary assassin. b. West Bosnia into a family of peasant serfs. His brother, Jovo, a small businessman, sent him to the Merchants' School in Sarajevo where, living in lodgings, he came under the influence of Danilo Ilič, a revolutionary social democrat. This, and the influence of revolutionary idealists among his school fellows, made him a Yugoslav nationalist and a socialist. He persuaded his brother to transfer him to Sarajevo high school where he joined *Rad,* a students' revolutionary secret society dedicated to ensuring political union of the Yugoslavs in a socialist state. He took a leading part in violent demonstrations against the Austro-Hungarian authorities, was expelled, went to Belgrade, there starved on charity until the outbreak of the Serbo-Turkish War (1912). Rejected for military service because of poor physique, he returned to Sarajevo determined to do some spectacular act for his cause. He decided to assassinate its arch-enemy, Franz Ferdinand, heir to the imperial throne and about to visit Sarajevo. The conspiracy spread and was finally directed by Danilo Ilič. Seven potential assassins were distributed along the route of the archduke's official drive but only two acted: the student Cabrinovič who threw a grenade at the royal car but blew up the one behind it; and Princip who shot the archduke and his wife dead. A month too young for execution under Austrian law, Princip was sent to prison for twenty years with hard labour and there died of tuberculosis.

Proletariat. From the Latin *proles*, meaning offspring, but referring, by Roman historical usage, to the numerousness of the offspring of the lowest social class, a *proletarius* being one who served the state not with property but with his offspring (*OED*). It is used in ◊ Marxist theory to mean the class of industrial wage-earners who, having no property, can get their living only by the sale of their labour to the capitalist class, but was in use by socialist writers before Marx's time.

Propaganda, indirectly from the Latin *propagare* and more directly from the Congregatio de propaganda fide, the committee of cardinals set up in 1622 by Pope Gregory XV to superintendent missions concerned with *propagation* of the faith. As first used by revolutionary movements propaganda had, accordingly, a missionary purpose and described material, printed or spoken, designed to convert people to the revolutionary cause by means of persuasive argument, rhetoric or ◊ dialectic. Owing to its continuous abuse by political parties of all colours and more recently by advertising agents hired to 'sell' political candidates to electorates, the word has become a pejorative: thus, to say of a claim made by a political opponent, or the enemy in war, that it is 'propaganda' implies that it is a pack of lies. But, as used by counter-revolutionary and above all by ◊ establishment publicists and persuaders it might fairly be defined as tendentious or insincere statements made regardless of, though not necessarily contrary to, the objective truth, by means of the written, printed or spoken word or by pictorial means, directly or by implication, and designed to make people think or believe what the propagandist wishes them to think or believe.

Although propaganda has been in use for centuries – some good examples will be found in the *Philippics* of Demosthenes – particularly in religious wars like those of the seventeenth century in which both Roman Catholics and Protestants published grotesque untruths designed to create a monstrous and repulsive image of the other (e.g. of the Roman Church as the Great Whore of Babylon), the first great modern exponent of the craft was Alfred Harmsworth, first Lord Northcliffe, founder-owner of the *Daily Mail*. His work in inventing and publishing the grossest lies about German behaviour in World War I – e.g. that the Germans were boiling the bodies of Allied war dead to make soap – created, in Britain, an image of the German which has not, even now, been entirely eliminated.

There are three serious dangers in the use of this type of propaganda: the first is that the true facts become obscured so that public opinion and ultimately political policy come to be founded on false premises; the second is that the propagandist and his clients may be convinced by their own lies, and so react towards the opponent lied about with an intransigent hatred which provokes a response in kind – a situation which has occurred between Israelis and Arabs in the Middle East; the third is that outrageous propaganda may provoke a reaction against the propagandist. In this case, people, becoming aware that they have been lied to, may dismiss as propaganda lies, perfectly true accounts of, e.g. enemy atrocities. Thus owing to the earlier work of Lord Northcliffe and his men, it was difficult in the 1940s, to convince the British public, and even their leaders, that accounts of the Nazi extermination camps were true.

A classic counter-revolutionary example of the use of propaganda was that of the 'Zinoviev letter'. In October 1924, just before a general election in Britain in which the Labour Party government was likely to increase its majority, certain Conservative newspapers published a forged letter purporting to be from the Bolshevik revolutionary Grigori ⊅ Zinoviev of the ⊅ Comintern, instructing the British left to stir up violent revolution. The implications were that under a Labour government there might be civil war and that a British political party was taking its orders from Moscow. This masterpiece of propaganda was successful and the Labour Party was defeated at the polls. A similar use of propaganda turned the progressive left's determination to emancipate women from domestic slavery and make them man's equals, into a widely believed story that the whole female population of Russia had been 'nationalized', i.e. made available to the ◊ Bolsheviks to quench their ravening sexual appetites.

World War II produced an even greater master of this distasteful art than Lord Northcliffe, the Nazi Minister of Enlightenment, Joseph Goebbels whose Ministry, like ◊ Stalin's analogous one, was satirized in George Orwell's *1984* as 'Minitrue' whose business was the continuous propagation of lies. Goebbels's method was to appeal to the basest instincts of mankind; he gave the ordinary man indulgence and public justification for behaving in such a way as to satisfy the sadistic 'instincts' which are normally kept strictly in hand. The 'Cold War' between the ◊ imperialist and communist power blocks is waged with propaganda of this kind.

Although revolutionary movements and parties have had some measure of success in the use of propaganda, for example, the transformation of the idea 'capitalism' from that of a more or less unjust social-economic system into a myth of evil, on the whole the anti- or counter-revolutionary establishments and dictatorships have been much more successful with it. The reasons for this are obvious: revolutionaries before and during the revolutionary phase are idealists with a commitment to such ideals as the truth, and a belief in the fundamental goodness of man: this is a serious and often crippling handicap. Their opponents, on the other hand, have only one object, to stay in office and destroy the revolution: they have no troublesome commitments to the truth, though they may well choose to tell it if it be expedient, nor any illusions touching the goodness of man, but deal solely in the realities of power. Needless to say, once the revolutionaries are successful they are soon behaving in the same 'realistic' way, since they then become the establishment.

But it does not follow that this must be so: propaganda in its original and honourable meaning – the education of the people in a particular ideology by the dissemination of truth as one sees it – is used by both liberal and ◊ New Left protesters; and it is worth noting that neither the People's Republic of China nor Cuba have sunk, in their propaganda, to anything like such depths of baseness as the ◊ Fascist, the Stalinist or even the parliamentary imperialist powers. It is at least possible that a New Left party in power would be saved, by a commitment to direct democracy entailing submission of the bureaucracy to unremitting criticism by the

Property

whole people, from the moral degradation which makes Orwell's 'Minitrue' a fair image of the various propaganda agencies of the principal power blocks, and even to some extent of the commercial advertising industry which has taught the political propagandists so much.

Wall writing. Revolutionary movements have long made use of walls as media for propaganda. There was an extraordinary outbreak of such revolutionary wall writing during the ◊ French Student Revolution of 1968, chiefly on the walls of university buildings at the Sorbonne and at Nanterre and on such other buildings as were seized and occupied by the revolutionaries as the Odeon Theatre. Many of the writings were original and witty; some involve too much play on words to be translatable, but here are some examples culled at random: *Anarchy is I; A man is not stupid or intelligent; he is free or he is not; Politics happen in the streets; Don't liberate me, I'll do it myself; The Economy is sick – let it die; Be realists, demand the impossible.*

Property. From the revolutionary socialist point of view, 'property is theft' (*see* Proudhon). This does not mean that nobody has the right to own anything whatsoever: although there is an extreme communist ideal state in which all property whatsoever would be held in common without any problems since there would be more than enough of everything for everybody regardless of the value of his work contribution – 'to each according to his needs'. For the time being socialism aims to bring all fundamental resources, land, minerals, the means of production, into common ownership, but does not discourage personal property in e.g. domestic machinery, motor-cars and jewellery, the only good title to such property being, of course, labour.

The 'property' intended to be understood when the socialist says that property is theft is land, mineral resources, all raw materials, and the means of production. This attitude to the problem of property can be traced back through a long line of socialist thinkers – ◊ Marx, ◊ Engels, ◊ Kropotkin, ◊ Chernychevsky, Rousseau, ◊ Proudhon (*What is Property?* 1840) and Mill (*Principles of Political Economy* 1848); to mention only some principal moderns, back beyond Thomas More's *Utopia* (1516) – to the discovery, at first no more than a kind of instinct but later confirmed by anthropology, that man in the primitive state which, although perhaps nasty, brutish and short, was not 'corrupt', had no property, and the land he lived off belonged to the community in common. Early stock-raising nomadic peoples had no notion of property in land even for the community ('the earth is the Lord's', i.e. in practice, all men's), though the ultimate sanction being force, they might be forced to limit their pastoral wanderings by treaty with neighbouring communities. Early agrarian peoples regarded land as being held in common; only the usufruct and very rarely all of that, was the individual farmer's property, that is, what he could produce from the share of the common land allowed him for his sustenance and only during his lifetime. As the institutions of priesthood and kingship developed, the king or the high priest became, as it were, the incarnation of common right, not so much the owner of as the trustee for all the land which was then 'held' from him by the subjects. Out of that developed various forms of feudalism. The power to alienate land, so that it became property, was a relatively late development in human history. In the case of the great Inca empire in pre-Colombian Peru, the once probably universal primitive communism was 'fossilized' into the sixteenth century, the conquering Spaniards introducing the idea of property. It is in any case manifest that since there was no primal legal authority which could confer title to land or any other natural resource on any man or group, all such titles can certainly be traced back to an original 'squatter's right' defended by force. Revolutionary socialism therefore seeks to right a wrong several millennia old and restore to common ownership the resources which mankind lives on.

The case of the 'means of production' is more complicated: the early socialists, when considering a 'worker', were considering an artisan, a man who with his own hands and simple tools produced goods for sale where production entailed the cooperation of a number of workers, the earliest known cases were not 'capitalist' but literally cooperative (the flint mine and manufactury at Grimes Graves, Cambridgeshire, is a prehistoric case in point). The worker who owns his tools has a clear socialist title to them: labour. But the moment he employs other men's labour, the case is altered, although not outrageously in the case of the very small employer who works with his men, and the case is only seriously altered by scale: when the means of production become a tool-plant costing large sums far beyond the individual worker's means to afford and requiring the labour of many men, then what the socialist regards as a morally, socially and economically objectionable situation arises: by owning the tools which a large number of men need in order to produce and so earn their living, a single individual or small group can exploit the labour of many, and by retaining the profit (surplus value) accumulate more and more capital and, in theory, by increase of economic power, continuously depress the living standard of more and more thousands of workers. Socialist justice requires that when the means of production are more than a single craftsman's tools used only by himself, they be treated as fundamental resources, i.e. common property; and, in common justice, it is a fact that those means have been created out of the surplus value of the workers' labour and therefore only the worker has title to them.

At the actual revolutionary stage of the change from capitalism to socialism, it is necessary, as one means of getting fundamental property (i.e. capital) out of private and into public hands, to abolish inheritance of property. Once the land and all other means of production are in public hands, there remains only personal property, i.e. chattels, and these, of course, can be transmitted by inheritance. In the USSR a private citizen may even own a house and the land it stands on: many higher paid people (e.g. artists, dancers and writers, not to mention high CP officials) own country cottages. These, moreover, can be bequeathed to the owner's children.

It is not only in socialist societies that, under the influence of socialist theory, property right has been severely curtailed. By taxation during life and at death the state continually erodes large accumulations of individual property and one of the most curious consequences of the revolutionary attack on the concept of property has been the imposition on the rich of the necessity to pretend that they are poorer than they really are; in other words, an element of shame has been introduced into the psyche of the man of property.

Proudhon, Pierre-Joseph (1809–65) b. Franche-Comté, France, s. of a cooper and innkeeper, largely self-educated, a printer by trade: anarchist philosopher and militant revolutionary. The key to his revolutionary thought is his implacable hostility to the state: 'All parties, without exception, in so far as they seek for power, are varieties of absolutism.' He proposed to replace it by voluntary contract, which he called 'association', between free individuals. Association is as central to his thought as absolute individual freedom, and in his *On the Creation of Order in Humanity* (1843) he emphasized its importance as the source of collective force and consciousness transcending those of the free individuals composing it. His ruling concern was with justice, which he conceived of as immanent, a part of the natural order: it is, he says, in *On Justice in the Revolution and in the Church* (1858), 'the central star which governs society ... the principal and regulator of all transactions, Proudhon's *What is Property?* (1840) was described by Karl ◊ Marx as 'the first decisive, vigorous and scientific examination of property': but the implied condemnation in his famous answer to his own question – 'Property is Theft' – is not a condemnation of those essentials for personal freedom, e.g. house, enough land for subsistence, the tools of one's trade; but of abuses of property, above all the abuse of using it to exploit the labour of others, i.e. capitalism. A man had a right to own the product of his labour; but the means of production other than the craftsman's tools must be held in common, for anything else led to degrading poverty on one side, demoralizing riches on the other. As for his ideas for ridding mankind of the two scourges, the state and the capitalist, like Marx (who hated his ideas), he saw salvation only in the working class: thus, in his *Warning to the Proprietors* (1841), he calls on the workers, the men of the people, to seize the initiative in the reformation of society; and since that will provoke a bourgeois reaction, he warns the magistrates and proprietors, those enemies of mankind, not to provoke these peaceful revolutionaries by police and military oppression or it will be the worse for them – worse, indeed, than such violences as regicide, assassination and insurrection. One of his letters reveals that he had in mind a secret society of just men, less like ◊ Bakunin's *Alliance* than like the medieval German Holy Vehm.

The workers' action which Proudhon envisaged was not political, but industrial: political action was dangerous, for the outcome of a successful political revolution could only be another tyrant state. The revolutionary struggle should be at the industrial level, with the people opting out of capitalism in favour of cooperative enterprises (*see* People's Bank). The world's economic system would ultimately consist in mutual exchanges of goods between voluntary associations of workers controlling industries (cf. ◊ syndicalism). Proudhon and Marx met and talked (Paris 1844–45), and because Marx was convinced that he could win the Frenchman over to his opinion they got on well together. But once they understood each other, the apostle of the all-owning and authoritarian state and that of the free individual could not possibly agree; and since Marx was the arch-exponent of political action by the working class, Proudhon of industrial action, not even their methods of overthrowing capitalism were the same. In his *Economic Contradictions* (1846) he clearly foresaw that communism, whatever its intentions could not but end by establishing a tyrannous monopoly of power.

In the 1848 revolution (⟡ Eighteen-forty-eight) Proudhon entered practical politics as a member of the Constituent Assembly. He did so for the specific purpose of getting his People's Bank established; for the rest, the experience confirmed him in his conviction that parliamentary government could not be used as a means to overthrow the state and replace it by his association network of free individuals, substituting arbitration for law courts and civil services by decentralized and direct administration. When the workers' insurrections against the ⟡ bourgeois wing of the provisional government broke out, he supported them: 'What,' he asked, 'is the capitalist? Everything. What should he be? Nothing.' Also in 1848 he founded the newspaper *Le Representant du peuple* and used it to propagate his ideas: it achieved the then very large circulation of 40,000. When it was suppressed by the government, he founded *Le Peuple*, and in 1849 he set about the founding of the People's Bank; it was soon supported by 27,000 'mutualists' but before it could be tried in practice Proudhon was charged with sedition for denouncing President (later Emperor) Louis-Napoleon Bonaparte for 'conspiring to enslave the people', and had to escape into Belgium. He returned secretly to liquidate the Bank and to continue editing *Le Peuple* from a hiding place.

Caught and imprisoned, he spent the three years of the very easy and mild prison regime in revolutionary journalism and writing, producing, notably, *The Confessions of a Revolutionary* (1850) in which he argued that there must be a quick end to the rule of man by man by the accumulation of capital; and *General Idea of the Revolution in the 19th Century* (1851) in which he developed the idea of revolution as a part of the natural order, inevitable. *Le Peuple* being suppressed in 1849, Proudhon founded, from prison and with money provided by Alexander ⟡ Herzen, *La Voix du peuple* which attained 60,000 circulation and, on days when the leading article was by Proudhon, sold at a premium. Repeatedly fined and sus-

216

pended, it was suppressed in May 1850. Proudhon refounded *Le Peuple*, but without enough money so that it appeared irregularly until suppressed after a few months for 'incitement to civil war'.

By the time of his release from prison he was isolated by fears aroused by his extremism, and for five years he was silenced and found it hard to get a living. But in 1858 came his *De la Justice dans la revolution et dans l'église* in which he compares transcendental and immanent justice and derives from that analysis the plan of a socially just society. It became a bestseller at once, but he was arrested, the remaining stock confiscated, and he was charged with numerous crimes against church (he argued that if there is a God he must be anticivilized, antiliberal, antihuman – in short, from man's viewpoint, evil), and state. Sentenced to three years in prison and a fine of 3,000 francs he appealed, and during his remand, escaped into Belgium where he became a 'lion', visited by Tolstoy, influencing and influenced by the realism of Courbet, writing the anti-militarist *La Guerre et la paix* (1861) whose title Tolstoy borrowed. In the 1860s groups of French working class men began to found mutual credit and other cooperative movements based on Proudhon's ideas which domi-nated French socialism until the rise of ▷ Marxism. But, as always, he stood outside and hostile to some of the major political movements of his time; for example, his distrust, even abhorrence, of nationalism was unpopular and his advocacy (in *Du Principe fédératif*, 1861) of loose federation between small regional associations as the maximum permissible political organiza-tion converted few, in that age of the unification of Italy and revolutionary support for Polish nationalism.

In 1862 he returned to France and devoted much energy to trying to persuade the working class to ▷ boycott the parliamentary elections by abstaining from voting. In this he did not succeed and the *Manifesto of the Sixty* (1864) issued by his followers rejected that part of his doctrine. Parliamentary representation for the workers by the workers was one of its aims: Proudhon would have none of it; the workers must boycott the whole bourgeois system, and create one of their own on Proudhonian lines beside it, which would ultimately replace it. That they could do so was argued in his last book, *De la Capacité politique des classes ouvrières* (1865) which he completed, exclaiming 'Despite the gods I will have the last word', by dictation, on his deathbed. The book, like his others, became a major influence on French socialism and the bible of ▷ syndicalism.

Puerto Rico, revolution in: There are two loosely linked revolutionary movements at work in this US colony. The MPI (Pro-independence Movement) led by Juan Mari-Bras has a Marxist- ▷ Leninist ideology, believes in a two-stage revolution, the first to be peaceful and preparatory, designed to create the political consciousness, social conditions, and crisis which would justify going over to the second, of armed struggle to destroy the ▷ bourgeois political and economic apparatus and replace it with socialism. The first stage would end with direct United States control being replaced by a fraudulent 'independence', i.e. a 'neo-colonialist' (*see* imperialism) native administration. MPI activities are therefore, for the time being, kept carefully within the law. But Mari-Bras is a Guevarist (*see* ▷ Guevara), contemptuous of orthodox, urban-based, 'revisionist' communist parties; he believes, therefore, in the proposition that the revolution can only be achieved by armed struggle; and that a measure of revolutionary violence even during the first stage should shorten that stage. He does not, consequently, repudiate the activities of the second Puerto Rican revolutionary movement, called Armed Commandos of the Liberation (CAL) which wages a campaign of urban ▷ guerrilla sabotage, e.g. the destruction of oil pipelines and the bombing and burning of American-owned business premises and tourist hotels.

Q

Quebec, revolution in: within the broad context of the turbulent Quebec nationalist or independence movement there is a small, growing, militant group which envisages not merely independence for Quebec from English-speaking Canada, i.e. a ⟡ bourgeois-nationalist coup d'état, but Marxist- ⟡ Leninist revolution aimed at installing a ⟡ New Left type socialist direct democracy. This is the Quebec Liberation Front (FLQ), with its armed wing, the Quebec Liberation Army (ALQ). In its manifesto, published in typescript 'underground' in 1967, Quebec is represented as a 'neo-colonized, underdeveloped country within the territorial domain of North American ⟡ imperialism'. The ALQ has carried out a number of terrorist acts as initiatives in the coming 'armed struggle' to bring about a 'revolutionary situation'. The leader of the movement is known as Mathieu Hebert. With some members of the FLQ he was arrested in 1967, charged with the murder of a woman who died accidentally in an ALQ bombing, and sentenced to life imprisonment. Mathieu Hebert is the *nom de revolution* of Pierre Vallières, a brilliant young journalist working officially on the establishment newspaper *La Presse* and unofficially as editor of the socialist theoretical journal, *Revolution Québecoise*. The FLQ and ALQ have the tacit support of the much larger Mouvement de Liberation Populaire which emerged from the serious social disturbances in 1965, when ALQ bombs exploded all over Montreal, tens of thousands of farmers marched on Quebec to demand a better return for their labour, and the trade unions mounted a series of protest demonstrations.

R

Rad: *see* Princip, Gavrilo.

Religion. In stable, established societies the higher clergy are part of the ruling class and may, as in e.g. Cyprus and the Irish Republic, even dominate it; as the revolutionary seeks to overthrow that class, he regards the Church as the enemy of the people. Thus, e.g. in those Muslim countries which were formerly part of some nominally Christian European empire, the clergy, being members of the subject race, were on the 'revolutionary' side; but following liberation, being required by the native ◊ bourgeoisie newly in power to help build up a nationalist ideology and being therefore elevated to the ranks of the new establishment, they became from the revolutionary point of view enemies of the people. Furthermore, there is in any society room for only a single official ideology: in pre-revolutionary societies that ideology is provided by the state-recognized religion, which must therefore (unless it can be won over), be regarded as an enemy by the revolutionaries who seek to set up a new ideology. ◊ Marx gave expression to this when he called religion 'the opium of the people', but there is nothing particularly ◊ Marxist about revolutionary anti-religious and anticlerical feeling. The 'infamous thing' which Voltaire called on his contemporaries to 'crush' was the Roman Catholic Church, and anticlericalism was part of the Encyclopaedist movement and therefore of the French Revolution. In the Spanish revolutions of the past 150 years not only have the clergy been a principal target of revolutionary violence, but so have the churches, and in all some hundreds have, at various times, been burned down by anarchists and anarcho-syndicalists. But in Spain, France, Italy and elsewhere revolutionaries have nearly always made a distinction between the higher clergy and the ordinary parish clergy, the latter often being more or less openly on the revolutionary side.

There are, however, some other aspects of this problem: anticlericalism does not necessarily imply atheism, and one great revolutionary, Robespierre, actually invented a new religion, the ridiculous Cult of the Supreme

Being which he tried to impose on his followers. But Marx's treatment of the subject goes much further: Marxism excludes belief in God as unscientific, irrational, in short grossly superstitious. In theory, therefore, communist states are bound simply to abolish the practice of religion as far as they can. For some years following the ⟡ Russian Revolution of October 1917, the ⟡ Bolshevik government of the USSR did all in its power to accomplish this. But once ⟡ Stalin had become all-powerful and the influence of the Old Bolshevists, those cosmopolitan intellectuals for whom Marxist theory was at least as important as practical politics, had declined, it was found expedient to relax the persecution of religion, or at least of the nationalist Russian Orthodox Church. The clergy were allowed a measure of liberty to practise their rites and were paid a stipend, though under rigorous state control: in short, the people, having failed to achieve the millennium by revolution, still needed their dose of opium. The antireligious aspect of Marxism is, of course, retained in theory, and there can be no religious teaching in the schools; nor, probably, could a man known to be devout attain high rank in the Communist Party; although, since all the monotheistic world religions frown, ideologically, on wealth, and Christianity specifically excludes the rich from heaven, it should be easier to serve God and socialism, than God and the mammon of capitalism. Indeed, non-Marxist socialism has not followed the antireligious line; there are numerous Christian socialist movements broadly based on the view that the compassion for the poor and determination to improve their lot which is the motive of socialism, can be equated with Christ's compassion for the poor – Christ is thought of as the first Socialist. Moreover, there are both Buddhist and Muslim movements which are at once religious and socialist, even militantly revolutionary.

A new development in the relations between the revolution and religion has occurred in some Latin American countries. Appalled and disgusted by the degree of misery imposed on the majority by the ruling minorities, and influenced also by the consideration that in the long run the revolution must triumph, a proportion of the parish clergy, and even certain of the higher clergy, like Bishop Helmer in Brazil, have allied themselves with the revolutionaries; and the revolutionaries, albeit nominally Marxist- ⟡ Leninist, have relaxed the doctrinaire antireligious rules to enable them to welcome this alliance.

In this development the RC clergy have been aided by such papal Bulls as *De rerum novarum* (Leo XIII. 1891) and by Pope John XXIII's critical attitude towards capitalist excesses. Protestant clergy, on the other hand, have remained firmly antisocialist and therefore antirevolutionary. This is an accident of history, the Protestant sects being confined to the rich industrial nations of northern Europe and North America where, capitalism being dominant, they would not survive economically were they to oppose it. The dominion of economic over transcendental considerations is clearly demonstrated, historically, in the case of the nonconformist Protestant sects of Christianity in Britain: when they were frowned upon by the Church of England, they were on the 'revolutionary' side in politics; but in the land of their emigration, the USA, they became the strongest allies of the ◊ establishment. This is so much the case that although the constitution of the United States excludes consideration of creed from politics, it had been regarded as impossible for a Roman Catholic to stand any chance of becoming President until the election, in 1961, of J. F. Kennedy as 35th President.

In short, since revolutionaries are obliged to make use, for economic and political ends, of an ideology hostile to that which is used by the ruling class in power, they are necessarily hostile to established religion whether in the name of humanism, as in the socialist case, or of a 'reformed' and 'purer' form of the religion of the society in question, as in the case of the English and French Protestants of the sixteenth century, of the Ismailis in Islam, or the Zen sect in Buddhism.

Revisionism, sometimes called Socialist Revisionism: it refers to the 'revised' form of ◊ Marxism first expounded by Edouard Bernstein at the Lübeck Congress of the German Social-Democratic Party in 1901. Bernstein argued that socialism can be attained by using the ◊ bourgeois parliamentary system to introduce progressive reforms, and that violent revolution was not, therefore, called for. (Karl ◊ Kautsky though he was Bernstein's chief critic, carried this a stage further, arguing that if Marx was right in his contention that socialism was historically inevitable, and that capitalism must decay of its own accord by reason of its internal contradictions, violent revolution was, clearly, unnecessary). But ◊ Lenin condemned this revisionism as a 'bourgeois corruption of the workers', and this denunciation was repeated at the 1961 Congress of Soviet Communist Parties. Revisionism is, therefore, heretical and consequently anathema, and as such it is used as a term of abuse among Marxists. The Chinese Communist Party's accusation that the USSR policy of 'peaceful co-existence' with capitalist countries is revisionist is clearly good, logical communist ideology. On the other hand, of course, Russian Communists argue that ▷ Mao Tse-tung's claim that every communist party is free to interpret Marxism- ▷ Leninism in such a way as to adapt it to particular national conditions, can be seen as opening the door wide to revisionism.

Revolution is defined by the *Concise Oxford Dictionary* as *complete change, turning upside down, great reversal of conditions*. Out of the large number of social and political revolutions recorded in history, five may be taken as prototypes: they are, in chronological order, the English, the American, the French, the Russian and the Chinese.

The English Revolution, 1688, after years of civil war and the short Commonwealth episode, finally substituted the power of a landed aristocracy and gentry for the power of a monarch ruling by divine right, who was the last relic of the feudal system which had been undergoing destruction for over two centuries, ravaged by plague (which by enhancing the value of labour raised the standards of the lowest class), and by strife among the feudal lords, and between the feudal lords and the king.

The American Revolution in theory substituted the power of a whole people self-governing democratically through representatives to a bicameral national assembly, the Congress, and an elected monarch, the President or Chief Executive, for the rule of an imperial power located overseas; it is thus the type of the anti-imperial revolution by a national ▷ bourgeoisie. There is a contradiction here: a people cannot effectively exercise power through representatives, but only by direct participation in decision-making. Because US democracy was not direct (as it had been in, e.g. Athens and early Republican Rome), but parliamentary and representative, in practice the American, like the English, revolution, gave power to an oligarchy, first aristocratic, later plutocratic.

In the French Revolution the power of a monarch ruling by divine right through and with the support of a feudal aristocracy exploiting a peasantry was replaced by that of a bourgeoisie more or less supported by a free, enfranchised and freeholding peasantry: it is, therefore, the type of the bourgeois-patriot revolution against a native, not an imperial, aristocracy.

The Russian Revolution in theory substituted the dictatorship of a

223

proletariat, in practice that of a one-party revolutionary elite claiming to act for the proletariat, for that of an absolute monarch ruling by divine right supported by a feudal, serf-owning, aristocracy: this was the first example of a two-stage revolution. In the first stage (*see* Russian Revolution, February 1917) the bourgeoisie, whose aim was to substitute urban capitalist for landowner control, with the French Revolution as its model, overthrew the feudal monarchy with the help of the peasants and the proletariat; and in the second stage (*see* ◊ Russian Revolution, October 1917), the proletariat overthrew the bourgeoisie, led by a militant socialist party, the ◊ Bolsheviks, whose aim was to substitute socialism for capitalism.

The Chinese Revolution was also a two-stage revolution, in the first stage the bourgeois-nationalists, with the support of the peasant and proletarian Communist Party, overthrew both the divine monarchy ruling through a bureaucracy and the foreign imperialist powers exploiting China, so that we have elements of both the French and American revolutions; thereafter the Communist Party, leading the peasants and proletariat, overthrew the bourgeois-nationalists, and therefore capitalism, and substituted socialism. But there were very large differences between the Chinese and Russian revolutions in the second stage as well as the first. The power base of the Bolsheviks was the urban proletariat and the army; the power base of the Chinese communists was the peasantry. Because the Russian Revolution of October 1917 was not preceded by a people's war, it was forced to defend its gains against a rebellious bourgeoisie in a civil war after the revolution. The Chinese Revolution was preceded and made by a people's war lasting twenty years, with the result that there was no subsequent bourgeois rebellion, the defeated bourgeois side taking refuge, with its Kuomintang army, in Taiwan.

Of the many theories advanced to explain revolutions of all five types, only two need engage the attention of serious students and only one the attention of realists: each can be defined in a word, one being 'idealist' and the other 'materialist' and then can be called, roughly and respectively, pre-Marxist, and ◊ Marxist. According to the idealist theory revolutions are attempts to realize ideals; those, e.g. of a religious sect, like the English or Scottish puritans or the Muslim Ismailis or, in the modern world, the humanist and social ideals of a political group or party: by the idealists, political and economic power are thought of as secondary gains, or as the mere necessary means to the ideological end. According to the Marxist theory revolutions are attempts by an economically exploited class to seize economic and political power from the ruling (exploiting) class, the ideological aim being achieved as a corollary.

A simple means of exemplifying this difference of emphasis can be found in the case of the English revolution: according to the idealist school, the revolutionaries were bent on substituting the new Protestant for the old Catholic ideology; in the course of achieving this they found that economic and political power had passed into their hands. According to the materialists, the ideology was a means to mobilize forces to wage a class war for control of economic and political power. The ideological factor was important since their revolution entailed a measure of sacrilege, e.g. in the killing of a king-by-divine-right, which needed the sanction of a new religion.

Realists confronted by these two theories of revolution will as a rule, and although they are not Marxists, find themselves obliged by observation of the facts to choose the materialist theory; for it cannot rationally be denied that whereas an ideology, whether religious, philosophical or humanist, has its roots in social conditions, or that social conditions are a product of economic and political forces, the converse is not true; ideologies do not of themselves generate particular economic and social conditions. The primitive hunter worships a god of hunting; he turns farmer to better his economy and then worships a goddess of fertility; he does not first become a sectary of that goddess and then, as a result of his conversion, turn farmer. The Arab armies of the sixth and seventh centuries were summoned to action in the name of Allah and had his name on their lips as they went into battle: but the purpose of their warfare was the conquest of territory and, quite simply, loot. From the fifteenth to the nineteenth century the European nations conquered the Americas, all Africa and a great part of Asia to increase their wealth and power and then justified this robbery with violence by reference to their religious duty to convert the heathen to their own ideologies. Sixteenth-century European princes and the rising seventeenth-century bourgeoisie of the northern European countries did not adopt the new protestant ideology and *incidentally*, perhaps by way of divine reward, find themselves more powerful or richer; they sought more power, more riches and turned to protestantism because it served that purpose: it does not follow that all those who did so knew just what they

Revolution

were doing: sincere ideologists, religious or political, have ever served the purpose of the few who saw more clearly and acted from strictly material motives.

So that ⟡ Marx and those predecessors in his field from whom he drew his conclusions were surely right when they saw history as a struggle in which those below, the exploited class, seek to oust and replace those above, the exploiting class. And the struggle is just, in that the majority is always striving against a minority for enjoyment of more economic and political power, so that, in material terms at least, it tends to promote the greater happiness of the greater number.

The French Revolution offers a clear demonstration of these truths: the ideology used to mobilize it was that of the *philosophes* or 'Encyclopaedists', and is expressed in the slogan 'Liberty Equality Fraternity', which appealed not only to the bourgeoisie, the class seeking to seize power, but to the masses who became their allies. An adherent of the ideological school would maintain that the Revolution was made to accomplish those three ideals: what it was actually made for appears both in its conduct and in the event: a greater measure of liberty than Frenchmen had formerly enjoyed was achieved, for it served the economic and political purpose of the bourgeoisie to let it be so. But then Bonaparte appeared to make sure that the masses, the allies of the bourgeoisie, should no longer be under any dangerous illusions that Equality meant more than equality of opportunity and before the law; and Fraternity anything at all. What Bonaparte did would have been done by another instrument had he not been available; Hoche, for example, only he died too soon. The point is that socially there would have been no difference, though the subsequent *events* would have been different. The Revolution Triumphant accomplished the material ends of the Revolution Militant; as for the failure to accomplish the ideals, it implies no ⟡ Machiavellian hypocrisy: it is all a question of what words mean at particular crises in history.

'Liberty' was also the ideal slogan of the American Revolution against the British ⟡ imperial establishment. But again, the word has rather a special meaning, in the context of the times: half the revolutionary leaders were slave-owners, yet it was never for a moment proposed to give liberty to slaves. The revolution was made, was declared and seen to be made, by a rising class of landowners and merchants, to take power out of British hands into their own. The liberty they had in mind was the liberty to

226

exploit on their own behalf: the liberty of a Brutus, a millionaire slave-owner, to be the boss; or the liberty of Athens where four-fifths of the population was unenfranchised and three-fifths were slaves (most of the American revolutionary leaders had had a good classical education). Liberty has always been one of the best rallying words used by ideologists to mobilize revolutionary forces: what it actually means is a matter for philosophers and they have never come to any conclusions. But of our five prototypical cases the American one leaves least room for doubt by even the most idealist of minds that the Marxist interpretation is the correct one.

In the Bolshevik October Revolution there was an exceptional measure of honesty (it might be fairer to the others to say, rather, a smaller measure of unconscious hypocrisy) in the original appeal to the masses. This was partly because the leaders, being Marxists, could not but be aware that while revolution needs to be inspired by an ideology, it is actually about material gains for the revolutionary class. 'All power to the Soviets!' was not some vaguely noble ideal. There was another factor making for honesty: as a result of the world war the condition of the masses was so atrocious that a simple promise of bread was more effective as a rallying cry than a promise of utopia; and for the 'ideal' ingredient there was the worldwide comradeship of the workers. But when, as a consequence of the civil war, of counterrevolutionary intervention by Britain, America, France, the USA, and Japan, and the Communist Party's gross mishandling of the peasants, bread was not forthcoming, the Revolution's leaders were obliged increasingly to rely on an ideological appeal: its positive element was the broadly humanist liberal aspirations which had been the pre-socialist and socialist cry for two centuries; the negative side was abuse of the enemies of the people, the alien interventionist bourgeoisie and its native counter-revolutionary allies: it has always been a sound rule of leadership, revolutionary or counterrevolutionary, to give the people someone to hate. It is instructive to compare the Bolshevik image of the monstrous, predatory, slavering foreign capitalist, with extreme Protestant propaganda against the RC Church in the English revolution, or with the hideous diabolical Jew of ⬧ Nazi mythology. With the exception of the Vatican's Congregatio de propaganda fide backed by the Holy Office, no social apparatus has ever been more successful than the CP of the USSR backed by the GPU (later KGB) in holding the masses loyal by ideological promises unsupported by any material and present reward. Though collective advantages were enjoyed earlier it was not for forty years that individual citizens began to enjoy the usual fruits of industrialization. The application of economic socialism has made the Soviet state the second most powerful – perhaps, now, taking its massive stability into account, the most powerful – state in the world: the material aim of the Revolution has, in that sense, been accomplished, provided the Russian people can identify with the state: but the noble, generous, humane ideal of socialism is still in the misty future.

The most recent major revolution, the Chinese, began as the Russian type, but with a longer bourgeois phase – 1911 to *c.* 1946; and a much longer civil war, which in this case preceded the second (socialist) phase, a difference with enormous consequences, and not the only one. For, with the emergence of ▷ Mao Tse-tung the revolutionary role of the peasants became far more important than that of the proletariat, and the countryside brought the revolution to the cities, not the cities to the countryside. Moreover, there was far more emphasis on the Leninist ▷ cultural revolution, and therefore on genuine democracy, than in the Russian case. Furthermore, the fact that the peasants, far from being a class alienated by the revolution, were its makers and in some measure its heirs (and the CCP has been much more successful than the CP of the USSR in involving the people and the intellectuals in the aims of the revolution), it has been easier for the CCP to keep some of its material promises much more promptly. It must in fairness be said that it has had one other very great advantage which the Russians never enjoyed: and one stroke of luck which the Russians did not have. The advantage was the very existence of the mighty communist USSR. However much the two powers quarrel, the mere existence of Soviet economic and military power has meant that the USA and the other capitalist powers have not dared to intervene in China since 1946. Just as the young American capitalism was free to develop in peace, protected by the power of the British Royal Navy from any question of a European adventure of the type which Napoleon III and his bankers attempted in Mexico, so the young communism of China has been free to develop in peace under the protection of the Soviet's H-bombs. As for the stroke of luck, how very often must millions of Russians, with ▷ Lenin and ▷ Trotsky and the Old Bolsheviks in mind, have cried from under the heel of the crafty boor Joseph ▷ Stalin, like Macbeth,

'They should have died hereafter!' Mao Tse-tung and ⟡ Chou En-lai, one a gentleman and the other a peasant, both scholars and the first a poet, men of Lenin's mettle, are, at the time of writing, still alive.

Revolutionary Catechism. This document, printed as a pamphlet and circulated in Russian and European revolutionary circles from 1869–70 was written in collaboration by ⟡ Bakunin and ⟡ Nechayev, based on an earlier *Programme of Revolutionary Action* by Nechayev and ⟡ Tkachev. Its opening paragraph reads: 'The revolutionary is a lost man; he has no interests of his own, no cause of his own, no feelings, no habits, no belongings; he does not even have a name. Everything in him is absorbed by a single, exclusive interest, a single thought, a single passion – the revolution.'

What else is the revolutionary? He is an implacable enemy of the world as it is, who lives in it only to destroy it; knows only one science, that of destruction; despises the social ethic and public opinion; for him whatever advances the revolution is moral, whatever obstructs it is immoral; there is no other rule. The revolutionary must always be prepared for torture or death; all tender feelings of family life, of friendship, love, gratitude and even honour must be stifled in him for the single cold passion for the revolutionary cause, and he must be ready at all times to kill with his own hands. He must remain free from romanticism, sentimentality, enthusiasm, private hatred or feelings of revenge. Revolutionaries, working together, must reach all decisions unanimously and when using lower grade revolutionaries for the cause must do so without regard for anything but the revolution.

In overturning established society the revolutionary should use different means according to the category into which people fall: (1) intelligent and important people will be assassinated; (2) important but unintelligent – let them live and flourish, for their bestial stupidity encourages the people to revolt; (3) the highly placed but incompetent – they can usually be blackmailed and the revolutionary must try to discover their discreditable secrets; (4) ambitious politicians and liberals – work with them, carefully involve them in conspiracies until they are so compromised that they cannot turn back but must, with their own hands, overthrow the state for their own sake; (5) those revolutionaries who are so only in their written and spoken words – they must be drawn or driven into deeds and involved

Rhodesia

in serious fighting in which the unfit will be killed while those that survive will be tempered revolutionaries. Women have a category to themselves: they make invaluable revolutionaries if they are 'open in deed and free from rhetoric', but otherwise are relegated to categories (3) or (4).

Paragraph 23 of the *Catechism* defines what the *tovarishchestvo* (revolutionary association) means by 'popular revolution'; there is no hope in reform or in revolutionary gradualism; every aspect of the old establishment, root and branch, must be destroyed, every tradition, order, class in the Russian state. Here are paragraphs 25 and 26: 'To do this we must draw close to the people; we must ally ourselves mainly with those elements which ever since the foundation of the state of Moscow have never given up protesting, not just in words but in deeds, against anything directly or indirectly tied to the state; against the nobility, the priests, the bureaucracy, against the world of guilds and against the rich peasants. We must ally ourselves with the doughty world of brigands who in Russia are the true revolutionaries. All our organization, all our conspiracy, all our purpose consists in this: to regroup the world-brigands into an invincible and omnidestructive force.'

Since the *Catechism*, in its published form, was certainly rewritten by ◊ Bakunin, although on the basis of the earlier Nechayev-Tkachev document, it has been held to be a fair, brief statement of Bakunin's political policy: *see also* International Brotherhood.

Rhodesia: *See* South Africa and Rhodesia, revolution in.

Rodgriguez, Manuel Ponte, Captain, former Commanding Officer of the Puerto Cebello Naval Base, Venezuela, and revolutionary leader of the ◊ FALN. *See* Venezuela, guerrilla movements.

Romania: *see* Iron Guard.

Russian Revolution 1870–1905. The miserable poverty of the Russian peasants under Tsarism, the starvation wages, wretched and humiliating conditions of the industrial proletariat, and refusal of all the fundamental rights of the subject to both classes, the numerical insignificance and political weakness of the ◊ bourgeoisie, coupled with the absolutism of the Tsar who was above all law, roused the consciences of many Russian

230

intellectuals who sought, at first by peaceful means and, when they failed, by violence, to liberalize social conditions and the political constitution. For this phase of the Russian revolutionary movement *see*: Land and Liberty; Narodnik movement; Nihilism; People's Will; Populists; Socialist Revolutionary Party.

Russian Revolution 1905. The activities of the revolutionary and reformist groups active in Russia from 1870 to 1905 (*see* Russian Revolution 1870–1905) had not been effective in obtaining fundamental rights of the subject or in relieving the misery of the peasants and industrial ▷ proletariat. Tsar Nicholas II (1868–1918), a stupid and obstinate autocrat, aggravated revolutionary activity by his persistent refusal to grant any kind of parliamentary constitution. The grotesque misconduct of the Russo-Japanese war by his generals and admirals brought widespread discontent into the open; this discontent was turned into revolution by an almost incredible blunder, the ▷ 'Bloody Sunday' (9 January 1905) massacre of peacefully demonstrating St Petersburg workers. It was ▷ Lenin's opinion that as a result of this atrocity 'the revolutionary education of the proletariat made more progress in one day than it would have made in years'. It was followed by mutinies in the armed forces, violent nationalist uprisings in the territories of the minority nations within the Russian Empire, strikes, thousands of peasant revolts, student riots, revolts in the universities and some assassinations. All these initial disturbances were put down by military intervention, there was a short lull and then revolution broke out again, with strikes involving hundreds of thousands. In August 1905 the government made some minor concessions and strikers began to drift back to work. The shattering naval defeat of the Russians at Tshushima and the signing of a humiliating peace with Japan freed the government's hands to deal with the revolt: it is significant that the news of Tshushima caused an average two point rise on the Moscow Stock Exchange; it was more important to crush the revolution than to go on fighting the Japanese.

In September there was a new wave of strikes and riots; printing works, all the railways, and most factories were paralysed; university staffs joined the students in demands for the fundamental freedoms, manhood suffrage, even votes for women. The workers demanded permanent ▷ Soviets and there was a movement to depose the Tsar and establish a Republic. Serious street fighting frightened Nicholas and his ministers into granting a constitution in a document known as the October Manifesto; it granted the fundamental freedoms, slightly broadened the franchise, and gave the Duma a legislative instead of merely consultative role. This Manifesto was at once denounced by ◊ Trotsky, a member of the St Petersburg Soviet of Workers, as 'a Cossack's whip wrapped in the parchment of a constitution'. To distract the public from the revolution and pick on the usual scapegoat, the Jew, the police organized pogroms on a gigantic scale all over Russia, but Nicholas dared not take any serious counter-revolutionary measures.

For some weeks there was peace, an unprecedented measure of freedom and a feeling that the new Duma might mean real parliamentary government. The Soviets in the two capitals grew daily in numbers and power. The St Petersburg Soviet demanded the withdrawal of troops and police from the city, a political amnesty, the lifting of martial law which had been imposed on the whole country, a constituent assembly, and the eight-hour day. But the workers had the employers as well as the government to reckon with :◊ lockouts, which meant hunger, were weakening them. The government scored a success when it crushed the mutiny of sailors in the Imperial Navy at Kronstadt. Trotsky tried to hit back by organizing a run on the banks, which was a failure. A new minister of the interior with more courage than most of the Tsar's ministers had Khrustalev-Nosar, president of the St Petersburg Soviet, arrested: Trotsky succeeded him. On 3 December troops surrounded the building where the Soviet was meeting. The members were armed and ready to fight; Trotsky then made what he later confessed to have been a revolutionary blunder; believing that if they fought the Soviet members would simply get themselves massacred, he ordered them to throw down their weapons; the members set about smashing up their guns, the entire Soviet was arrested by the troops, and the revolution in St Petersburg was over.

At this point the Moscow Soviet called a general strike in their city, with the intention of turning it into an armed insurrection. The revolutionaries were badly led; there was street fighting for a week, but the military got the upper hand by shelling the working-class residential districts with heavy artillery and by shooting thousands of prisoners taken in the street fighting.

No sooner was the revolution crushed in the two capitals than it broke out in the Baltic and Far Eastern provinces, with huge strikes, serious and destructive riots, and pitched battles with army units. But the government had recovered its nerve: strong punitive expeditions were sent to the four major 'fronts'; firing-squads and flogging parties did their work well. Nicholas, in his *Diary,* recorded that his formerly liberal prime minister, Witte, 'now wants to hang and shoot everybody'. Last to be crushed were the millions of peasant revolutionaries: between 1 November and the end of December 1905 there were 1,372 peasant risings, accompanied by the looting and burning of manor houses all over Russia. This state of war between Tsarism and the people lasted well into 1906, but in due course the recipe of hanging and shooting restored the old order.

The revolution was a failure, but it taught the revolutionaries an important lesson. Next time they must have the soldiers on their side. It did score some small and temporary gains, e.g. the concession of a legislative role for the Duma and a broadened franchise which gave the workers representation in that house. But in the following years these gains were neutralized by the Tsar's implacable hostility to the Duma and determination that it should not erode the imperial autocracy.

Russian Revolution, February 1917. From the suppression of the Revolution 1905 (*see* preceding entry), for the next decade the social and economic situation in the Russian Empire remained continuously potentially revolutionary: there were innumerable strikes, some of them on a huge scale; urban riots, peasant revolts, and, in retaliation, Cossack and Guards massacres of the rebels and strikers. On the non-violent level there was the struggle between the progressive wing of the Duma and the Tsar Nicholas II for a genuine parliamentary and more or less democratic constitution, the former supported by the liberal ⟡ bourgeoisie often represented by the Kadet and Octobrist parties; the latter by the Tsarina who urged her husband to be another Ivan the Terrible, her *âme damnée,* Rasputin, and the reactionary wing of the nobility. The political, social and economic fever came to a head after two years of the 1914–18 war, chiefly because the people's miseries were aggravated by ever worsening conditions: the appalling hardships suffered by millions of soldiers ill-supplied and worse led; severe shortages due to mismanagement of the economy, leading to starvation at home; more strikes in all the industrial centres; defeat on the German and Austrian fronts; industrial breakdown; and grotesque bureaucratic muddle and inertia and general defeatism leading to loss of all interest in the war, combined to create an explosive revolutionary situation, especially in Petrograd. The Duma progressives warned repeatedly of impending revolution and denounced the Tsarist absolutism which was exasperating the people; even the British ambassador warned the Tsar, in a private audience, of what would happen if he did not grant an an immediate constitution and hand the executive power to a responsible administration. Nicholas remained obstinately blind to the truth, even when plots to depose him in favour of his son or his brother were exposed, and when Rasputin was assassinated. ⟡ Social revolutionaries, Mensheviks and the few ⟡ Bolsheviks organized street demonstrations. By 22 February tens of thousands of starving, striking workers were on the streets. Troops and police were attacked, but soon began going over to the revolution; even the Cossacks proved 'unreliable'. On 27 February the crack Volynsky regiment mutinied and a few days later the whole Petrograd garrison of 170,000 were refusing orders and shooting officers. Michael Rodzyanko, president of the Duma, telegraphed the Tsar that the city was in anarchy, the people starving, the troops in full mutiny and asked for the government to be dismissed and a new, responsible, administration appointed to meet the demands of the revolution. Nicholas prorogued the Duma. It refused to disperse and asked the Grand Duke Michael to declare a military dictatorship. Michael wasted time trying to persuade Nicholas to agree, and so lost his chance. On 27 February (a) the Duma party leaders formed themselves in a provisional government, mostly Kadets and Octobrists, and (b) the socialist revolutionaries formed their own 'government', the Temporary Executive Committee of the Soviet of Workers' Deputies, mostly social revolutionaries, Menshevik and Bolshevik social democrats. The principal men of the Provisional Government were Milyukov, Guchov, and Kerensky; they immediately promised the people an amnesty; freedom of speech, press and assembly; a people's militia to replace the police and no victimization. It forced the Tsar to abdicate, with the intention, later frustrated by the Soviet, of crowning the Tsarevich under the regency of Michael.

The Soviet Executive Committee held an election of workers' and soldiers' deputies: one worker for every thousand per factory; one from every factory with fewer than 1,000 workers; and one soldier from every company. The 1,500 strong Soviet which resulted consisted mostly of

Menshevik or social revolutionary soldiers; fewer workers of the same persuasion; and only forty Bolsheviks. Its executive committee immediately organized companies of soldiers to protect the revolution, who were to obey the Provisional Government only for so long as the Soviet endorsed its orders. The Soviet was inclined to support the Provisional Government provided it carried out its promise and added to its programme equality of rights, abolition of minority nationality disabilities, democratic elections for a Constituent Assembly; and no Romanov restoration. It was not yet demanding socialist measures, the Menshevik majority holding that it was their duty at this ◊ 'bourgeois' stage of the revolution to support the bourgeois liberals. The real differences between the two bodies did not emerge until late April: the Soviet, representing the war-weary workers, peasants and soldiers, wanted immediate peace with Germany; the Provisional Government, under severe Allied diplomatic and financial pressure, wanted more efficient prosecution of the war. Meanwhile, outside the capital the revolution was welcomed, in some places with reservations; peasants and industrial workers set up their own soviets. By the end of April it was clear that, having completed its basic programme of legislation, the Provisional Government had accomplished nothing in the fields of economics and war politics; was jibbing at fixing a date for the Constituent Assembly; was hostile to the enfranchisement of the soldiers; and was still playing with the idea of a Romanov restoration. This meant stalemate, for as Prince Lvov, the idealistic but otherwise useless president of the Provisional Government, put it, 'The Soviet has power without authority; the Government has authority without power.' This was the uneasy situation which ◊ Lenin and ◊ Trotsky were able to exploit from May until their triumph in October.

Russian Revolution, October 1917. Almost as soon as the news of the ◊ Russian Revolution of February 1917 reached Germany, Alexander Parvus, Russian-born German ◊ Marxist social-democratic leader of European repute, suggested to the German High Command that ◊ Lenin and other ◊ Bolshevik leaders then exiled in Zürich be helped to return to Russia. His object was to exploit in the service of international social democracy the High Command's wish to weaken the Russian home front by aggravating the revolution. As a result Lenin and thirty-two other Bolsheviks were moved across Germany in a sealed train and reached Petrograd on 3 April.

(George ◊ Plekhanov, doyen of Russian ◊ Marxists, was given similar godspeed and cruiser transport by the British who knew him to be a German-hater who would advocate Russian continuance in the war at whatever cost.) Of the other most effective Russian socialist revolutionaries, ◊ Trotsky had set out to return to Russia from New York in March, but had been put into a concentration camp by the British, in Halifax, Canada, and did not reach Petrograd until May; Kamenev and ◊ Zinoviev were already there.

The Bolsheviks had set up their HQ in a villa near the Peter-and-Paul fortress. From there Lenin promulgated his 'April Theses': no support for the war effort, since the Provisional Government was still capitalist; concentration on the immediate overthrow of capitalism in Russia; all power to the ◊ proletariat and the poorest peasants, and therefore overthrow of the Provisional Government; expropriation and nationalization of the land and its control and management by peasant soviets; a formation of a revolutionary International to spread the revolution abroad. These theses, at first rejected as too extreme, were accepted by the end of April. The task then became to win control of the Petrograd Workers' Soviet from the Menshevik and social revolutionary majority. The first open breach between the Petrograd Soviet and the Provisional Government occurred when the government published its war aims including 'adherence to all obligations assumed towards our Allies'. The war-weary people and soldiers broke out into riots and street fighting (18 April). The Bolshevik Central Committee seized the chance to point out that the Provisional Government was 'bound hand and foot to Anglo-French and Russian capital'. The government knew that it was losing control of the armed forces even at the fronts where troops were becoming mutinous. It decided to save itself by taking three social revolutionary and Menshevik ministers from the Soviet into the administration. The small Bolshevik minority in the Soviet rejected the idea of any such cooperation with the ◊ bourgeoisie; in Lenin's view the two socialist parties which consented to this arrangement were putting themselves 'outside the revolutionary pale'. On 5 May, while the Executive Committee were commending the proposed coalition to the Chamber, Trotsky, arriving from concentration camp in Halifax, Canada, was given a standing ovation and at once spoke against the coalition, though he was not yet a Bolshevik. It was, he said, 'a capture of the Soviet by the bourgeoisie'.

The coalition continued its predecessor's war policy. Even the All-Russian Congress of Soviets held in June rejected proposals for an immediate separate peace with Germany made by the Bolsheviks, and Lenin was denounced as a German agent. Nevertheless, Bolshevik committees were steadily gaining strength in the armies and factories and their press under Trotsky's guidance was growing in influence. When the Congress elected a new Executive Committee it included 35 Bolsheviks, 104 Mensheviks and 99 social revolutionaries. But the principal Congress resolution – for complete workers' control of industry and confiscation of capitalist profits – carried by an enormous majority – was drafted by Lenin and Zinoviev. Now the Bolshevik cry of 'All power to the Soviets!' was raised. As these cries grew louder Lenin, suffering from overwork, went for a short holiday to Finland. Soldiers were everywhere deserting the fronts, peasants seizing the land, workers the factories. When, in mid-June, Kerensky, as War Minister, ordered a general Russian offensive against the German fronts, the soldiers showed extreme reluctance to obey orders, and the moment the Germans counterattacked, ran away and kept on going until they reached home. By July the Petrograd streets were crowded with revolutionary soldiers and sailors ready to attack the government. But neither Lenin, back from Finland, nor any other Bolshevik, despite the cry of 'All power to the Soviets', thought the moment had come; whereas a new, socialist-dominated but bourgeois-orientated government now decided on firmness, suppressed all publications calling for disobedience to military orders or violent overthrow of government; banned street meetings and processions; condemned land seizure by the peasants; took powers for arrest and deportation of violent revolutionary leaders; published partly authentic and partly forged documents connecting Lenin with Parvus and thus raising again the cry that Lenin was a German agent. The Soviet Executive Committee and the Executive Committee of the Peasant Soviets joined heartily in this denunciation; Lenin was forced to go 'underground' and Trotsky and other Bolsheviks were arrested and imprisoned, though soon released.

As a result, Lenin now proclaimed a new Bolshevik policy: no longer 'All power to the Soviets', the Petrograd Soviet's leaders had turned it into 'a fig-leaf of counter-revolution', and it was unfit to hold power. Instead, 'Victory for the workers': armed uprising must transfer power into the hands of the proletariat and the poor peasants, 'to put into execution the programme of our party' (Trotsky, *History*). In short, a revolutionary dictatorship of the proletariat. ⟡ Stalin put this policy to the 6th Bolshevik Party Congress held illegally in June, but the majority was still too unsure to take the leadership of an insurrection. But the people were soon pushing them into that coveted but uncomfortable position: as shortages became worse, prices rose three times as fast as wages, and tension between labour and employers became intolerable; workers seized control of the factories and employers retaliated by lockouts. Factory workers' committees became increasingly Bolshevik while in the country the peasant Soviets were seizing not only land but control of local business, over-ruling or ignoring government agencies. When Chernov, the social revolutionary leader in the cabinet, tried to legalize their seizures, there was a cabinet split and Prince Lvov resigned. The right-wing Kadets, dominating the next administration, tried to veto 'all basic social reforms' until the calling of a Constituent Assembly which they had no intention of calling. Kornilov, the only Russian general still effectively fighting the Germans, called for a 'restore order' programme; Kerensky appointed him C-in-C, whereupon he announced from Moscow that the time had come to hang Lenin, the German agent, disperse the Soviets and restore the death penalty for soldiers disobeying orders. When it looked as if he was trying to impose a military dictatorship, Kerensky dismissed him (26 August). Kornilov refused to go and made a cavalry advance on Petrograd. This caused a strong pro-Bolshevik swing in public opinion. The Soviet, that 'fig-leaf of the counter-revolution', organized workers' defence squads and sabotage of the railway communications Kornilov would need. The would-be dictator was arrested without bloodshed.

The Soviet called a conference of all democratic organizations to decide what form of effective government was now possible; all that emerged was another coalition under Kerensky and an advisory Council of the Republic. Trotsky immediately denounced it and again proclaimed the Bolshevik programme: workers' control of industry; transfer of land to peasant committees; denunciation of secret treaties; an immediate armistice; arming of the workers; establishment of a Red Guard; self-determination for the nationalities. All over Russia there were lootings and arson, banditry, rioting, mutinies and pogroms. Such authority as existed was in the hands of local Soviets. With two million army deserters at large, predatory bands of soldiers roamed the country. Among the seven million men still under arms, defeatism, and then Bolshevism, rose like a tidal wave and swept aside all military discipline.

In these conditions only Lenin, to suit his own purpose, revived the slogan 'All power to the Soviets', and declared that the Bolsheviks would take no office in a Menshevik-Social-Revolutionary administration, since they stood for the dictatorship of the proletariat. Those two parties, bound in the coalition with the bourgeois parties, failed, as he knew they must, to respond. At the September local elections in Moscow the Bolsheviks were the largest party with a small overall majority. In Petrograd and elsewhere the story was much the same, although they were still in a minority in the country as a whole. Trotsky became president of the Petrograd Soviet and a vote of no confidence in the Provisional Government was passed by a large majority. On 13 September Lenin summoned the Bolshevik Central Committee to prepare at once for an armed insurrection. It took him a month to persuade them.

It was Trotsky who found the instrument for the coup d'état: when, on 9 October, the Mensheviks proposed forming a committee for revolutionary defence, he backed them, and then seized on the Committee and turned it, despite their protests, into a Military Revolutionary Committee. Many of the Petrograd garrison troops and the Kronstadt sailors were already Bolsheviks; many more came over when the Bolsheviks first attributed to Kerensky the intention of sending them to the front, then intervened to prevent this. On 24 October Colonel Polkovnikov, OC Petrograd garrison, ordered all army units to rid themselves of the political commissars appointed by the Soviet, while Kerensky, declaring Petrograd in a state of insurrection, summoned loyal troops to garrison the Winter Palace, government HQ, and take control of all key points in the city. On 25 October the Council of the Republic resolved by a small majority to call on the government to invite the Allies to stop fighting and negotiate a peace with Germany; to legalize all land-seizures by the peasants; and to advance the date of the oft-postponed Constituent Assembly. In short, to steal Lenin's thunder. But it was too late, the Military Committee's soldiers and Red Guard factory hands were seizing every strategic point in the city, including the State Bank; the government troops handed over to them without a struggle. On the afternoon of 25 October Trotsky was able to proclaim to the Soviet: 'In the name of the Military Revolutionary Committee, I announce that the Provisional Government no longer exists.' On the night of 25/26 October the second Congress of Soviets met. The Bolsheviks were the largest single party, but in a slight minority to the social revolutionaries, who were split into a left and right, and the Mensheviks, split into Menshevik-Internationalists (left) led by Martov and Mensheviks (right). Martov proposed a commission to form a joint Socialist government; Lenin, playing for time, agreed. The right-wing social revolutionaries and the Mensheviks walked out, combined with some peasant leaders, members of the Council of the Republic, and trade union leaders, to form a Committee of Public Safety and denounce the Bolshevik coup d'état as undemocratic. This enabled Trotsky to tar Martov with the same brush as the dissident social revolutionary rightists, and repudiate the coalition agreement. During the morning of 26 October a newly elected Central Executive Committee dominated by Bolsheviks appointed an all-Bolshevik government, the first Council of People's Commissars, headed by Lenin and with Trotsky at Foreign Affairs.

It was a minority government: at the long-delayed election to the thereafter aborted Constituent Assembly the Bolsheviks won 168 seats, the social revolutionaries 299 and all other parties 153. But that was no longer the point: the Bolsheviks had the soldiers, and they ruled as the executive of the proletarian dictatorship; their first decrees were immediate armistice, and abolition of private property in the means of production and in land. Moreover, as all their opponents, left and right alike, showed their willingness to call in foreign allies, even Germans, against the Bolsheviks, both the new glamour of the Revolution and the older charisma of nationalism came to reside in the Bolsheviks. Furthermore, Lenin and Trotsky, having published the secret treaties and exposed their iniquitous horse-dealing were appealing over the heads of governments to people everywhere, for open diplomacy and 'a just and democratic peace without annexations or indemnities' (it is Trotsky speaking, not Woodrow Wilson), which was what a majority of the world wanted. The Revolution still had to fight the civil war but by 27 October 1917 it had triumphed, and it was to take Stalin twenty years to throw away the pride and joy of the Russian workers and peasants in what they imagined they had created for all time: a reasonably just society.

S

Sabotage. There are two published derivations of this word and it is not impossible that both are valid. An industrial machine could be halted and damaged by 'clogging', i.e. by jamming a clog – *sabot* in French – into its works. Clogs (wooden shoes) were worn by industrial workers in Britain, France and many other countries in the nineteenth century, and such use of clogs by malcontent or revolutionary workers may be the origin of the verb *saboter* and hence of its derivative (cf. the French *savate*, literally an alternative for *sabot*, but which also means a form of boxing in which kicks are allowed). But the word *sabot* is also used in French to mean the 'chairs' which hold railway lines to sleepers: in the great French railway strike of 1910 workers cut the (then) wooden *sabots* to prevent trains from being run by blacklegs. The use of the word by the ◊ Industrial Workers of the World to describe the act of damaging or wrecking industrial plant as a revolutionary act, brought it into currency in its now accepted sense, when the IWW stand against war, in the US in 1917, led to their being described as 'sabotaging' the US war effort. In its official military sense it was first used during the Spanish Civil War to describe the activities of ◊ 'fifth columns' on both sides.

Sacco and Vanzetti. The most famous names in the anarchist martyrology. Farnandino (but known as Nicola) Sacco (1891–1927) b. Torremaggiore, Italy, s. of a prosperous peasant. Left school at fourteen, worked on farm, migrated at 17 to join some cousins at Milford, Mass., USA; worked as unskilled labourer while studying bootmaking; qualified, obtained high paid work 1910–17. Took an active part in cultural anarchist activities, reading the anarchist newspaper *Il Proletario* edited by the poet-revolutionary Giovanitti; and with his young wife Rosa Zambolli playing in socialist amateur theatricals. Joined (1913) the anarchist 'Circolo di Studi' and worked to spread anarchist doctrine. Arrested and fined, 1916, for 'breach of the peace', i.e. supporting a strike. Bartolomeo Vanzetti (1888–1927) b. Villafalleto, Italy, s. of another prosperous peasant.

Sacco and Vanzetti

Although brilliant enough at school to become an academic, he was apprenticed to a baker and thus early had the harsh realities of working-class life forced on him; reading widely, he became a ◊ Marxist anarchist. Migrated (1908) to New York, where he earned his living as a dishwasher, quarryman, gardener, and in other casual labour, while reading revolutionary authors. He obtained regular employment at a ropemaking factory in North Plymouth, but following a strike in which he took an active part, did not return to work there but became a fish pedlar, earning a fair living at it and meanwhile extending his reading to include Darwin, Spencer, Hugo, ◊ Proudhon, ◊ Kropotkin and ◊ Malatesta.

In 1917 when the US declared war on Germany, both Sacco and Vanzetti, to avoid conscription to which they mistakenly believed themselves liable, fled to join an anarchist cooperative undertaking in Monterrey, Mexico. Later in the year both realized that they would not be conscripted and returned to the USA, Sacco to resume bootmaking, Vanzetti to wander the eastern states taking various jobs.

In 1919 there were numerous acts of revolutionary violence in the US. Following the loudly protested deportation of the anarchist Galleani, Emma ◊ Goldman, and other revolutionary leaders, some of these acts, including the destructive bombing of Attorney-General Palmer's Washington house, were attributed to anarchists and their ◊ IWW allies, who had openly declared their intention violently to resist the US government's antisocialist and antiliberal policies. It became easy for the police, and politically expedient, to attribute common law crimes to social revolutionaries. On 5 May 1920 a number of Italians, most of them anarchists, including Sacco and Vanzetti, were arrested and charged with a hold-up and double murder. A very complex chain of coincidence, mistaken identity, guilt-by-association and police malpractice enabled the state to bring forward a sufficient semblance of evidence. Vanzetti, tried separately, was at first convicted of attempted robbery with violence and condemned to 12–15 years hard labour. Retried, together with Sacco, on another murder charge in the following month, their case was prejudiced when, five days after being charged, thirty people were killed in Wall Street by an anarchist bomb outrage. Thayer, the judge at the trial, whose conduct of the case during the next seven years was condemned as outrageously unjust by leading men of both the bench and the bar, had decided that they were guilty before the trial began and was determined on their death;

the jury was deliberately packed with extreme antisocialists. The accused men were condemned to death. Appeals, delaying 'supplementary motions' and mercy petitions to the Governor of Massachusetts, Fuller, followed during the next seven years, long before the end of which time it had become perfectly clear that both men were innocent of the crimes they were charged with as of any other crime; and equally clear that Thayer and Fuller would use every means, including suborning of witnesses, manipulation of juries and refusal to accept the confession of the real murderer, to put the two self-confessed socialist-anarchists to death. During this period of seven years the Sacco and Vanzetti case, like the Dreyfus case in France, at an earlier date, became a bone of contention between opposing doctrinaires both in the USA and abroad, the simple matters of justice, and of the martyrdom of the two gently ideological Italians, being entirely lost sight of. Abroad, there were mass demonstrations and riots in support of the two anarchists: these, and the increasingly alarming bomb-outrages by protesting anarchists in half a dozen major American cities, served to harden the determination of the Massachusetts authorities to kill their two victims. They were sent to the electric chair, together with Madeiros, the real and self-confessed killer, on 23 August 1927. Subsequent and extremely thorough analysis of the case has confirmed that these executions were politically motivated judicial murders.

Saher, Manuel. Venezuelan communist and ◊ guerrilla leader known as Comandante Chena, now serving a prison sentence of fourteen years imposed at the instance of his father, the Governor of Falcon State, whom he had denounced as 'an assassin of the Venezuelan people': *see* Venezuela: guerrilla movements.

Sandino, Augusto (1895–1934) Nicaraguan revolutionary leader, past-master of ◊ guerrilla warfare against regular troops. b. Niquinohomo, bastard s. of an Indio girl and a wealthy landowner and member of the Liberal party, who gave the boy a good education and made him administrator of his estate until 1920 when Sandino had to leave the country following a violent personal quarrel with a politically powerful man who had insulted Sandino's mother. Nicaragua was governed by a Conservative Party dictatorship subservient to US capital and maintained in power by US Marines. From 1920 to 1926 Sandino worked in Mexico as an oil

Sandino, Augusto

man, getting to know the workers and developing vaguely socialist ideas. He returned to Nicaragua at his father's suggestion (1926) when the liberal General Moncada rose in arms against the dictatorship. He obtained work at an American-owned gold mine and began to agitate for better pay and conditions for the miners, but deciding that only violent revolution would be effective, raised a guerrilla band, armed it (from Honduras) with his savings, and began to wage war on the government, while propagating an anti-US ◊ imperialist, strongly nationalist, and more or less socialist doctrine, with undertones of syndicalism. His army grew rapidly to several thousand men, and his help enabled Moncada to put the government troops on the defensive and threaten the capital, Managua.

At this point the US government intervened and tried to patch up a coalition in which the leaders of both political parties would get fat perquisites in place and pay to ensure that US enterprises in Nicaragua could continue to draw large profits from the country. Moncada and all the 'generals' in the field agreed to this peace, excepting Sandino who declared that he would not lay down his arms until the US ceased to intervene in Nicaragua (July 1927 Manifesto); and that he was fighting for the people of all Central America. The US shipped more Marines into Nicaragua and provided them with air cover. After defeats inflicted on him by US dive-bombers, Sandino devised a system of guerrilla tactics which made him less vulnerable from the sky, split his forces into small, mobile bands under independent 'generals' not all of whom were Nicaraguan, refused pitched battles and for seven years waged increasingly successful war against the Marines, their airforce, and the American-raised and officered National Guard. The war was a foreshadowing, *in petto*, of the US–Vietnam war, with Sandino playing Ho Chi Minh, his *guerrilleros* the Vietcong, and the National Guard the South Vietnamese. Sandino became a charismatic hero all over Latin America and even beyond, including in the US among liberals and radicals who clamoured for the withdrawal of US forces from Nicaragua. ◊ Chang Kai-shek, at that time also hostile to the forces of US capital, named a regiment after Sandino, and the ◊ Comintern sang his praises. But although he sent a delegation to the Anti-Imperialist Congress (Frankfurt 1928) and his brother Socrates Sandino joined the CP, Sandino refused to affiliate 'Sandinismo' to communism. By 1928 the US was reduced to terrorist bombing of villages in an effort to shake peasant loyalty to Sandinismo.

In 1929 Sandino was tricked into Mexico by an bogus offer, made in collusion with the U S government, although in response to an appeal from Sandino, from President Portes Gil, of Mexican financial and weapons aid. He was kept hanging about for months in the hope that his forces would melt away in his absence. The CP made another effort to recruit him and failing, denounced him as a mere bandit, in emulation of U S official propagandists. He realized that he was being fooled, and managed to escape across the country and on to a ship at Vera Cruz, returned to Nicaragua (April 1930) to resume his command and intensify the war. When Herbert Hoover succeeded Calvin Coolidge as U S President in 1929 he found he needed all his Marines for the China service and, moreover, following the great Stock Exchange panic of that year, was soon short of money for the 'pacification' of Nicaragua. Sandino was urged to stop fighting with the promise that if he did, the Marines would be withdrawn. The National Guard had proved no match for Sandino's *guerrilleros*, and both the Conservative and Liberal leaders implored the Americans to remain to defend them. Sandino continued to declare that he would fight until all U S forces were withdrawn, and by 1933 he had made his point: the U S Marines would be withdrawn and when they had gone he would lay down his arms.

Before withdrawal the U S persuaded Liberals and Conservatives to sink their differences and form a national government under the Liberal Sacasa; and placed the National Guard under the command of a man they could rely on to keep far to the right, General Somoza. Sandino kept his promise and by treaty with President Sacasa was allowed to retain control of one northern province, and to keep 100 men under arms. He at once set about organizing, planting and settling an 'agrarian commune' on something like syndicalist lines at Guiguili in the Segovia mountains, but the deliberately provocative behaviour of the National Guard towards Sandinistos threatened to produce a civil war again. Sandino went to Managua to confer with President Sacasa, was kidnapped, after dining with the President, by Somoza and, with members of his staff, murdered. It has not been proved that Somoza was acting on American orders; it seems to be true that the U S Ambassador tried to save Sandino, but he may have been in ignorance of Somoza's clandestine relations with the U S government which remained discreetly inactive when Somoza proceeded to depose Sacasa and make himself dictator. The beneficiaries of his dictatorship

Seale, Bobby

were US capital; himself (he died worth 60 million dollars and owning one-tenth of all the agricultural land in Nicaragua); and his son Luis, who succeeded him as dictator.

Sandino's influence is very far from dead: Bayo, the Spanish colonel who trained Fidel ⟡ Castro and Che ⟡ Guevara in guerrilla warfare and wrote a handbook on it, cited Sandino as the great master of that military craft, whose example his pupils must never lose sight of. And so strong was his hold over his countrymen's imagination, and that of millions of other Latin Americans, that the revolutionary spirit of Sandinismo must long continue to inform guerrilla movements in the subcontinent.

Seale, Bobby (1937–   ) b. in Dallas, Texas. American black revolutionary, founder and later Chairman of the ⟡ Black Panther Party and a cult figure of such power that Panther captives being tortured by the police of various US cities used the thought of him to give themselves strength to endure (see, e.g. the statement of Jomo Raskin, a teacher at New York State University who was tortured by the police after being arrested 9 December 1969, quoted by J. Gerassi in *Towards Revolution*, 1971). By his own account Seale had no idea of what communism was until he was told that it deprived men of their liberty, whereupon he identified it as the creed of the US government. He was given a crash-education in Marxist-⟡ Leninism by Huey P. ⟡ Newton whom he met at Merrit College in 1962, and in the Afro-American Association. With Newton he worked out a ten-point programme for an Afro-American political party, out of which emerged, five years later, the Black Panther Party. Seale earned his living first in the US Army Air Force, then as a sheet-metal worker, and later as a draughtsman in an electronic plant. He became Chairman of the Black Panther Party, was arrested as a result of defending himself against a police assault in Chicago and killing a policeman, and, after a trial during which he was bound and gagged while his lawyer was excluded from the court, was sentenced to a 2–15 year term. Escaping, he was arrested again, charged (the original charge was quashed on appeal) with unlawful flight between states and conspiracy to kidnap and murder a defecting Panther. Of these charges he was acquitted by a Connecticut court, but sent to prison for four years for contempt of the Chicago court which had had him bound and gagged during his earlier trial. In prison he remained Chairman of the vestige of the Black Panther Party which had been more or less effectively paralysed by police action.

Secret Societies, Revolutionary. During the past two centuries revolutionary movements in Europe and America have been of two kinds: open organizations, or at least as open as police repression would permit; and secret conspiracies. The major example of the open organization is that of ◊ Marxist ◊ socialism, with its usually legal political parties organized to win power whether by evolution or revolution; and, of the secret society, Bakunist anarchism. The forming and use of secret societies for revolutionary ends has an ancient history in both China and Europe – the medieval Holy Vehm in Germany, for example, was, if not exactly revolutionary, certainly political. In modern times in China the 'Fists of Harmony' (Boxers) society had a very ancient ancestry of conspiratorial movements with similarly impressive names, e.g. the 'Avenging Knives'. The Boxers were formed (*c.* 1890) to drive out the foreigners who were battening on the decrepit Empire and at first had the secret support of the Dowager Empress. The movement collapsed after the British Navy had relieved the foreign concessions, besieged by the Fists of Harmony forces in Pekin. Such ◊ nihilist movements as 'The ◊ People's Will' in nineteenth-century Russia were organized as secret societies. In the Balkans secret revolutionary societies were flourishing until World War II: outstanding was the Black Hand society of Serbian army officers, formed with the object of liberating the Slav provinces of the Austro-Hungarian Empire by means of terrorism; this notorious society was responsible for the assassination of King Alexander Karageorgevic I and his Queen Draga of Serbia, and it is probable that it had a hand in the assassination of the Archduke Franz Ferdinand of Austria at Sarajevo in 1914. Both the Committee of Union and Progress or ◊ Young Turk movement (1920) and the Romanian ◊ Iron Guard (1927) began as secret societies. The former was responsible for the revolution which brought down the Ottoman Empire and established the Turkish Republic; the latter a Fascist Party. The earliest Arab revolts against Turkish rule, e.g. the Mesopotamian Ahad and the Syrian Fetah also began as secret societies. Most notorious in Europe were such Italian revolutionary secret societies as the Camorra and the Carbonari: the Camorra was formed in Naples in 1820 to protect political prisoners from the brutality of their Bourbon jailers by bribery or terrorization, or both, of prison officers. The Carbonari (char-coal-burners) was also Neapolitan in origin and its initial purpose was to protect the peasantry against vicious exploitation by feudal landlords. Carbonari were mercilessly hunted down by the political police of Papal and other Italian states, tortured and hanged (1820–30). In 1827 they succeeded in raising an insurrection in Naples against the Bourbon monarchy, but it was easily crushed and the ringleaders were hanged. It was on Carbonari 'lodges' that ◊ Mazzini founded his Young Italy republican movement. The Mafia, now a criminal organization which exists solely for gain, was founded late in the eighteenth century to fight for Sicilian independence. From time to time the most successful and respect-able of all secret societies, the Freemasons, have played a political role: Leon ◊ Trotsky's first book, written in prison, was a study of political Freemasonry which had been a power in Russia since the reign of Catherine the Great; and that same power was regarded as a major enemy by the powerful clerical establishments in several Roman Catholic countries, while by many liberals it was regarded as the white hope of the enlightened and progressive elements. In Ireland such secret societies as the fanatically Protestant White Boys or Peep O'Day Boys (1784); and Roman Catholic Defenders, Ribbon Society and ◊ Fenians, were all organized on secret society lines to use violence, including assassination, for political ends. The Invincibles who assassinated Burke and Lord Frederick Cavendish in Phoenix Park, with the probable help of the Fenians in the matter of money, was supposed to be a secret society, but its members were so incapable of secrecy that they gave themselves away and were hanged.

The history of the USA is bedevilled by secret societies, several of Italian or Sicilian origin, like the imported Camorra and Mafia and the Sicilian-American Cosa Nostra. The most dangerous and persistent was the Ku-Klux-Klan (*kuklos*, Gr. a circle) formed *c*. 1886 to oppose, if necessary by violence, the emancipation of Negro slaves. Later it adopted a broader policy which included antisemitism and, under Northern Irish Protestant (Orange) influence, anti-Roman Catholicism. ◊ Bakunin's Revolutionary Alliance was an anarchist secret society on a very consider-able scale, with active branches from Russia to Spain; it was Bakunin's revolutionary protégé ◊ Nechayev who drafted the ◊ *Revolutionary Catechism* ◊ . The Alliance infiltrated the First International and nearly wrecked it by splitting it into factions for and against conspiratorial methods. In the Kenya independence struggle (1954–60) the Kikuyu secret society, ◊ Mau-Mau, used the imposition of secret oaths to gain recruits to its bands of forest fighters and ensure the silence and 'loyalty' of the villagers on whom the military bands depended for support and supplies.

The strong and persistent opposition of ◊ Marx and ◊ Engels to the conspiratorial type of revolutionary organization – although Marx was a member of a revolutionary secret society in his youth – discredited that type of revolutionary activity among serious socialists and until recently all socialist and communist movements have been open until forced 'underground' by police persecution. But today the use of violence by political police forces, National Guards, and military dictatorships in repressing the peaceful propagation of socialism has produced a reaction towards conspiratorial organization of revolutionary movements, e.g. the ◊ Weathermen in the USA and the ◊ Tupamaros in Uruguay. This however is more a matter of necessity than a taste for and belief in the 'hidden hand' kind of revolutionary militancy which seems to have had a special appeal for nineteenth-century revolutionaries.

Sekou Touré, Ahmed (1922–) s. of a Muslim peasant in French Guinea: *see* African power transfers. But since the trade unions and the political parties founded and directed by this militant African nationalist, were and are more or less ◊ Marxist; and since, as President of Guinea, he and his Guinea Democratic Party have followed a policy of national-ization and state control of industry and commerce, there is more reason to consider Sekou Touré a revolutionary than most of the African politicians who have received political power from the former European imperial powers.

Sinn Fein, meaning 'Ourselves Alone'. A revolutionary society, later political party, founded 1902 by Arthur Griffith (1872–1922) to win freedom, or at least autonomy, for Ireland, from the UK. Griffith was a moderate, but in 1914 the party was joined by so many Irish Nationalist extremists that their leader, James Conolly, won control of it and, colla-borating with the ◊ Fenians Society (Irish Republican Brotherhood) organized and launched the Easter Rising in Dublin, 1916. In 1917, with Griffith still leading the moderates, leadership of the militants fell to

Eamonn ◊ De Valera who, unwilling to accept the Irish Free State compromise negotiated with the British by Griffith and Michael ◊ Collins, took the militants out of the party (1920) to form them into, first the Irish Republican Army (◊ IRA) and then the Fianna Fail political party. But Sinn Fein remains as the political wing of the revived IRA.

Slato: Secretariado Latinamericano de Trotskismo Orthodoxo: *see* Galdos (Hugo Blanco).

SNCC: Student Non-violent Coordinating Committee. The most militant of the US black civil rights organizations. The method which it favours for obtaining full civil rights for black Americans is the founding and recruiting of active black political parties at county level which could later develop into larger parties at state and possibly Federal level. Its first successful task was to persuade black citizens to resist terrorization by white racists, and to register as voters; to help them overcome the psychological and physical obstacles put in their way; and to cast their votes despite violent threats and action against them. SNCC's first operation of this kind was at McComb, Mississippi in 1961, where it later founded the Mississippi Freedom Democratic Party (Jackson 1964) following the passing of the 1964 Civil Rights Bill into law. SNCC was also responsible for founding a second political party at County level, the Lowdnes County Freedom Organization, Alabama (1965) as a model for future operations. The Committee is thus committed to putting ◊ Black Power theory into practice. The SNCC is not specifically 'revolutionary' but there is a revolutionary element in its philosophy and social revolution is increasingly implicit in the militancy of Black Power which faces the fact that if the ◊ bourgeois capitalist society is incapable of changing itself to accommodate Black Power aspirations, then Black Power must set about getting rid of bourgeois capitalism.

Social Democracy. In 1869 two German political parties with revolutionary socialist programmes, the General German Workers' Union founded by ◊ Lassalle and the Social Democratic Workers' Party founded by ◊ Bebel and Liebnecht united to form the Socialist Workers' Party, commonly known thereafter as the Social Democratic Party. Its aim was to install ◊ Marxist socialism – officially adopted as the Party's programme in

1891 at Erfurt – by parliamentary means, i.e. by winning a majority in the Reichstag. It very quickly became the most successful and fastest-growing socialist movement in the world, and therefore the leader of world Socialism, whose aims, organization and method were copied in numerous other countries. In 1871 two socialists, one being Bebel, were elected to the Reichstag, the first socialists elected to a national assembly in any country. The progress of the movement by the year 1914 and the outbreak of World War I (1914) can be shown in tabular form:

Country and national assembly	Total membership	Socialist members
Austrian Reichsrath	516	82
Belgian Chamber	166	39
British House of Commons	670	42
Danish Folketing	114	32
Finnish National Assembly	200	87

(Women received the vote in Finland 1907; 9 of the above Socialist MPs were women)

French Chamber of Deputies	597	102
German Reichstag	397	110
Holland's Lower House	100	7
Italian Chamber of Deputies	508	40
Norwegian Storthing	123	23
Russian Duma	432	16
Spanish Cortes	?	1

(Failure of the Social Democrats in Spain was due to the powerful attraction of the much more revolutionary anarcho-syndicalist movement which boycotted elections)

Swedish Lower House	230	87
Swiss National Council	167	15

It should be emphasized that these figures are those only of the socialist parties which repudiated violent revolution and relied entirely on parliamentary methods. They cannot be used to measure the strength of socialism since all these countries also had revolutionary non-parliamentary parties or movements.

Outside Europe, social democracy was also influential: it played a part in the teachings of Dr ↔ Sun Yat-sen and therefore in the original Kuomintang and the ↔ Chinese revolutions. Some of its ideas were adopted by the left wing of the Indian Congress Party. It has been important. n the foundation and political development of Israel. In Australia the Labour Party was founded on social democratic principles which were, however, progressively abandoned when the Party took power: it formed the Commonwealth Governments in 1904, 1908 and 1910 – but the socialist part of its programme was defeated on referendum. In the USA socialism was always weak at the political level, chiefly because it was repudiated by the very conservative American Federation of Labour. In the presidential election of 1912 the Social Democratic candidate polled 800,000 of the 17,000,000 votes.

The year 1914 has been taken as the terminal date in the above table because World War I produced major changes. At the Second (Social Democratic) International Congress (Stuttgart, 1907) it had been resolved that socialists in national parliaments must, when the occasion arose, refuse to vote war credits. The German Party ratted on this obligation in 1914, with the result that so did most other SD parties, with the honourable exception of the British Independent Labour Party. As a result social democracy was discredited as a revolutionary movement; it attracted reformers and liberals but socialist revolutionaries gravitated into the communist Parties which originated in the majority, i.e. ◊ Bolshevik wing of the Russian SD Party. This change in pattern inevitably shifted the SD parties to the right; and they now occupy that band of the political spectrum formerly occupied by the Liberal and Radical parties.

Social Democratic parties. A social democratic revolutionary is a ◊ Marxist socialist who wishes to bring about revolutionary social, economic and political changes on Marxist lines but to do so by peaceful, parliamentary means. The designation was used by all European continental Marxists excepting the French and British, from about 1860, including the Russian Marxists until the split (1903) into Menshevik and ◊ Bolshevik parties which made the name Social Democrat ambiguous when applied to a Russian socialist. The first formally entitled social democratic political party was the German Sozialdemokratische Arbeitpartei founded 1869 by Wilhelm Liebnecht (1826–1900) and August ◊ Bebel (1840–1913) at the Congress of all German socialist movements held in Eisenbach. It was brought to its remarkable zenith of numerical strength by ◊ Lassalle, and by 1912 was polling a majority (4,293,000) of the votes in elections. It was

Socialism

only kept out of office by coalitions of the centre and right-wing parties, just as today the majority (communist) party, is kept out of office in Italy. During the following two decades social democratic parties were founded in Belgium, Austria, Romania, Hungary, Holland, Bulgaria, Russia (1898), Finland and Serbia. In France the characteristic chauvinism combined with a socialist tradition older than the German, kept French socialism non-Marxist and peculiarly French. In Britain the working class had politically left ideas rooted in Chartism and in early trade unionism (in turn strangely rooted in Christian nonconformism), rather than Marxism; furthermore the innate humility of the British working class, a product of the strong caste system, and the skill with which the ⬦ bourgeois parties conceded a fraction of the workers' demands, a measure and even, of welfare, a share of power to the Labour Party (e.g. by not forming anti-left coalitions), on condition that its leaders repudiate socialist measures, kept positively social democratic action to a minimum.

More interesting in the context of social democracy have been the histories of the Danish (1889), Norwegian (1887) and Swedish (1889) social democratic parties which, although developing on non-revolutionary lines as regards means, have, in terms of ends, written a very large measure of social democratic policy into the national ⬦ establishments, although far short of the really revolutionary measure of abolishing Capitalism.

It is this falling short of the ultimate revolutionary aim, combined with the refusal to use revolutionary means, that so weakens the present social democratic parties face to face with bourgeois-capitalist willingness to resort to violence. As a consequence of that weakness these parties are repudiated by all genuine ⬦ New Left revolutionaries.

In general, the social democratic parties now occupy that band of the political spectrum formerly occupied by the Liberal and Radical parties; the old social democratic band is occupied by the orthodox Communist Parties; and the Marxist-Leninist parties of the New Left alone remain revolutionary.

Socialism. The economic system in which the means of production, distribution and exchange, i.e. all natural resources, land, industrial plant and trading institutions are owned by a collective of the people, which may be the state or municipalities, but can be e.g. cooperatives or, as in ⬦

253

syndicalism, the trades unions. Politically socialism has no predetermined form, since collective ownership can, in theory, be managed by a parliamentary democracy, a single political party claiming to act as the people's executive, or even by a divine monarchy as in Inca Peru. But since a capitalist society cannot be transformed into a socialist one without expropriation of the individual private owners of the means of production, distribution and exchange, or of the companies of shareholders which, more commonly, own them, revolutionary political parties have come into existence to effect the change, some of them dedicated to the use of violence, others to the use of peaceful, parliamentary means.

The origins of socialism are complex. In the first instance it appears to have been conceived as an idealistic reversion to the primitive communism which is believed to have preceded the regime of private property which, according to the French socialist ◊ Proudhon, originated in theft: that is to say, in the appropriation by powerful individuals of what by natural law belonged to everybody. Industrial plant, product of labour by brain and hand applied to natural resources belonging to all, only labour, the workers, have any title to it and it becomes the common heritage of mankind.

But the idea that the earth, and everything made of its substance, must belong to every man in common, has a powerful appeal to the sense of justice. In Thomas More's *Utopia* (1516) all property is common. During the seventeenth-century rise of Capitalism, the idea does not seem to have attracted the support of any writer of consequence, but in the eighteenth century, perhaps as a byproduct of the romantic revival of admiration for the noble savage, and what was supposed to be the basic goodness of human nature, explicit in the writings of J-J. Rousseau and implicit in his *Le Contrat social* (1762), it found powerful advocates. Jean Meslier in his *Testament* (1764), Mably in *De la Législation* (1778), Morelly in his *Code de la nature* (1755), Thomas Spence in his *The Mode of Administering the Landed Estate of the Nation* (1775), William Ogilvie in his *The Right of Property in Land* (1782), all these put forward political-economic ideas which we should now call socialist, although the word had not yet been invented.

William Godwin's *Enquiry Concerning Political Justice* (1793) (*see also under* Anarchy) condemned private property as immoral and inexpedient. Although the French Revolution was in no sense socialist, but, as a ◊

bourgeois revolution using an alliance with the 'people', very respectful of the idea of private property, it did produce in Gracchus Babeuf and his 'Society of Equals', communists before communism, advocating industrial cooperatives, community of goods, and equal sharing of all wealth; and it is even true to say that all these ideas had their advocates in more way-out partisans of the English revolution a century earlier. In 1799 a German jurist, Hugo, made the first reasoned attack on the institution of private property from the juridical point of view; and Tom Paine, in his *Agrarian Justice* (1797) indicted private property differentials as the gravest injustice.

The Frenchman Saint-Simon first set forth the socialist ideas developed in the body of his later work in a pamphlet entitled *Letters from a Resident of Geneva to his Contemporaries* (1802) and laid stress for the first time, half a century before Karl ♢ Marx, on the importance of a scientific approach to political economy. In his last work, published posthumously, *The New Christianity* (1826), Saint-Simon laid the foundations of various Christian socialist edifices which have since been erected, for the most part rather jerrybuilt. Another brilliant Frenchman, François Charles Fourier who, incidentally, foreshadowed Sigmund Freud in his theory that crime and even vice were due to repressed passions, published in his *Théorie des Quatres Mouvements* (1808) the first theory of economic planning, though he was not hostile to capitalism – unlike his English contemporary Charles Hall who indicted it in his *Effects of Civilization on the People in European States* (1805). Hall was probably the first thinker to point out in so many words that since the workers are the only producers of wealth, but themselves enjoy only a small fraction of it, they constitute an unjustly exploited class.

The actual word 'socialism' appears to have been coined about 1820, but by whom is not clear. It seems not to have been used, for example, by Robert Owen, the British industrialist and social reformer who denounced organized religion as a major source of social injustice and evil and believed that if you give people good living and working conditions and fair wages, they will behave morally; in other words, that environment determines character. Owen ran his own factories on very advanced and enlightened principles, and he tried, but failed, to establish colonies run on socialist lines in America. The earliest use of the word yet traced is 1827: it occurs in a discussion of Owen's theories in the *Co-operative*

Socialism

Magazine, the monthly organ of the London Co-operative Society founded in 1824. Owen denied that competition in industry was either beneficial or constructive: cooperation, he said, was not only juster, it was more efficient.

In France, also, at about the same time, the word *socialisme* came into use, and the theory into fashion among many intellectuals and many practical men.

David Ricardo's *Principles of Political Economy* first dealt scientifically with the labour theory of value proposed by Hall and on which Sismondi, in *New Principles of Political Economy* based a reasoned attack on 'laissez-faire' or, as we should say now, 'market' capitalism. Sismondi's attack was extended and expanded in William Thompson's *Inquiry into the Principles of Distribution of Wealth* (1829).

It was from Sismondi and Thompson that Karl Marx ◊ took the theory of surplus value which is the cornerstone of his criticism of capitalism, and therefore of ◊ Marxism.

The first consciously socialist revolutionary insurrections were those of the Lyon weavers in 1831 and 1834. It was in the course of analysing these risings that the Saint-Simonian socialist Pierre Leroux first used the words 'bourgeoisie' to designate specifically the capital-owning employers of labour, and ◊ 'proletariat' to mean the majority of the workers who had no capital and must sell their labour to live; Marx borrowed both usages from him. Louis ◊ Blanc carried Leroux's ideas a stage further, producing the fundamental socialist slogan 'From each according to his capacity, to each according to his work', which implies, of course, a continuance of inequality and therefore also implies, if complete social justice is the aim, the advance to communism – 'From each according to his capacity, to each according to his needs' predicated by Marx.

In 1840 came Proudhon's *What is Property?*, to which his answer, mentioned above, was 'Property is theft'. Next came Pecqueur's *New Theory of Social and Political Economy*, advocating abolition of private ownership and monopolization of capital and management of all industrial plants by the state.

It was from these forerunners that Marx learned his socialism; something else was needed to give it drive, and this he found in the romantic if grim emotionalism of the German League of the Just, later known as the Communist League, which he joined in Brussels in 1847, the year

256

before he and ⋄ Engels produced the *Communist Manifesto*. It was Marx, certainly, who first presented the struggle for control of the economy between the bourgeoisie and the proletariat in terms of war, a class war which could not be avoided.

From the mid-nineteenth century onwards socialism became the doctrine and policy of organized political movements and parties seeking power either by revolution, as in Russia; or, as in Germany and Britain, by winning a majority in the national parliament; or, as in Spain and, to some small extent in the USA (*see* ⋄ Industrial Workers of the World), by gaining control of the trade unions. Revolutionary socialist parties have gained control of more than half the world; evolutionary socialist parties have succeeded in introducing a measure of welfare legislation into capitalist societies and a not inconsiderable measure of redistribution of wealth: *see also* Social Democracy.

Socialist Labour League. A British Trotskyist revolutionary group: *see* New Left; Student power.

Socialist Realism. The only art style tolerated in the USSR since the rise of ⋄ Stalin whose death it unfortunately survived. The theory is that the work of an artist must depict the lives of the workers not only realistically but in such a way as to support and emphasize the moral of socialism as interpreted by the CP of the USSR; and the achievements of the ⋄ proletariat, thanks to CP leadership, in the building of socialism. Any work of art which does not conform to this theory, e.g. modern abstract painting and sculpture, is ⋄ 'bourgeois decadent'. Socialist Realist art might be described as the orthodox Soviet communists' equivalent of commercial art in the West, a form of advertising designed to sell to the people the illusion that the dictatorship of the proletariat is alive and well.

Aesthetically, the worst consequences of the theory are to be seen in paintings: in deliberate opposition to all stylistic developments since World War I and blind to the brilliant *avant garde* painting which flourished 1917–24 under ⋄ Lenin, Socialist Realist painting relies on a bland form of nineteenth-century 'naturalism' with overtones of Impressionism and Expressionism by way of spice. This kind of painting cannot be attributed solely to Stalinist restraint. Russia's graphic art has always been weak, except between 1900 and 1924, tending always to be literary, isolated and backward: the one strong artistic tradition is in icon-painting and since icon-painting is didactic it is a form of propaganda. Even such as it is, Socialist Realism has produced no painter of talent in the USSR, but there are a few communist painters outside the USSR who have managed to produce, within the same constraining rules, works of merit, e.g. the Italian Renato Guttoso, by leaning heavily on Van Gogh, Millet and Daumier.

In literature the case is different, for Russian literary traditions are strong, rich and of the highest excellence. The Socialist Realist novel or poem is, like the Socialist Realist painting, 'Victorian' but may be good of its kind. But the Russian writer of really original and powerful talent is, of course, quite incapable of working within the Socialist Realist rules since those rules exclude sincere criticism of Soviet life, of the Communist Party, of the society ⇨ 'establishment'. Thus the best of the USSR's poets and novelists, jealously watched by the hacks who compose the Writer's Union, are for the most part unable even to publish their works in the USSR, are ostracized and persecuted – to the point of imprisonment or confinement to psychiatric hospitals as mad, if they allow their books to be published in translation abroad – and are treated as pariahs by the establishment's hack literary critics. The cases best known to the public at large are those of the Nobel Prize winners Pasternak and Solzhenitsyn.

Russia also has a rich and powerful musical tradition and happily for composers it is very much more difficult, at least for the sort of boorish dogmatic bureaucrats who are the guardians of the rules, to identify deviation from those rules in music than in painting or literature. Nevertheless, Soviet composers even of the rank of Prokoviev have repeatedly fallen into disgrace for composing works not immediately comprehensible to every peasant and worker; and have been constrained to write for public celebrations music which was a disgrace to their own talent.

The sins against the light resulting from Socialist Realism in the People's Republic of China must be judged by a different criterion. 'Westernization', consequent upon the adoption of Western technology, has had the same lamentable consequences for art in all the non-Western cultures, whether communist or capitalist, as a result of the illusion that the terms of art, like those of science, are universal. In a revolution involving throwing out the dirty bath water of traditional forms and terms in the fields of science, politics, economics and social life, the baby – art – may inadvertently be thrown out as well. It is at least possible that in China what seems to be the aesthetically appalling consequence of Socialist Realism is no more than an oversight, and this 'Zhdanov dogma' will in due course be repudiated by a people with so splendid a tradition in the visual arts as the Chinese.

Socialist Revolutionary Party. One of the developments out of the ▷ populist movement was the foundation, at Saratov (1896) of the Union of Socialist Revolutionaries, later known as the Northern Union. Its HQ was moved to Moscow in 1897. From the beginning it had two aspects: one, clandestine and conspiratorial, involved in every kind of illegal political activity from the publishing of illicit ▷ propaganda to ▷ assassination; the other open and legal, providing political articles for such respectable journals as *Russkoe Bogatstvo* and promoting candidates for the *Zemstvos* and, later, the *Duma*. In 1900 it combined with other populist groups to form the Socialist Revolutionary Party (SRP), with its own newspaper, *Revolutionary Russia*, published first in Finland, later in West Europe, and smuggled over the frontier. Its 'combat organization' which existed to plan and mastermind assassinations and acts of industrial ▷ sabotage, was remarkably efficient, and its 'bag' included, as well as a number of lesser lights, two Ministers of the Interior, Sipyagin (April 1902) and Plehve (July 1904), the Grand Duke Sergei (February 1905), Stolypin, a Liberal prime minister (and still thought by some to have been assassinated by the police), and ▷ Lenin (1920), although Lenin did not die of his wound at once. The SRP held its first congress in 1905, by which time it had had remarkable success in recruiting peasant support and had a great deal to do with the revolutionary programme of the newly formed All-Russian Peasants' Union. Its agrarian doctrine was based on the declaration that 'The land belongs to no one and labour alone confers the right to use it', which meant that land must be nationalized and thereafter controlled by elected local authorities. No compensation would be paid to landowners, but a dole would be paid to them pending their retraining for useful work.

The SR Party Congress established firm links with the revolutionary nationalist parties and groups in the 'nationalities' – the Social Democrats in Finland, the Social-Federalists in Georgia, the Dashyaks in Armenia, the Social-Democratic League in Latvia, and the Polish Socialist Party.

Socialist Revolutionary Party

Moreover, despite the distrust with which it was regarded by the German Social Democrats, it was affiliated to the Second ◊ International.

It was at this first Congress that the Party's twofold nature developed into schism very like that which had divided the Russian Social Democratic Party: there was a moderate wing, those who wanted the party to be open and legal and to use peaceful means of winning power; and an extremist, revolutionary wing which favoured the use of secrecy, violence and conspiracy, the latter being in the majority. The moderates broke with the main body of the Party to form the Popular Socialist Party which sank into insignificance, while the real revolutionaries were confirmed by the Congress in the use of violence, including assassination. The final act of the Congress was to elect a five-man Central Committee (Chernov, Argunov, Rakitnikov, ◊ Azev and M. A. Natanson).

When in 1906 Tsar Nicholas II conceded a Duma (October Manifesto), the Socialist Revolutionaries, believing armed insurrection to be imminent, ◊ boycotted the election. (The Social Democrats would have done the same had the Bolshevik view prevailed, but were persuaded by the Mensheviks to participate.) But so successful had their propaganda in the rural area been, that the peasants insisted on voting for candidates who expressed Socialist Revolutionary views without being party members, so that the Duma had an *ex officio* Socialist Revolutionary Party; in the 1907 election the party changed its policy, put up official candidates, and won 34 seats out of 288, while the Social Democrats, Bolshevik and Menshevik, won 65.

In 1908 the SRP was badly shaken by a scandal: Vladimir Zurtsev, its counter-police espionage expert, charged Azev, one of the principal leaders who also served on the 'combat organization' with being a police informer. He was tried by a 'court of honour' and found undeniably guilty. The trial revealed a very extraordinary state of affairs: it was proved that Azev had informed on the group which was charged with the assassination of Plehve; and had *then* undertaken that assassination himself, successfully. He was condemned to death but escaped into Germany where he died in 1918.

On the outbreak of the ◊ Russian Revolutions of 1917 which they had done so much to prepare, the socialist revolutionaries were much stronger in the country at large, in the Petersburg and Moscow Soviets, and, ultimately, in the Constituent Assembly, than the Bolsheviks. But, dedicated, now that the Revolution had come, to respect for direct democracy, that is to doing nothing until they had the mass of the people with them, they were hamstrung by their own principles when faced with the dictatorial will to power of Lenin and the Bolshevik leaders. Power, as always, went to the men who really wanted it and believed they knew exactly how to use it. Until the Social Revolutionary Dora Kaplan shot at and wounded Lenin, the Bolsheviks gave the Socialist Revolutionaries a small share of power and were willing to tolerate them; but they were the first victims of the Bolshevik terror which followed the attempt at assassination and by 1925 had either been exterminated or absorbed into the Communist Party.

Soledad Brothers. Specifically, three Black Marxist-Leninist convicts in Soledad (California) prison, Fleeta Drumgo, John Clutchette and George ◊ Jackson made famous by the latter's published writings and by Jonathan ◊ Jackson's attempt to force his brother George's release by an armed raid on a San Raphael court and the seizure of hostages, using weapons which Angela ◊ Davis was later accused of supplying, a charge of which she was subsequently acquitted. After revelations of shocking prison conditions; of the Californian judiciary's discrimination against Blacks and social revolutionaries; the deaths of Jonathan Jackson and two other Blacks, and of the judge, during the San Raphael raid; and the publication of George Jackson's writings, the words *Soledad Brothers* became a potent symbol of New Left revolution and especially of the revolt of the American Blacks against White oppression.

Sorel, Georges (1847–1922) French revolutionary theorist, an engineer by trade, who tried to syncretize the philosophies of Karl ◊ Marx, Henri Bergson, and the syndicalist theorists and thus arrived at an existentialist theory of revolutionary violence which can be studied in his *Réflections sur la violence* (1908) and *Les Illusions du progrès* (1909). It was his opinion that the class war was of positive value because it kept society active and vigorous; and that its violent aspects should be encouraged because violence provides those great liberating crises, the only moments of true freedom, 'when we make an effort to create a new man within ourselves ... and when we take full possession of ourselves'. Sorel conceives the class war as everlasting and he presents certain syndicalist concepts, notably the ⊅ general strike, as valuable less for what they can achieve by way of positive revolution, which is probably very little, than for their value as 'myths' – there seems here to be a faint foreshadow of certain aspects of Jung – which feed the hopes and courage of the proletariat and make them feel their strength. His syncretism of several socialist and anarchist theories was never accepted by any considerable body of revolutionaries, and Sorel was always an outsider; but his writings had some influence on anarchist and anarcho-syndicalist intellectuals; some critics have seen in him the spiritual ancestor of both J-P. Sartre and André Malraux.

South Africa and Rhodesia, Revolution in. The African liberation movement dates back to before the foundation of the African National Congress (ANC) in 1912. It was led by rich, educated Africans and by tribal chiefs and was, accordingly, pacific and reformist. The advent of the Afrikaner Nationalist government, however, gave younger and more militant Congress members such as Nelson ⊅ Mandela their chance to push the Congress to the left, e.g. in the Freedom Charter (1955) which called for universal suffrage, redistribution of the land, and nationalization of the mines and other sources of wealth. Like the South African Communist Party which was forced underground (formally, it disbanded) by the Suppression of Communism Act (1950), the ANC was committed to non-violent means of bringing about these social changes. But in 1959 a group of Congress members broke away to form the Pan-Africanist Congress (PAC) which repudiated the ANC policy of cooperation with organizations representing non-black oppressed groups, holding that such cooperation was retarding the cause of black liberation.

In March 1960 a PAC demonstration against the pass laws ended in the massacre of demonstrators by the police at Sharpeville and the banning of both the PAC and the ANC. They went underground and late in 1961 the ANC set up an armed, militant wing, ⊅ Umkhonto we Sizwe, to carry out acts of sabotage against government installations, a campaign which continued until the arrest of the leaders in 1963 in which year also a PAC plan for nationwide attacks on whites was aborted by thousands of arrests. Since then the leaders have been in exile but in Tanzania and Zambia have trained units designed to penetrate South Africa and carry on the revolution from bases beyond its borders. In 1966 PAC units joined with units of the Zimbabwe African National Union and were in action in Rhodesia; and in 1967 Umkhonto and units of the Zimbabwe African People's Union were in action against Rhodesian and South African forces at Wankie, Rhodesia. The problems of penetrating South Africa, have not yet been solved, but action against Rhodesia was resumed in 1973.

The Rhodesian revolutionary movement gathered real impetus after the breakup of the Central African Federation in 1961, and the imprisonment of the established African political leaders following the rebel Smith Administration's Unilateral Declaration of Independence in 1965. It was only then that the ZANU and ZAPU movements decided to use armed force as the only means of overthrowing the white supremacist regime. Neither has published a political programme but they are loosely allied with PAC and ANC respectively.

PAC is said to have a ◊ Maoist ideology, to receive financial support from China, to regard the South African Communist Party as counter-revolutionary and condemns the ANC for following the Moscow line of peaceful coexistence with ◊ imperialism.

Soviet, Russian for 'council'. But in at first revolutionary and later established political practice in Russia, more specifically, the revolutionary committees elected by factory workers in the ◊ Russian Revolution 1905 and again in the ◊ Russian Revolution, February 1917, first in St Petersburg and Moscow, then all over Russia. It was by gaining control of the Petersburg Soviet and using it to overthrow the Provisional Government led by Kerensky, that the ◊ Bolsheviks were able to seize power in October 1917, the Soviet then becoming the elected justification for the 'Dictatorship of the ◊ Proletariat'. As a result the name Soviet was applied to all primary government bodies, at national, provincial and municipal levels, with a Supreme Soviet composed of delegates from all the Soviet Republics of the Union.

Spanish Civil War 1936-39. After half a century of struggle led by the revolutionary movements, the anarchists, anarcho-syndicalists and, later, ◊ Marxists, and particularly the anarcho-syndicalist trade unions united in the revolutionary Confederacion Nacional del Trabajo, the dictatorship of Primo de Rivera was overthrown in 1931, the monarchy ended, King Alfonso XIII sent into exile, and a Spanish Republic established. A provisional government of republicans and socialists ruled until the general election of 1936, from which the parties of the left emerged with an overwhelming majority. A Popular Front government excluding communists at once initiated a programme of urgently needed reforms, notably in landholding (a landowning class of 1 per cent of the population owned about 51 per cent of the land). To put a stop to and reverse these social reforms, a group of high-ranking army officers strongly supported by the landowning aristocracy, the higher clergy and the big industrialists, invaded Spain from Morocco under General Sanjurjo, with Moorish troops and some regiments of the Spanish army, to overthrow the government and install a ◊ Fascist dictatorship on the Italian model. Sanjurjo was killed in September 1936 and the command of the insurgents fell to General Francisco Franco, military governor of the Canary Islands. He received help from Italy in the form of 50,000 troops sent by Mussolini, later reinforced to 100,000; and from Germany in the form of a powerful airforce of bombers whose pilots perfected their skill for the war which Hitler was planning with the democracies, by totally destroying the Basque 'holy' city of Guernica. Since the parliamentary democracies refused to help the Spanish government, using the excuse of non-intervention to give Franco his chance to exterminate those dangerous revolutionaries, European communists organized the recruiting, transport and training of communist, socialist and liberal volunteers from a dozen countries, who were organized into the International Brigade, which became the symbol of socialist revolution in arms. The U S S R sent military advisers, commissars to ensure that the anarchists were checkmated, and some supplies. Spain thus became the battlefield in which socialism and fascism at last confronted each other with weapons in their hands. The Fascists swiftly won control of the south and west, but were checked in the north and east by what remained to the Madrid government of the regular army, by the embattled industrial workers and miners, by Catalan and Basque nationalists including their clergy, and the International Brigade, which inflicted a defeat on the Italian army at Guadalajara and later enabled Madrid to stand siege for a year.

The Fascists were steadily strengthened by more and more aid from ◊ Nazi Germany and Fascist Italy. The Republicans were weakened by inability to obtain essential supplies, denied them by France and Britain and, for some obscure reason hatched in the secret, brooding mind of

Josef ◊ Stalin, withdrawal of all aid from the USSR; but above all by the determination of the Stalinist communists to treat the revolutionary anarchists and syndicalists as much more dangerous enemies than the Fascists. At all events, Barcelona fell on 26 January 1939 and Madrid on 28 March.

For a decade after these events the Spanish Civil War and the International Brigade remained the most potent symbols for the Left of the struggle against Fascism – the bourgeoisie in arms; and were not replaced in the canon of symbols until the rise of ◊ Mao Tse-tung and Castro-Guevara.

Spartacus League. Student wing of the International ◊ Marxist Group.

Spartakusbund. The German Spartacus League, named after the leader of the gladiators' and slaves' revolution against Rome (73–71 BC) was the breakaway extreme Left wing of the German Social Democratic Party, and was so called by Karl ◊ Liebnecht and Rosa ◊ Luxemburg when they made the break in 1916. In 1918 it became, under the same leaders, the German Communist Party and for fourteen days, after its formation and before the murder of the two leaders, constituted the German Socialist Republic which, but for those murders, might conceivably have snatched power from the feeble hands of the young Weimar Republic, and created a communist Germany led by the two most humane social democratic leaders of their time.

Stalin, Joseph (Joseph Vissarionovich Djugashvili, 1879–1953) s. of a cobbler, b. Gori, Tiflis, Georgia. He was intended for the church and sent first to the Gori Ecclesiastical School, thereafter to Tiflis Theological College, from which he was expelled for spreading revolutionary ideas among the other students. He became a ◊ Marxist and joined the Tiflis branch of the social democratic movement in 1898, devoting himself to working wholly for the revolution as an agitator and organizer at Batum and Tiflis. He was arrested for these activities in 1902, imprisoned, escaped, and during the next ten years was arrested, imprisoned and escaped no less than five times. He first met ◊ Lenin at a Party conference in 1905 when the ◊ Bolshevik leader was briefly in Russia. Lenin seems never to have liked or completely trusted him; at all events Stalin did not, when the revolution finally broke out, become one of the leader's immediate circle of colleagues. Stalin continued his work for the Party and in 1912 was editing *Pravda* (Truth), the home edition of the Russian revolutionary exiles' paper for which both Lenin and Trotsky were writing, and the official organ of the Central Committee of the Communist Party of the USSR. His name does not appear as one of the prime movers among the Bolsheviks who made the ◊ Russian Revolution of October 1917, although he was certainly actively involved, and was appointed Commissar for Nationalities (that is, for ethnic minorities) in the first Council of the People's Commissars. He spent 1918–19 fighting in the civil war and became a member of ◊ Trotsky's War Council in 1920. His skill and determination as a politician manipulating his colleagues and intriguing for supreme power were of the highest order, and when it became clear that Lenin was dying of overwork and the aftermath of Dora Kaplan's bullet, he was elected to replace him as First Secretary of the Communist Party by henchmen who looked to him for advancement. There is a story, originating in Trotsky's autobiography, that Lenin, realizing that Stalin would abuse his power to the terror of the Russian people and the ruin of the Party's ideals, advised strongly against his election, a remarkable instance of foresight, if true.

Stalin's method of securing supreme power was to play on the veneration with which the rank and file and lesser leaders of the Party regarded every word that Lenin had ever uttered or spoken, to get rid of rivals for the leadership by accusing them of deviation from Leninism – the doctrine implicit in the body of Lenin's writings on Marxism, to which Stalin himself adhered with tedious dullness in his own copious writings. His principal rival was Trotsky: the manifest difference between them, although from Stalin's point of view any stick would have done to beat a dog, was that whereas Trotsky was a true international revolutionary, believing that socialism could not be achieved short of world revolution; and was a sort of ◊ Mao in his view that power should be in the hands of continuously revolutionary but firmly disciplined people, Stalin was a nationalist, advocating the idea of 'socialism in one country', which he was to transform into a reign of national communist terror. Trotsky and ◊ Zinoviev and other old Bolsheviks would have been willing to see the revolutionary lead taken away from them by revolution in one of the industrially advanced countries; Stalin was not. This antithesis was not new in Russian history: opposed to such 'Europeanizing' cosmopolitans as Peter the Great in politics, Turgenev in literature, there have always been the arch-Russians, fearful and contemptuous of Europe and cosmopolitanism, such Tsars as Ivan the Terrible, and such writers as Dostoyevsky.

In 1925 Stalin began on a programme of industrialization on a vast scale, in a series of Five Year Plans, concentrating on the heavy industries and making use of foreign engineering specialists. Meanwhile the peasants were failing to produce the food which the USSR needed. For a while, during the NEP period (see ▷ Russian Revolutions) when the *kulaks* – farmers employing labour – had been able to make profits, there had been some improvements in food supplies. But Stalin's reversal of NEP, in the first instance by the imposition of crippling taxes, put an end to that. Stalin therefore initiated a programme of farm 'collectivization', the grouping and nationalization of farms into large units to be run on industrial lines. In the ensuing disturbances a large number of *kulaks* were 'liquidated' (the Stalinist word for murdered), a great many peasants died of starvation, and there was famine on a colossal scale.

In 1936, however, things had improved and Stalin was strong enough to introduce a new constitution, the ostensibly liberal Stalin Constitution, which in practice gave him absolute dictatorial power. This enabled him to destroy all political rivals, opponents and critics, including the best of the USSR's soldiers of the highest rank, in a series of remarkable show trials in which, by means which have never become clear, the accused persons were induced to confess to the most abject and improbable crimes against the people and the state, thus justifying their own execution. Meanwhile hundreds of thousands of ordinary people, victims of delation or the whim of the secret police (see ▷ Russian Revolutions), were herded into labour camps where, under the atrocious conditions, they either died or survived to be released and rearrested, being regarded as permanently tainted wethers of Stalin's flock of 180 million slaves.

When the ▷ Nazis invaded the USSR Stalin stood forth no longer as a revolutionary but as the strongly conservative tyrant he increasingly became. He reintroduced strict division between officers and other ranks, restored the Orthodox Church to a measure of favour, had those foreign communists who were genuine Bolshevik revolutionaries, and whom he could get into his power through the ▷ Comintern, murdered; had Trotsky, last of the great revolutionary Bolsheviks, assassinated; deliberately left

Stalin, Joseph

◇ Tito, the Yugoslav communist leader, without help in his terrible struggle with the German-Italian-Croat (*Cetnik*) alliance, once he realized that Tito was not only waging a patriotic war but making a communist revolution; abolished the instrument of world revolution, the Comintern; and conducted the war and foreign affairs in the spirit and with the aims of a nationalist patriot, like any Tsar.

He was, despite subsequent accusations that he failed to prepare for the war and made numerous costly blunders in directing it, at least as responsible for the successful Russian resistance to the gigantic German war machine, as Churchill was for that of the British.

The victories of his armies over the Germans enormously enhanced the international standing and power of the USSR and therefore of Stalin personally. He was equally successful in his diplomatic work, ensuring, at his meetings with the United States and British leaders at Teheran (1943) and Yalta (1945), that all Eastern Europe should become, after final victory, part of the new Soviet Empire, under communist governments.

In the postwar period Stalin, no longer a revolutionary, appeared as one of the world's most conservative and chauvinistic nationalist leaders. He rid himself of possible rivals and opponents in another series of 'purges' directed by his police chief, Beria, and extended the use of labour camps to maintain his 'terror'. By imposing strict restraints on movements of Soviet citizens, and by suppression of all the freedoms, he brought about those conditions which Winston Churchill described when he said: 'From Stettin in the Baltic to Trieste in the Adriatic, an iron curtain has descended upon the Continent.'

It was at the start of a new purge directed primarily against a number of doctors accused of plotting his death, and which had strong anti-semitic overtones, that Stalin did, indeed, fall ill and die. At first he was, like Lenin, deified. But three years after his death he was denounced by his successor and former henchman, Nikita ◇ Khrushchev, at a CP congress meeting held in secret, for a long list of crimes and blunders and, above all, for fostering a cult of his own personality which had destroyed that collective leadership proper to a communist party and a socialist state. This denunciation led to a decline in Stalinism – the brand of narrow-minded, stupid, conservative and repressive national communism which was Stalin's creation and to which the USSR and other communist states in East Europe are only too apt to revert whenever any relaxation of

Stern, Abraham

extreme Soviet communist conservatism shows signs of producing demands
for more liberty of thought, speech and press.

Stambolisky, Alexander (1879–1923). This Bulgarian peasant was the
first revolutionary of modern times who succeeded in leading a peasantry
to victory over the middle class and the urban ◊ proletariat. The son of a
peasant, he went to Germany to study advanced methods of agriculture
and on his return to Bulgaria, having discovered that he had all the
qualities of a brilliant demagogue, he set about promoting and organizing
a peasant revolution to overthrow the power of the cities. Efforts to prevent
Bulgaria from joining in World War I led to his imprisonment (1915) but,
released in 1918, he was one of a group of politicians who forced the
abdication of King Ferdinand; and in 1919 he became prime minister.
For four years he used virtually dictatorial powers to remove all taxation
from the peasants and load it on to the bourgeoisie and the urban proletariat. But when, in 1923, he agreed to help the government of Yugoslavia
to crush the Internal Macedonian Revolutionary Organization, which was
making too free a use of ◊ assassination, he was, predictably, himself
assassinated.

Stern, Abraham (1907–42) Israeli revolutionary terrorist b. Poland
whence he made his way to Palestine and joined ◊ Jabotinsky's ◊ Zionist
Revisionist movement which aimed at winning Palestine for the Jews, and
Jewish statehood, by force of arms. A brilliant classicist, he studied and
taught Greek and Latin at the Hebrew University, and wrote Hebrew
poetry with a strongly patriotic tone. A scholarship took him to Rome
where he conceived a great admiration for ◊ Mussolini. He returned to
Palestine in 1929 and fought against Arab rioters. From 1933 he gave up
academic life and took to underground revolutionary terrorism, as an
extreme Hebrew imperialist, on more or less ◊ Fascist lines, with visions
of a great Israeli empire in the Middle East, founding the Hebrew Liberation Movement which became known to the British mandate authorities
as 'the Stern gang'. In 1937 he helped to found Irgun Zvai Leumi
(National Military Organization) and in 1938 went to Poland where he
tried to arrange for the training and arming of a Jewish commando which
was to invade Palestine and seize it for the Jewish nation. Arrested on his
return, by the British, he was released in 1940. He wrote and published

Stirner, Max

more patriotic poetry, and took the *nom-de-guerre* of Yair, the legendary hero of Masada. In association with Nathan Friedman-Yellin, he organized and carried out terrorist activities against the British and Arabs, in which a number of lives were lost and much property damaged or destroyed. The majority of the Jewish population was hostile to his ruthless methods, including the other militant but more chivalrous organizations, and when two Jewish policemen, sent by Captain Geoffrey Morton of the CID, who was hunting him down, were killed, they turned completely against him and helped in the hunt. As a result he was located in a hideout in Tel Aviv, arrested and handcuffed by Morton and his men, and 'shot while attempting to escape'.

Stirner, Max (Johann Caspar Schmidt, 1806–56) Bavarian school-teacher and revolutionary anarchist theorist who only became important three decades after his death because of revived interest in his extra-ordinary and only important book *The Ego and his Own* (Munich 1843). As a poor student he was a mild, undistinguished member of the Freien ('The Emancipated') group of Young Hegelians, (*see* ⟡ Marx), whose first published works, on educational methods, were printed in Marx's *Rheinische Zeitung*. *The Ego and his Own* was written when he was teacher at a girls' school: in it he turned ⟡ Hegel upside-down, denied the existence of all natural law and the claims of common humanity, claimed that the *only* reality we can experience is the 'selfness of the self'; in this there is a curious foreshadow of existentialism. Every man is at war with every other; voluntary association with others for mutual advantage is possible, and may even be desirable, but it will be a 'cold war', an expedient union of egotists without law or rules in which the balance of power is maintained by the tension between equally strong, mutually hostile, purely selfish wills. Again, here there is a curious foreshadow, this time of the physical universe in terms of Einsteinian mathematics. To bring this about valid social, economic and, of course, religious, institutions must be destroyed as soon as possible and by resort to immediate violence of every kind. Stirner also analysed and contemptuously rejected every philosophical system, including those of Hegel, whose lectures he attended, and Marx, whom he knew as a Young Hegelian. In short, he utterly denied the honesty or viability of every kind of 'collective', abstract or concrete, even the viability of the abstraction 'mankind', leaving as the only reality the free, elemental, devotedly selfish individual, loyal to nothing and to nobody but the Self. As a result of this book Stirner was briefly famous, but since it offered nothing but Nothing, and caused a scandal which cost him his job and barred him from others, he sank into obscurity and debt and died poor and miserable. Thirty years later *The Ego and his Own* was inspiring violent, libertarian anarchists all over Europe and America, and it still has its admirers.

Student Non-violent Coordinating Committee. *See* SNCC.

Student power. In the advanced industrial countries of the West a progressive proportion of the students at universities and other institutions of higher education, including many who are, by reliable accounts, among the ablest and most intelligent, give expression to a revolutionary rejection of the established bourgeois-capitalist-managerial-corporation-affluent society, in their lifestyle: long hair, unconventional clothes, total sexual freedom, use of drugs and of particular kinds of music, pacifism and, in extreme cases, quietism and the establishment of communes for living at the simplest possible level without private property. The origins and nature of this phenomenon in America have been described and analysed by Charles Reich in *The Greening of America*, which gives it far greater significance than other writers have done; if that work is valid for the US it is probably valid for Britain and West Europe, but there is little reason to suppose that it is. This lifestyle is taken to be the outward and visible sign of an inner state of grace which alienates the subject from the affluent society stigmatized as repulsive and degrading in all its aspects. But that is only one aspect of the student revolution: there are two others more conventional and formal: the first concerns the university itself; the second society at large. First, student revolutionaries seek to transform the university from an institution which prepares the student for a place commanding a large salary in the affluent society, into one which prepares him or her for the fullness of a rich spiritual and aesthetic life; and in the second place they seek to win administrative control of the university for the student body, in other words a democratic university like that of, e.g. Salamanca in the sixteenth century where the 7,000 students elected their own professors and the professors elected the rector who held office for only one year.

Sun Yat-sen

As regards society at large, the student revolution seeks to overthrow the present political and economic establishment and replace it with a democratic socialist society so contrived that it cannot harden into a parliamentary oligarchy or into a dictatorial establishment. The organs by whose means active expression is given to this purpose are numerous and small, and are not working together. But they have, for the most part, certain things in common, e.g. some kind and measure of ⋫ Marxism as their philosophy and equal hostility to the capitalist and communist establishments (see New Left). In Britain the most important are the Trotskyist I S (International Socialists); the ⋫ Spartacus League, which is the student wing of the I M G (International Marxist Group) affiliated to the ⋫ Fourth International; and the Y C L (Young Communists League) which is Moscow-oriented. In France the organizations are the J C R (Jeunesse Communiste Revolutionaire), Trotskyist; F E R (Fédération des Etudiants Revolutionaires), also Trotskyist; U J C (ML) Union des Jeunesses Communistes (Marxist-Leninist), Maoist; U E C (Union des Etudiants Communistes) Moscow-oriented; C A L (Comité d'Action Lycéen) the teenage New Left: see also French Student Revolution, 1968.

Sun Yat-sen (1867–1925) Chinese democratic revolutionary, leader of the Kuomintang nationalist movement which overthrew the Manchu Empire and founded the Republic of China. b. Macao, s. of a peasant; ed. Honolulu by missionaries; converted to Christianity. Further studies, U S A where he became a citizen, and Hong Kong where he studied medicine. In the 1890s he founded a number of political movements, chiefly among moderate revolutionary exiles, to promote republican revolution in China and introduce social and economic reforms; the most important was the 'Save China League'. While he was in London in 1897 he was seized by Manchu agents and imprisoned in the Chinese consulate, but released when the Foreign Office intervened. His 'Save China League' seems to have become absorbed into the earlier, Kuomintang party: *min* means 'people': *kuo* means 'state' and the compound means 'republican'. In 1898 Sun gave his party its three principles: Nationalism; Democracy; Socialism. Yet another of his foundations, The League of the Common Alliance, was active in China from about 1905 and when its work culminated in revolution (see Chinese Revolution 1911) he hastened back to

272

China, from New York, to assume the leadership. In Nanking a Revolutionary Assembly proclaimed him President (not of a republic, but of the 'United Provinces of China', on the model of the USA). Meanwhile Yuan Shih-kai had been made prime minister by a National Assembly in Peking and, for the sake of unity, Sun stood down. Unity was not achieved, however, and Sun continued as head of a provisional government in Nanking until Yuan died (1915) six months after proclaiming himself Emperor (*see* Chinese Revolution 1911). This left Sun Yat-sen nominally President of China; but his government was not in control of much of the country, which had fallen into the hands of provincial warlords who ruled as military dictators and waged war on each other for the supreme power, so that Sun was not able to implement the three principles outside a relatively small area. However, moving to the left, he began to receive some aid in 1922 from the USSR, on condition of modifying the rules of the Kuomintang to admit communists who thenceforth gave the party much more driving force and manpower. Sun did not live long enough to reap the benefit of this reform of his party, but it was with communist help that his successor and brother-in-law, ⧫ Chiang Kai-shek was eventually able (1927) to establish something approaching central government control by defeating the warlords or coming to terms with them.

Syndicalism. From the French *syndicat*, trade union; a revolutionary doctrine whose sectaries, unlike the socialists and communists, aim not at capturing the state apparatus from the ruling, middle class, for the ⧫ proletariat, but, ignoring politics and political methods, at seizing worker control of the means of production, distribution and exchange. Each plant within an industry is to be run by the workers represented by a council of their trade union; individual plants are to be connected by a sort of loose federation of plants; and all the industries, trades and professions, likewise self-governing, to be connected together in a similar federation of their executive councils. This federation of trade union councils will form the only fabric of the economic community; and the political state will be extinguished as being oppressive and therefore evil, and moreover, unnecessary. Thus, syndicalism, while it is not identical with anarchism, has affinities with it which have led to the syncretism called anarcho syndicalism.

As a revolutionary movement, at first without a theorist, although under

the influence of ◊ Proudhon, syndicalism arose among French revolutionary trade unionists in the second half of the nineteenth century, and for
some seventy years it flourished there, in Italy and in Spain. In Britain,
in a version slightly medievalized and with the element of revolutionary
violence removed to suit the national character, called Guild Socialism, it
found a great advocate in Professor G. D. H. Cole. It also found expression
in the USA, between 1905 and c. 1920, in the economic and social philosophy of the ◊ Industrial Workers of the World.

Syndicalism found its intellectual prophet in the French philosopher
Georges ◊ Sorel whose *Reflections on Violence* (1908), written after he had
become a convert to a ◊ Marxism which ◊ Marx would hardly have
recognized, developed the idea of revolutionary violence and the ◊
general strike as 'myths' to be used to inspire and move the proletariat
to revolutionary action. Sorel glorified revolutionary violence as the only
effective denial of the existing order; but he denounced violence when
used by the state, through its police, as intolerably oppressive.

Syndicalism concentrates solely on industrial action, to culminate in the
general strike, as the means to revolution, but does not exclude more
militant forms of violence, since it expects the bourgeoisie to wage war on
the workers to put down the strike. But it is as firmly opposed to ◊
communism as is the ◊ bourgeoisie itself, holding, what experience has
shown to be true, that state control and organization of industry are
incompatible with working class freedom. On the other hand, syndicalists
agree with those communists not infected with ◊ revisionism touching the
inevitability of violent class war. And syndicalists are to the left of orthodox
communism in preaching the absolute necessity for world revolution,
envisaging an international extension of the federation of *syndicats* as
making political foreign relations as unnecessary as the political State
itself.

Like other non-communist revolutionary movements syndicalism lost
most of its momentum in the 1920s with the rise of communism following
the successful ◊ Bolshevik revolution in Russia; it foundered on the hard,
jagged realism of Marxism, even Sorel himself, after a curious flirtation
with the ◊ Action Francaise, becoming an enthusiastic supporter of the
◊ Bolsheviks.

T

Terrorism. A revolutionary, or, sometimes counterrevolutionary ('police terrorism') method by means of which a population is induced to cooperate with revolutionary outlaws by inspiring it with terror: rich men may be induced to contribute money to the revolutionary funds by threats against their lives or those of their families; the poor may be induced to find them food and shelter, or at least to refuse information to the police or military, by similar treatment; small groups or single individuals of the opposing forces may be trapped or ambushed and killed; members of the government may be assassinated; and confidence in the forces of the law and stability of the regime may be undermined by the violent destruction of public buildings or the armed robbery of banks. In extreme cases terrorism may be extended to indiscriminate destruction which may be justified by ◊ Bakunin's dictum: 'Let us put our trust in the eternal spirit which destroys and annihilates only because it is the unsearchable and eternally creative source of all life. The passion for destruction is also a creative passion' (*Reaction in Germany*, 1846).

Terrorism may be simply a means of propaganda by deed instead of word: it was used more or less in that spirit by The ◊ People's Will and the ◊ Socialist Revolutionaries in Russia in the nineteenth century.

It was much used by anarchists, although disapproved of by many of them, from about 1870 to 1900 in France, Italy, Spain and the US. The spirit of terrorism was even manifest in the names chosen by some French anarchist groups, e.g. *La Panthère, La Haine, Les Terribles*; and in such revolutionary songs as, e.g. *La Dynamite*:

> Nos pères ont jadis dansé
> Au son de canon du passé
> Maintenant la danse tragique
> Veut une plus forte musique
> Dynamitons, dynamitons.

275

Thakin Than Tun

Representative members of the bourgeoisie and their clerical allies were assassinated more or less at random; churches, and the houses occupied by the managers of capitalist enterprises were blown up; shops were looted to feed the poor; a French president, an American president and an Italian king were assassinated.

The Bakunist (Italian) Federation of the Anarchist branch of the International (the anarchist and anti-Marxist wing which was so strong in Italy and Spain), and such anarchist movements as the Committee of the Social Revolution, adopted terrorism as a deliberate policy, despite all that such gentler souls as Kropotkin, Costa and the greatest Italian anarchist, ◊ Malatesta could do to dissuade them.

In the revolutionary history of France, and to some extent Italy and Spain, it is not always easy to distinguish genuine anarchist conspiracies from 'anarchist' plots, initiated by *agents provocateurs*; 'anarchist' newspapers were founded and financed by the police to trap real anarchists into their hands (the situation is satirized by G. K. Chesterton in *The Man who was Thursday*). One such doubtful case is that of the *La Mano Negra* movement in Spain: it was almost certainly a police-inspired movement and the seven 'anarchists' who were publicly garrotted in Jerez de la Frontera (1883) were probably innocent peasants.

In the twentieth century terrorism has been used chiefly in nationalist revolutions, e.g. by the Irish against the British; by the Arabs and the Jews against the British in Palestine; by the Algerians against the French. Counter terrorism was a favourite weapon of the Nazis, is used by the ◊ CIA, and is in almost continuous use by the South African government against their black and coloured citizens.

Thakin Than Tun (1915–1968). Chairman and military leader of the Communist Party of Burma, s. of a landowner, ed. Rangoon University and led a Marxist group within the bourgeois-nationalist Thakin Party before the Japanese invasion. Held office in the Japanese sponsored puppet government. He became Secretary-General of the Anti-Fascist Peoples Freedom League, 1946, and in 1947 of the BCP, when he adopted and persisted in a ◊ Maoist line hostile to the CP of the USSR and from 1965 guided his Party on the lines of the ◊ 'Lin Piao' theory of revolution, making the Burmese countryside rather than the cities the base of his revolutionary operations. By 1950, after two years of civil war, he controlled most of the

Burmese rural areas, several major cities and a number of smaller towns, but not Rangoon. The government of U Nu and of his successor Ne Win received modern weapons including napalm from the UK and US governments and by 1965 had regained most of the territory lost to the revolutionaries. But in 1965 Thakin Than Tun resumed the offensive and was making a good recovery when he was killed in action (1968). With his death the communists again lost ground but have slowly regained their hold on some parts of Burma under the leadership of Thakin Ba Thein Tin.

Tierra y Libertad. A Mexican-American, i.e. 'Chicano' revolutionary movement in the USA which tends to identify with the Tricontinental (OSPAAAL) and, in general, with the ◊ New Left of the Third World. Names of leaders are secret. The revolutionary Chicanos believe that what they call 'Anglo' civilization, i.e. the civilization of white Americans, is and always has been deliberately bent on exploiting the labour of all Americans with coloured skins for specifically capitalist- ◊ imperialist ends, cheapening that labour by treating these coloured people as second-class citizens with fewer rights than the whites, or no rights at all. The Chicano revolutionary programme includes the setting-up of study groups, anti-imperialist propaganda among the Chicano people of all the south-western states, especially through their already considerable 'underground' press, and a theatre of revolutionary propaganda; creation of a Third World Liberation Front with other revolutionary minorities within the USA; the gaining of political control, by electoral means, of regions where Chicanos are in a majority; recovery of the land granted to their *pueblos*, communally, by the Treaty of Guadalupe Hidalgo (1848) and of which they have since been expropriated by various more or less illegal means; organization of ◊ boycott of all 'Anglo' business undertakings and deliberate use of industrial action to sabotage 'Anglo' businesses and industries; formation of Chicano political parties; and armed groups to organize counterviolence and to carry out 'revolutionary justice' on 'collaborationists, accommodationists and agents', i.e. those of their own people who, by working within the white rules, play a 'neo-colonialist' role.

Tito (Josip Broz, 1892–   ) b. Croatia, to a peasant family, father Croat, mother Slovene. Primary ed. (village school) only. Apprenticed to a locksmith in Sisak (1907–10); metalworker in various cities of the

Austro-Hungarian empire and member of the Metal Workers Union affiliated to the Social Democratic Party of Croatia (1910–13). In 1913 began
military service and was promoted corporal. Imprisoned (1914) for anti-
Austrian subversive talk, he was released to fight on the Galician front
against the Russians, wounded and captured. Released from PoW camp by
the Russian Revolution of February 1917, lived for a while with a Polish
Bolshevik railway worker, went to Petrograd, was arrested on suspicion of
Bolshevism, imprisoned, escaped to Omsk and became a Red Guard
following the October 1917 Revolution. When White Russian forces took
Omsk he escaped and lived (1919) with Khirgiz nomads, later returning
to Omsk where he married a Russian girl. In 1920 he returned, with his
wife, to his native village, Kumovec, now in the new Yugoslavia where the
Socialist Workers (Communist) Party had already been founded under the
aegis of the ▷ Comintern. Broz did not join it at once and was not yet even a
convinced communist. He rejoined the Social-Democratic Party, got his
living as engine-mechanic at a mill, lived in one room where his wife bore
him three children of whom one survived infancy, until, in 1923 he was
called on by a Comintern agent who knew Broz as a former Bolshevik
sympathizer and Russian-speaker, and now recruited him as a CP agitator.
Using trade union organization as a front, Broz began work for the CP,
and by hard work, ambition and readiness to risk his freedom, climbed
through the Party hierarchy, meanwhile changing location and jobs
frequently in order to keep a step ahead of the police and do the Party's
work in various places. His first revolutionary newspaper article appeared
in *The Organized Worker*, 27 March 1917. Thereafter he became a full-
time professional revolutionary. Arrested (June 1927) and held without
trial, he forced the authorities to try him (October) by hunger strike.
Released pending appeal against his sentence, he 'went underground', for
the dictatorship of King Alexander Karageorgevic was becoming increasingly tough with communists.

It is significant for Broz's later career that the Comintern, which
financed the Yugoslav CP, already regarded it as tiresomely independent,
but that 'independence' was largely a reflection of the inconsistencies
arising out of the conflicting nationalisms of the Croat, Slovene and
Macedonian CPs (1928/29). Broz emerged as a leader when, at the Zagreb
CP conference 25/26 February 1928 he frankly exposed these differences
and, with an ambitious eye on the main chance, appealed to the Comintern

for 'guidance'. Hunted by the police, he was again arrested when grenades were found in his room. He turned the trial into a forum for passionate communist propaganda and was sentenced to five years in prison. Allowed books, he used the time to complete his education, with the help of a fellow-prisoner, the ◊ Marxist philosopher Mosa Pijade. A year after release he went to Moscow to work in the Balkan Secretariat of the Comintern, and there got to know many leading communists and the leaders of his own party. The Yugoslavs were repeatedly 'purged' for indiscipline and as a result of one such purge, Broz was made Organizing Secretary, a case of driving out Satan with Beelzebub but that was not yet clear to the Russians. During the next few years, working in Yugoslavia, Paris and Moscow for the Party, his self-preservatory discretion, penetrating understanding of ◊ Stalin's madness, and the friendship of the great Bulgarian communist, ◊ Dimitrov, enabled him to survive the purges in which about 100 Yugoslav CP leaders were murdered by the NKVD. As a result he was Secretary-General of the Yugoslav CP when war broke out in 1939.

Hitler had decided that before attacking the USSR he should neutralize Yugoslavia by putting pressure on the government of Prince Paul, Regent since his brother's ◊ assassination, pro-Nazi but restrained from open support of Germany by the Serb opposition to his policy. But on 25 March 1941 he signed the Tripartite Pact. There were serious Serb riots, a group of anti-German army officers forced Paul to abdicate and go into exile, and formed a new government in the name of the boy King Peter. Hitler ordered the conquest of Yugoslavia which, after the heavy bombing of Belgrade on 6 April, was accomplished in ten days. Peter and his government fled the country. The Germans occupied most of Serbia and Slovenia; Italy the rest of Slovenia, the Dalmatian coast and the islands, Bosnia and Montenegro; Hungary was given some Yugoslav territory; and a state of Croatia was set up under the sadistic Ustasi leader, Ante Pavelič, subservient to Germany.

Tito's subsequent partisan war was waged against all these governments, but chiefly the Germans and their Ustasi allies; his conscious aim was a communist Yugoslavia. Starting with a few small militant communist groups in various parts of the country, he ended the war with about quarter of a million partisans under arms most of which had been captured from the enemy, holding down as many as ten enemy divisions. Not the least remarkable of his successes were those of persuading the half

Tito

dozen different nationalities under his command to work amicably together; and of consistently maintaining his independence of Stalin who was prepared to sacrifice the revolution in Yugoslavia to the prejudices and policies of his western allies, and by no means anxious to have, in the Balkans, a communist state owing nothing to the Red Army, and everything to its own communists. The Western allies had at first supported the resistance movement of the royalist General Mihailovič and his Cetniks. But when, at last, it became clear that the Cetniks were as often fighting with the Germans against the communists, as against them, Winston Churchill insisted on shifting military aid, supplies and liaison to Tito, despite American opposition and Russian coolness.

By 1943 Tito had a skeleton civilian government, known as AVNOJ (Anti-Fascist Council) working and was confident of imposing his communist revolution on the whole country once the Germans had been defeated. He infuriated Stalin by informing him that he would not tolerate any attempt to restore the royalist government, which Stalin had been prepared to agree to in return for more important concessions from the US and Britain. In August 1944 Tito went to Italy to meet Churchill and British aid was stepped up. At the end of the war he was in a position to make his own terms. In return for recognition of his (communist) Federal Republic of Yugoslavia he agreed to accept some royalist ministers into his first postwar government, knowing that he could get rid of them as soon as it suited him, which he did.

While Tito continued nominally to accept Soviet leadership of world communism, in practice he would not accept Russian dictation in foreign and economic policy. From 1945 to 1947 his relations with the USSR were amicable and he was Stalin's cold war ally. But his growing independence, in such matters as negotiating a possible federation with Bulgaria, and insisting on helping the communists in the Greek civil war although Stalin had sacrificed them to the West in his international horse-trading, was such that in 1948 an even more infuriated Stalin broke with him and threatened to bring Yugoslavia to heel, conducting a loud hymn of hate sung by the whole communist world against Yugoslavia. Tito refused to be bullied or intimidated, made it quite clear that the Yugoslavs would fight if invaded by the USSR, obtained economic aid from the West, considerably liberalized his internal regime and continued to defy the USSR until two years after Stalin died. He only consented to be reconciled with the Russians and then on his own terms, when ◊ Khruschev visited Belgrade and publicly apologized for the Soviet attitude (1955).

Since Lenin, Tito has been the most able and successful communist revolutionary with the one exception of ◊ Mao Tse-tung. He remains a convinced, but has never been a dogmatic, Marxist and has given Yugoslavia a measure of prosperity based on an idiosyncratic and highly empirical Socialism. As a man, his pleasure in wine, women and song, especially women, his love of fine clothes, and his luxurious homes have added to, rather than detracted from his popularity and extraordinary hold over all the ethnic groups composing the federal republic he created.

Tkachev, Pyotr Nikitich (1844–86) b. Velikiye Luki, s. of a Russian petty noble. 'Blanquist' revolutionary theorist who served his first, three-year, prison term at the age of nineteen for advocating violent revolution, while associated with the group of students who, under the leadership of P. G. ◊ Zaichnevsky, formed the ◊ Young Russia movement, and who are sometimes known as the 'Jacobins' of the Russian revolutionary movement. It is probable that Tkachev had a hand in the writing of the Young Russia manifesto, but unlikely that he was among those who were accused of burning down part of St Petersburg in a series of mysterious and devastating fires in 1862. In St Petersburg University circles he met ◊ Nechayev and with him wrote (1868) *A Programme of Revolutionary Action* which, rewritten by ◊ Bakunin, became *The ◊ Revolutionary Catechism*. After he had read ◊ Marx Tkachev broke with his anarchist associates and began to propound, in a series of writings which lasted almost for the rest of his life, or rather until he went mad, revolutionary theories of his own, broadly based on the writings of ◊ Blanqui. He spent most of 1869–73 either in prison or in exile, chiefly in Siberia, but in 1874 took refuge in Switzerland. Although his sympathies lay with the 'communist' populists and ◊ Marxists, he isolated himself as a revolutionary thinker by insisting, like the Young Russia adherents, on the value of the conspiratorial revolutionary elite in bringing about revolution, rather than on mass movements.

In economics he was a complete Marxist for whom the basis of society and the motive force of history was economic materialism. He consistently

Tkachev, Petr Nikitich

attacked the value of positivism in social science and particularly the evolutionary ideas of Herbert Spencer. He was a rigorous egalitarian. Taking his own trade: 'Intellectual activity must be paid for and its price falls heavily on the shoulders of the peasants. Each page of a review is paid for by the sacrifice of those who will never read it . . . for . . . whoever has more than the average income is eating somebody else's bread.' Unlike Marx he believed that revolutionary propaganda should work on the peasants, not the proletariat; the only hope of revolutionary salvation for Russia was in the peasants. In 1875 he founded, in Geneva, a Blanquist group with their own paper *Nabat* (Tocsin) subtitled *The Organ of the Russian Revolutionaries*. A single paragraph from an article in that journal (1876) outlines his basic revolutionary ideas: 'The essence of the first stage is the fight, and therefore violence; the fight can be carried out successfully only on the following conditions: centralization, severe discipline, speed, decision and unity in action. Any concession or doubt, any compromise, multiplicity of command or decentralization of the forces in the fight, can only weaken their energy, paralyse their work and do away with any chance of victory.' There we have the early 'Jacobin' Tkachev; he continues: 'Constructive revolutionary activity on the other hand, though it must proceed at the same time as the destructive activity, must by its very nature rely on exactly opposite principles. The first is based mainly on material force, the second is based on spiritual force; the first relies mainly on speed and unity, the second on the solidity and vitality of the changes it has brought about. The first must be carried out with violence, the second with conviction. The *ultima ratio* of the first is victory, the *ultima ratio* of the second is the will and reason of the people.' What Tkachev repeatedly warned against in the second, constructive phase, was falling into ◊ Utopianism, a danger about which he had written analytically and at length.

In 1880 he became convinced that the peasant *jacqueries* all over Russia would shortly combine into revolution and he shifted his *Nabat* and its printing press, and his Society for the Liberation of the People, an ineffectual revolutionary action group which he had founded in 1876, into Russia. The revolution failed to materialize, he lost his printing press and in 1881 he gave up and went to Paris to join the editorial board of the Blanquist *Ni Dieu ni maître*. But a year later he fell seriously ill, his brain was affected and he spent the last four years of his life in a lunatic asylum.

282

Torres, Father Camilo (1929–66). Colombian revolutionary sociologist and militant ◊ guerrilla fighter. b. Bogota into the upper middle class. He read law at the National University, Bogota and then theology at a Dominican seminary, where he took holy orders. Next he went to Louvain, Belgium, to read sociology. He became Chaplain, National University and founder of its Faculty of Sociology; Dean, Advanced School of Public Administration; Founder, Institute of Social Administration, Cardinal's representative on the Board of the Colombian Agrarian Reform Institute. His first political interest was in arousing the mass of the peasantry to political consciousness by a programme of education: 60 per cent of Colombians took no part in politics, not even casting their votes in elections; they should be taught to formulate and state their own demands instead of having policies thrust on them from both Right and Left. Without such awareness, liberal reformist and left revolutionary movements were bound to fail as, indeed, by 1960 (*see* Colombia; guerrilla movements) they had done.

In March 1965 Torres published his 'Platform for a United Popular Movement'. The Hierarchy at once dismissed him from his Deanery and demoted him to a minor post on starvation salary, and his 'Platform' was pronounced to be 'irreconcilable with the doctrines of the Church'. Torres challenged this, publicly denounced the Hierarchy, and called, in a broadcast, for expropriation of the wealth of the Church. The Hierarchy warned all Catholics to have no dealings with this turbulent priest. A meeting between Torres and the Cardinal-Archbishop achieved nothing, and Torres asked to be unfrocked; this was conceded and he then set about organizing a United Front of Popular Movements which was to include the Liberals and Christian Democrats on the right, and the communists, both orthodox and ultra-left, on the left. The group most inclined to take the idea of a mass movement seriously was the Fidelista Ejercito de Liberacion Nacional (*see* Colombia guerrilla movements) with which he cooperated. He founded and wrote for the journal *Frente Popular* which had a spectacular initial success. But the task of producing a moderate socialist programme which all the elements of his Popular Front could subscribe to, proved impossible. He was suspected of trying to turn the Front into a political party in which all the others would lose identity and policies. Group after group seceded from the Front. Forced to admit defeat, Torres joined the National Liberation Army (*see* Colombia, guerrilla movements) as a *guerrillero* and issued a call to all Colombians to arm, prepare and train for a war of revolution with the slogan '*Liberation or Death!*' His ⬦ guerrilla group was ambushed by a unit of the government's anti-guerrilla forces, and Torres was killed in action 15 February 1966.

Trade unions and trade unionism. In Britain, the trade union movement first started in the woollen industry in the eighteenth century, was forced into clandestinity by the Combination Laws during the Napoleonic Wars, but was legalized in 1825; it has not been revolutionary. It is true that the men who tried in the 1830s to form the Grand National Consolidated Trades Union were Owenite socialists and did aim at putting an end to capitalism by what was, in fact, the earliest form of ⬦ Syndicalism. But their attempt failed, never attracting enough working-class support. Since then the British trade unions have not, even in their most militant moments, e.g. in the ⬦ General Strike of 1926, aimed at the overthrow of governments or the destruction of capitalism and the Trades Union Congress (TUC), like the American Federation of Labour (AF of L) and the CIO in the USA, has long become a part of the national ⬦ establishment, a bulwark of the Welfare State and bourgeois parliamentary democracy.

On the European continent, however, the trade union movement has, chiefly by its early connection with anarcho-syndicalism, from time to time adopted a revolutionary attitude. In the 1890s the doctrine of anarcho-syndicalism, originating in France, spread into Italy, Spain and northern Europe. According to this doctrine, the pure anarchist plan for workers' 'communes' as the primary organs first of the revolutionary struggle and thereafter of the new society, was no longer appropriate, since it took no account of the fact that in an industrial society the centre of a worker's life was not his home but his place of work; the 'commune' must therefore be replaced by the 'syndicat', i.e. the trade union: (*see* Syndicalism; Proudhon). The revolution itself would be accomplished not by political action, but by economic action or what we now call 'industrial action', and above all by the ⬦ general strike. So attractive did this doctrine prove in France that by about 1900 the anarcho-syndicalists led by Fernand Pelloutier had become extremely powerful in the Confédération Générale du Travail (French equivalent of the TUC or AF of L) whose daily newspaper, *La Voix du Peuple*, was edited by an anarcho-syndicalist. From 1900 to 1910 the CGT under this influence led the French workers in a series of strikes and sabotage actions which were revolutionary in intention and to which the bourgeoisie reacted by police violence. By 1906 the syndicalist movement felt strong enough to announce, in the Charter of Amiens, that the French workers repudiated all political parties however 'left' and would adopt a go-it-alone revolutionary policy of industrial action. But this proved to be a zenith; and from that date anarcho-syndicalist influence waned, Marxist influence waxed, with the result that industrial action by the *Syndicats* tended to be used only to obtain higher wages or better conditions, while the workers' revolutionary action became political.

Outside France, the country most affected by syndicalist ideas was Spain. In fact the anarchist trade union movement there led the revolutionary struggle for forty years and had a greater appeal for a majority of the workers than Marxism. Anarchism was already popular and widespread among both workers and intellectuals: syndicalism gave it a new dimension and the anarcho-syndicalist general strike in Barcelona in 1902 had a revolutionary, not a merely welfare, purpose. By 1908 the syndicalist Solidaridad Obrera was the strongest working-class movement in Catalonia and all the more dangerous to the central government in that it supported the Catalan Separatists. When, in 1909, the government desperately needed army reservists to try to reverse the disastrous course of its war with the Riff in Morocco, it tried to kill two birds with one stone by confining the call-up to Catalonia. Solidaridad Obrera reacted by calling a general strike which was supported by the socialists; there followed a week of street fighting directed, on the workers side, by the unions; fifty or more convents and churches were burnt down, about 200 workers were killed, thousands were taken prisoner and many tortured or shot out of hand. So atrocious was the government's repression, that protests poured in from all over Europe as well as from the Spanish people, and the Conservative Government was forced to resign in favour of a Liberal one. In 1910 the anarcho-syndicalist trade unions all over Spain united in the Confederacion Nacional del Trabajo with the deliberate intention of creating an organ of revolution on a national scale: it initiated and led strikes, including general strikes which developed into armed insurrections; at least one city was declared a workers' 'commune'; and when in 1912 the Liberal prime

Tricontinental

minister Canalejas declared the CNT illegal and broke a railway strike by calling up the strikers for military service, he was shot dead by an anarchist assassin. In 1920 the CNT had about three-quarters of a million members and these militant anarchist trade unionists, rather than the Marxist socialists and communists, led the revolutionary struggle in Spain until it was finally crushed by Franco's victory in the Civil War of 1936–9. That victory he owed as much to the enmity between anarcho-syndicalists and communists on the other side, as to any other cause.

In Germany, trade unionism was a late and rather weak growth; the class struggle was left to the social-democrats and later communist parties, the unions confining themselves to negotiating wages and conditions of employment. In the USA, too, the so-called 'craft' unions were anti-revolutionary and even, in their maintenance of differentials and their policy of exclusiveness, reactionary. The great industrial unions were, in the last decades of the nineteenth century and the first decades of the twentieth, more liberal and occasionally inclined to a mild version of socialism, but were at no time genuinely revolutionary and by their acquiesence in such measures as the Taft-Hartley Act, showed themselves to be ⟡ 'bourgeois' in their ideology. In the West, as in the USSR, the trade unions are a part of the Establishment and as hostile to revolutionary parties and policies as is the 'management'.

Tricontinental: *see* OSPAAAL

Trotsky, Leon (Lev Davidovich Bronstein, 1879–1940) s. of a prosperous Jewish farmer in Kherson province. The village school taught him Russian, arithmetic and Hebrew, but in 1888 he was sent to the St Paul *Realschule* (German Lutheran) in Odessa where his principal extracurricular interest was writing poetry. Suspended for a year for leading a demonstration against an act of injustice, his schooling was further interrupted by ill-health and his father provided him with a private tutor. Returned for a final school year to the Gymnasium at Nikolayev where he read political economy and became a socialist. On leaving school he engaged in political agitation and propaganda among the workers and was a founder of the South Russian Workers' Union. In January 1898 he was arrested and imprisoned, first in Kherson, then Odessa where he did his first revolutionary writing, then Moscow where he first read ⟡ Lenin, and where he

Trotsky, Leon

married a fellow revolutionary, Alexandra Lvovna. They were exiled (1900) to Siberia where he continued to engage, with other political exiles, in revolutionary writing and organizing, and where two daughters were born to them. After reading Lenin's *What is to be Done?* Trotsky decided to escape in order to engage in more effective revolutionary work. He reached Samara and joined the London-based *Iskra* (both a journal and a revolutionary movement); his work attracted the attention of Lenin who wrote urging him to join him in exile. He was smuggled into Austria, given money by Victor Adler, leader of the Austrian social-democrats, and reached London, where Lenin was living, in autumn 1902. There he worked with ◊ Lenin, Martov, Sedova and others, writing for *Iskra*, and lecturing in the East End to Russian and German immigrants. He was sent to lecture in Brussels and Paris, where he met more Russian political exiles. At the Congress of the Russian Social Democratic Party which met in London (1903) he was delegate for the Siberian Union branch, and when the Party split into ◊ Bolsheviks (Lenin) and Mensheviks (Martov), Trotsky took a middle position attempting to reconcile both factions, though at first favouring the Mensheviks with whom he later broke.

He was in Geneva in January 1905 when the ◊ 'Bloody Sunday' massacre of workers led by the priest Gapon occurred. Accompanied by his second wife, N. D. Sedova, a leading social-democrat, he returned to Russia, on a false passport, wrote pamphlets for the underground Bolshevik press in Kiev, worked with both Bolshevik and Menshevik factions in St Petersburg, went into hiding in Finland when hunted by the police, returned to St Petersburg to organize and edit a revolutionary press, and became president of the Workers' Soviet. Arrested in December 1905, he continued his revolutionary studying and writing in prison, relaxing occasionally with French novels. He acquired fame by his conduct at the trial of the Workers' Delegates, which was described as 'heroic', and discovered his great gift for oratory. Exiled again to Siberia, at Berezov *en route* he evaded the guards and made a spectacular escape, by reindeer sledge and on horseback, 700 kilometres to a railhead in the Urals, met Sedova in St Petersburg and with her and their children went into exile lasting ten years. He continued his revolutionary work, with Rosa ◊ Luxemburg, Karl ◊ Liebnecht, ◊ Kautsky, ◊ Bebel, ◊ Lenin, ◊ Zinoviev, etc. in Germany, France, England, Belgium, Romania and other countries.

Trotsky, Leon

In October 1908 in Vienna he founded *Pravda*; and it was in this period that he developed those ideas of 'permanent revolution' which separated him from Stalinist Russian communism. He also wrote for the legal, liberal press in Russia. On the outbreak of World War I Trotsky moved his family to Switzerland but was able, as war correspondent of the *Kievskaya Mysl*, to work in France until expelled, at the instance of the Tsarist government, for editing the revolutionary *Nashe Slovo* for Russian political exiles.

He and his family were put over the Spanish frontier, arrested by the Spanish police and put on a ship for New York; there he wrote and spoke for the socialist cause and joined the editorial board of *Novy Mir*, a Russian language socialist paper. On the outbreak of the ⟡ Russian Revolution, February 1917, the family set out to return to Russia, but were arrested by the Canadian (he himself says British naval) authorities and put into a concentration camp at Halifax, Nova Scotia. At the instance of the Russian Provisional Government under pressure from the Petrograd Workers' Soviet, they were released and went to Petrograd where Trotsky became president of the Soviet in which the Bolsheviks were in a minority.

In the following months he took the leading Bolshevik role, and in the ⟡ Russian Revolution October 1917), a role second only to Lenin's. Their names became inseparable in the popular understanding of the Revolution. He was appointed, by the CP Central Committee, Commissar for Foreign Affairs in the first Communist Government, turned his brilliant negotiations at Brest-Litovsk into propaganda for world revolution, and signed the Treaty, against his will and only at Lenin's insistence. On the outbreak of civil war he was appointed Commissar of War, and created the Red Army out of the remnants of the Tsarist army, revolutionary workers and peasants. From his 'war ministry', a special train composed of offices, radio station, supply wagons, workshop and garage – the '*Predrevoyensoviet* train' – he rushed from one to another of the sixteen war fronts during more than two years; he organized the victory of the revolution, taking personal command in crises, e.g. when Petrograd was besieged by the 'White' General Yudenich. It was during the war that the opposition between Trotsky and Stalin became clear, and that Stalin, taking advantage of Lenin's illness following the attempt on his life in which he was wounded, began creating the personal following and bureaucratic 'apparatus' which was to give him supreme power and destroy Trotsky. Following the victory of the Red Army (1920–21), Trotsky undertook the reorganization of the shattered national transport system.

Even before Lenin's death, Stalin's skill in manipulating his Central Committee colleagues and creating a bureaucracy which identified its interests with his, succeeded in partially isolating Trotsky. This was a struggle for personal power but there was a real political difference; Stalin's policy was 'socialism in one country' and his apparatus a rigid bureaucracy of the established revolution: Trotsky's was 'the revolution in permanence' (until the total destruction of capitalism), and death to bureaucracy. Following Lenin's death in January 1924, Trotsky was seriously ill and unable to be at the centre of events in Moscow or to take charge of the Leninist cause in the Central Committee, which enabled Stalin progressively to deprive him of offices, power and followers; he lost the Commissary for War in January 1925 and was given an important technological post. But, almost continuously ill, with a permanently high temperature, he went, in 1926, to Berlin for special treatment. He returned late in the year to try to organize the angry opposition to Stalin's pro-Kuomintang China policy which had led to a massacre of communists by ▷ Chang Kai-shek; and in 1927 became leader of such opposition as there was, in the Central Committee and the CP at large, to Stalin's majority faction which controlled the GPU; this involved him in 'illegal' political agitation which Stalin characterized as 'counter-revolutionary'.

At the 15th Congress of the CP, December 1927 he and his party were expelled from the Central Committee, later from the CP, and Trotsky and his family were exiled to Alma-Ata in Central Asia. He was still a focus of the anti-Stalinist 'pure' Leninists and acted as such, with the result that in January 1929 he was charged with counter-revolution and forcibly deported to Turkey. During his Istanbul exile he wrote *The Permanent Revolution* (1929); the first part of *The Spanish Revolution* (completed 1939); *The Struggle against Fascism in Germany* (not published in book form until 1970); vol. I of his great *History of the Russian Revolution* (1931), completed during later exiles elsewhere; and *The Stalin School of Falsification* (1932) which led to his being stripped of Soviet citizenship, 1932, in which year he visited Copenhagen to deliver a lecture, and published *Problems of the Chinese Revolution*. In 1933 he founded the International Communist (▷ Bolshevik- ▷ Leninist) League from which later derived the Fourth ▷ International. In 1933 he was granted a visa for France,

T

there continued his work as an anti-Stalinist pamphleteer, but was so harassed by Stalin's agents, the French government and the ▷ bourgeois press, that he took refuge in Norway when its socialist government invited him to do so, there completing the *Life* of Lenin started in France. He organized the first Conference of the Fourth International, although it was not officially founded until later; and wrote *The Revolution Betrayed* (1936).

The first of Stalin's great show trials by which he rid himself of the old Bolsheviks took place in 1936, and Trotsky was convicted *in absentia* of conspiring to overthrow the Soviet government. As a result of threatening pressure from the USSR and from Norwegian ▷ Nazis led by Quisling, the Norwegian government deported Trotsky, on an oil tanker, to Mexico where President Cardenas had offered him asylum. In 1937 Stalin charged him, still *in absentia*, with being a Fascist agent: Trotsky not only exposed the purge trials in the world press as faked, he also defended himself against the charges by arranging for a commission of enquiry to retry the case, in the USA, under John Dewey: the commission acquitted him and declared the Moscow trial a frame-up. One of his sons, still in Russia, was put into a labour camp where he died; in 1938, another, Leon Sedov, was poisoned by a GPU agent, in Paris. In the same year Trotsky published *The Death Agony of Capitalism and the Tasks of the Fourth International*; other works of this period were *In Defence of Marxism* (1939) and *Marxism in our Time* (1939); several other books were left unfinished at his death. In May 1940 a first attempt by Stalin's agents to murder him failed, but on 20 August a more competent agent succeeded in driving an icepick through his brain.

Inferior to Lenin as a philosopher and Marxist theorist, and to Stalin in the baser arts of politics, Leon Trotsky was the greatest revolutionary man of action of the twentieth century. He believed that without Lenin the October Revolution would have failed; and that with Stalin it was betrayed; what is likely is that without Trotsky, the supreme organizer of victory in the Civil War and supreme advocate of its cause with the workers and socialist intellectuals all over the world, it would have perished in its infancy. Without Trotsky, too, its original purpose and ideal would have been even more completely abandoned and obscured than they were by Stalin – the purpose being socialist revolution continued until the extinction of capitalism everywhere, the ideal, an international, worldwide, communist community, humanist, egalitarian, free from the evils of class and state, and therefore of war. That ideal is very remote and perhaps unattainable; but it remains the hope that springs eternal in the revolutionary breast and Trotsky did more than any other Bolshevik to keep it alive: *see also* Trotskyism.

Trotskyism. A manifestation of ⟡ communism based on the revolutionary principles of ⟡ Trotsky who accepted the ⟡ Leninist opinion that nationalization of the means of production, distribution and exchange had not accomplished ⟡ socialism in the USSR and therefore urged that the revolution was not over when that had been achieved, but must, in order to combat the natural tendency of the bureaucracy to rule from above, excluding the people from power, continue. Socialism, which implies direct democracy involving all the workers in the business of making economic and political decisions, could be installed only by a condition of 'permanent revolution'. (Cf. Lenin's argument that the principal revolutionary duty of the workers was to use their trade unions to check the growth and abuses of bureaucratic power.) Trotskyism also entails internationalism: ⟡ Stalin's 'Socialism in one country' was a fraud, and all socialists, including those of the USSR, must carry on the revolution until it was worldwide. Trotskyism therefore implies antinationalism, antibureaucracy and world revolution to achieve a dictatorship of the proletariat – that is of the world's productive workers – completely emancipated from national governments and from any Party bureaucracy.

Tupamaros. A small but effective movement of revolutionaries active as urban *guerrilleros* in Uruguay. The name is based on that of Tupac Amaru, the last royal Inca to revolt against the Spaniards. There are believed to be about one thousand Tupamaros and many of them, like the ⟡ Weathermen in the USA, drawn from the rich upper ⟡ bourgeoisie. Nor are they only from the youth of that social class: the group is directed by highly placed professional men and even civil servants, people holding important posts in banking, the unions, ministries and above all universities. The ultimate object is Marxist- ⟡ Leninist revolution. Funds are obtained by bank robberies, and the group has blown up government radio stations, successfully raided government establishments for supplies of arms and explosives, fermented and led strikes and caused riots. Like other Latin American,

Turcios Lima, Lieutenant Luis Augusto

and like the Palestine ◊ guerrilla movements, this one is intended less to cause and lead an immediate mass revolution, than to create the conditions for revolution. Its activities may in some respects be compared with those of the ◊ nihilists and the ◊ People's Will militants in late nineteenth-century Russia, rather than with those of organized and self-conscious communism. The Tupamaros were pioneers in the technique of kidnapping important members of the diplomatic corps and holding them as hostages while forcing the government to release political prisoners or pay large ransoms. During 1972 police *and* paramilitary action against the Tupamaros was so successful that they have for some time been inactive.

Turcios Lima, Lieutenant Luis Augusto. ◊ Guerrilla leader in Guatemala, killed in October 1966. *See* Guatemala.

U

Umkhonto we Sizwe – Spear of the Nation. The armed revolutionary wing of the (South) African National Congress. Following the Sharpeville massacre the leadership of the S A resistance movement decided to meet violence with violence as the only means of overthrowing the *apartheid* State and in 1961 opened a campaign of sabotage against government installations all over the country. Following the arrest of key leaders in 1963 and the sentencing of Nelson ◊ Mandela and his comrades to life imprisonment, the movement's leaders in exile adopted a new strategy. Armed units of Umkhonto were trained in Tanzania and Zambia and, together with units of the ◊ ZAPU were first in action against Rhodesian and South African forces at Wankie, Rhodesia in 1967: *see also* South Africa and Rhodesia, Revolution in.

Unceda, Luis de la Puente (1926–65) Peruvian revolutionary guerrilla leader, s. of a landowner. As a schoolboy he became a supporter of the American Popular Revolutionary Alliance (APRA), a party which offered a mildly liberal and wholly ineffectual opposition to the ruling oligarchy. When in 1948 it was made illegal by the dictator Odria, Unceda was sent to prison for protesting and later exiled. He went to Mexico where he mixed with other South American political exiles, but remained a liberal and strictly Roman Catholic reformer; he did not at that stage turn to socialism. In 1954 he returned secretly to Peru to prepare a liberal democratic revolution against the dictatorship, was caught and again imprisoned. Released with other *politicos* some months before the 1956 elections, he went to Trujillo University and there wrote an agrarian reform thesis, *La Reforma del Agro Peruano* (published 1966). Attending the First National Agrarian Reform Forum at Havana, he still defended the system of capitalist landowning, although calling for very great liberal reforms and limitation on the size of holdings. His next political concern was with an attempt to move APRA policy to the left and make it effective. Failing, he led a breakaway left-wing of the party into independence first as

URD

'APRA Rebelde', which tried to get an agrarian reform bill through Congress and predictably failed; and then to mark a complete divorce from APRA, as the Movimento de Izquierda Revolucionaria (⟡ MIR). In 1961 he was again imprisoned for a year, and during that time became convinced of the need for armed insurrection by the peasants, to install a socialist government. He had difficulty in carrying MIR with him. He went (1962) to visit Hugo Blanco (⟡ Galdos); but as he had by now become a communist, whereas Blanco was a ⟡ Trotskyist, this conference with the more experienced organizer of peasant revolution was unfruitful. By 1964 de la Puente's political position was nearer to the Pekin than to the Moscow line, and he had some support from Fidel ⟡ Castro. He believed that the Marxist-Leninist conditions for revolution were present, and he began to organize armed insurrection by rural guerrillas, to be supported by a political campaign in the towns. His guerrilla groups bore such Inca (Quetchua) names as 'Tupac Amaru' and 'Pachacutec'. A Revolutionary Proclamation was widely publicized, calling for dissolution of Congress; general amnesty; agrarian reform, the land to be given to the peasants who worked it; a living wage for all workers, adjustable to the cost of living; an end to landlordism in the towns; nationalization of oil resources; and recovery of full national sovereignty from the US ⟡ 'imperialists'. De la Puente's guerrilla activities included the raiding of Civil Guard posts for arms; the blowing up of strategically important bridges, the sacking of large *haciendas*; fighting and capturing police detachments; fighting army patrols; recruiting the military alliance of the warlike Campa Indians; and even capturing small towns. Such were his successes that they led, in the absence of that mass rising which he seems to have expected, or at least hoped for, to his downfall: for the government made use not only of large numbers of infantry, but of artillery, and air-force bombing with HE and napalm, against the guerrilla-controlled regions; and the guerrilla bands were wiped out and their peasant and Indian allies cowed. Luis de la Puente himself was taken alive but murdered by the police two days later.

URD: Unidad Revolucionaria Democratica. Venezuelan non-communist party of the left: *see* Venezuela: guerrilla movements.

USA, Revolution in. A number of revolutionary movements are active

294

in the USA. Most, although not all, are derivatives of the oppression of coloured minorities, among whom the original movement for assertion of equality of rights within the US system has developed, as a result of white repressive reaction to their claims, into a revolutionary movement tending to the destruction of that system. The Communist Party of America is no longer regarded by the ⟡ New Left groups as revolutionary, having long since been convicted of Stalinist ⟡ revisionism. Although all the militant revolutionary groups, whether black, brown, red or white are divided by differences in their analysis of the revolutionary potential, they share much common ground: all regard capitalism, and especially US ⟡ imperialism (in the ⟡ Leninist sense), as the arch-enemy of mankind which it is essential to destroy; all have a Socialist ideology, whether Marxist- ⟡ Leninist as interpreted by ⟡ Marcuse, ⟡ Trotskyist, ⟡ Maoist, or ⟡ Guevarist. All see the Kremlin bosses as a sort of Great Whore of the Babylon of Unrighteousness, only a shade less evil than the White House–Pentagon–CIA triumvirate of devils. All, finally, insist on the importance of cultural revolution (again in the Leninist sense) and therefore aim for a direct democracy within a socialist framework: *see also* Bay of Pigs; Carmichael, S.; CIA; Cleaver, E.; Davis, A.; Forman, J.; Jackson, G.; Jackson, J.; Marcuse, H.; Newton, H. P.; Seale, B.; Tierra y Libertad; Weathermen; Williams, R. F.

Utopia, Utopianism. Utopia is the society which every true revolutionary has in mind when he sets out to change the existing order. From the Gr. *ou-topos*, i.e. 'nowhere' or 'no-such-place', but the more immediate derivation is from the *Utopia* (1516) of Sir (later Saint) Thomas More, a work of fiction emulating Plato's (428–348 BC) *Republic*, in which the author describes an, in his view, ideal society. In Utopia the relationship between the individual and the state is balanced and harmonious, inequitable differences between social classes no longer exist, health, longevity and learning are universal, material plenty is assured for ever but good taste has eliminated vulgar luxury, intelligence and goodwill rule under the government of the just, men are good, women virtuous and children obedient. This being so, the commonsense and self-knowledge of ordinary unregenerate men has given the word *utopian* a meaning rather different from that which More intended, and it is now used to describe political and social (and by extension other) ideas which are held to be impractical, impracticable, romantic to the point of absurdity. A serious flaw in all Utopias is that once you have *perfected* society it cannot improve but must remain static, which is in conflict with the fact that life implies ceaseless change. More's book was intended seriously to advance certain ideas of how an ideal society should be organized and the same yearning for a somewhat austere perfectionism is to be found in its spiritual descendants, e.g. in William Morris's *News from Nowhere* (1891) and the works of H. G. Wells (1866–1946). It is even to be found in the works of authors of Utopias whose purpose was primarily satirical comment on existing institutions and manners; for example, in the Brobdingnagian and Houhynnihym chapters of Swift's *Gulliver's Travels* (1726), the El Dorado part of Voltaire's *Candide* (1759) and in Samuel Butler's *Erewhon* (1872). Modern social novelists have carried the ordinary sceptic's attitude to Utopia to its logical conclusion by reversing Plato's intention in the *Republic*, and using the imaginary state as an awful warning that, if we do not at once change our foolish ways, to this horror will existing social and political trends inevitably lead. The outstanding examples in this *genre* are both English: Aldous Huxley's *Brave New World* (1932) which exposes the social dangers of bowing down to science; and George Orwell's *Nineteen-Eightyfour* (1949), a warning against the consequences of failing to oppose the growth of one-party ideological governments.

V

Varela, Juan de la Cruz. Colombian ◊ guerrilla leader, founder of the communist peasant republic of Sumapaz: *see* Colombia; guerrilla movements.

Venezuela: guerrilla movements A pastoral letter delivered by Archbishop Blanco of Venezuela in 1957 describes the economic and social conditions under the government of President Jiminez, which gave rise to the ◊ guerrilla movements in that country: the mass of the people were living in 'scarcely human' conditions; wages were 'inexcusably low'; the level of unemployment was 'intolerable'. First to revolt were the military who forced Jiminez to dismiss his hated Chief of Police. This sparked off revolt by university students, a number dissident factions, and the Communist Party, organized into a single effort by the Patriotic Junta of Fabricio ◊ Ojeda, who called for a ◊ general strike; the response was good, and Jiminez fled the country. A military Junta led by the liberal Admiral Larrazabal seized power. He held elections, standing for President himself, his chief opponent being the exiled Romulo Betancourt, Leader of the Accion Democratica Party, who was elected, although in Caracas itself five out of six votes were cast against him. He had promised an all-party coalition government, but broke his word by excluding the CP, and, in the same spirit which disappointed hopes of his liberalism, put down student demonstrations by force, used the army to prevent peasants from taking over the land which had been promised them; and the National Guard to break up political meetings of oil and industrial workers.

Fidel ◊ Castro's success in Cuba encouraged the Venezuelan left to rally, and a breakaway faction of Accion Democratica led by Moses Moleiro, the Movimento de Izquierda Revolucionaria (◊ MIR), including fourteen deputies in Congress, tried to give legal expression to the left reformist feeling in the capital. Betancourt used violence to put down the MIR, closed down the CP newspaper *Tribuna Popular*, arrested and gaoled CP deputies, and moved troops into the oilfields where revolutionary feeling ran high. These were the events which in 1962 provoked the guerrilla movements. A number of these groups began to operate against government forces and to recruit peasant support. The communist Chirino Front was led by Douglas ¢ Bravo, a trained CP man, and Fabricio ¢ Ojeda of the MIR. The 'El Charal' Front was led by Vincent Cabazas, and two communists, Luben ¢ Petkoff, and Manuel ¢ Saher, known as 'Comandante Chena', son of the Governor of Falcon State: in an open letter to his father, Saher had denounced the Governor as 'an assassin of the Venezuelan people'. An orthodox CP 'Simon Bolivar' Front was led by Tirso Pinto. In Caracas itself urban guerrillas, for the most part students, were organized as Tactical Combat Units.

Government military and paramilitary forces, 'advised' by CIA officers, were easily able to deal with such small, scattered groups which were therefore driven into union as the National Liberation Army comprising communists, MIR and groups adhering to the non-communist but leftist Unidad Revolucionaria Democratica (URD). This militant organization was strengthened by the many dissident professional army and navy officers who joined it, following the seizure of the Carupano Naval Base by its own officers, and of the principal Naval Base, Puerto Cabello, by a group led by the base's Commanding Officer, Captain Rodriguez. As a result of these actions the CP was banned, which forced it, for the first time, to adopt a policy of armed insurrection by formal resolution of its Politbureau (December 1962). The seven principal guerrilla groups were now recombined into the Fuerzas Armadas de Liberacion Nacional, known as FALN, and promulgated a manifesto condemning Betancourt's government as antidemocratic, oppressive and responsible for the serious economic and social crisis in the country; proposing to overthrow it by revolution and to set up a 'revolutionary, nationalist and democratic' government; setting up an elaborate Code of Honour to guide guerrilla conduct of the struggle; and appointing Captain Rodriguez as its C-in-C. Political decisions were to be made by the affiliated FLN – *Frente de Liberacion Nacional*. Aspirant guerrillas were sent for training to Cuba, China and the USSR. Militant operations were directed against US interests by burning down the big Sears Roebuck store and the US military Mission HQ in Caracas. An attempt was made to assassinate Betancourt, who next withdrew parliamentary immunity from police action from all CP and MIR Deputies in Congress, and had them arrested. Attacks were made on army and police posts all over the country.

On 1 December 1963 elections were held; the FALN had called on the people to boycott them, but this appeal failed. The *Accion Democratica* candidate Raul Leoni was elected President and he at once offered the CP an amnesty if they would forego the use of revolutionary violence. Differences about this offer split the FALN; but some guerrilla activity continued and it was not until 1965 that the CP decided to revert to peaceful means of reforming the State, a decision strongly opposed by Douglas Bravo speaking for guerrilla groups which accused the CP of ◊ 'revisionism'. The FALN rump reorganized itself with Bravo as C-in-C and Ojeda as chairman of the FLN executive. A newly promulgated programme, the Iracara Manifesto, demanded amnesty for all political prisoners; legalization of all political parties; a programme of industrialization to enable Venezuelans to own and process their own natural resources; land, credit and machinery for the peasants; emancipation of foreign policy from US imperialist control. The CP refused to support Bravo and Ojeda, but agreed to meet them for a discussion of problems. Coming down from the mountains to Caracas for this meeting, Ojeda, possibly betrayed by the CP Politbureau, was captured by the military police and later murdered in his cell.

Luben Petkoff, leading a group of trained guerrillas who had been assembling from training centres on an island off the Venezuelan coast, landed in Venezuela and after being detected and strafed by government aircraft, took refuge in the mountains (1965). He and Bravo have since continued operations on a reduced scale with some help from Cuba, but they have had only minor successes.

Vietcong. Military wing of the South Vietnamese Marxist- ◊ Leninist National Liberation Front. It was responsible for waging the most protracted, courageous and successful ◊ guerrilla war against the world's greatest military power, the USA. The Chinese People's War against the Kuomintang was as long, but the Kuomintang never received anything like the amount of military support given by the US to the South Vietnamese 'neo-colonialist' (*see* imperialism) governments: the Vietcong was faced with something like 600,000 American soldiers, their Australian and South Korean allies, all magnificently equipped and supplied; a very powerful U S air force, and an equally powerful war fleet. Yet by 1971, after more than a quarter of a century of war, the revolutionary guerrilla forces had forced the U S to begin withdrawing its armies, leaving the defence of imperialism in South Vietnam to the South Vietnamese armies which they had trained and supplied. The failure of this policy of 'Vietnam-ization' became clear in 1972 when the combined forces of the Vietcong and the North Vietnamese Army repeatedly defeated the South Vietnamese. But in 1973 the U S government was forced by public opinion and the drain on resources, which led to dollar devaluation, to abandon South Vietnam after negotiating a cease-fire which was unenforceable.

Viet-Minh. Marxist- ⟡ Leninist revolutionary political organization founded, Vietnam 1941, by ⟡ Ho Chi Minh to resist the Japanese following their seizure of Indo-China from the French in World War II. It was the army politically educated and directed by the Viet-Minh which, under General Giap, defeated the French attempt to resume possession of their old colony, at Dien Bien Phu (1954), after a nine years war. Before that date the Viet-Minh and its army had been transformed into the Fatherland Front (Lien Viet Front): *see* Vietnam.

Vietnam. At the time of writing the communist revolution in Vietnam has been in progress for a quarter of a century. It has been successful in North Vietnam and clearly will be in the South. The revolution is of the Chinese, rather than the Russian or Cuban type: i.e. a protracted 'people's war' manned chiefly by peasants first against foreign ⟡ imperialist domi-nation (France succeeded by the USA), secondly against the 'neo-colonialist' government in Saigon. There have been two stages in the first successful part of the revolution and these are being repeated in the next part: a nationalist revolutionary war in which non-communists joined with communists to drive out the French, and which culminated in the French defeat at Dien Bien Phu, followed by a socialist revolution which put power into the hands of the Communist Party.

The first phase: when, in 1940, the French imperial masters of Vietnam (i.e. Annam, Tonkin and Cochin-China) were driven out by the Japanese who occupied the country in their place, a number of resistance move-ments, waging guerrilla warfare on the Japanese became active in Annam and Tonkin. In 1945 these movements, nationalist and communist, or

simply anti-Japanese, together overthrew the emperor of Annam, Bao
Dai, and proclaimed the Republic of Vietnam, (it is an old Chinese
designation meaning 'Farther South'). The strongest element in the new
government was the Communist ⟫ Viet-Minh led by ⟫ Ho Chi Minh. It
was the Viet-Minh, under General Vo Nguyen Giap, which led the
revolutionary war against the returned French (1946–54). As a result of
Giap's victory at Bien Dien Phu (1954), France asked for an armistice: in
the negotiations at Geneva (July 1954) Giap agreed to division of the
country at the 17th parallel of latitude into North Vietnam and South
Vietnam; this partition was to end in July 1955 and free elections for a new
unified government of all Vietnam had to be held. The 1954 negotiations
also transferred sovereignty from France to Vietnam, Cambodia and Laos:
Ho Chi Minh refused to sign these conventions and never recognized the
division of Vietnam.

The French had installed Bao Dai, the deposed Emperor of Annam, as
Vietnamese Chief of State. His government, seated in Saigon, was recognized by the UK and the USA as the only legitimate government of
Vietnam. In January 1955 the USA undertook to train and supply its
armed forces; in October a referendum replaced Bao Dai with Ngo Dinh
Diem. His government was autocratic and corrupt and weakened by
opposition from the Buddhist Hoa-Hoa sect, the ultra-Catholic Cao Dai
sect, the Binh Xuyen party which controlled the police and the brothels;
and above all the National Liberation Front (communist) whose Vietcong
forces, supplied and supported by North Vietnam, soon controlled most
of the country outside the cities. The US repudiated their puppet Diem,
who was promptly murdered (November 1963) and for the next nine years
there was a series of ineffectual governments, more or less helpless against
the growing strength of the Vietcong, under the Presidency of the Buddhist
General Nhuyen Khanh. In June 1965 he was overthrown by the Council
of Armed Forces and with US support (probably rather more than mere
support), General Nguyen Van Thieu installed as Chief of State and Air
Marshal Nguyen Cao Ky as prime minister, heads of a government which
the US could use as the instrument of their attempt to crush the revolution
in Vietnam. In the next three years the US built up its counterrevolutionary
armies until, by 1968, it had half a million American soldiers and about
50,000 Australians, New Zealanders and South Koreans.

The epic struggle of the Vietcong in what is, perhaps, the greatest guerrilla-type revolutionary war ever waged and with inadequate means and against the world's greatest and richest military and imperialist forces, has become the focus of the ⬦ New Left revolutionary spirit all over the world. Ho Chi Minh was, in his lifetime, a sage of the left with the charismatic power almost of ⬦ Mao Tse-tung himself; the war has converted millions of social democrats and even mere liberals to the cause of the Vietcong and of North Vietnam; has sparked off revolutionary action, and given it identity, in many parts of the Third World; has been at the origin of revolutionary movements even in the U S itself; and has alienated many more millions, in the capitalist West, from the pro-American governments of their own countries. So powerful and worldwide was the disgust of ordinary people with the American and South Vietnamese counterrevolutionary war, that British governments, friendly to U S governments for sound capitalist reasons, were nevertheless forced to resist American demands for military aid in Vietnam.

In the present phase of the revolution (Spring 1973), the U S forces have been withdrawn – the Nixon policy of 'Vietnamization' is a convenient name for 'retreat' – there is a cease-fire in force, it is being repeatedly broken by both sides and socialist revolution in the south seems likely.

Although the North has maintained a united front in its struggle against the Americans and their southern Vietnam 'colonialist' allies, there are at least three ideologies at work there with different approaches to the revolution. The orthodox Moscow-orientated communist group is led by Le Duan, Secretary General of the CP; there is a ⬦ Maoist group which includes the editors of the CP's theoretical journal, *Hoc Tap*; and a 'Cuban' or Guevarist (*see* Guevara) group whose leading figure is General Giap, the soldier who beat the French and is said to have directed the Vietcong war against the Americans and their Vietnamese allies. Like the Chinese CP the Vietnamese Maoists dismiss the threat and fear of nuclear war as bluff and cowardice and welcome the prospect of a violent fight to the finish on the grounds that it will eliminate in advance all possibility of a post-revolutionary civil war and counterrevolution. Le Duan's position seems to be somewhere between the Chinese and Russian attitudes in the matter of coexistence with capitalism; it differs chiefly from that of the other two groups in its insistence that the revolutionary aim must be political and economic centralization, in short an all-powerful, institutional communist state – whereas the others, and particularly those who follow

Giap, see that aim as decentralization, with political power in the hands of the people operating by means of direct democracy, and economic power in the hands of collectives. Giap and the Maoists regard the people of the rural areas, the peasants, as the principal revolutionary fighters whose task it is to 'liberate' the cities (*see* Cultural Revolution); and they play down the role of the urban proletariat; Le Duan, on the other hand, holds that the revolution can only be led effectively by the urban proletariat organized and led by the CP. But the differences within the Vietnamese communist movement, between old and new left, are not as great as they are in the countries of their origin and the world at large, and just as the revolution itself has been on Chinese lines, it seems likely that a 'Chinese' outcome is to be expected rather than a 'Russian' one.

Villa, Francisco (Pancho, 1878–1923) Mexican bandit-revolutionary; real name Doroteo Arango was abandoned when he became an outlaw. b. San Juan de Rio, Durango. There is a category of outlaws who are half social revolutionary, half professional brigand. ♢ Nechayev and ♢ Bakunin declared that the brigands of Russia, with their tradition of robbing the rich and helping and protecting the poor, were the true revolutionaries and should be emulated by all dedicated social revolutionaries. In Britain their mythical archetype is Robin Hood; they are numerous in Chinese folklore; the greatest Russian examples are Pugachev and Stenka Razin; two interesting modern examples are the Sicilian Juliano and, above all, ♢ Sandino.

Pancho Villa was of this kind. Conditions in Mexico were peculiarly favourable to the sort of violent operations for which he and the relatively more sophisticated and intelligent ♢ Zapata became famous. The illiterate, largely Indio, landless and frequently destitute peasants had no means of protest against the oppression of the white, Spanish-speaking masters of their country, and no hope of betterment, but in banditry. It was among the more energetic, or at least apathetic victims of the ruling landowner class and its chiefly foreign capitalist allies, that Villa recruited his band of peasant warriors.

He was first obliged to take to the hills when, at the age of sixteen, he killed a man who had raped his sister, and for sixteen years he was no more than the leader of a band of cattle-rustling outlaws, politically conscious only in the sense that his depredations were confined to the proprietors of the great *rancheros* who flourished at the expense of the poor peasantry during the dictatorship of Porfirio Diaz. But when in 1910 Francisco Madero, the liberal leader, raised an armed insurrection against the dictator Porfirio Diaz and drove him from the country, Villa led his mounted band to Madero's support and when Madero became President, constituted himself a leader of patriotic 'irregulars'. But, incapable of submitting himself to military discipline of even the most rudimentary kind, his persistent insubordination led General Huerta to arrest and condemn him to death. Madero commuted the sentence to imprisonment, from which he escaped (1913) to take refuge in the US. When Huerta had Madero assassinated and became dictator, another general, Carranza, rose against his brutally oppressive regime and Villa immediately joined him and turned his force of outlaws into a regiment of irregular cavalry which became famous for its bold and successful exploits in the continuing civil war. Carranza having defeated Huerta with Villa's help, and assumed the Presidency, Villa turned and waged war on him, was defeated in a series of battles, but continued in control of a considerable part of the north. To demonstrate that he was indeed the master, he seized and 'executed' sixteen US citizens and then invaded the US (1916). The US Army drove him back across the frontier and followed him into Mexico; but this counter-invasion infuriated Carranza, who refused to cooperate in catching Villa; the latter was also helped by the peasantry of the Chihuahua province, whose hero he was. He continued at war with the Mexican government until Carranza's death in 1920, when he made peace on condition that he be given a large ranch to retire to. The government agreed and as soon as he had disbanded his troop, had him assassinated.

Violencia, La: *see* Colombia: guerrilla movements.

Weathermen. An illegal anarchist movement of American youth dedicated to the destruction of established US society by violence. The name is derived from the line *You don't need a Weatherman to know which way the wind blows*, from the Bob Dylan song 'Subterranean Homesick Blues'. The movement emerged as the militant faction of the 40,000 strong Students for a Democratic Society (SDS). Although this was a legal organization, by 1967 it was being closely watched for 'subversion' by the FBI and police and by 1968 its militant faction was taking to the use of revolutionary violence, in some ways reminiscent of the ▷ nihilist and People's Will movements in late nineteenth-century Russia. At the SDS national congress, Chicago 1969, this faction became dominant and was able, e.g., to expel the 'reformist' (i.e. non-violent) ▷ Marxists from the student movement. Adopting a policy of immediate violent action and the name Weathermen, it was responsible for the bombings of banks, court buildings, police stations, universities, and the disruption of high schools; and for leading riots and battles with the police. The leaders, who were from the rich upper ▷ bourgeoisie, some of them sons or daughters of millionaires, were all wanted by the police and FBI and are forced to live and work 'underground'. They regard US ▷ imperialism as the arch-evil and aim to destroy it, and Capitalism, by forcing it to take ▷ Fascist means of oppression which will ultimately become intolerable and thus rouse the masses. The principal leaders were Mark Rudd and Bernardine Dohrn, both children of rich parents and in their late twenties. The Weathermen worked in cells of three to minimize the danger of infiltration, so that each Weatherman knew only two others. They saw their task as the destruction of existing society rather than the building up of a new one, for which indeed, their broadly Marxist- ▷ Leninist ideas were few and vague. They had no connection with the Communist Party despised as bureaucratic and dogmatic. They had an extremely tough, ▷ guerrilla-type training for recruits, including forty-eight-hour total fasts and abstention from sleep, based on a special manual of revolutionary violence. To eradicate all trace of their own bourgeois upbringing they deliberately outraged carefully inculcated feelings: e.g. they would kill and eat stray cats, wreck gravestones in cemeteries, neglect their teeth, and personal and domestic hygiene and cleanliness. The use of alcohol and drugs, excepting 'pot', was discouraged. Recruiting was among the intellectual top flight of high school children in the 16–18 age group. The Weathermen had links with the black revolutionary movements, and more tenuous ones with the ⬦ Vietcong, Cuban Communism, Al-Fatah and other Palestinian guerrilla groups, (*see* Palestine, revolution in) the Quebec Liberation Front, and similar organizations. Funds for their operations were obtained by robbery.

Whether their organization is still extinct is uncertain.

Weizmann, Chaim (1874–1952) Russian Jewish, later British scientist who became the leader of ⬦ Zionism and first President of Israel.

Wijeweera, Rohan (1944–   ). *See* Janatha Vimakthi Peramuna

Williams, Robert F. (1925–   ) Black American revolutionary leader b. Monroe, NC; served in the US Marines. Returned on discharge, 1953, to Monroe where he joined the local chapter of the National Association for the Advancement of Coloured People and later became its President. In 1957 the Ku Klux Klan began a series of armed raids on NAACP HQ and on the homes of its leaders. Williams reacted by forming an armed defence unit and on the occasion of the next KKK raid, returned the raiders' fire. This was the first instance of black Americans resorting to planned, deliberate revolutionary violence. As a result he was hunted by by the police and the FBI, arrested on a charge of kidnapping which was patently a frame-up, escaped, was posted wanted as a dangerous criminal, and sought asylum in Cuba. Although he had at one time much influence on the whole ⬦ Black Power movement with his book *Negroes with Guns* (1962) and his newsletter *The Crusader*, his extreme advocacy of violence and his quarrels, accompanied by wild accusations of treachery with the Cuban and Chinese leaders have discredited him in the eyes of serious black revolutionaries.

Women's Liberation Movement. American in origin; a generic name applied to many groups of radical neo-feminists which are for the politicizing and mobilizing of the female majority against male dominion; the movement has no organization structure and no official leadership. Although statements of principle appeared as early as 1952, e.g. with Selma Jones's pamphlet *A Woman's Place*, its origin is traced to a critical paper written (1964) by a young black woman founder of ⟡ SNCC on the position of women in SNCC; and to an article, in the same spirit, in *Studies on the Left* (1966) by two white women SNCC members. These writings inspired the formation of small groups of militants while at the same time Betty Friedan, author of *The Feminine Mystique* (1963), and others founded the National Organization for Women, NOW, 'To bring women into full participation in the mainstream of American society . . . exercising the privileges and responsibilities thereof in truly equal partnership with men', a moderate reformist organization which has had some successes, e.g. in obtaining the appointment of the US Equal Employment Opportunities Commission. The more important part of the movement consists of groups, cells and chapters which hold 'consciousness-raising', otherwise known as 'bitching', sessions designed to help women to know themselves, each other and their true relationship to male-dominated society, without cant; to clarify the liberationist aims; and to prepare for effective revolutionary action.

Awareness of the movement became widespread when (1967) the UNO passed its Declaration of Equal Rights for Women and with the march on Washington organized by the Jeanette Rankin Brigade to protest against the Vietnam war; of the thousands who marched a fraction split off to form an autonomous women's revolutionary movement. This holds that a male-dominated socialist economic and cultural revolution would be no revolution at all but only another coup d'état among men. It points to the connection established by scientific anthropology between the concept of property and the oppression of women. It emphasizes women's historical achievements, e.g. the inventions of agriculture, pottery and weaving. It maintains that the family, as an institution, is oppressive to women (and also to men and children), but has yet to settle upon a suitable alternative. It maintains that if the planet is to be salvaged from ecological disaster and nuclear war at the hands of male-dominated powers, women must seize control of the revolutionary movement at large because even the revolutionary left is badly tainted with male supremacism. Women's Liberation claims also to be engaged with the class problem in a unique way since

'Women are the only oppressed people whose biological, emotional and social life is totally bound to that of the oppressors', (New York Radical Feminists) and the family structure probably constitutes the earliest power paradigm.

The event which attracted sudden and unfortunate publicity for the movement and gave it an image it has had trouble in shaking off was the picketing of the Miss America Contest at Atlantic City in July 1968. Women threw symbolic bras, girdles, lipsticks and high-heeled shoes into 'Freedom trash cans'; an advance report declared that bras would be burned and although there appears to be no evidence that they were, the 'bra-burning' tag has stuck. So too has the man-hating image, since the publication of Valerie Solanas's semi-satirical 'manifesto' SCUM (Society for Cutting Up Men). No such society of course exists, but Solanas's attempt to maim pop-artist Andy Warhol distracted media attention from the serious aims and work of the movement and possibly inspired other subversive demonstrations such as the 'hexing' of Wall Street, etc. by WITCH (Women's International Terrorist Conspiracy from Hell).

In England the movement was slower to gain momentum. It was given some impetus by the Ford women workers' strike in July 1968. Groups began to form and a demonstration at the Miss World contest in 1969 followed by the first national conference at Oxford in February 1970 announced that a national movement now existed. United recently by the fight for equal pay and anti-discrimination legislation, the movement has now, although still working for the most part separately, allied itself to some extent with the already established liberal feminist voice – for example, the joint production of a bi-monthly newspaper by the Fawcett Society and the Women's Lobby. It is nationally committed to demands for equal pay, improved education, twenty-four-hour nurseries, free contraception and abortion on demand. Discussions among individual groups go further and are most frequently concerned with the inadequacy, from a woman's point of view, of family structure and sexual mores.

Women's Lib is strongest in the USA where there are between fifty and two hundred cells or groups in every major city and every considerable town and cells in all the universities. It is also active in Australia, Britain, Canada, Finland, France, Germany, Holland, Japan, Mexico, Sweden and Tanzania. Primarily a white middle-class movement, it is beginning to attract recruits from the black community because the ⟡ Black Power movement is male-supremacist; and from the working-class because women workers are repeatedly sold out by trade unions which invariably and inevitably favour their male members.

Thus, Women's Liberation is far from being simply a militant feminist movement; although it has its liberal-reformist wing it is increasingly anti-capitalist and socialist-revolutionary if only because oppressive exploitation of women is and cannot but be inherent in any corporation capitalist or state capitalist society.

Y

Yon Sosa, ◊ guerrilla leader: *see* MR 13; Guatemala: guerrilla movements.

Young Russia. Both the name of the Central Revolutionary Committee and the manifesto of a group of extreme socialist Russian revolutionary students and intellectuals active in the 1860s. The manifesto, circulated from a clandestine press, proclaimed that Russia was entering (1862) a revolutionary phase; that the revolution must be bloody and pitiless and would destroy the feudal landowning, and the young (in Russia) capitalist system. Although it borrowed ideas from ◊ Herzen, the manifesto severely condemned his moderation as mere liberalism. The aim of the Revolutionary Committee was a Russian Social and Democratic Republic in the form of a federal-republican union of the regions, governed by popular assemblies elected by universal suffrage. Factories and farms would be run by their own workers, education would be free, women emancipated to the status of full citizenship, monasteries abolished, military service reduced and soldiers' pay raised and the republic would be ◊ nihilist in the sense of being hostile to such institutions as the family and religion. Above the assemblies would reign the Party, the executive élite of dedicated incorruptibles prepared to interfere with the democracy if it showed any sign of betraying the revolution by the kind of weakness that, e.g. had put Louis-Philippe on the throne of France. The Young Russia movement and its manifesto were chiefly the work of P. G. ◊ Zaichnevsky its prime mover. Because it propounded the idea of a revolutionary élite of dedicated extremists, it was stigmatized by moderate ◊ populists as 'Jacobin' which became a term of abuse used, e.g. by ◊ Plekhanov against ◊ Lenin. But its influence on the development of Russian revolutionary history was considerable for two decades.

Young Turks. *c.* 1900 liberal Turkish exiles in Europe formed a movement, the 'Committee of Union and Progress', which became known by this name, to introduce radical reforms into the Ottoman Empire, an absolute tyranny under the Sultan Abdul Hamid, significantly nicknamed Abdul the Damned. The Young Turks made use of dissident movements in Armenia and Macedonia where (1908) they had their first success with a revolt of young army officers which spread across the empire, finding a number of able leaders, but notably Enver Pasha who unified the revolts into a national movement and forced the Sultan to restore (July 1908) the constitution which had been imposed on him by the great powers at the Treaty of San Stephano following the Russo-Turkish War (1876–78). The first Turkish parliament met in December 1876 but the returned exiles of the Young Turk party found their liberal ideas swept aside by the nationalist chauvinism of the military Young Turks led by Enver. The Sultan attempted a counterrevolutionary coup, was again forestalled, and deposed and exiled (April 1909). In 1914 Enver took the Turks into World War I on Germany's side against the opposition of the Young Turk liberals, and only fell with the defeat of Turkey and the rise of Mustapha ◊ Kemal.

Z

Zaichnevsky, P. G. (1843-?) Founder and leader of the Young Russia movement of 'Jacobin' student and intellectual revolutionaries.

Zaire, revolution in. On 3 January 1959 in Leopoldville (now Kinshasa), Belgian Congo, during a mass rally of the Congolese National Movement, the movement's leader Patrice ⟡ Lumumba demanded that the Belgian government grant immediate independence to the Congo. A street demonstration of tens of thousands of people supporting this demand on the following day was violently dispersed, with much loss of life, by government forces. This hardened the determination of the nationalists, pressure was maintained and in 1960 independence was conceded, Lumumba becoming prime minister of the new republic on 29 June 1960. The Belgians meanwhile organized the secession of the very rich Katanga province, taking advantage of tribal differences, and using as their instrument a puppet secessionist government led by Moise Tshombe: this was in order to retain the profits and control of the Union Minière du Haut Katanga for Belgian, French, British and American capital. Net mining profits in 1960 were $407 million. This move resulted in a sharp shift to the left of the Lumumba government and a bloody civil war. At Lumumba's request the United Nations intervened with a mixed force of Swedish, Irish and Indian troops: according to the nationalists and Katangans this was in order to impose a peaceful settlement and stop the fighting; according to the Lumumbaists the UN betrayed its mission and protected the Union Minière from being taken over by its only legitimate owners, the people of Congo-Kinshasa including Katanga. The Katanga army consisted largely of European mercenary troops paid, according to the Lumumbaists, out of Union Minière funds. Lumumba himself was kidnapped by Tshombe's troops and later murdered in Tshombe's presence. Following the imposition of 'peace', the revolution was left in the hands of a number of ⟡ guerrilla bands with a more or less ⟡ Maoist Marxist- ⟡ Leninist ideology. They had, at first, a considerable success, and China-trained Pierre Mulele who had been Lumumba's Minister of Education, and Christophe Gbenye, set up a Revolutionary Congolese government with their capital in Stanleyville. The US government, or at all events, the ▷ CIA, became alarmed at the prospect of a movement under Chinese communist influence gaining control of the Congo, and financed a Belgian-backed force of counterrevolutionary mercenaries with arms and funds, to destroy the revolutionary government. Che ▷ Guevara and a small force of veteran Cuban *guerrilleros* joined the revolutionaries and trained and led the Patrice Lumumba Battalion, but they proved to be no match for the better trained, disciplined, armed and well-paid mercenaries supporting the nationalist forces of General Mobuto. The revolutionary movement finally collapsed at least for the time being, when Mulele accepted from Mobuto an amnesty, free pardon and a place in the Nationalist Cabinet (September 1968). This was justified ideologically by the Maoist rule that in the sort of conditions obtaining in the Congo the revolution must be in two stages, in the first of which the ▷ Marxists should support the ▷ bourgeois nationalists in their struggle against imperialist control, and submit to nationalist leadership, proceeding to the second, socialist stage only after the country had been liberated from the foreigners.

ZANU: Zimbabwe African National Union: *see* South African and Rhodesia, Revolution in.

Zapata, Emiliano (1877–1919) Mexican revolutionary, b. Anenecuilco, Morelos. For the background to his revolt, *see* Villa, Francisco. As a smallholder championing the rights of his class and of the landless peasants, he was persecuted and finally imprisoned by the police of the dictator Porfirio Diaz. When the liberal leader Francisco Madero led a rising which drove Diaz from the country, Zapata became the Maderisto leader in Morelos, but when Madero as president failed to implement his promise of land tenure reform and land redistribution, Zapata continued the fight, first against the Liberal government, then against the dictatorships of Presidents Huerta and Carranza which succeeded it, allying himself with Carranza's guerrilla enemy Pancho Villa. During all three presidencies Zapata controlled Morelos and was able to initiate his own programme of reform: he drove out the rich *haciendados*, burnt down their great houses, and divided the land of their vast estates among the peasants. He set up schools and made a start at establishing social services. One of Carranza's generals was sent to deal with him, trapped him in an ambush, and shot him in April 1919.

ZAPU: Zimbabwe African People's Union: *see* South Africa and Rhodesia, revolution in.

Zelyabov, Andrey Ivanovich (1851–81) Russian ▷ nihilist revolutionary, b. Odessa, s. of a peasant. Expelled 1872 from Odessa university for organizing a student protest against an unpopular professor, he devoted himself to propagating socialism among workers and intellectuals, was arrested and convicted of subversion and served a year in prison. After his release (1875) he was recruited into the terrorist wing of the *Narodnaya Volya*, the ▷ People's Will, one of the ▷ populist movements, in the full knowledge that he would be involved in a plot to assassinate the Tsar Alexander II. In the event he became the chief organizer of the assassination, but was arrested a few days before the date for which it was planned, 1 March, 1881. His place was immediately taken by his comrade Sophia ▷ Perovskaya who carried the plan through. As soon as she and other comrades were arrested, Zelyabov signed his own death warrant by writing to the authorities to claim sole responsibility for the assassination. The purpose of his life and the gallantry of his bearing during the trial and on the scaffold were exemplary.

Zetkin, Clara (née Eissner, 1857–1933) b. Wiederau, Saxony, daughter of a village schoolmaster; ed. at the feminist Leipzig Teachers' College for women. In Leipzig she met and married the Russian Socialist revolutionary Osip Zetkin, was converted to socialism and joined the German Social Democratic Party (1881). She took her revolutionary work seriously, and was a founder delegate to the Second ▷ International (Paris 1889). From 1892 she was editor of the socialist women's magazine *Gleicheit* published in Stuttgart and she was a co-founder of the International Socialist Women's Congress (1907). From 1907 to 1917 Zetkin was on the Executive Committee of the German Social Democratic party and became a close friend of Rosa ▷ Luxemburg. In 1915 she organized an international women's congress against war, convening it in Berne; as a result she was arrested for pacifist subversion on her return to Germany and served a prison term. With Luxemburg and Karl ◇ Liebnecht she founded the revolutionary ◇ Spartakusbund in 1916. This led her (1919) into the German Communist Party and in 1920 she was elected to its central committee and, as a communist member, to the Reichstag. In 1924 she went to Moscow to serve in the Presidium of the Comintern Executive Committee, but was nevertheless re-elected to the Reichstag at every election thereafter until by August 1932 she was 'mother of the House' and as such presided over the last opening of the Reichstag before its destruction by the ◇ Nazis some months later. Her health and eyesight had been failing for nearly ten years when she died in a Soviet clinic.

Zimbabwe. The name by which South Rhodesian black revolutionaries know their country: hence, e.g. Zimbabwe African People's Union (◇ ZAPU): *see* South Africa and Rhodesia, revolution in.

Zinoviev, Grigori (Grigori Radomylsky, 1883–1936) Russian ◇ Bolshevik revolutionary leader, a member of the party accompanying ◇ Lenin (April 1917) when the Germans helped the Bolshevik exiles to return to Russia following the February ◇ Russian Revolution. Zinoviev was Commissar responsible for the Third International (◇ Comintern), and a member of the Politbureau (1920–26). In the great schism which divided the Communist Party leadership in 1926 in the course of which ◇ Stalin and his bureaucracy defeated and destroyed ◇ Trotsky and the old Bolshevik international revolutionaries, Zinoviev first took Trotsky's side and as a result lost his membership of the Politbureau. After a period of wavering, he saw which way the wind was blowing, and submitted to Stalin. But he was too late, and was one of the victims of the 'purge' whereby Stalin rid himself of all opposition to his dictatorship. Having been tried and imprisoned for 'treason' in 1935, he was brought from prison to be tried again and executed (August 1936). His name became well known in Britain during the general election campaign of October 1924 when a letter purporting to be from him and bearing his signature, but which was a forgery, in which the British left was urged to resort to violent revolution, was published by the Conservative press to create a 'Red Scare' and so defeat the Labour Party.

Zionism. The name given to the worldwide movement among the Jews for return to their ancient home in Palestine. It had and has two chief sources, one in sentiment, tradition and religious feeling, the other in the need to find safe refuge from manifestations of antisemitism ranging from civic disabilities in some East European countries, to the pogroms of Tsarist Russia and Poland and the ◊ Nazi extermination camps.

Zionism does not come within the definition of revolution implied in the introduction: it is a nationalist movement and does not aim at making radical changes in the social or economic orders. On the other hand, it has provoked such revolutionary changes in the Middle East; has manifested itself in such revolutionary institutions, e.g. the *kibbutzim* many of which are austerely socialist; and provoked the rise of such revolutionary ◊ guerrilla movements among the Palestine Arabs by its success, that it would have been unrealistic to omit all reference to it.

As a dream Zionism is as ancient as the Diaspora, but as an active and finally militant organized movement it owes its start to the writings of a Hungarian Jew living and working in Vienna, Theodor ◊ Herzl (1860–1904), which inspired the First Zionist Congress (Basle, 1897) whose object was announced as 'to secure for the Jewish people a home in Palestine guaranteed by public law'. The movement long remained primarily an Austrian and German one, supported by some British, American and French Jews many of whom, on the other hand, and almost all of whom among the rich were opposed to Zionism and preferred assimilation into their particular adopted community, not always but usually short of conversion to Christianity. During World War I the Zionist centre shifted to England owing to the zeal, powerful personality and intellectual brilliance of one man, Dr Chaim Weizmann (1874–1952), later official leader of World Zionism, and still later first President of the Republic of Israel (1948–52). He was a Russian-born, British naturalized Jew whose scientific importance as a biochemist and whose brilliant war service in the explosives department of the Admiralty gave him the weight and influence to secure the support of the British government for Zionism. In this he was much helped by another Russian Jew, the fiery Zionist militant, Vladimir Jabotinsky, raiser and commanding officer of the Jewish Legion which fought for the Allies (1914–18). British Foreign Office support was made manifest in the Balfour Declaration (1917), named after the Foreign Secretary, A. J. Balfour, which declared British support for a Jewish National Home in Palestine; the subsequently disastrous fact that Palestine was being promised to the Arabs at the same time, inexplicable by the ordinary honest man in the street is explicable by and to politicians as the *raison d'état* of a country at war. The Declaration was given substance, after confirmation by the other Allied governments, as the British Mandate from the League of Nations (1920) to overlord a Palestine shared by Jews and Arabs. This, of course, involved Britain in a permanent civil war first with the Arabs, then with the Jews, who, meanwhile, were also fighting each other. After the outbreak of World War II and when the British authorities, to satisfy the Arabs, refused to allow Jews fleeing from the Nazis to land in Palestine, the revolutionary Irgun Zwei Leumi movement planned all-out war against the British authorities; the secret revolutionary society Lohmey Heruth Israel organized the assassination of Lord Moyne within whose Egyptian proconsulate Palestine was included; and the poet-patriot terrorist Abraham ▷ Stern organized urban guerrilla warfare on both British and Arabs. Meanwhile, the much larger and more popular, moderately socialist Haganah, the home-guard movement initiated by Jabotinsky, which developed into the Israeli Army, insisted that the arch enemy was ▷ Hitler's Germany and that all Jews should help the lesser enemy, Britain, in her war to the death against the Nazis.

Once the world war was over, all the Zionist movements combined to fight the British and the Arabs, until the British, in despair, gave up the Mandate as unworkable and the Jewish leaders, by a unilateral declaration of independence, created the Republic of Israel (14 May 1948). The success of this creation, and of the Republic's wars with the surrounding Arab powers which it has twice defeated decisively has provoked a number of Arab revolutionary guerrilla movements, of which the most important is Al-Fatah, whose aim is to recover Palestine (now Israel) for the Palestine Arabs: *see* Palestine, Revolution in.

INDEX

Index

Index